One Nation, Two Realities

One Nation, Two Realities

DUELING FACTS IN AMERICAN DEMOCRACY

MORGAN MARIETTA AND DAVID C. BARKER

OXFORD
UNIVERSITY PRESS

OXFORD
UNIVERSITY PRESS

Oxford University Press is a department of the University of Oxford. It furthers
the University's objective of excellence in research, scholarship, and education
by publishing worldwide. Oxford is a registered trade mark of Oxford University
Press in the UK and certain other countries.

Published in the United States of America by Oxford University Press
198 Madison Avenue, New York, NY 10016, United States of America.

© Oxford University Press 2019

CIP data is on file at the Library of Congress
ISBN 978-0-19-067717-6

9 8 7 6 5 4 3 2 1

Printed by Sheridan Books, Inc., United States of America

To Jordan, Mason, and Forthcoming

–MM

To Meg, Matt, Jackson, and Johnny Cash (loyal Newfie)

–DCB

PROLOGUE

"Global warming is the greatest hoax every perpetrated on the American people."

—Senator Jim Inhofe, Republican from Oklahoma
Senate Speech, July 2003

"Global warming is real, global warming is real. . . . Senator Inhofe is dead and dangerously wrong."

—Senator Bernie Sanders, Independent from Vermont
Senate Speech, July 2012

"Race and racism are still critical factors in determining what happens and who gets ahead in America."

—Touré, author of Who's Afraid of Post-Blackness
The New York Times, *November 8, 2011*

"While there are racists in America, America is no longer a racist society, and blaming disproportionate rates of black violence and out-of-wedlock births on white racism is a lie and the greatest single impediment to African-American progress."

—Dennis Prager, syndicated columnist
August 2008

"I've always believed that people are born with the predisposition to be homosexual. And so I think if someone is born that way it's very difficult to say then that's a sin."

—Chris Christie, former governor of New Jersey
CNN interview, June 15, 2011

"People who are gay say that they're born that way. But one thing I know, that the behavior one practices is a choice."

—Mike Huckabee, former governor of Arkansas
CNN interview, December 30, 2007

CONTENTS

PREFACE

A merican perceptions of reality have divided in a deep and consequential way. While many may see the phenomenon of dueling facts as a temporary aberration from the normal consensus, we see it as a long-term and unavoidable reality . . . a fact you might say. Our studies of its origins suggest it is not going anywhere anytime soon, and we must learn to navigate the landscape of dueling fact perceptions.

Any important cultural and political phenomenon presents two vital questions: *What are its causes? And what are its consequences?* Much of the emerging discussion of disputed realities focuses on the political environment—partisan leadership and fragmented media—as the source of the problem. However, we argue that the origins are psychological as well as environmental, grounded not only in the designs of manipulative elites but also in the impulses of ordinary citizens. Hence, it is not merely the easier target who is to blame (*them*: politicians and pundits) but also the more sensitive target (*us*: everyday flawed citizens).

When it comes to consequences, we argue that the ramifications of dueling fact perceptions are not merely a matter of ineffective governance but also stretch into the degradation of civil society. As ordinary citizens come to recognize that others hold contrary perceptions of reality, they react with personal disdain and social disengagement, which leads to spiraling polarization. Perhaps even worse, DFPs disrupt the positive relationship between education and democracy in a way that defies the normal expectations we place on greater schooling and knowledge. The contemporary democracy of facts has led to some negative facts of contemporary democracy.

Of course, the causes and consequences of any phenomenon can be examined only after the *concept* itself is clear. For an emerging area of study such as facts in politics, the concepts themselves may be in development or in dispute. We argue that the problem of dueling facts is broader and somewhat different than the emerging discussion among political science scholars suggests. Much of that research focuses on *misinformation*, or distortions of the limited collection of demonstrable facts for which we can identify correct and incorrect answers, such as the current rate of inflation. Instead, this book offers a broad conceptualization of dueling fact perceptions (DFPs). Citizens' *perceptions* of facts, regardless of what the accepted facts may be, are our focus. Perceived facts can range from the easily verifiable, such as recent changes in the stock market, to the utterly unknowable, such as essential facets of human nature. The continuum between these poles is inhabited by many blurred realities that are characterized by challenges to the legitimacy of the relevant data, competing perspectives on the meaning of recognized evidence, and disagreement among opinion leaders, presenting no small problem for ordinary citizens to formulate a clear perception. This conceptualization allows us to recognize that the number and range of DFPs are larger and more influential than previous research suggests. The phenomenon is *broader than misperception* of verifiable information and *deeper than misdirection* from partisan leaders.

A fourth social science question focuses on *correctives*. Can we suggest government policies or institutional changes that will address the causes or ameliorate the consequences of DFPs? Our answer at this point is *No*. Dueling facts are more entrenched than can be solved by simple expedients like more education or extensive fact-checking. Greater education and political knowledge are employed by citizens to *project their priors more accurately onto their perceptions*. Disappointing as this is to educators such as ourselves, it seems to be the case. Fact-checking doesn't seem to help either; the psychological forces driving fact perceptions are not counteracted by the claims to expertise and neutrality offered by professional fact checkers.

More broadly, we see no reason for optimism about the role of facts in American democracy. Facts are fractured into competing perceptions; instead of attention to evidence, divided perceptions are driven by deeply entrenched divisions in core values; the positive relation between education and consensus facts is also fractured; and our factual divisions lead to disdain of our fellow citizens and disengagement from civil discussion, creating spiraling polarization. The current situation is bad, and the prospects are worse.

We should note at the outset the role of Donald Trump in all of this. We began to consider the dueling facts phenomenon around 2010 and started collecting data in 2013. By the end of 2016, *post-truth* had become a normal adjective, while *alternative facts* and *fake news* had become widely employed phrases. But Donald Trump did not create the problem of dueling fact perceptions, which preceded his presidential campaign and will likely be with us long after he is gone. He may have made the problem worse by accelerating the decline of trust in news media, but there are now and have always been those who are fundamentally uninterested in facts or details. An influential American once said, "I am sure that I never read any memorable news in a newspaper." That was not Donald J. Trump but Henry David Thoreau.[1] We think Trump is more of a chapter in the contemporary story of dueling fact perceptions than its author.

The combativeness of factual disputes led us to the metaphor of dueling facts—two opponents violently contesting their public honor. We conceptualize factual conflict as an advanced form of polarization, moving beyond partisan, ideological, cultural, or geographic division to polarized perceptions of reality. However, divisions over ideologies or policies are one thing, while deep disputes over reality itself are another. This phenomenon seemed to us to be somewhat different from, and maybe more important than, the kinds of polarization that were being discussed throughout political science. *What is driving this?* Is it just advanced partisanship or something else? And *what happens in a society when citizens make competing claims about reality?* How does it affect how we deal with each other? And finally, *can this be corrected?*

Climate change is the dominant example of a deeply influential DFP, *on which perceptions became more divided rather than less as greater evidence accumulated over the last decades.* How, we discussed many times, were perceptions of global warming and climate change moving not toward consensus but toward greater division? A similar dynamic seemed to also apply across a broad range of realities. One of the most prominent is the enduring power of racism in American society. This divided perception took on new importance after the shooting of Trayvon Martin in 2012. Again and again in the following years—in regard to Michael Brown and Eric Garner in 2014, Freddie Gray in 2015, Alton Sterling in 2016,

---

[1] Thoreau 1854, page 71. Though deeply influential on later scholars, Thoreau was famously uninterested in facts from experts or news from journalists but was sure he could *feel* his way to truth; as he phrased it in *Walden*, "Sometimes, when I compare myself with other men, it seems as if I were more favored by the gods than they, beyond any deserts that I am conscious of; as if I had a warrant and surety at their hands which my fellows have not" (page 99). Cf. Trump: "I'm a very instinctual person, but my instinct turns out to be right" (*Time* interview March 23, 2017). For a critical view of Thoreau's epistemology, see Schulz 2015.

Jordan Edwards in 2017, Stephon Clark in 2018, and too many others—Americans could not avoid the knowledge that their fellow citizens held deeply different perceptions of those events as well as of the broader facts of race and racism in American life.

But DFPs go far beyond climate and racism, encompassing a broad range of realities influencing political debate: the origins of sexual orientation, the consequences of vaccines, immigration, the national debt, minimum wage increases, gun control, the prevalence of violent crime and false convictions, the degree of threat from terrorism, and too many other examples to list. To be sure, in previous time periods there were examples of divided perceptions of important events and prevailing conditions. To name just two, Americans disagreed about what likely happened between Anita Hill and Clarence Thomas (as illustrated by opinion polls at the time of his confirmation hearings to the Supreme Court in 1991), and Americans held very different perceptions of the intent and capabilities of the Soviet Union during the Cold War. But the breadth and depth of divisions over perceived facts seem more pervasive now.

In studying this phenomenon, we did *not* embrace a postmodernist vision in which each person's beliefs are just as good as anyone else's—and we don't think most ordinary citizens think that way either. In a fully postmodern condition, we would have thousands of competing facts, which amounts to having no facts at all. The contemporary era is not a world of *no facts* but instead a world of *dueling facts*, with two separate camps entrenched in their own positions and backed by their own authorities.

Neither did we embrace the opposite pole of thinking about facts: that they are clearly and decisively within easy reach most of the time. Many educated people harbor hubristic certainty that their perceptions are surely accurate (even those far outside their areas of expertise) and that others who perceive things differently are ignorant or dishonest. Our middle ground between throwing up our hands and fully trusting our own perceptions reflects our fundamental respect for epistemology—the view that a knowable reality exists but that it is difficult to know. The current dilemma could be summarized in the observation that *the polarization problem has increased the epistemological problem*; facts are always hard to discern and to hold in consensus, but when core beliefs are polarized it becomes much harder. Nonetheless, we believe that legitimate evidence and data can be gathered, accepted, and applied to social science questions, even to the question of disputed perceptions, of which both sides seem certain though both cannot be correct. Our goal is to collect empirical evidence and testable theory in a collective enterprise that will convince citizens and scholars from any ideological perspective, recognizing that the process is fraught with (surmountable) difficulty and (correctable) error.

We are well aware that each side believes its perceived facts to be the correct ones and would prefer that any book of this nature endorse them. A colleague commented on an early draft of these pages: "The liberal facts are more often, perhaps even always true. That has to be acknowledged." Several of the conservatives we know feel the opposite way. Neither side will find solace here on this question because our point is not to establish which side is correct. Instead, it is to point out that for ordinary citizens, truth-claims by established authorities are not decisive. There is more to the problem than simple true and false, information and misinformation. We offer extensive evidence on the politics of fact perceptions (about which we have some degree of expertise, especially in regard to evidence garnered through surveys and experiments) but very little evidence on the accurate reality of various disputed facts (on which we have much less, and not enough, expertise). As two scholars with similar trainings and bases of knowledge, we do not even agree with each other when it comes to the fact disputes that we examine in this book. For many of the disputed facts we agree on their likely direction, but for some we (vigorously) do not. Reasonable people can and do arrive at different perceptions of facts in the current political environment. This is a thing to explain, and we believe that two scholars who do not always agree on perceived facts—but do agree on social science methods—are an appropriate team to examine this phenomenon.

We aim to do so in an evidence-driven way. Our approach was to gather as much empirical data, across as much time and as many perceived facts, as possible. Through the Cooperative Congressional Election Studies conducted by YouGov, we collected data from multiple national surveys over a five-year period from 2013 to 2017. We also conducted several rounds of survey experiments on a regional sample of California residents (through the *CALSPEAKS* panel). There are several discussions of psychological theory and strands of the philosophy of knowledge, but at heart this is an organized presentation of collected data on perceptions of facts. In the full scope of the volume we attempt to address the *causes, consequences*, and possible *correctives* of DFPs in a comprehensive examination grounded in extensive empirical evidence.

We collected debts along with data during the six years of this project. The Political Communications Group at the University of Massachusetts Lowell (UML)—John Cluverius, Joshua Dyck, Mona Kleinberg, and

Jenifer Whitten-Woodring—contributed generously to the ideas presented here. The UML Center for Public Opinion directed by Josh Dyck and Frank Talty sponsored several of the national surveys discussed in the book. Without these colleagues at UML, this work would be much poorer and less persuasive. The Institute for Social Research at the California State University at Sacramento (formerly directed by David) supported several surveys on the *CALSPEAKS* panel, which allowed us to conduct the experimental research that informs some of our arguments. Many other scholars inspired or criticized the ideas or writing in the volume, including Jeffrey Friedman, Shterna Friedman, Jennifer Hochschild, Jon Krosnick, Jennifer Lawless, Jan Leighley, Danielle Joesten Martin, Kim Nalder, Robert Shapiro, Liz Suhay, Phil Tetlock, and Joe Uscinski. We would also like to thank the participants in The Politics of Truth Conference at American University on March 28, 2018, including Kevin Arcenaux, Adam Berinsky, Kim Fridkin, Alan Gerber, Justin Gross, Donald Haider-Markel, Danny Hayes, Greg Huber, Jennifer Jerit, Scott Keeter, Nathan Lee, Arthur Lupia, Lilliana Mason, Joanne Miller, Diana Mutz, Kim Nalder, Brendan Nyhan, Ethan Porter, Justin Reedy, Jason Reifler, and John Sides, as well as the National Science Foundation and the School of Public Affairs at American University for their generous support of the conference. We would like to recognize the tireless efforts (and endless patience) of our editor, Abby Gross. A special thanks goes to Bert Rockman, our friend, colleague, and mentor. A real gentleman and scholar Bert is. Many friends also critiqued these pages, including Jeffrey Condran, Tyler Cote, Tyler Farley, Robert Holzbach, Glenn Kent, Paul Murphy, and Ellen Schaefer. Marietta also thanks the much missed, much admired Mark Perlman. Most of all, our wives—Jordan and Meg—and our children—Jackson, Mason, and Matt—were our greatest support during these years, our most important and certain facts.

One Nation, Two Realities

1 | Introduction

TRUTH AND TRUST

FACTS RELY ON TRUST. To a greater extent than many of us would like to admit, our perceptions of facts are not grounded on unchallenged observations but instead on trust in others' reports about things that can be disputed. Even if we witnessed an event ourselves, we trust that our own observations were not faulty or biased, mistaken or misremembered. In the more common case that we hear or read about a political reality, we trust that the source—mainstream journalist, government official, political leader, college professor, personal friend, ordained clergy, midnight blogger—is reliable. And if we hear of two dueling accounts of the truth, we must decide which report we trust and which we ignore. Given the necessity of trust, do we trust *your facts or mine*? For most citizens it is not a hard choice—we trust *our* facts. Our facts are the ones that match *our* values. Our facts are the ones that are endorsed by *our* political party and *our* social groups. *Your* facts do not have these characteristics, which allows them to be discounted easily, even if they have empirical evidence or expert opinion on their side.

The Meekness of Facts, the Aggressiveness of Facts

One of the core characteristics of facts is meekness. They do not assert themselves but must be found and often dragged from concealment. They can be pushed around by stronger beliefs like values and ideologies, and they often retreat from loud voices. As value conflict, ideological polarization, and the uncivil discourse of recent American politics have grown stronger, facts have cowered. In *Public Opinion*, Walter Lippmann applauded the occasional "murder of a Beautiful Theory by a Gang of Brutal Facts."[1] But since Lippmann's 1920s, facts have become lazier and less inclined to fight theories. We now have relatively passive facts. By the 1960s, the psychologist Abraham Maslow argued that "the facts are very soft-spoken."[2] By now, they can barely be heard at all above the noise.

On the other hand, we offer the metaphor of dueling facts—violent physical conflict between contenders. American politics now includes continual conflict over fact perceptions, including sometimes perplexed and sometimes uncivil exchanges on television news, online, and in personal conversations over contradictory understandings of reality. We call them *dueling facts* because they come in recognized pairs engaged in combative contests for respect, often over perceived insults to each other's standing. Perhaps the image of dueling pistols is too decisive because the contest seems to drag out without a clear victor. Even a duel with swords seems to offer a more clear-cut winner. Perhaps the better metaphor for the state of factual conflict in American democracy is a boxing match without a referee: a long, bruising fight with many rounds and knockdowns but no knockouts, resulting in bloodied competitors each convinced of victory and an audience equally certain and divided. Any decision from the judges will be split and only lead to accusations of bias and immediate demands for a rematch.

How do we square this contradiction between meek and aggressive facts? Like many facets of facts in the current day, their alternating pacifism and militancy is difficult to comprehend clearly. Part of the problem is the frequent assumption that facts really do speak for themselves. John Milton put it this way in 1644: "Let her and Falsehood grapple, who ever knew Truth put to the worse in a free and open encounter?"[3] The more contemporary sentiment that "the truth will out" is phrased *res ipsa loquitur* ("the thing speaks for itself") in legal jargon and "we hold these truths to be self-evident" in the Declaration of Independence.

Indeed, many a politician wishes he had the power to assert that facts are self-evident and need no justification. But quite the contrary is true in a less trusting political culture. Contradicting the many assertions that facts are stubborn things (as John Adams phrased it in his famous defense of the shooters in the Boston Massacre),[4] we argue that facts are elusive

---

[1] Lippmann 1922, page 10.

[2] Maslow 1963, page 130.

[3] Milton 1644.

[4] "Facts are stubborn things; and whatever may be our wishes, our inclinations, or the dictates of our passions, they cannot alter the state of facts and evidence: nor is the law less stable than the fact; if an assault was made to endanger their lives, the law is clear, they had a right to kill in their

and malleable, more like warm Jello in the hand than a cold statue on a pedestal.

However, while the facts themselves are meekly contented to be wallflowers, *assertions* of facts are often aggressive. Facts are quiet; Fox is loud (and MSNBC is no Zen garden). We suggest that the apparently contradictory nature of facts results from conflating *truth* (actual reality) with *facts* (human approximations of the truth), mixed with *the unwarranted assumption that one or both are easily within our grasp*. To explain this, we can begin with a controversy between two major sources of facts: CNN and *The New York Times*.

CNN versus *The New York Times*: Differing Perspectives on Truth and Facts

In October 2017, CNN began its "Facts First" campaign. The first ad on television, Twitter, and Facebook shows a perfect apple in the middle of the screen while the voiceover explains, "This is an apple. Some people might try to tell you that it's a banana. They might scream banana, banana, banana, over and over and over again. They might put BANANA in all caps. You might even start to believe that this is a banana. But it's not. *This is an apple*."[5]

CNN doesn't question that the perception of the apple is anything but obvious and easy. Other facts are presumably equally clear to them. If fact perceptions are obvious and easy, someone who sees things differently is motivated to deceive and is not to be trusted. The print ads in this campaign state, "Facts are facts. They aren't colored by emotion or bias. They are indisputable. There is no alternative to fact. Facts explain things. What they are, how they happened. Facts are not interpretations. Once facts are established, opinions can be formed. And while opinions matter, they don't change the facts. That's why, at CNN, we start with the facts first." Therefore, the ads imply, listen to

---

own defence." Adams is, of course, arguing that the stubborn fact is that the British soldiers were attacked and therefore it was not a massacre at all, exactly the opposite fact most Americans were taught in school.

[5] https://www.cnncreativemarketing.com/project/cnn_factsfirst. Version 2: "This is an apple. You can look at it from the left; you can look at it from the right. But it doesn't change the fact that this is an apple." Version 3: "This is an apple. And this is a distraction. (chattering teeth move across the screen) But while the distraction might grab your attention, it will never change the fact that this is an apple." Several variations on the theme have followed.

us, "the most trusted name in news" (as their long-standing ad campaign phrases it).

Eight months earlier, *The New York Times* presented a very different set of ads: the "Truth is Hard" campaign, which debuted during the broadcast of the Academy Awards in February.[6] The signature television ad is also stark and simple, featuring black sentences on a white background. It begins with "The truth is *our nation is more divided than ever*" and slowly changes the text following "The truth is . . ." to "*alternative facts are lies*," to "*the media is dishonest*," with a faster and faster rendition of competing claims to truth across the political spectrum. When it slows down again, the now bold type says, "**The truth is hard**," then "**The truth is hard to find**," "**The truth is hard to know**," and finally, "**The truth is more important now than ever**."

At first glance, CNN and *The Times* seem to suggest a similar conclusion: listen to us. However, the characterization of reality offered by the two news outlets is quite different. To CNN, reality is easily recognized and reported, like the nature of the apple. To *The Times*, on the other hand, understanding reality is not easy but hard, specifically because people have different perceptions and because they often haphazardly blend opinions with facts, as in the series of statements in the ad. Those claims are intentionally fuzzy, like everyday arguments, rather than crisp and clear like the apple. *The Times'* nickname, the "Gray Lady," refers to the newspaper's age as the paper of record (and some claim because its close-set typeface makes the entire page look gray rather than black and white), but it also fits the argument of the ad campaign—things are gray and nuanced, requiring a trusted guide such as itself. We agree more with the Gray Lady than with CNN on this one; reality is often difficult to discern, especially in the current political environment.

Before we conclude this comparison of CNN and the paper of record, we would like to call attention to another subtle difference in the two media authorities' ad campaigns, which might go unnoticed but is important: *they employ different terms to describe empirical reality. The Times* focuses on *truth*, while CNN focuses on *facts* ("Truth is Hard" versus "Facts First"). There is an important distinction to be made here, which reflects the competing claims that one is easier to recognize than the other.

---

[6] https://www.youtube.com/watch?v=gY0Fdz350GE.

Truth versus Facts

We often use these two words interchangeably, but they are significantly distinct. *Truth* refers to what really exists, the actual state of things. We would desperately like to know the truth, but philosophers and scientists from the beginning of philosophy and science have recognized that we have only limited and flawed access to it. Errors are rampant, and disagreements are profound. What we do have are *facts*, or *socially determined approximations of the truth*. Facts are as close as we can get to the truth, but they might not be *that* close sometimes. Accepted facts may be somewhat incomplete or even completely wrong. They may be shown to be false and replaced by other facts. No reasonable person asserts that all of the known facts of the current moment are the truth without error or that none of them will ever be withdrawn.

Perhaps more importantly, for most ordinary citizens, the facts are not at all clear. Facts are routinely disputed by political leaders. Facts are sometimes disputed by experts. Even when experts demonstrate a consensus, that consensus is often difficult for ordinary citizens to perceive when they hear opposing views from seemingly respectable sources. There is a great deal of available information on politically relevant facts—too much to handle—but very little clear guidance on which pieces of information are legitimate and which are not. Trust in the traditional sources of authority that are able to provide that guidance—academia and media—has been falling. Many people, perhaps especially the highly educated, may feel that regardless of the public dispute, *they* know the truth or that when in doubt they can sort through the legitimate and illegitimate evidence and come to the right conclusion. It seems clear to them that others who disagree must be misled by elites or misdirected by their friends or are simply misrepresenting for their own benefit (who, after all, could really believe such obvious falsehoods?). We suggest that such epistemic hubris is dangerous. When we assume that the facts are easy to know and that those who dispute us are fools and knaves, negative democratic consequences ensue.

One can pretend that these difficult problems are simple: assume that the known facts reflect the truth, and assume that we can trust a favored source to report the known facts grounded in expert consensus (just trust CNN or *The New York Times*, as their ads suggest). If we make these leaps, they are grounded in trust of various forms. Trust is a large part of the dilemma of dueling facts, largely because trust is in short supply.

To provide a fuller and more common-language understanding of what most contemporary Americans mean when they speak of facts, they are *descriptions of reality that reflect the best available objective evidence as endorsed by the prevailing authorities of society.* The problem is that reasonable people can disagree about whether we have enough evidence to make a claim to owning a fact at all, as opposed to uncertainty or admitted ignorance. What one person considers to be a fact may be seen as an estimate, a guess, or a supposition by someone else who does not recognize the strength of its foundations. When we hear a claim to a fact, reasonable people can disagree about whether those asserting it have established the key elements of "reality," "objective," "evidence," and "prevailing authorities."

Reality simply refers to the world around us. The term assumes that the truth exists outside of human perceptions, even if we have trouble perceiving the truth accurately. Jennifer Hochschild and Katherine Einstein take this common-sense position in *Do Facts Matter?* and describe two forms of these realities: "states of affairs" and "causal statements."[7] The first describes *what exists*, while the second describes *what brings these things into existence.* An example of a factual claim describing a state of affairs would be "the global mean temperature is higher now than 50 years ago," while an example of a causal statement would be "human activity causes climate change." Both are assertions of facts in the sense that *X exists* and *X leads to Y* are descriptions of empirical reality.

While we can break the two apart analytically, more often in the political world these two forms of facts are conflated together. For example, the op-ed headline in *The New York Times* of February 21, 2015—"Obamacare Is Working"—was partly a claim about a state of affairs (the number of insured Americans is higher, and the growth of healthcare costs is lower) and partly a claim about a causal mechanism (aspects of the Affordable Care Act have created these positive outcomes). Rather than being pure statements of either the first kind of fact or the second, more often it seems that political assertions are entangled hybrids of the two. In our view, this makes the project of disentangling states of affairs from causal claims not only difficult but also unhelpful for understanding politics. Like Hochschild and Einstein, we are content to treat both kinds of statements about reality (and their mixture) as claims to facts.

---

[7] Hochschild and Einstein 2015, pages 35–36.

Objective refers to existing without regard to personal perspective. If *the perception relies on the perceiver*, then it is subjective rather than objective. Only if many observers with various backgrounds and beliefs perceive the same thing do we consider it to be objective. Of course, it has become normal in some circles to reject this possibility and insist that all things are subjective at heart. The common-language understanding of facts rejects this insistence on the dominance of subjectivity, whether labeled postmodern or deconstructionist or perspectival or any of the other terms that deny the existence of objective facts. We take the position invoked since Plato's allegory of the cave: we suspect one reality to exist and only doubt our ability to perceive it. The fault is likely ours for being poor at perceiving rather than the world's for being poor at existing in a stable fashion. Another way of phrasing this is that the problem is not about existence but about *epistemology* (can we perceive accurately?). When people refer to a "fact," they are asserting the objective state of affairs, often because they know that the inherent subjectivity of humans creates alternative claims that are false.

Evidence refers to the full range of legitimate information that bears on a claim. Perhaps most importantly, the existence of a fact requires that there *is* evidence. No fact can exist if no evidence is available. In that case we can have opinions, guesses, or hopes but not facts. Even if evidence is available, it can be incomplete, contradictory, or of questionable legitimacy. If enough evidence exists (and cannot be discounted too heavily), we can assert a position with some degree of confidence along the continuum from *possible* to *likely* (more than 50%) to *very likely* to *certain* (which humans almost never reach). In social science, we have pretty much agreed on 95% as a standard of likelihood, which suggests that something is a fact when it is less than 5% likely to *not* be a fact. Insisting on 100% would mean that almost nothing would ever be called a fact, so we are forced to accept a bit of an error rate. But when we call something a fact we are as confident as humans can be that it is grounded in the best available evidence.

So if a fact is a description of reality supported by the objective evidence, when someone claims that something is *not* a fact, he is in essence asserting that it is not objective or not backed up by the available evidence. It may not be objective because it is biased or dependent on other beliefs. It may not be accurate because there are no legitimate data available or because the data are fraudulent or because some other data have not been considered. If any of these objections are believable, then the claim in question is *not* a fact but instead a misperception, mistake, illusion, or some other form of error.

Another common way of defining a fact is *an empirical statement that can be falsified but we are confident has not been.* This is the Popper standard of falsification, which has been extremely influential in social science. The problem is that who *we* are and *how confident* we need to be are not at all agreed upon. Some would argue that the majority is the standard; a consensus perception is a fact. Others argue that the appropriate *we* must be experts; facts are what the experts believe, regardless of how the majority sees it. When someone asserts that "facts are not democratic," she generally has the second standard in mind. But relying on experts to define facts requires that we can identify those experts and trust them to provide authoritative facts about things the public cannot verify for themselves. When citizens trust different sources (or none at all), this conception of facts leads to dispute. The problem of trust is unavoidable: Do we trust specific sources to be authoritative? News media? University faculty? Scientists? Clergy? Government agencies? Hochschild and Einstein define objective facts as those "determined by nearly unanimous agreement among experts who have relatively little ideological or partisan motivation."[8] The difficulty is that citizens may have very different views about which authorities are ideological or non-ideological, partisan or non-partisan, making this understanding of factual authority problematic for citizens to agree upon.

Some have great confidence, trust, or faith in our ability to recognize objectively accurate reality; others have much less confidence and are much less willing to recognize authoritative facts because they do not accept that we have the means to know them or do not trust those who claim to know them. These problems of perception and perspective create disputed claims to reality. When examining this phenomenon, what is the best way to conceptualize it and the best set of terms to employ?

Throughout this book, we employ the following definitions:

Truth is what really exists, though it may or may not be within human observation.

Facts are descriptions of reality reflecting the best available objective evidence endorsed by prevailing authorities.

---

[8] Ibid., page 36.

Epistemology is the process and study of establishing facts, which is important specifically because truth and facts are not necessarily the same.

Dueling fact perceptions (DFPs) exist to the extent that people perceive facts differently, regardless of whether they are established facts or not. DFPs of established facts include *misperceptions* on one side. However, many DFPs make claims for which no clear and indisputable facts have been established—what could be called *blurred realities*. DFPs encompass both *misperceptions* and *blurred realities* (which can be difficult to distinguish and the distinctions between the two can change over time as new information becomes available). Hence, DFPs are the broadest category and the focus of our attention. As we will show, when perceptions of reality are divided, serious democratic consequences follow—regardless of who happens to be right or wrong in any given instance.

The focus on *perceptions* is a key aspect of DFPs as a concept. What exists in citizens' minds is the source of political consequences; perceptions guide political actions, and therefore it is those perceptions we seek to understand. *Misinformation* (false data) would be irrelevant if it did not lead to *misperceptions* (false beliefs). When we or others employ terms like *dueling facts* and *partisan facts*, the additional word *perception* seems to be implied even when it is omitted. There are really no *partisan facts* or *dueling facts*, per se, because an established *fact* (in common language and as we define it) has no legitimate counterpart with which to duel, but there certainly are *dueling fact perceptions*, which is what is implied by the shorthand (and slightly imprecise) term *dueling facts*.

Facts, Truth, and Trust

> Where all the facts are out of sight a true report and a plausible error read alike, sound alike, feel alike. Except on a few subjects where our own knowledge is great, we cannot choose between true and false accounts. So we choose between trustworthy and untrustworthy reporters.
>
> —*Walter Lippmann*[9]

---

[9] Lippmann 1922, pages 142–143.

Public Opinion was published in 1922, but it is a brilliant anticipation of the contemporary politics of truth. In some ways it lays out a starting point for our book:

1) Facts cannot be known easily
2) Conclusions drawn from personal knowledge often fill the gap, and
3) Perceptions of the impersonal world reduce to whom we trust

The trust on which we are forced to rely takes several forms: trust in traditional sources of authority such as universities, trust in government agencies to report information accurately, trust in journalistic fact checkers to establish the truth. And trust in our own personal knowledge and core values as guides to reality. Trust in our social groups and party leaders to fill in the gaps in our knowledge. *Distrust* of the seemingly self-serving and distorted assertions of our political opponents. Distrust of fellow citizens who see the facts differently.

Some kinds of trust have fallen, while others are rising. Which are which can be summarized in the question, *Your facts or mine?* Forms of trust grounded in others—the *your* category—include specific media outlets, universities, government agencies, and fact checkers, all of which are perceived by many to be compromised. Forms of personal trust—the *mine* category—include an individual's own experience, identity groups, information found in personal searches online, and especially a citizen's core values. *Your* facts are trustworthy only to the degree that their sources appear to have connections to *my* groups and beliefs.

In a fascinating book on the origins of contemporary claims to expertise (*A Social History of Truth*), Steven Shapin argues that trust is at the heart of modern epistemology. The goal of the book is "to draw attention to how much of our empirical knowledge is held solely on the basis of what trustworthy sources tell us." Our search for "a world-known-in-common" reduces in many ways to a search for "a reliable spokesman for reality."[10] Who can be trusted to tell the truth? The clergy? The government? Children (as in "The Emperor's New Clothes")? Shapin's argument is that in the early modern period it was gentlemen, who were believed to be so independent (both financially and morally) that they had no incentive to lie. Hence their statements—without any proof the public could understand—would be believed. Eventually this trust was transferred to

---

[10] Shapin 1994, pages 21, 36, and xxvii.

scientists in general, who are the modern-day gentlemen of leisure who do not lie. That trust, however, seems to be time-bound—and its time seems to be ending.

The question of the tree falling in a lonely forest applies here but in reverse. The usual framing of the question assumes that we know a tree has fallen. If we do not have knowledge one way or the other and one person says he heard it fall, while another insists that the noise was not a tree at all but instead something else entirely, do we believe a tree fell? Do we believe it if the earwitnesses in favor outnumber those opposed by a small margin? What if they are 4 to 1? What if the one dissenter is a friend of ours? Perhaps the harder and more appropriate framing for our current politics is, *Do we believe it if we heard something tree-like and we expected a tree to fall, but the experts say it didn't?* Or the reverse—*the experts say it fell, but we did not hear it?* Whom do we trust?

One example of this dilemma is the infamous reporting scandal on George W. Bush's National Guard service, which more or less ended Dan Rather's long career in journalism. The *truth* of the situation—whether Bush did or did not use family influence to gain a National Guard spot that would keep him out of Vietnam and whether he did or did not fulfill his training duties—remains stable but unknown. What changed were the known *facts*. Until *60 Minutes* aired the accusations, the known facts were that Bush served honorably, if not in combat. Then the facts endorsed by a major national institution (CBS News) were otherwise. Then CBS retracted the accusations and fired several influential reporters and editors, changing the known facts again.

The 2015 film about the saga, oddly entitled *Truth*, insists that the *60 Minutes* story really *was* true, even if its sources were false. For his part, Rather continues to defend the story.[11] His position is that even though the sources cannot be documented and may have been falsified, the story they substantiated was in essence true (just not demonstrated by *those* sources). So to summarize, CBS initially said the sources were *facts* and the story was *truth*; CBS later said the sources are *not* facts, so the story cannot be said to be truth; Rather says the sources *may not* be facts, but the story still is truth. No agreement on this will be forthcoming. Rather's 2015 statement for *Variety* magazine was "Don't take my word for what it is; don't take CBS's word for what it is; go see it and make up your own mind."[12] But citizens making up their own minds—grounded in what matches their

---

[11] See Stahl 2012.
[12] Lenker 2015.

prior beliefs more than the legitimate evidence—may be the heart of the problem.

As difficult as it is to forge a consensus, socially created facts endorsed by authoritative institutions are all we have as approximations of the truth. Our current dilemma facing democratic society is that the declining weight of traditional sources of authority allows citizens to follow their own inclinations. Either forced to fend for themselves or freed to follow their own desires, we know what citizens will do: *employ their priors to dictate their perceptions*. And priors in the current day—core values, partisan attachments, social identities—are deeply divided. As we will demonstrate throughout this book, polarized values lead to DFPs. This in turn leads to disdain toward those who perceive facts otherwise and to disengagement by citizens with more moderate views. The polarization of perception leads to a downward spiral of distrust, cynicism, and further political polarization.

Under these conditions, facts are not as obvious as many citizens believe they are. Politically engaged citizens often feel that their obvious perceptions of facts must be asserted; they must speak *truth to power*, by which they mean that obvious truths must override the equally obvious distortions being attempted by the powerful. But majority perceptions are themselves quite powerful, especially when driven by deep feelings of certainty. When they are wrong they may be speaking *power to truth* rather than the reverse. Discerning between the two possibilities has become a problem.

Almost everyone who cares about the trajectory of American democracy bemoans the phenomenon of DFPs. Many recognize—either implicitly or, as in our case, explicitly—that trust is the bridge that allows us to conclude that offered facts are close to actual truth, but that bridge is damaged, collapsing, or perhaps entirely washed away. Nonetheless, many observers have expressed hope that with different media or improved incentives for partisan leaders or better fact-checking or more civic education trust can be restored, facts can become less politicized, and we can all get closer to the truth.

To put it bluntly, we are here to dash those hopes. In the coming chapters, we offer much more psychological background and analyze a great deal of data from surveys and experiments. We end up as pessimistic as Lippmann. He saw it coming, but we are living in it. And we suspect it is going to get worse, not better. Our conclusion is that the core divisions between facts and values have not just been smudged; they have been effectively erased. Before conducting these studies, we might have thought that education was the marker that could redraw the lines. As it turns out, it is the eraser. The only hope for a less factually polarized republic, in our view, is if the public becomes *less* sophisticated and *less* engaged—which is not an inspiring democratic slogan.

Why Now?

A final question to ask at the outset of this inquiry is whether DFPs are really more prevalent and powerful now than they were in times past. The psychological mechanisms described in the following chapters are certainly not *new*. The mechanisms of selective cognition, group conformity, and motivated reasoning (see Chapter 5) have always been with us. But the conditions that allow them to flourish have clearly expanded and deepened in recent times. While many things are the same, there are at least three ways in which conditions are very different: *polarization*, the *information environment*, and the *demise of trust in authority*.

The most influential change may be the extreme moralization of politics and the polarization that has flowed from that. Our core argument that value projection plays a major role in the origins of DFPs is related to the rising polarization of public values. According to a broad range of scholarship, our values are far more divided now than they were through most of the twentieth century. Some scholars disagree about how recently the shift began to occur, but the evidence of rising divisions grounded in core personal and political beliefs is overwhelming.[13] The religious divide is an especially influential part of this story; the rise of public secularism complicated a more uniformly religious public culture. While atheists were once excluded from much of public discourse, secular culture now has a clear voice in American politics. Similarly, other competing voices of racial minorities, feminists, recent immigrants, LGBTQ citizens, and other groups were also once not a part of mainstream political conversation but now very much are, bringing with them a broader set of competing values. These movements of ideas and ideologies have shifted American politics to a more polarized place. Partisan loyalties have also polarized. No doubt partisan attachments have deepened, become more affective, and coalesced across a range of issues that were once less unified within partisan groups. Multifaceted polarization as a

---

[13] See, for example, Hunter 1991, Layman 2001, White 2002, Abramowitz 2011, 2013, Jacoby 2014, Campbell 2016, Garrett and Bankert 2018.

dominant feature of American life and politics is at the heart of the historical changes driving DFPs.

A second influential change is clearly in the information environment. The rise of alternative and partisan media sources aided the rise of opposing perceptions of reality. But these changes are linked to the first change; partisan media did not spring out of the ether. In an important sense, ideologically specific media rose to meet the demand from the divided citizens those media serve (and from whom they profit). Polarization is profitable, for media moguls seeking advertisers, reporters seeking an audience, and politicians seeking votes. Media companies may have risen to supply a divided demand as much as they created it.

Another important development in the information environment is the proliferation of online and social media. The availability of an explosive amount of online information in unguarded form no doubt contributes to DFPs. But the influence of unsupervised information flows is dependent on the third major change that has encouraged DFPs: the decline of trust.

New technologies do not *make* citizens do anything; instead, they *allow* us to do what we are already inclined to do. For example, cars didn't force people to move to the suburbs, but cars did make it easier to do so—which changed American communities in many profound ways. Likewise, the Internet doesn't force people to believe in its wisdom and to disregard traditional sources of knowledge. If citizens continued to trust traditional sources of information authority, the reach of the Internet would be more limited. What it offers fills the void left by the abandonment of the previous gatekeepers. Falling trust in traditional media (the disseminators of knowledge) is one facet of the story. Another is distrust of universities (the producers of knowledge). One of the major changes leading to DFPs was in the character of the university. Chapter 12 (on the role of education and trust in its institutions) is an important part of our argument not only because of the demonstration of the inability of education to unify fact perceptions but also because of the demonstration of the lack of trust in universities. Once regarded as bipartisan and non-ideological institutions, universities have come to be seen as dominated by one side of the ideological spectrum. The polarization of the public leads half of it to distrust an institution it sees as representing an opposing ideology rather than presenting non-ideological facts. The result is an openness to alternative offerings of knowledge, online or in person, legitimate or not.

While we offer three answers to the question of why now—the rise of divided values, the expansion of media and Internet sources, and the decline of trust in authorities to sort it out—all three could be understood as facets of polarization. The polarization of beliefs, the polarization of information sources, and the polarization of trust are deeply interconnected. The psychology of dueling fact perceptions was always available, but the polarized conditions driving that psychology have flourished in our time.

Summary and Plan of the Book

In the chapters that follow, we consider four main questions about dueling fact perceptions: *How should we think about this phenomenon? Why are perceptions of facts so polarized? How consequential is factual polarization? And what are the odds of correction?* The following brief sections provide an overview of the four parts of the book, focusing on the concepts, causes, consequences, and possible correctives of DFPs in the not-so United States.

Concepts (Part I, Chapters 2–4)

Most political science research has focused on "misinformation" and "misperceptions," or the problem that many citizens hear and hold incorrect facts, regardless of the clear verifiability of the correct ones. But the problem of dueling facts is far broader than merely those that are verifiable without controversy. Our aim here is not to understand who is right or wrong but rather to understand how ordinary citizens perceive reality. Part I of the book outlines our conception of DFPs and the empirical evidence we will use to examine them.

Causes (Part II, Chapters 5–9)

The more vital question is, *Why is it so hard to tell which of the competing perceptions are accurate?* While part of the story is surely misdirection by party leaders and media pundits, we argue that this isn't the whole story or even the most important part. Drawing causal arrows is always difficult, so we attempt to distinguish between the *clear* and the *controversial* causes. One clear cause is our current national polarization. Scholars argue about whether Americans are polarized more around values, ideology, partisanship, religion, identity, geography, or media consumption; but each facet of polarization seems to reinforce the others, cycling toward ever greater division. Polarization enhances several interwoven psychological mechanisms of selective cognition that create divided perceptions. The polarized environment also increases the psychological motivation to be accepted by our social groups rather than to be correct about our fact perceptions; holding accurate perceptions of a public controversy has little personal payoff, while belonging to a social group has much greater direct benefits. And while it may be hard to know if the experts agree with us, it is relatively easy to know if our friends do.

More controversial is the extent to which dueling facts are driven by *polarized leadership* or *polarized values*. The first is an external mechanism grounded in the political environment, while the second is an internal mechanism created by citizens' own deeply held beliefs. This is a critical distinction because one mechanism relies on elite manipulations that could be curtailed or counteracted, while the second flows from citizens' own values that are likely entrenched.

The term *partisan facts* reflects the argument by some scholars that the origin is largely the influence of opinion leaders taking advantage of partisan tribalism. In this view, party politicians and the ideological personalities of Fox News and MSNBC (and the like) distort facts for their political ends and drag susceptible citizens along with them. Our view is that the origin of divided perceptions is also divided value systems. Extensive analyses of national survey data suggest that while the external mechanisms are important, so is the internal mechanism of polarized value systems. As public values have polarized over the last decades, facts have followed. Top-down leadership is not necessary if bottom-up beliefs are powerful enough for citizens to project their preferred values onto their perceived facts.

The role of value projection in the creation of dueling facts brings us to one of the other psychological contributions of the volume: a *theory of intuitive epistemology*. The starting point is Philip Tetlock's observation that individuals bring distinct frameworks for discerning knowledge, not merely about expected probabilities and trusted sources but also about the core questions they ask. In other words, we do not end up with the same answers because we do not begin with the same questions. Tetlock theorized that these intuitive epistemologies come in distinct categories, to which we add that those categories reflect distinct value systems. We argue that *value systems carry intuitive epistemology*. A specific value is not merely a predisposition for what we would like to exist but also a predisposition for how we discern its existence. And the stronger the value commitment, the stronger the epistemological framework: *absolutist values lead to absolutist facts*, which makes it even harder to correct misperceptions.

Consequences (Part III, Chapters 10 and 11)

Another argument of the book is that dueling facts have a range of negative consequences that are more difficult to alter than the obvious prescriptions suggest. Some of the clear consequences seem to be miscommunication and mistrust, fostering further division and deadlock. With no agreement on basic realities, we have little chance of a consensus on the national problems to be solved, let alone how to address them. DFPs foreclose the potential for broad policy agreement as well as fruitful deliberation.

Another set of negative consequences are social, extending beyond politics to the coffeeshop and workplace. In our experiments, when people are faced with others who see reality differently, they tend to react with contempt, refusing to share space with them—even workspace, one of the last remaining environments in which many Americans interact with others across the political divide. Factual disagreement even appears to skew the electorate, mobilizing ideologues but silencing moderates. The result is further retreat into like-minded bubbles, creating more distance and distrust, fostering greater polarization.

Correctives (Part IV, Chapters 12–15)

For these reasons, the most commonly offered *correctives*—education and fact-checking—are not effective and may actually be counterproductive. Perhaps the most consistent (and sobering) finding across many recent empirical studies is that specific fact perceptions are *not* predicted by education or political knowledge. The evidence demonstrates that as citizens rise in political sophistication, motivated reasoning becomes stronger rather than weaker. Our findings regarding value projection reach the same conclusion. As cognitive resources grow, citizens simply become more adept at attaching their priors to their perceptions.

Contributing to education's lack of efficacy in reducing DFPs is the erosion of trust in traditional sources of knowledge. Recent national surveys demonstrate that a surprisingly large proportion of Americans hold a low degree of trust in the knowledge created by universities. When the primary institution that discerns and disseminates knowledge for the nation is no longer trusted, this fosters a susceptibility to alternative sources of information. Our data bear this out more precisely. The changes in the perception of the university as an external source of authority are another foundation for pessimism about the effective role of education in creating a consensus.

For some of the same reasons, fact-checking does not amelio-rate divisions in fact perceptions in the intuitive way we might expect. In Chapter 13, we provide a critical assessment of the epistemological foundations of the fact-check industry, and in Chapter 14 we reinforce other scholarly findings that citizens tend to reject the fact-checks that dispute their prior beliefs. Greater education merely facilitates this pro-cess. This is the case even among people who are predisposed to trust fact checkers, even when the perception relates to a candidate from the same political party. These findings further reinforce our conclusion that politically motivated fact perceptions are at least as much about value differences as they are about partisan tribalism and external leadership.

Finally, we find that the durability of DFPs is a reflection of the ideolog-ical symmetry of their origins. While some scholars have suggested that dueling facts are essentially a phenomenon of the Right, driven by con-servative values and Republican leadership, it became clear in analyzing several years of survey data that this is simply not the case. As we show in Chapter 15, the influence of value projection and partisan leadership is remarkably symmetric across various DFPs, and in some ways we find ev-idence of *liberal asymmetry*.

Conclusion (Chapter 16)

The book concludes with the role of dueling facts in the contemporary par-adox of knowledge and democracy. Perceiving the world accurately has always been difficult, but *the polarization problem has increased the epis-temological problem*. Unfortunately, there is more to the origins of dueling facts than laziness by the public and lying by elites; the core problem is not merely miseducation or misdirection but divided values projected onto perceived facts. Greater education and political sophistication are em-ployed to sharpen rather than dull the connections between the strength of internal beliefs and the perception of external realities. The consequences of the dueling facts phenomenon include a degeneration of the close tie between education and democracy.

I | Concepts

2 | What Smarter People Have Said About Facts

PHILOSOPHICAL AND PSYCHOLOGICAL FOUNDATIONS

NIETZSCHE FAMOUSLY SAID "there are no facts, only interpretations." Like many others, we have trouble understanding Nietzsche. We have a sense that he is saying something profound, but exactly what is hard to grasp. This also seems to be where our political culture stands in regard to the phenomenon of dueling facts. It seems to represent a shift, but where it comes from and where it is going are unclear. Many important scholars and thinkers before and after Nietzsche have offered important insights into the nature of fact perceptions. This chapter highlights some of those contributions, which we believe illuminate important aspects of the contemporary predicament. The discussion here does not merely recognize previous thinkers but also explains some of the crucial ideas that frame this study. It provides some deeper insights into what we think is happening and why we are pessimistic about the future of facts.

Presented in general order from older to more recent ideas, we discuss ancient Greek and Norse approaches to facts, the rise and demise of the fact/value distinction, the John Adams/Benjamin Franklin controversy over known facts, the famous Dewey/Lippmann debate over the ability of democratic citizens to perceive facts, and the infamous discussion of bullshit as a rhetorical category.

Two Eyes, One Lie: Deception in the Contemporary Cave

Premodern humans had a relationship with knowledge very different from the one we claim today in the post-Enlightenment world. The ancients believed that knowledge was limited and hard-won. Norse mythology is especially striking in this regard. Odin, the All-Father, was obsessed with gaining knowledge, to the point that when asked to pay the price of one of his eyes for a substantial gain in wisdom, he took the bargain willingly (hence Odin is usually portrayed as wearing an eyepatch).[1] To many modern readers it seems that Odin chose a contradiction: he gained knowledge by giving up a major source of it (clear eyesight). But one point of the myth seems to be that the Norse did not see it that way. They were convinced that what we saw with our eyes was often false; our eyes tricked us to such a degree that eyesight was a trap. If one could stop relying on the eyes and move to a deeper form of knowledge, that was the better choice.[2]

Many of the ancient Greeks were also deeply skeptical about the extent of human knowledge. One of the first metaphors taught to philosophy students is Plato's allegory of the cave: humans attempt to understand the world without being able to observe much of it directly, relying instead on shadows projected on our cave wall from the objects outside. Like many undergraduate students, we were taught the allegory of the cave, only to see it quickly dismissed in favor of Enlightenment hopes for increasing access to knowledge through modern methods. In graduate school, the optimism of Auguste Comte—who coined the term *social physics* in the early 1800s to imply that the social world could be understood and predicted as well as the physical world—replaced the skepticism of the Greeks.[3] Universities as creators of new knowledge promised to take us out of the cave with advanced social science methods. This was especially the case for the topics amenable to quantitative data collection, in which vague claims to knowledge were replaced by the specific levels of confidence provided by statistical analysis.

---

[1] "Long, long ago, when the worlds were young, Odin travelled through the land of the giants, risking his life to get to Mimir, to seek wisdom. . . . 'One drink. With a drink from your well, Mimir, I will be wise. Name your price.' 'Your eye is my price,' said Mimir. . . . Odin's face was set. 'Give me a knife,' was all he said" (Gaiman 2017, pages 45–46).

[2] Contra the advice of the Odin myth, see the discussion in Chapter 5 of the persuasiveness of personal knowledge.

[3] See Comte 1830–1842.

However, these Enlightenment methods of data collection, experimentation, and statistical analysis have produced substantial evidence raising doubts about the optimism created by the Enlightenment. One of the recent critics of strong claims to knowledge is Philip Tetlock, whose research on expert judgment and forecasting amply demonstrates the hubristic over-reach of the expert class.[4] In regard to non-experts, scholars in the years since the rise of mass polling have demonstrated the profound public ignorance of political events, regardless of rising levels of education and falling costs of information.[5]

Pre-Enlightenment (or anti-Enlightenment) thinkers have added other influential challenges to our confidence in obvious perceptions of facts. Perhaps the most influential was Vico's principle of *verum factum*, often translated as "what is true is made" or, as Isaiah Berlin phrases it, "the true [*verum*] and the made [*factum*] are convertible": facts are created by people, and different groups of people create different ones.[6] In *The Future of Fact* (discussed in Chapter 3), Michael Herzfeld puts it more bluntly: "facts *are* made up. And that *is* a fact" (italics in original).[7]

This line of thinking is often traced to Berger and Luckmann's *Social Construction of Reality* or Searle's *Construction of Social Reality*. Both the sociologists (Peter Berger and Thomas Luckmann) and the philosopher (John Searle) argue that many of the things that we think of as objective reality rely instead on consensus beliefs; they are "only facts by human agreement," as Searle phrased it. "There are things that exist only because we believe them to exist," though "they seem as natural to us as stones and water and trees."[8] Berger and Luckmann famously argued that these social realities gain their objective quality by being created by one generation and then accepted by the next.[9] As Berger phrased it in *The Sacred Canopy*, this process of socialization "achieves success to the degree that this taken-for-granted quality is internalized." Hence, some of the aspects of society that we perceive as real, fixed, and enduring depend on the discussion that surrounds us; in this way "the subjective reality of

---

[4] See Tetlock 2005, Tetlock and Gardner 2015.

[5] See most notably Converse 1964, Delli Carpini and Keeter 1996, and Lupia 2016.

[6] Giovanni Battista Vico published his great work—the *Scienza Nuova* (*The New Science*)—in 1725. Isaiah Berlin chose this quote as the best single representation of the concept: "The rule and criterion of truth is to have made it." See Berlin 2000, especially pages 43–51.

[7] Herzfeld 1998, page 71. "Why do we so strenuously resist that insight?": because "it violates a deeply held conviction in the commonsense basis of all claims to factuality."

[8] Searle 1995, pages 1, 4.

[9] This concept may be more familiar in the language adopted by constructivists in political science and international relations: facts are constructed; see Wendt 1992, Hopf 1998.

the world hangs on the thin thread of conversation."[10] Many social facts have this quality: marriage (obviously one man/one woman, until it obviously isn't), paper money (really just paper, unless we all grant it value, until our collective belief falters and paper money hyperinflates into just paper again), or tenure (our personal favorite, which again relies on the collective agreement that scholars have permanent jobs regardless of their annoying habits).

Searle distinguishes *brute facts* from *institutional facts*. While brute facts result from clear evidence and repeated observation, institutional facts are closer to frozen arguments about what is the case. These assertions about reality have hardened into facts, appearing for a time to be solid and indisputable (like brute facts). But they are instead institutional facts that rely on the endorsement of powerful social groups, possibly thawing or shattering when faced with social change. They may change slowly (thawing) or quickly (shattering) but are not as stable as the common-sense understanding of facts suggests.[11]

John Locke—one of the more important Enlightenment thinkers from the American perspective—argued that human knowledge originates in only two fashions: from direct perception through the five senses or through the operation of the mind as we reflect on these perceptions.[12] What is curious about this argument is that it leaves out the major source of contemporary perceptions: what we are told by people we trust. While some of what we know of the world comes from personal observation and experience, a large share of what we know comes from reports we have heard or read or watched, about things we will never perceive directly. Many of the most salient facts of contemporary politics—wars, revolutions, peace talks, the state of the economy, climate change, well-known police shootings, terrorist attacks—are all in the third category of things we learn from external reports rather than sensory experiences. We

---

[10] Berger 1967, pages 24, 17.

[11] See the discussion in Marietta 2012, pages 11–14. One could also reference the Nominalist/Realist debate in medieval philosophy, which was about how much the world exists outside of our beliefs about it. If reality exists independent of our conceptions, then we are back to Plato's cave: we can perceive things correctly or incorrectly, but that doesn't alter what they are. To quote a favorite story told by Mark Perlman about Neils Bohr (the Nobel Prize–winning nuclear physicist), a fellow scientist on the Manhattan Project at Los Alamos visited Bohr at his house and noticed a horseshoe above the garage. "You can't possibly believe in that sort of thing," the visiting scientist said. "Of course not," replied Bohr, "though I hear it works whether you believe in it or not." But that story may not be true.

[12] "So that's my thesis: all our ideas take their beginnings from those two sources—external material things as objects of sensation, and the operations of our own minds as objects of reflection" (Locke 1690, book II, chapter i.4).

now operate in a realm of trust, but not trust in our own faculties; instead we trust in reports from others. And those reports are not merely of the reporter's own perceptions but are reports of reports (of reports). The number of steps between any sensory experience and what we hear is so large that trust has many gaps to fill.

Locke agreed with the Norse and the Greeks on the eyesight metaphor of human understanding: "The perception of the mind is most aptly explained by words relating to eyesight."[13] In Locke's view, "understanding strikes me as being like a closet that is wholly sealed against light, with only some little openings left to let in external visible resemblances or ideas of things outside. If the pictures coming into such a dark room stayed there, and lay in order so that they could be found again when needed, it would very much resemble the understanding of a man."[14] This metaphor is a bit more civilized than the cave, but not much more laudatory of human perception. Locke agrees with the Norse and the Greeks that eyesight is an important metaphor but mostly in the sense of our limitations rather than our abilities.[15]

We may no longer live in caves, but we do live in their parable. In the contemporary cave, the shadows on the wall are now television and the Internet. The image is sharper but does not necessarily provide clearer information. There are important differences that make the current scenario *worse* than the Greek cave. Unlike in Plato's metaphor, in the contemporary cave *we do not know* that we are bound by the neck and unable to turn our heads or leave the cave, limiting our perception. Quite the opposite: we feel superior compared to past ages about how much we know and the easy availability of knowledge should we choose to look it up. And unlike Plato's cave wall, on which was projected only a single image, our living room television depicts *two* competing images, one from the Right and a different one from the Left. Hence, we are faced with potentially greater difficulties of perception. All of this suggests that the Norse were on to something. Perhaps we should be more aware of the lies of the eyes, or at least of the limitations of claims to factual knowledge.

---

[13] Ibid., book II, chapter xxxix.2.

[14] Ibid., book II, chapter xi.17.

[15] Antisthenes to Plato: "I see a horse, but I don't see horseness." Plato: "You have the eye with which a horse is seen, but you have not yet acquired the eye to see horseness." See Guthrie, page 214; see also Campbell 2002, page 75.

The Fact/Value (Non)Distinction

While claims about verifiable facts are problematic, claims about worthy values have the advantage of not pretending to be based on empirical evidence. The long philosophical tradition of the fact/value distinction stretching back to David Hume makes a strong claim of separation between the two.[16] One of our starting points for this book was that facts and values are *philosophically* distinct but *psychologically* intertwined. Even those who believe that the two should be kept separate fall prey to the psychological mechanisms that combine them ruthlessly together. The problem was a philosophical separation that did not hold up empirically. On greater reading and reflection, however, it turns out that even philosophically the division is deeply questionable. Several important thinkers have rejected the separation of facts and values in favor of recognizing their interdependence.

Perhaps the best place to start is Hilary Putnam's *The Collapse of the Fact/Value Dichotomy*, probably the clearest recent statement of the long-standing conflict over the relations between facts and values.[17] The title suggests an unfolding event or transition; the fact/value dichotomy *collapsed*, but it once appeared to be stable, even unquestioned. When we began this study, we too assumed that the dichotomy was stable. However, between Hume's view in the 1700s and Putnam's in the early 2000s, perspectives on what can be known about reality have changed radically, more than once. Putnam points out that Hume understood a fact to be something for which we have a sense impression—if you could see or touch something, it could be said to be a fact. This limited view of facts distances them handily from values. But social science practice advanced far beyond personal observation of visible conditions, incorporating much more distant and abstract social realities. We not only hold the facts we stumble upon personally but also develop perceptions about distant and difficult facts. And the facts we (and others who report them to us) choose to seek out (from the vast multitude of possible facts) are motivated by the values we prefer. Facts and values are connected in the sense of *one motivating the other*. Why any given question would be worth asking is dependent on value judgments. As Putnam phrases it, *"theory selection always presupposes values."*[18] Claims to value-free social science apply to

---

[16] See especially Hume 1739, Weber 1946, Putnam 2002.
[17] Putnam 2002.
[18] Ibid., page 31, italics in original.

the methods of *answering* questions rather than the methods of *choosing* them. Even when the methods of answering questions are value-neutral, the method of selecting questions almost never is because human scholars can choose their questions grounded in what concerns them, driven by their beliefs. Observation of social reality is not neutral but, as Putnam phrases it, "comes to us screaming with values."[19]

When presenting and discussing these distant facts, Putnam argues that "evaluation and description are interwoven and interdependent," such that facts and values are hopelessly connected.[20] To cite a simple example, to call something "cruel" is both a description and an evaluation.[21] We could agree on the action but disagree that it should be evaluated as cruel or agree on what would normatively count as cruel and disagree about whether those conditions occurred. *Cruel* as a term means nothing without *both* the condition and its evaluation being present. Putnam concludes, contra Hume, that in many cases "factual description and valuation can and must be *entangled*."[22]

Putnam also recognized that the fact/value distinction is itself a value statement. It may be so engrained in our thought patterns that we take it as an empirical statement, but it is a philosophical construct that is boldly normative: we *should* think of values and facts as separate so that we can work toward making the facts fit our values (i.e., improve the world). The fact/value distinction was offered by moral philosophers (including Hume) who believed that we should not be lazy about assuming that facts were already in conjunction with values. The world can diverge from our wishes, which is why we should remind ourselves that things are not already as they should be. The fact/value distinction carries very clear value intentions.

Once we recognize Putnam's arguments about the broader contemporary conception of facts, the dependence of factual observations on value motivations, the interweaving of fact and value assessments in everyday description, and the fundamentally normative command in the fact/value dichotomy, it begins to collapse.

Another advocate of the conjunction of facts and values—from a completely different perspective—was the psychologist Abraham Maslow, best known for his theory of a hierarchy of needs. Maslow's approach to

---

[19] Ibid., page 103.
[20] Ibid., page 3.
[21] Putnam also offers the example of wine descriptions: "Think, for example, of the fantastic combinations of fact and value in a wine taster's description of a wine" (ibid., page 103).
[22] Ibid., page 27, italics in original.

facts and values was also an original one. In a remarkable essay entitled "Fusions of Facts and Values," Maslow criticizes "the dichotomy between fact and value which is conventionally and unthinkingly held by most scientists and philosophers to be a defining characteristic of science itself."[23] He notes that "facts don't just lie there, like oatmeal in a bowl."[24] They do not just wait on the table to be found, obvious and self-defining. Instead, we must assign them to categories pre-laden with meaning *simultaneously* with observation. The facts immediately suggest patterns or missing elements; hence, the facts don't speak for themselves, but they do speak. The more we apprehend facts clearly, the more they invoke attention to their value-laden qualities: "the increase in the factiness of facts, of their facty quality, leads simultaneously to increase in the oughty quality of these facts. Factiness generates oughtiness, we might say."[25]

Maslow argues that this inseparableness, or demandingness, of facts toward values is not merely psychologically unavoidable but *preferable*. In both of the best states of humans, this is our aspiration. The first state is peak experiences (self-perceptions of the best moments of a human life), during which we are very happy and perceive the world to be beautiful and complete. The second state is the goal of psychotherapy—to accept ourselves as worthy even with our flaws—what Maslow describes as "a fully loving acceptance of humanness."[26] These are the two preferable ways in which facts and values are brought together: the facts of the world rise up to become closer to our values, or we reconcile our expectations to match what already exists in the world; in either case we perceive facts and values simultaneously and in conjunction. Each of us may achieve neither peak experiences nor acceptance, but *what humans aspire to* is the fusion of facts and values rather than their separation ("the possibility of deliberately, voluntarily fusing facts and values").[27]

To sum things up so far, contrary to the frequent assertion of the fact/value dichotomy, the philosophical distinction is not as sharp as it may first appear. It is not the case, as Putnam explains it, that "fact is fact and value is value and never the twain shall meet"; the two merge frequently,

---

[23] Maslow 1963, page 126.

[24] Ibid.

[25] Ibid., page 127; "Facts create oughts! The more clearly something is seen or known, and the more true and unmistakeable something becomes, the more ought-quality it becomes—the more requiredness it acquires, the louder it 'calls for' particular action . . . the easiest and best guides to the most decisive actions are very more facty facts; the more facty they are, the better guides to action they are" (page 127).

[26] Ibid., page 122.

[27] Ibid., page 125.

sometimes in secret, but often they don't even try to hide their liaison.[28] As we will argue later, the interweaving of the two allows values to frame fact perceptions in the normal process of life and politics. Even the educated and elite are not immune to this syndrome, as suggested by a famous story about two of our Founding Fathers.

The Adams/Franklin Controversy

John Adams and Benjamin Franklin—no ordinary citizens—were forced to share a small room in a crowded inn during the early days of the Revolutionary War (September 1776). Their famous disagreement over prevailing facts was recorded in Adams' autobiography.[29] Though each would have been considered among the most educated members of American society at that time, they held deeply different views of medical facts. The gist of the debate was whether cold temperatures cause colds or some mechanism related to human behavior causes the common illness:

> But one bed could be procured for Dr. Franklin and me, in a Chamber a little larger than the bed, without a Chimney and with only one small Window. The Window was open, and I, who was an invalid and afraid of the Air in the night, shut it close. Oh! says Franklin don't shut the Window. We shall be suffocated. I answered I was afraid of the Evening Air. Dr. Franklin replied, the Air within this Chamber will soon be, and indeed is now worse than that without Doors: come! open the Window and come to bed, and I will convince you: I believe you are not acquainted with my Theory of Colds. Opening the Window and leaping into Bed, I said I had read his Letters to Dr. Cooper in which he had advanced, that Nobody ever got cold by going into a cold Church, or any other cold Air.

In short, Franklin contended that colds are caused by humans polluting enclosed air by respiration: "We should imbibe the real Cause of Colds, not from abroad but from within." Adams does not buy it, because it does not comport with his personal observations: "the Theory was so little consistent with my experience, that I thought it a Paradox. . . . There is much

---

[28] Putnam 2002, page viii.
[29] See the Massachusetts Historical Society archives, dated September 9, 1776. The autobiography is believed to have been written by Adams in the early 1800s (after Franklin's death in 1790), even though recorded in diary form.

Truth I believe, in some of the things he advanced: but they warrant not the assertion that a Cold is never taken from cold air." Adams concludes with an anecdote at Franklin's expense: his death at 84 was likely due to catching a cold. Franklin had long suffered from painful kidney stones but died from complications of a chest cold:

> And I have heard that in the Opinion of his own able Physician Dr. Jones he fell a Sacrifice at last, not to the Stone but to his own Theory; having caught a violent Cold, which finally choaked [*sic*] him, by sitting for some hours at a Window, with the cool Air blowing upon him.

Adams is sympathetic and respectful to Franklin's theories but does not see how they account for the data. This is a clear case of the interplay of theory and evidence in epistemology: Franklin has a theory, but it is incomplete and lacks empirical backing; Adams is not buying it without further evidence. He thought Franklin made some good points but nonetheless maintained that his own views were probably correct, even asserting that Franklin's theory likely killed him.[30]

Several fascinating aspects of this famous dispute illuminate our current concerns about dueling fact perceptions:

1) The two disagree about facts, even though each would be considered among the most knowledgeable citizens.
2) They maintain civility and mutual respect regardless of their factual dispute, with Adams even agreeing to humor Franklin and listen to his justifications. This is not the contemporary norm, as we will discuss in Chapter 11.
3) Adams' resistance to Franklin is grounded in contradictions with his personal observations, even if the theory appeared to be sound. (We will return in Chapter 5 to the influential role of personal knowledge in fact perceptions.)

---

[30] In the final analysis, both men lived to very old ages for their time. Adams passed away at 90, and Franklin at 84 (and Thomas Jefferson live to be 83). George Washington, on the other hand, died at 67, after developing a sore throat following several hours on horseback in a cold rain. However, it may have been the extremity of the bloodletting performed by his doctors that really killed him. This was a normal practice, believed to remove the bad blood that was causing health problems. The most prestigious doctors of that time—including Washington's personal physicians, one of whom had been Physician General of the US Army—believed it to be effective, what we might call an accepted fact endorsed by the reigning authorities of society.

Lippmann versus Dewey: The Epistemology of Democracy

LIPPMANN: "Public opinion deals with indirect, unseen, and puzzling facts, and there is nothing obvious about them."[31]

DEWEY: "The main facts of political action, while the phenomena vary immensely with diversity of time and place, are not hidden even when they are complex. They are facts of human behavior accessible to human observation."[32]

Walter Lippmann and John Dewey conducted a famous debate in the 1920s about the nature and future of American democracy. Dewey was the most famous American philosopher of the time; Lippmann was the younger journalist and shaper of popular opinion. Lippmann wrote first, with a book in 1922 (*Public Opinion*) and a second in 1925 (*The Phantom Public*); Dewey responded to both in 1927 (*The Public and Its Problems*). The debate was ostensibly about the capacities of democratic citizens to meet the demands of democratic citizenship, and therefore what shape American democracy should take (elitist or participatory). This public dispute foreshadowed the extensive political science discussion of citizen competence, from Converse's "Nature of Belief Systems in Mass Publics" in 1964 to Zaller's *Nature and Origins of Mass Opinion* in 1992 to Achen and Bartels' *Democracy for Realists* in 2016. On the question of whether ordinary citizens were up to the task, Lippmann said *No* and Dewey said *Yes*. But the core of their debate was really about the public's ability to perceive facts. Lippmann describes facts as "events that are out of sight and hard to grasp," "unseen," and "invisible"; to Dewey, "the facts are simple and familiar."[33] How could two such distinguished thinkers see the nature of facts so differently?

Dewey's first sentence focuses on "the distance which may lie between 'facts' and the meaning of facts." He goes on to discuss the problem citizens face in comparing brute facts and the competing perceptions of the proper role of government. Lippmann's first sentence invokes a metaphor closer to Gilligan's Island than Plato's cave: a hypothetical "island in the ocean" at the opening of World War One, which was populated with both English and Germans and received little news. If a cannon booms in Europe and no

---

[31] Lippmann 1922, page 17.
[32] Dewey 1927, page 19.
[33] Lippmann 1922, pages 8, 19, 125, Dewey 1927, page 17.

one hears it on an island, can they know they are at war? Lippmann sees the limits of public knowledge as insurmountable, imposed by the complexity of the topic, the flaws in journalism, the limited time citizens can devote to public affairs, and the psychology that leads people to substitute preferred stereotypes for disfavored pieces of knowledge, all contributing to the ocean between established facts and perceived facts. While Dewey and Lippmann never fully account for their different understandings of ordinary citizens' abilities to perceive facts accurately, we offer an interpretation of their differences grounded in their underlying arguments about the distribution of values.

Dewey admits that Lippmann is correct that "political facts are not outside of human desire and judgment," such that "there is a likelihood that we shall unwittingly have doctored the facts selected in order to come out to a predetermined point."[34] Nonetheless, he concludes that the facts are quite accessible. Both thinkers see epistemology as hard, but Dewey is optimistic that we can do it if we try (emphasizing "we"). Dewey is convinced that democracy is a team sport and that collectively the public is quite capable of reaching a consensus perception. It is the public, not the individual, who must act in a democracy, just as the public must act cooperatively to perceive accurate facts.[35]

Lippmann, on the other hand, focused on the problem of the individual citizen: "it is the individuals who act, not society; it is the individuals who think, not the collective mind."[36] Lippmann's disdain for the "mystical democracy" of group wisdom seems to be deeply connected to his view that values are pluralistic and contradictory, providing no basis for an American collective of any meaningful form. There are only individuals, and maybe groups, but no singular public: "There is no human point of view, but only the points of view of men. None is valid for all human beings, none for all human history, none for all corners of the globe. . . . Against this deep pluralism thinkers have argued in vain."[37] Nonetheless, many thinkers "are most reluctant to admit that there is room in the world for different and more or less separate purposes."[38]

---

[34] Dewey 1927, pages 6, 9. "The local face-to-face community has been invaded by forces so vast, so remote in initiation, so far-reaching in scope and so complexly indirect in operation that they are, from the standpoint of members of local social units, unknown. . . . They act at a great distance in ways invisible to him" (page 131).

[35] This argument foreshadows Page and Shapiro 1992.

[36] Lippmann 1927, page 162.

[37] Ibid., page 87.

[38] Ibid., page 151.

Dewey is one of those thinkers, his faith in the public's abilities grounded in his belief that they share collective values. In his view, the error of the individualists is that "current philosophy held that ideas and knowledge were a function of a mind or consciousness which originated in individuals by means of isolated contact with objects. But in fact, knowledge is a function of association and communication."[39] Dewey saw the public as fully capable of consensus, arrived at through collective action and thought. He offers several striking turns of phrase connecting effective democracy and knowledge creation: "Democracy is a name for a life of free and enriching communion,"[40] as well as "faith in the capacities of human nature; faith in human intelligence and in the power of pooled and cooperative experience."[41] It is the process of "organized intelligence,"[42] creating "a kind of knowledge and insight which does not yet exist."[43] Democracy is a method to "read what we call reality (that is to say the world of existence accessible to verifiable inquiry),"[44] which requires "the participation of every human being in the formation of the values that regulate the living of men together."[45] Democracy creates consensus knowledge, which supports consensus values, which reinforce democracy, etcetera.

At heart, the dispute is not about the *facts of democracy* as much as it is about the *democracy of facts*. Dewey believed that democracy (collective decision-making) created consensus perceptions (but he also recognized that this depends on consensus values). Can all of us know reality in the same way and arrive at recognized facts? Dewey said *Yes* because we start with consensus values (and continue to reinforce them together). Lippmann said *No* because our values are divided. Who was correct about consensus versus conflictual values? We believe it is hard to argue in current polarized America that it was not Lippmann who saw the future: American values are not merely plural but deeply divided and antagonistic in contemporary politics. As Carl Bybee phrased it in an incisive essay in 1999, Lippmann "saw the post-factual world and feared it. The absence of facts and the primacy of subjective perceptions meant for Lippmann a world paralyzed by relativity."[46]

---

[39] Dewey 1927, page 158.
[40] Ibid., page 184.
[41] Dewey 1937, page 460.
[42] Dewey 1935, page 79.
[43] Dewey 1927, page 166.
[44] Dewey 1919, page 42; see also Morris 1999.
[45] Dewey 1937, page 462.
[46] Bybee 1999, page 60.

Lippmann provides a vivid description of how divided values create disputed facts, grounded in "the habits of the eyes" or "the human habit of accepting foresight for sight."[47] "For the most part we do not first see, and then define, we define and then see"; therefore, "what is alien will be rejected, what is different will fall upon unseeing eyes. We do not see what our eyes are not accustomed to take into account. Sometimes consciously, more often without knowing it, we are impressed by those facts which fit our philosophy."[48]

We suspect values are the key elements of our belief systems that do this work (along with partisan identity and ideology):

> Rationally, the facts are neutral to all our views of right and wrong. Actually, our canons determine greatly what we shall perceive and how. . . . The orthodox theory holds that a public opinion constitutes a moral judgment on a group of facts. The theory I am suggesting is that, in the present state of education,[49] a public opinion is primarily a moralized and codified version of the facts. I am arguing that the pattern of stereotypes at the center of our codes largely determines what group of facts we shall see, and in what light we shall see them.[50]

This explains "why a capitalist sees one set of facts, and certain aspects of human nature, literally sees them; his socialist opponent another set and other aspects, and why each regards the other as unreasonable or perverse, when the real difference between them is a difference of perception."[51] Divided beliefs (values, ideologies) are the structure on which the superstructure of fact perceptions are built. Hence, dueling fact perceptions are as sincere as they are difficult for others to understand.

To summarize the Dewey/Lippmann debate from the perspective of facts: democracy relies on epistemology; collective epistemology depends on consensus values; and if we do not have consensus values, then epistemology will fracture. These observations frame our perspective on the

---

[47] Lippmann 1922, pages 54, 60.

[48] Ibid., pages 55, 78.

[49] Lippmann's reference to "the present state of education" reflects his endeavor in *Public Opinion* to frame an answer to the lack of capacity of democratic citizens; the book ends with a hope that professional social science might solve "the failure of self-governing people to transcend their casual experience and their prejudice, by inventing, creating, and organizing a machinery of knowledge" (ibid., pages 229–230), but by the publication of *The Phantom Public* Lippmann had abandoned the idea that professional journalists and scholars would transcend their own ideological biases of perception.

[50] Ibid., pages 79, 81.

[51] Ibid. page 82.

origins of dueling fact perceptions (Chapters 5–7) and on the concept of intuitive epistemology (Chapter 8).

While Lippmann and Dewey differed on whether accurate public perceptions were possible, they seemed to assume that individuals had similar conceptions of what they were trying to perceive. But what if different individuals have different goals of perception? Both philosophers and psychologists have suggested that one method of perception does not fit all, as highlighted in the philosophical and psychological debates over *correspondence* versus *coherence*.

The Epistemology of Facts: Correspondence versus Coherence (versus Pragmatism)

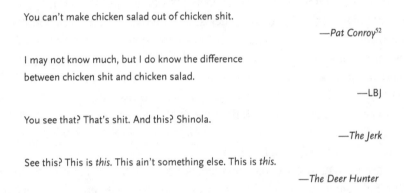

You can't make chicken salad out of chicken shit.

—*Pat Conroy*[52]

I may not know much, but I do know the difference
between chicken shit and chicken salad.

—LBJ

You see that? That's shit. And this? Shinola.

—*The Jerk*

See this? This is *this*. This ain't something else. This is *this*.

—*The Deer Hunter*

"Wassat?," two-year-olds ask repetitively, pointing to something in the vicinity. "Wassat?," they ask again, pointing to something else. The fascination with what things are (and the satisfaction that each thing—and others like it but not things different from it—has a singular name) can take up a lot of our time, both at home and on campus. Recognizing things for what they are, and not mistaking them for something they may seem like but are not, is one of the core roles of scholars as well as parents naming things for children. This endeavor is deeply complicated by epistemological disagreements over *how*, but also over *why*, we are doing that. Is chicken salad distinct from chicken shit, or are they the same thing? Why do we want to know? When it comes to food, this knowledge is not just idle curiosity but has a much more pragmatic purpose. Do we have to know the names and facts of many things (like a fox), or as LBJ and Steve Martin suggest, only the most important ones (like a hedgehog)?

---

[52] *Prince of Tides*, page 92.

A traditional question yelled by drill sergeants in army boot camp is, "Private, what's the white stuff in chicken shit?!" The correct response is, "That's chicken shit too, Drill Sergeant!" This means that small pedantic distinctions are not important; every part of chicken shit is chicken shit and has no excuse for its behavior. Another example of this graphic practical epistemology is in the famous scene from *The Deer Hunter*, in which Robert DeNiro's character explains to one of his hapless buddies that things have consequences and people should know what they are. His way of phrasing it—"This is this, this ain't something else"—makes little sense on its face but is also an evocative statement about the stable nature of the world, who understands it, and who is a fool.

The ease and accuracy of public epistemology—as in the case of Dewey versus Lippmann—are deeply disputed. Not only the facts but also the methods by which we can discern facts (as well the purposes for which we do so) are not agreed upon. In order to see some of the core disagreements, we have to take a brief and somewhat depressing tour through some of the highlights of the philosophy of truth. To put the conclusion up front, there are distinct legitimate goals of perception, on which individual philosophical traditions—and likely individual citizens who know nothing of philosophy—differ substantially. One of the core competing distinctions is the difference between *correspondence* and *coherence* as the definition of reality (and goal of perception).

Carl Bernstein gave the keynote address at the 2017 White House Correspondents' Association Dinner. He focused on his signature phrase: "the best obtainable version of the truth." Bernstein attempted to define this goal of journalism in the age of Trump (who broke tradition by not attending the dinner but was still its main topic of conversation): "It's a simple concept, yet something very difficult to get right because of the enormous amount of effort, thinking, persistence, pushback, logical baggage and, for sure, luck that is required, not to mention some unnatural humility. . . . The best obtainable version of the truth is about context and nuance, even more than it's about simple existential facts." Context and nuance require the reporter (or scholar) to add interpretation and meaning: What are the other important things connected to this thing? Why do we care? What does it mean? And here values come into play. This would cause little comment if those values were shared, but in the current day they are not.

The Correspondents' Dinner advocated (perhaps unsurprisingly) a correspondence theory of truth. *Correspondent* as a noun can mean both "a person employed by a news agency to send reports" and "a thing that corresponds to something else." The linguistic connection does not seem accidental. The correspondence theory argues that we can only determine the accuracy of a statement by its connection to empiricism; a belief is true to the degree that it fits with accepted observations. But standards of truth, like so many other things in social science, have a robust competition. At least three other competing understandings have influenced how we see facts: *coherence* (rather than correspondence), *pragmatism*, and *postmodernism*. As scholars we tend to reject all three of them, but they nonetheless have had great influence and explain something important about contemporary dueling fact perceptions.

Philosophers of science have engaged in a long debate over *coherence* versus *correspondence* as the "best available version of the truth." Simply put, the coherence theory argues that we can only determine the truth or accuracy of a statement by its compatibility (coherence) with other statements that we already accept; a belief is true to the degree that it fits with our other beliefs.[53] Coherence is prized in theory-driven research; congruence among accepted theories is demanded for believability.[54] Consider the role of coherence in our perceptions of lying. If someone alleges that *X* lied, but you think he is an honest person, the assertion is not coherent with your priors, so you are likely to not believe it. This raises the critical role of *trust* in both approaches to truth. Coherence is more obviously grounded in trust of ourselves and others: we accept as true the things that fit with what we already believe, and we accept as reliable sources those whom we already trust.

Correspondence *also* relies on trust for any assertion of empirical agreement that we cannot examine ourselves (which is a large number of important things in our contemporary specialized society). When we cite a consensus of scientific belief as evidence, we are really asserting a form of mediated correspondence grounded in trust of a group of scientists.

---

[53] "Two grand metatheories have been persistent rivals in the history of science in general and in the history of research in judgment and decision making in particular. . . . The goal of a correspondence metatheory is to describe and explain the process by which a person's judgments achieve *empirical accuracy*. The goal of a coherence metatheory of judgment, in contrast, is to describe and explain the process by which a person's judgment achieves logical, or mathematical, or statistical *rationality*. . . . Scientific research seeks both coherence and correspondence but gets both only in advanced successful work. Most scientific disciplines are forced to tolerate contradictory facts and competitive theories. Researchers must, therefore, live with the tension caused by those who wish to pursue the reconciliation of facts and those who wish to resolve the contradictions of theories" (Hammond 2000, page 53). See also Rescher 1973, Kirkham 1992, Hammond 2007.

[54] "Theories must be coherent. That is, theories cannot be self-contradictory and generally, they must be consistent with other widely held beliefs within that scientific community" (Dunwoody 2009, page 119). See also Young 2001.

We assume that the views of those scientists correspond with reality; but that assumption is grounded in trust, and it falters if that underlying trust diminishes. To the extent that trust in the knowledge communicated by accepted authorities (academia, media) is grounded in perceived agreement with values or ideology, the foundations of coherence creep into the standard of correspondence. (We will return in Chapter 12 to the variation in trust in academic authority as a crucial aspect of dueling fact perceptions.)

So we recognize truth either because it matches our priors that we already accept as true (coherence) or because it matches observations that we accept as valid (correspondence). The core problem with coherence as a standard of truth is that claims of facts can be logically connected to things that we already believe are true *but still be false*. The core problem with correspondence is determining *which observations* are the correct ones to consider; for many questions of fact there are multiple possible indicators.[55] Much has been written about these two concepts of truth, and we would only like to make a small proposition: while most contemporary social scientists endorse a correspondence theory—which asserts that reality is knowable through observation, even if it is difficult to perceive accurately and we should often default to admissions of ignorance—what many people *really do* much of the time is follow a coherence theory, which is easier, is more satisfying, and does not require the frequent admission of uncertainty or ignorance (which people hate). It is much more difficult to know if a proposition corresponds to objective reality than if it coheres with our other beliefs (or if it coheres with the beliefs of people we trust). Looking outward for evidence is much more problematic and time-consuming than looking inward for connections to what we already believe. Even when attempting to look outward with integrity, we most often rely on the word of others with whom we cohere. *Correspondence is hard, while coherence is relatively easy.*

Earlier we discussed the famous Adams versus Franklin controversy over the facts of the night air as an example of how the most educated and intellectual members of a society can still disagree on facts (and, at that time period at least, still respect each other). This dispute is also an

---

[55] The dual dilemmas are "the possibility of a coherent set of beliefs that do not correspond to reality, and the difficulty in selecting and identifying facts for correspondence" (Dunwoody 2009, page 121). See also Tetlock 2005 on correspondence with observations as a foundation for truth compared to coherence with priors.

example of correspondence versus coherence as competing standards. Adams is arguing correspondence (the idea that cold temperatures are not related to colds does not correspond with his observations), while Franklin is arguing coherence (his prior theory of colds logically means that cold air is not harmful).

It is important to note that Dewey was not an advocate of either correspondence or coherence as an approach to truth and fact. He had his own approach: pragmatism. Dewey saw the purpose of knowledge as social utility: what is effective in achieving collective goals is true. As Bybee phrases it, "the test of truth must be in its consequences for the people and judged by the people who experience those consequences."[56] The pragmatic epistemology of facts leads to a problem: if the truth of a belief is gauged by its effectiveness, then the goals that we seek are a core element of truth. In other words, the values we wish to achieve shape the truth (effectiveness) of facts. Those who embrace different values and goals will embrace different facts. Dewey did not see this as a problem because he assumed a functional set of consensus values in American culture and politics. With consensus values, a pragmatic approach is a viable competitor to correspondence. However, with polarized values, pragmatism leads directly to factual divergence, aided by a respectable philosophical perspective. We do not have the capacity in contemporary American politics for consensus pragmatism, only *polarized pragmatism.*

As we mentioned, postmodernism is a fourth approach that has influenced American culture. It is more a theory of anti-knowledge or the impossibility of facts, and we think it is fair to say that most social scientists reject it as foolish on the face. However, it seems to have had broad influence in the humanities and even in mainstream culture. Postmodernism thrives on the lack of a clear definition, though it generally includes not merely the denial of the availability of knowledge but the accusation that knowledge production is really about power.[57] In *Respecting Truth*, Lee McIntyre argues that the problem with postmodernism is that some "have

---

[56] Bybee 1999, page 61.

[57] This includes a broad range of "deconstructionists" as well as postmodernists (Derrida 1981, Foucault 1977, Rorty 1979, etc.), who take more radical positions against any existing or knowable objective reality. These views are taken more seriously in the humanities than social sciences as they at heart assert that reality does not exist in a stable form, rather than the more common social science assumption that a relatively stable reality exists but is difficult for humans to perceive and agree upon. The problem is either that reality is does not exist (postmodernism, which is insurmountable) or that reality is hard to discern (epistemology, which is merely difficult).

interpreted it more radically as a claim not just about the impossibility of objective knowledge, but a denial of independent reality itself. Thus there is no truth, because there is no objective fact or reality to which it could correspond. Why then would anyone insist that they know the truth? In order to assert their power."[58] McIntyre blames part of the problem of the contemporary disrespect for university knowledge on the negative influence of postmodernism bleeding out beyond academia. Postmodernism is insidious because, like conspiracy theories, it is hard to engage with evidence. In conspiratorial thought, the lack of evidence is considered evidence that a conspiracy has swept that evidence under the rug.[59] As students of ours have asserted, the lack of evidence of the Illuminati is actually evidence of their power to erase their tracks. Likewise, "How can one hope to engage in rational argument over the truth of the 'social construction of knowledge' claim against science when it is a fundamental truism of relativism and postmodernism that there is no such thing as truth?" McIntyre concludes that "promoting fashionable academic notions, even though the arguments for them are weak, is playing with fire and can cause real damage."[60]

To summarize the conflictual history of the epistemology of facts, *correspondence* is what most ordinary people and social science scholars most often think is correct, but it is difficult; *coherence* has more support within philosophy than social science and is easier psychologically, leading to polarized facts; *postmodernism* may be nonsense but has been influential, also leading to polarized facts; and *pragmatism* has some support and leads directly to polarized facts grounded in competing values. Which approach is followed by ordinary citizens in their perception of facts has never been fully examined. Only correspondence leads toward consensus fact perceptions—but if and only if we agree on which empirical evidence to employ, which we often do not. The other three approaches to knowledge lead directly to dueling fact perceptions. Even though correspondence may be what most social scientists (and journalists) believe people *should* do, when we combine the legitimate arguments in favor of coherence with the easier cognitive burden it presents, we suspect that coherence with values is what people *actually* do.

---

[58] McIntyre 2015, page 104.
[59] See Uscincki and Parent 2014.
[60] McIntyre 2015, pages 105, 107.

The Nature and Importance of Bullshit

Returning to the Nietzsche quote at the beginning of the chapter—"there are no facts, only interpretations"—did he really say that? He seems to have written it in his notebooks, which were only published after his death in collected fragments that he never put in finished form.[61] For someone who wrote a remarkable amount, the quote is not in his official works, so did he really mean it? And didn't he go insane? We heard that. With these observations we have discounted the event and discredited the source, so maybe we don't have to take it seriously. So facts can easily slip into not existing, even the fact of possibly the most famous assertion that they do not exist. This, one might say, is bullshit. It is more clever than meaningful or, as they say in the law, "more prejudicial than probative" (more likely to mislead than inform). One might think that this is not a scholarly topic, but it has become so in recent years because of its broad cultural significance. In order to understand contemporary knowledge claims—especially by politicians—we suggest that one should consider the relevance of *On Bullshit* by Harry Frankfurt.

Frankfurt wrote an influential essay first published in the *Raritan Review* in 1986 and later as a brief book in 2005. It argues that we should recognize the nature and boundaries of bullshit as a category of prevalent communication. Bullshit is not *truth* (accurate reality) or *fact* (empirically supported and institutionally endorsed reality), but neither is it *lying* (intentional falsehood). Lying has the goal of giving a false impression about the *subject* of the statement; bullshit has the goal of giving a false impression about the *speaker* of the statement. The goal is personal aggrandizement or status enhancement, regardless of the truth or falsity of the statements made. This is done by making the speaker appear smart, witty, or amusing (socially desirable traits) but only incidentally accurate. A bullshitter's bullshit might be true, or it might not be; but the speaker is simply unconcerned about accuracy as a goal. As Frankfurt put it, "what he cares about is what people think of *him*."[62]

Frankfurt suggests that bullshit is both prevalent and on the rise (in 1986 and then in 2005). Why? Because the actual facts, which allow for telling the truth or lying, are less available: "Bullshit is unavoidable whenever circumstances require someone to talk without knowing what he is talking about."[63] Given that under these conditions "it makes

---

[61] Nietzsche (1886) 2003, page 139.
[62] Frankfurt 2005, page 18, italics in original.
[63] Ibid., page 63.

no sense to try to be true to the facts, he must therefore try instead to be true to himself."[64] Frankfurt makes an important observation for understanding contemporary politics in the Trump era and perhaps beyond: "people do tend to be more tolerant of bullshit than of lies." Lying is dangerous to one's reputation, while bullshitting is less so; hence, "never tell a lie when you can bullshit your way through."[65]

To summarize, perhaps there is a large category of fact assertions that have status value rather than truth value; their goal is being impressive rather than being accurate. An interesting article by Rasmus Kleis Nielsen argues that we should expect to find more bullshit on social media: "The gulf between the supply of justified beliefs and the demand for much more . . . creates space for bullshit." He concludes that "we need to take bullshit seriously as an intellectual and analytical problem."[66] We concur.

The concept has certainly come into discussion in popular culture. Jon Stewart gave a well-known discussion of the prevalence of bullshit in his final monologue on the *Daily Show* in August 2015:

> Bullshit is everywhere. There is very little that you will encounter in life that has not been, in some ways, infused with bullshit. Not all of it bad. Your general, day-to-day, organic free-range bullshit is often necessary. Or at the very least innocuous. 'Oh, what a beautiful baby. I'm sure it'll grow into that.' That kind of bullshit in many ways provides important social-contract fertilizer. It keeps people from making each other cry all day. But then there's the more pernicious bullshit. Your premeditated, institutional bullshit, designed to obscure and distract. Designed by whom? The bullshitocracy. . . . The best defense against bullshit is vigilance. So if you smell something, say something.

Stewart seems to understand the concept very much like Frankfurt does: assertions for social value rather than truth value, which are problematic when they are confused with assertions intending to convey actual reality.

---

[64] Ibid., page 66. Cf. Polonius' famous advice to his son in *Hamlet*: "This above all: to thine own self be true, And it must follow, as the night the day, Thou canst not then be false to any man" (Act I, Scene iii). This sentiment can be interpreted several different ways.

[65] Ibid., page 50.

[66] Nielsen 2015, page 2.

A Note on Trump and Bullshit

In the Preface, we argued that this book is not about Donald Trump: dueling fact perceptions preceded him and will likely continue long after his presidency. However, the Trump presidency is part of the story of dueling facts. In an important sense, the Trump election may be a product as well as a cause of divided perceptions.[67] However, Trump also seems to have added to the dueling facts phenomenon through his use of language, which we believe is aimed at persuasion rather than accuracy. In other words, Trump's rhetorical success and bullshit are deeply connected: Trump seems to reflect the bullshit goal of amusement/persuasion/social status rather than the academic goal of accuracy.[68] Given that political science scholars frequently argue that the primary aim of politicians is to be elected (rather than to be correct, including during the governing/permanent campaign phase), this should not be a surprise.

As Trump phrased it to *Time*, "I'm an instinctual person, I happen to be a person that knows how life works."[69] And as Tony Montana phrased it in *Scarface* in 1983, "Me, I always tell the truth. Even when I lie." If a politician can choose between saying something that is *literally true* (and likely verifiable), *possibly true and possibly not* (but difficult to verify), *entertaining* (without reference to its veracity), or *authentic* (true that I think it), the first category may have much less political value than some combination of the other possibilities. This may be especially the case if the literally true thing does not serve his social/electoral purposes. We suspect that Trump follows the opposite of the academic practice in choosing factual assertions: rather than attempting to find areas where there is dispositive evidence and make a defensible claim, Trump focuses on areas in which there is little accepted evidence (or that are characterized by contrary assertions) and then makes claims that are difficult to verify. Those factual claims can be described as bullshit in the sense that their primary

---

[67] See Swire et al. 2017, Gunther et al. 2018.

[68] Cf. Fareed Zakaria on CNN, March 17, 2017: "I think the president is somewhat indifferent to things that are true or false. He has spent his whole life bullshitting. He has succeeded by bullshitting. He has gotten into the presidency by bullshitting. It's very hard to tell somebody at that point that bullshit doesn't work because look at the results, right? But that's what he does. He sees something, he doesn't particularly care if it's true or not, he just puts it out there." See Vales 2017. See also Dawsey et al. 2018, who reported in the *Washington Post* that Trump admitted to making up factual assertions when meeting with Canadian prime minister Justin Trudeau: "Nice guy, good-looking guy, comes in—'Donald, we have no trade deficit'—I said, 'Wrong, Justin, you do.' I didn't even know . . . I had no idea. I just said, 'You're wrong.'"

[69] *Time* interview, March 22, 2017.

goal is not empirical accuracy but social acceptance, a likely pervasive and persuasive form of political and social communication.

Conclusion

This chapter offered some foundational ideas that influenced how we see the concept of dueling fact perceptions. To summarize:

1) While we initially assumed that the fact/value distinction was correct philosophically but incorrect empirically, it turns out that it has serious philosophical flaws as well.
2) Knowing facts is hard, which was pointed out not only by the Norse and the Greeks but also by contemporary philosophers and social science scholars. This highlights the importance of *epistemology*— the study and practice of knowledge claims—a concept we will discuss often in the upcoming chapters. (See especially Chapter 8 but also Chapters 12, 13, and 14.)
3) The Adams/Franklin controversy teaches us that even the most educated elites of other eras were also not immune from factual disagreement, though even in the combative and slanderous time of the American Revolution these two gentlemen maintained civility in the face of dueling facts. (In contrast, see Chapter 11.)
4) Dewey and Lippmann had a much more public and influential disagreement in the 1920s over whether ordinary citizens could accurately comprehend political facts; in the end, their dispute is about the underlying degree of value conflict as well as the epistemology of democracy. (See Chapter 7 regarding why Lippmann was correct.)
5) While many scholars assume that *correspondence* with empirical observation is the touchstone of truth, rival philosophers (and psychologists) offer the competing standard of *coherence* with prior beliefs. While correspondence with evidence may be what empirical scholars tend to prefer, coherence with values is what many citizens likely practice. (See Chapter 6.)
6) The prevalence of bullshit as an influential facet of how humans often argue (for social value rather than truth value) is no bullshit. (See especially Chapter 5.)

3 | Dueling Facts in Political Science

"It was no part of political science to think out how knowledge
of the world could be brought to the ruler. . . .
It was not necessary to consider how to
inform the heart and feed the reason.
Men took in their facts as they
took in their breath."

—Walter Lippmann[1]

W E AGREE WITH LIPPMANN THAT, once upon a time, professional political science ignored the role of facts, but not anymore. Just as scholars once assumed the aggregation of policy
opinions was simple and seamless—until Kenneth Arrow discovered
that preferences do not aggregate easily and Philip Converse observed
that consistent preferences may barely even exist—scholars and pundits
once assumed that facts were easily identified, conveyed, and believed.
But the polarization of fact perceptions has become a manifest feature of
American politics. Over the course of the last two decades, many prominent scholars have addressed the role of facts in politics, and the pace has
accelerated in recent years. However, just as fact perceptions are disputed
in American politics, the study of factual disputes is characterized by core
disagreements yet to be resolved. This chapter discusses some of the dominant perspectives and highlights the ways in which our approach is different and more comprehensive.

---

[1] Lippmann, 1922, page 164.

Competing Concepts

Facts have always played a role in political science analyses but not clearly focused on the problem of factual *dispute*. In John Zaller's extremely influential book *The Nature and Origins of Mass Opinion*, he notes that "every opinion is a marriage of information and predisposition: information to form a mental picture of a given issue, and predisposition to motivate some conclusion about it."[2] But he quickly leaves the topic of facts, assuming that political information was something a citizen either had or didn't have, rather than something over which there was disagreement. The contemporary classic work on knowledge in politics is Delli Carpini and Keeter's *What Americans Know About Politics and Why It Matters* (1996). They catalogue the vast lack of information held by American citizens but again see knowledge as something that runs from very little to a lot (usually very little) but not *competing* pieces of mutually exclusive knowledge.[3] Arthur Lupia's more recent book *Uninformed* (2016) updates and expands Delli Carpini and Keeter's study of political knowledge. Again, it focuses on the public's *lack* of information rather than *disputed* information.[4]

Since the late 1990s, scholars have increasingly recognized the role of dueling facts. This literature employs the terms *misinformation, misperceptions, partisan facts*, and *cultural cognition*, among others. Several of these terms carry a theory of origins or an argument about the nature of the phenomenon itself. We briefly review this scholarship, focusing on how each of these terms restricts understanding of the broader phenomenon. We conclude by offering the term *dueling fact perceptions* (DFPs) as the broadest and most neutral conceptualization that allows us to study the phenomenon without prejudgment.

---

[2] Zaller 1992, page 6.

[3] Also see Bartels 1996, Althaus 1998, Gilens 2001, Barabas and Jerit 2009, Jerit and Barabas 2017, Barabas et al. 2014.

[4] Lupia's book is more nuanced about what counts as useful information from different perspectives and recognizes the role of value projection on factual perception: "Values have a strong and deep effect on how people see the world. . . . Values often affect our responses to new information before we realize that they are having this effect" (pages 108, 111).

Misinformation and Misperceptions Restrict the Range of Inquiry

Two of the commonly employed terms in the emerging political science literature are *misinformation* and the resulting *misperceptions*.[5] One of the earliest and most influential studies of misinformation was by James Kuklinski and colleagues, which defined *misinformed* citizens as those who "firmly hold beliefs that happen to be wrong . . . not just in the dark, but wrongheaded."[6] Brendan Nyhan and his colleagues define *misperceptions* as "factual beliefs that are false or contradict the best available evidence in the public domain."[7] In the same vein, Jennifer Hochschild and Katherine Einstein's important book begins with the "premise of a sharp and important divide between individuals who know the facts and those who believe something else."[8] Subspecies of misinformation and misperception include *disinformation, malinformation, propaganda, fake news, rumors, conspiracy theories*, and even *damned lies*.[9]

The focus on misinformation/misperception and its cousins channels inquiry into only those fact perceptions for which just about any reasonable, intelligent, and sane person would reach a similar conclusion, such

---

[5] See Berinsky 2017, Hochschild and Einstein 2015, Kuklinski et al. 2000, Nyhan and Reifler 2010, 2015, Reedy et al. 2014, Wells et al. 2009.

[6] Kuklinski et al. 2000, page 793.

[7] Flynn et al. 2017, page 128.

[8] Hochschild and Einstein 2015, page 38.

[9] While misinformation is simply wrong, *disinformation* is deliberately and intentionally false (see Habermas 1984, Lewandowsky et al. 2013). Another category, *malinformation*, is true information that is shared to cause harm; an example is the public release of the Clinton campaign emails by WikiLeaks (see Derakhshan and Wardle 2017). When false information is shaded in such a way as to unfairly discredit one point of view, it is often termed *propaganda* (see Lasswell 1927, Sproule 1997). *Fake news* is fabricated reports by disreputable sources, especially online, which mimic the appearance of credible news sources (see Allcott and Gentzkow 2017, Lazer et al. 2018; of course, this is not what everyone means by the term—it is also used regularly to discredit a mainstream news story that one does not like). *Rumors* are unverified claims that tend to spread rapidly "because other people seem to believe them" (Sunstein 2009, page 6), providing psychological comfort in contexts of ambiguity, rapid change, or perceived threat (see DiFonzo and Bordia 2006, Gidda 2014, Berinsky 2015, 2017). *Conspiracy theories* resemble rumors, but they emphasize the agency of secretive, powerful cabals (see Sunstein and Vermeule 2009, Uscinski and Parent 2014, Miller et al. 2016, Uscinski et al. 2016, see also Marietta and Barker 2018 on the relations between conspiratorial thinking and DFPs). Finally, Robert Shapiro distinguishes *damned lies*, which he defines as intentional and authoritative falsehoods put forward when there is a lack of balance in the information environment, meaning that the lie goes unchecked. Prominent examples of damned lies include (1) the 1960 claim by the Kennedy campaign of a "missile gap" between the United States and the Soviet Union, (2) the Gulf of Tonkin incident that precipitated US escalation of the Vietnam War, and (3) the claims of Iraqi weapons of mass destruction and connections to al-Qaeda that were used to justify the invasion of Iraq (see Page and Shapiro 1992; see also Lewis 2014).

as changes in the rate of inflation or unemployment. Many of the prominent studies of misperceptions focus on precisely these economic facts because they can be ascertained with accepted certainty based on government figures.[10] This approach allows for clear determinations of when individual citizens are in error and the damage such misperceptions can do to democratic health. However, there are many realities for which dispositive conclusions are not available or remain disputed among experts. For ordinary citizens, these facts are immensely difficult to sort out, even when the available evidence is weighted heavily to one side. The evidence is often hard to understand, seemingly credible information often exists to support both sides, and the credibility of sources is often difficult to judge.[11] As Thomas Gilovich phrases it in his classic work on perception *How We Know What Isn't So*, "for nearly all complex issues, the evidence is fraught with ambiguity and open to alternative interpretation."[12]

In addition to the challenges associated with the many blurred realities that we face, conceptualizing the core problem as misinformation or misperception gives the impression that a corrective is easily available; accurate information can be provided and misperceptions can be corrected. However, one of the clear conclusions of the existing studies of fact perceptions is that the problem is not simply one of a lack of exposure to authoritative facts, and their correction is not simply a matter of providing the legitimate information (see Chapters 12–14). As Lewandowsky et al. phrase it, "the framing of the current post-truth malaise as 'misinformation' that can be corrected or debunked fails to capture the full scope of the problem."[13]

Partisan Facts Prejudges the Mechanism

In 2002, Larry Bartels published an influential study of dueling facts, identifying partisan bias as the core cause. Focusing on perceptions of the

---

[10] See Bartels 2002, Bullock et al. 2015, Gerber and Huber 2010, Khanna and Prior 2014, Prior et al. 2015, Anson 2016, Schaffner and Roche 2017.

[11] In Walter Lippmann's discussion of facts in politics, he emphasizes that "the pictures inside people's heads do not automatically correspond to the world outside" (1922, page 19). This is the case because "the truth about distant or complex matters is not self-evident" but is instead bedeviled by "indirect, unseen, and puzzling facts" that are part of "the world beyond our reach" (pages 202, 17, 158). Experts may have more clear access and insight, but ordinary citizens have little ability to sort out these "unseen and complicated affairs" (page 98).

[12] Gilovich 1991, page 83. On the prevalence of differing interpretations of the same facts, see Gaines et al. 2007.

[13] Lewandowsky et al. 2017, page 355: "the current state of public discourse can no longer by examined through the lens of misinformation that can be debunked but as an alternative reality that is shared by millions" (page 358).

state of the economy, Bartels concludes that "partisanship is not merely a running tally of political assessments, but a pervasive dynamic force shaping citizens' perceptions of, and reactions to, the political world. Partisan bias in political perceptions plays a crucial role in perpetuating and reinforcing sharp differences in opinion between Democrats and Republicans."[14] The problem is not merely the mischiefs of faction, as Madison phrased it, but the mischiefs of factions' facts. Several scholars have followed in employing terms like *partisan bias* and *partisan facts*.[15]

However, in the same fashion that the term *misperception* restricts the range of inquiry into the phenomenon, the term *partisan facts* restricts investigation into their origins by prejudging the outcome and discouraging discussion of other possible causes.

Cultural Cognition Conflates the Causes

Dan Kahan and his colleagues provide a richer account of the causal mechanisms underlying DFPs, which they call *cultural cognition*.[16] The term embraces partisanship, group belonging, and value projection, gathering them all under the cultural cognition umbrella. We share important foundations with this perspective, including that "cultural commitments are prior to factual beliefs on highly charged political issues," which have "less to do with differences in knowledge than differences in values."[17] We also agree that "if one starts with the intuitive but mistaken perspective that public disagreement is an artifact of insufficient or insufficiently available scientific information, the obvious strategy for dispelling disagreement, and for promoting enlightened democratic decision-making, is to produce and disseminate sound information as widely as possible. But . . . this strategy will be futile."[18] However, we think it important that scholars distinguish rather than conflate the influence of values, identities, and partisanship. As we briefly describe in the current chapter and will

---

[14] Bartels 2002, page 138.
[15] See Bullock et al. 2015, Jerit and Barabas 2012, Prior et al. 2015, Weeks 2015. Achen and Bartels 2016 describe the mechanism of partisan facts: "Our account of partisan perception implies that people's political views and factual judgments are likely to be significantly and pervasively influenced by their partisan predispositions" (page 284).
[16] See Kahan 2013a, 2013b, 2016, Kahan and Braman 2006, Kahan et al. 2012.
[17] Kahan and Braman 2006, pages 149, 169. They note that "the directives of leadership figures are clearly invested with cultural authority" but also that "individuals accept or reject empirical claims about the consequences of controversial policies based on their visions of a good society" (i.e., values) (pages 161, 148). In Chapter 7, we attempt to untangle these mechanisms to gain some purchase over the balance between party leadership and value projection.
[18] Ibid., page 148.

discuss more thoroughly in Chapter 7, the democratic implications of one or another mechanism being dominant are profound.

Dueling Fact Perceptions Covers It

To overcome the conceptual restrictiveness and causal imprecision of other terms, we offer *dueling fact perceptions* (DFPs). What is most important and influential in the politics of facts are not the facts themselves—not who is right or who is wrong—but citizens' dueling *perceptions* of them. It is fact *perceptions* that have political ramifications. And for many fact perceptions with clear political ramifications, Americans are in an uncompromising duel. That contest is fueled by more than just partisan leadership. It is also about values and the deeply internalized psychological processes that we examine in the chapters to come.

Competing Perspectives on the Origins of DFPs

Political science may have concluded that American citizens are largely "innocent of ideology," but they have been proven guilty of holding questionable facts.[19] Political scientists have begun to describe and evaluate the dueling facts phenomenon with some initial narratives. The more prolific view—characterized by the *partisan facts* literature discussed in the previous section—can be described as *environmental* or that DFPs are mostly a product of external forces: polarized elite partisans and polarized information sources lead to polarized perceptions. The minority perspective, which we are championing here, does not deny the role of these external forces but also sees a large role for *individual*, or internal, processes: polarized core values, associated with declining trust in consensus authority and the replacement with trust in value-laden social groups, lead to the projection of preferred values onto perceived facts. These two competing narratives suggest different perspectives on the concepts, causes, consequences, and correctives of DFPs.

If the concept is best characterized as misperceptions and if it is a product of the external environment of misinformation, then we may be able to correct it through education, fact-checking, or other reforms. On the other hand, if the concept is best characterized as DFPs and if it is

---

[19] For the classic ideological innocence conclusion, see Converse 1964; for a recent update, see Kinder and Kalmoe 2017.

the product of ordinary individuals projecting their divided values, then it likely cannot be corrected easily through known mechanisms. In our view, the phenomenon is not merely misperceptions but includes a broader range of DFPs, many of which are not verifiable; is not just the result of party leadership (the external or environmental cause) but also the result of value projection (the internal or individual cause); and is not amenable to correction from education and fact-checking but is instead a more lasting problem for the future of the relation between knowledge and democracy. These additional insights into the nature and origins of DFPs suggest different conclusions about future prospects, less optimistic about their amelioration and more pessimistic about spiraling polarization.

Initial Findings and Influential Works

To summarize some of the major findings of the emerging political science scholarship on dueling facts, we know three core things about DFPs: they are prevalent, they are resistant to correction, and they are associated with political sophistication.[20] In addition to the state of the economy, other topics about which large numbers of Americans appear to hold erroneous beliefs include (1) demographic population percentages,[21] (2) foreign affairs,[22] (3) HIV information,[23] (4) crime rates,[24] (5) local initiatives,[25] (6) political scandals,[26] (7) climate change,[27] (8) gun control,[28] (9) the welfare state,[29] (10) vaccines,[30] (11) genetically modified foods,[31] (12) healthcare,[32] and (13) evolution.[33] When presented with various attempts to alter or correct their perceptions, little effect has been found on citizens' entrenched fact perceptions in our polarized society.[34] And confirming

---

[20] For a summary of the current literature, see Flynn et al. 2017 or Lewandowsky et al. 2017. See also Ramsay et al. 2010, Southwell and Thorson 2015, Southwell et al. 2018.

[21] Hochschild and Einstein 2015.

[22] Kull et al. 2003, Gaines et al. 2007.

[23] Price and Hsu 1992.

[24] Hochschild and Einstein 2015.

[25] Wells et al. 2009, Nalder 2010, Reedy et al. 2014.

[26] Hochschild and Einstein 2015.

[27] McCright and Dunlap 2011, Hochschild and Einstein 2015.

[28] McCright and Dunlap 2011, Thorson 2016, Aronow and Miller 2016.

[29] Hofstetter and Barker 1999, Kuklinski et al. 2000, Thorson 2016.

[30] Freed et al. 2010, Uscinski 2015.

[31] Entine 2015, Uscinski 2015.

[32] Nyhan 2010, Pasek et al. 2015.

[33] Haider-Markel and Joslyn 2008.

[34] See Nyhan and Reifler 2010, Thorson 2016. See also Redlawsk et al. 2010.

the expectations of the more pessimistic researchers, education and political knowledge are employed most often to increase the tight connection between predispositions and perceptions, with the result that more informed and sophisticated citizens are more divided rather than closer to consensus.[35]

Several illuminating books by political science and political communication scholars as well as popular-press writers have addressed these emerging conclusions. The most important original book-length treatment of factual polarization is Jennifer Hochschild and Katherine Einstein's 2015 *Do Facts Matter*? In their view, "the temptation to use misinformation can deeply damage the fragile system of democratic decision-making."[36] They focus on the negative ramifications of the "engaged misinformed."[37] Citizens can be informed or misinformed and active or inactive.[38] Hence, they fall into four categories: the active informed, the inactive informed, the inactive misinformed, and the *active misinformed*. That last category is the real problem. This is reminiscent of an old military joke about the difference between lazy and incompetent officers: if you have to have an incompetent leader, it is better if he is lazy because the hard-working incompetent ones are much more dangerous. While this category may be rare in the US military, Hochschild and Einstein's point is that it is unfortunately common in the US population. The incentives for politicians to mobilize the active misinformed are so great that when misinformation dominates, Hochschild and Einstein suggest that "public officials should seek ways to work around, ignore, or reject public opinion."[39] In other words, some aspects of misinformation are so negative that we may even need to advocate *against* democracy.[40]

We were influenced deeply by *Do Facts Matter?* and by an older and remarkably prescient book published in 1998: *The Future of Fact*, edited by Jeffrey Strange and Elihu Katz. This volume resulted from a conference conducted over twenty years ago, when these questions of DFPs were just beginning to be recognized. Nonetheless, the contributors to this volume—including James Kuklinski and John Zaller—had tremendous foresight.

---

[35] See Barker 2002, Hamilton 2011, Joslyn and Haider-Markel 2014, Kahan 2015, Nalder 2010, Nyhan et al. 2013, Shani 2006, Taber and Lodge 2006.

[36] Hochschild and Einstein 2015, page 6.

[37] Ibid., page 14.

[38] Ibid., figure 1.1, page 14.

[39] Ibid., page 142.

[40] "That strategy is not very democratic on its face, but it may be essential for good democratic governance understood more broadly" (ibid., page 142).

The combined effect of the book's individual chapters is a grim vision of the future of facts: a factual dystopia, not as jack-booted as *1984* or as drug-addled as *Brave New World*, but bad. They identify several facets of the current situation, including the political polarization that would drive divided perceptions, the decline in consensus authority, and the rise in the influence of alternative sources of information online.[41]

Even in the late 1990s, several of the authors saw facts as increasingly slippery: "Facts are all around us, of course, but they are hard to recognize"; "Our factual worlds are more like cabinetry carefully carpentered than like a virgin forest inadvertently stumbled upon"; "I think you cannot deny that, now, at the end of the century, fact has become a problematic notion."[42] James Kuklinski expresses skepticism about our ability to identify objective facts: "political facts are less straightforwardly factual in the Joe Friday ["just the facts, Ma'am"] sense than we often recognize. They are problematic in various respects. To a great extent, the criteria for and relevance of political facts are determined within, not outside, politics."[43] As psychologist Marcia Johnson phrases it, "the fact that the relationship between cognition and reality is not a one-to-one mapping creates the core epistemological dilemma we face."[44] Katz and Strange summarize the future as dominated by "the fragmentation of society into particularisms that command more loyalty than the center," in which "the Internet is leveling traditional structures of authority."[45] If that was the predictable future of facts twenty years ago, what can we perceive about the future of facts twenty years hence?

One pessimistic assessment of the situation comes from the Rand Corporation.[46] Jennifer Kavanagh and Michael Rich provide a broad survey of the causes and consequences of what they call "truth decay" or "the growing imbalance in political and civil discourse between, on the one hand, trust and reliance on facts and current analytical interpretations of facts and data and, on the other, opinions and personal attitudes—a balance that seems to be increasingly shifting in favor of the latter."[47] They summarized the existing literature to offer four contributing

---

[41] "While there is much ballyhoo about how the Internet will improve education and make all our lives better, it is quite apparent that the Internet poses new problems for how we traditionally create, consider, and act on facts" (Strange and Katz 1998, page 199).

[42] Ibid., pages 8 (Katz and Strange), page 18 (Jerome Bruner), and 57 (Joseph Margolis).

[43] Ibid., page 147.

[44] Ibid., page 180.

[45] Ibid., pages 9, 12.

[46] Kavanagh and Rich 2018.

[47] Ibid., page 4.

causes: polarization, cognitive biases, changes in the information environment (especially online), and failures of the school system to keep up with these new inputs. Consequences include a broad array of declines in the efficacy of democracy, including paralysis of decision-making, erosion of civil discourse, and civic disengagement.[48]

Another noteworthy contribution, this time from philosophy, is Lee McIntyre's *Respecting Truth*. McIntyre argues that we should address the problem by respecting the conclusions of social science scholarship: "I will make two proposals for how we might begin to reap the benefits of respecting truth: first by allowing science to have a more prominent role in influencing public policy and second by committing ourselves more fully to the pursuit of empirical social science."[49] He also spends several pages describing the doleful influence of postmodernism inside and outside of the academy as a source of the public difficulty in identifying demonstrable facts.[50]

Several popular-press books have also added insights. In chronological order, some of the significant ones are *The Post-Truth Era* (2004),[51] *True Enough: Learning to Live in a Post-Fact Society* (2008),[52] and *Fantasyland: How America Went Haywire—A 500-Year History* (2017). A shorter version of *Fantasyland* appears in an extended essay by Kurt Andersen in *The Atlantic* (September 2017). Andersen is a novelist, author of a satire about Donald Trump coauthored with Alec Baldwin,[53] and

---

[48] "Without agreement about objective facts and a common understanding of and respect for data and analytical interpretations of those data, it becomes nearly impossible to have the types of meaningful policy debates that form the foundation of democracy" (ibid., page 14).

[49] McIntyre 2015, page 132. See also McIntyre 2018.

[50] McIntyre 2015, pages 103–110. This argument is also a core theme of Michiko Kakutani's *The Death of Truth: Notes on Falsehood in the Age of Trump* (2018). From the literary rather than philosophical perspective—Kakutani was the chief book critic for the *New York Times*—she argues that "It's safe to say that Trump has never plowed through the works of Derrida, Baudrillard, or Lyotard (if he's even heard of them), and postmodernists are hardly to blame for all the free-floating nihilism abroad in the land. But some dumbed-down corollaries of their thinking have seeped into popular culture and been hijacked by the president's defenders, who want to use its relativistic arguments to excuse his lies, and by right-wingers who want to question evolution or deny the reality of climate change or promote alternative facts" (page 45).

[51] Ralph Keye's assertion that "we live in a post-truth era" (2004, page 13) was one of the early mainstream uses of the term (he credits a 1992 essay by Steve Tesich in *The Nation* as the origin). Keyes bemoans the decline of honesty and the rise of alternative ethics. Many years before Trump's political career, Keyes discusses his tendencies toward exaggeration; even back then, Trump called this approach "truthful hyperbole."

[52] Farhad Manjoo (2008), a journalist for *The New York Times*, provides a clear rendition of the psychological foundations of DFPs. In his view, citizens follow their inclinations and shortcuts to arrive at what is not necessarily true but "true enough."

[53] Andersen 2017, Baldwin and Andersen 2017.

cofounder of *Spy* magazine in the 1980s with Graydon Carter (who famously referred to Donald Trump in the magazine as a "short-fingered vulgarian"). Andersen's view is that factual misperception is an American phenomenon, driven by virtues turned vices. Americans believe in liberty and self-determination but have taken that to mean that the same qualities should guide perceptions of facts.[54] This obviously understates the degree to which the residents of other developed nations also hold misperceptions and disputed facts.[55] Andersen believes that there are clear perceptions and misperceptions, correct and incorrect observations, facts and "facts," as he phrases it. The book assumes that sorting out correct facts is not so hard (his perceptions are obviously the correct ones). Andersen offers little modesty about his epistemological claims and no broader understanding that identifying the accurate empirical facts is not always so easy (or as likely to match what an educated person already believes). This is perhaps the core aspect of Andersen's approach, as well as that of several political science scholars, with which we disagree.

Conceptualizing the phenomenon as DFPs suggests that the problem is broader and harder to resolve than is sometimes assumed; it is not limited to a small number of easily verifiable facts but encompasses a larger number of blurred realities. In addition to embracing a broader range of fact perceptions that are influential in contemporary politics, the term takes a neutral position on possible causations, which is the subject of some of the core analyses to be discussed in upcoming chapters. With this concept in mind, we turn to describing some of the most salient DFPs in American politics.

---

[54] "Americans have given ourselves over to all kinds of magical thinking, anything-goes relativism, and belief in fanciful explanation . . . much more than the other billion or so people in the developed world, we Americans believe—*really believe*—in the supernatural and the miraculous"; "Why are we like this? . . . The short answer is because we're Americans, because being American means we can believe any damn thing we want" (pages 5, 7).

[55] See Flynn et al. 2017: "Because studies in this field have typically been conducted in the United States, one might be tempted to believe that misperceptions are a uniquely American problem. They are not" (page 129).

4 | Dueling Facts in American Politics

> "We used to have disagreements about the best way up the mountain.
> We now have disagreements about the existence
> of two different mountains."
>
> —*Michael Gerson*[1]

THE PROLOGUE TO THIS BOOK illustrates the contemporary dilemma of dueling facts from the perspective of ordinary citizens: they hear strong and certain assertions of contradictory realities at the heart of American political debates. A US senator asserts that "global warming is a hoax," while another US senator insists that denial of global warming is "dead and dangerously wrong"; one state governor argues that "people are born with the predisposition to be homosexual," while a different governor is certain that "the behavior one practices is a choice"; one pundit argues that racism is still a powerful force in American life, while another pundit argues that racism no longer holds back African Americans from success. Each side of each dueling fact has prominent proponents, and each has arguments that show up immediately on an Internet search. But only one of the competing perceptions matches our core values; only one of the combative facts is held by our closest friends and social groups; only one is stated absolutely by the leaders of the political party we identify with; only one therefore feels like *our* fact rather than *their* fact.

Grappling with these concerns led the *Oxford English Dictionary* to declare *post-truth* the word of the year for 2016, defined as "circumstances in which objective facts are less influential in shaping public opinion than

---

[1] Chief speechwriter and senior policy advisor to President George W. Bush (2000–2006), keynote speech at The Politics of Truth Conference at American University, March 28, 2018.

appeals to emotion and personal belief." Oxford's usage metrics recorded *post-truth* rising by 2,000% in a single year across many forms of media.[2] But even before the 2016 election year, several observers had begun to comment on the decline in consensual perceptions of reality. In 1999, in a prescient article entitled "Can Democracy Survive in the Post-Factual Age?" Carl Bybee wrote that "we appear to have moved into a post-factual age where the border between fact and fiction, news and entertainment, information and advertisements has increasingly blurred."[3]

And in 2005, on the inaugural episode of *The Colbert Report*, Stephen Colbert famously introduced the term *truthiness*—subsequently a Merriam-Webster word of the year in 2006. He defined it as "the belief in what you feel to be true rather than what the facts will support." Colbert's character explained, "I don't trust books. They're all fact, no heart. And that's exactly what's pulling our country apart today. Let's face it folks, we are a divided nation. . . . We are divided between those who *think* with their head and those who *know* with their heart."[4]

One way to conceptualize the problem facing citizens is an advanced form of polarization. John Adams famously worried that "There is nothing which I dread so much as a division of the republic into two great parties, each arranged under its leader, and concerting measures in opposition to each other. This, in my humble apprehension, is to be dreaded as the greatest political evil under our Constitution."[5] We seem to have reached Adams' feared outcome.

Several scholars have written persuasive books about polarization as a defining and growing feature of American life and politics. Some argue that the core form of polarization is partisanship, others that it is the division of core values, religion, race, wealth, geography, media consumption, taste, or simply affect.[6] We can't dispute any of those characterizations. But polarization has clearly broadened to include polarized perceptions of reality as well.[7]

---

[2] Steinmetz 2016. See McIntyre 2018.

[3] Bybee 1999, page 29.

[4] Colbert 2005. After *post-truth* was awarded the Oxford word of the year, Colbert responded, *"Post-truth* is clearly just a rip-off of my 2006 word of the year, *truthiness"* (November 18, 2016 broadcast).

[5] Adams letter to Jonathan Jackson, October 2, 1789.

[6] See Abramowitz 2011, 2013, Barker and Carman 2012, Bishop 2008, Brewer and Stonecash 2007, Brownstein 2007, Campbell 2016, Hetherington and Weiler 2009, Hunter 1991, 1994, Jacobson 2007, Layman 2001, Mann and Ornstein 2012, McCarty et al. 2006, Schier 2016, Sunstein 2009, Theriault 2008, White 2002, but see also Fiorina et al. 2005 for a dissenting perspective.

[7] Kahan also describes factual dispute as a form of polarization: "Polarization over questions of fact is one of the significant features of contemporary democratic political life"; "today's politics of 'fact polarization'" (2016, page 1). See also Flynn et al. 2017: "The polarization that our politics must confront is thus not just over issues and public policy, but over reality itself" (page 144).

Thomas Mann and Norman Ornstein, authors of one of the influential books on American polarization (*It's Even Worse Than It Looks*), reject "the old notion that Americans can share a common set of facts and then debate options" because citizens now "view the political world through such sharply different lenses—with different perceptions of reality."[8] In short, *the polarization problem has increased the epistemological problem.* Even with advanced forms of research, advanced educational opportunities, and advanced forms of information delivery, for the ordinary citizen knowing is not as easy as it used to be.

Three Prominent Dueling Fact Perceptions: Climate, Racism, and Sexuality

The range of dueling fact perceptions is quite broad, and in this book we examine a lot of them. However, in order to keep things relatively clear and focused, we spend a disproportionate share of our time on three highly influential DFPs: *climate change, racism*, and *sexual orientation*. These three DFPs are at the heart of contemporary American political conflicts, spanning a range of political domains. They are broad and influential fact perceptions that infuse political thinking about large issues of equality, social justice, threats to society, and government priorities. To be clear, we do not see each of these as dueling *facts* for which there is no consensus among experts about the correct answer. But, as we will describe, they are certainly *dueling fact perceptions* in the sense that the American public is deeply divided about them and the truth is not easy for ordinary citizens to discern.

Climate Change

The best-known and perhaps most illustrative example of a DFP in contemporary politics may be climate change. There is a consensus among mainstream scientists that the Earth is warming at a faster pace than is attributable to long-term weather cycles and that human consumption of fossil fuels is at least partially responsible.[9] However, scientists are reluctant to phrase these things absolutely, and a quick Internet search will reveal some scholars with elite-sounding titles who will confidently challenge

---

[8] Mann and Ornstein 2012, pages 46, 61.
[9] See Intergovernmental Panel on Climate Change 2014.

the validity of the data or offer alternative theories of non-anthropogenic causes, which opens the door to alternative interpretations.[10] Gallup data on perceptions of global warming reflect this problem. In response to the question, *Do you believe increases in the Earth's temperature over the last century are due more to the effects of pollution from human activities or natural changes in the environment that are not due to human activities?* 61% of Americans reported in 2001 that human activities were to blame, while 33% thought natural causes were more likely. In 2014, these numbers were 57% and 40%, respectively. Contrary to many expectations, perceptions of global warming did *not* move closer to consensus throughout the early 2000s.

Gallup has also been tracking a question on how much Americans worry about global warming. When the question was first asked in 1989, the percentage who reported being worried "a fair amount" or "a great deal" was 63%. In 2016, after decades of increasing evidence, the number was 64%. The *Annual Review of Political Science* in 2017 summarized the state of public opinion on climate change: "A review of research findings and polling data about Americans' attitude on climate change reveals a lack of meaningful long-term change in mass opinion. . . . Despite an overwhelming scientific consensus about climate change's causes and consequences, Americans remain divided over whether the problem even exists . . . notably, there is no evidence of consistent long-term movement in public opinion toward a belief in human-caused global warming."[11]

As a broad concept, it may be important to distinguish among different facets of what citizens may or may not perceive to be a fact about the climate. Perhaps the most basic aspect is the existence of global warming, or whether the Earth's mean temperature has risen in the past decades. A second aspect is climate change more broadly, including fluctuations of both cold and hot temperatures, rising sea levels, decreasing ice caps, and extreme weather patterns such as droughts and hurricanes. A third aspect is origins, or whether the climate changes are the result of human activity. A fourth way in which factual assertions about climate change are often framed is the degree of threat. How much of a threat is climate change—and hence how much political and financial capital should we invest in it—compared to other threats such as terrorism, ISIS, weapons of mass destruction, the possibility of future warfare with other nations such as China or Russia, the growing lack of clean water in many parts of the

---

[10] See Hulme 2009.
[11] Egan and Mullin 2017, pages 209, 210, and 213.

globe, diseases (especially superviruses or the bacteria that are untreatable with existing antibiotics), energy crises, or the national debt? Assertions of comparative risk—that climate change is the biggest threat to the global economy or to American national security or to the future of humans on the planet—are the most difficult to demonstrate with persuasive evidence or expert consensus.[12] The core DFP seems to be a combination of the first three aspects: confidence or lack of confidence in the existence of human-caused global warming and climate change. This is reflected in Gallup's core question, *Do you believe increases in the Earth's temperature over the last century are due more to the effects of pollution from human activities or natural changes in the environment that are not due to human activities?* We will employ a similar approach to this DFP.

Racism

> "It's just a fact that if you're a young African-American man
> and you do the same thing as a young white man,
> you are more likely to be arrested, charged,
> convicted, and incarcerated."
>
> —*Hillary Rodham Clinton, first presidential debate 2016*

Another disputed reality that is highly polarized and politically relevant is the degree to which racism continues to shape the prospects of minority citizens in our society. It is not difficult to find public arguments that racism (a) has gone down meaningfully in both presence and influence, (b) has gone down in overt presence but not enough to change many outcomes, or (c) has not gone down but instead morphed into new forms, worsening in important ways.[13] Public perceptions of the influence of racism are tremendously significant for policies ranging from diversity in university admissions to legal protections for voting rights, both of which have been disputed in recent Supreme Court cases and *both argued on the grounds of the continuing prevalence and influence of racism.*[14]

---

[12] "Climate Change Is Biggest Threat to Global Economy," UN Climate Change, January 14, 2016 (https://cop23.unfccc.int/news/climate-change-biggest-threat-global-economy); "Our Climate Is Our Security," *US News and World Report* opinion column, August 1, 2017 (https://www.usnews.com/opinion/world-report/articles/2017-08-01/the-pentagon-finally-gets-it-climate-change-is-a-national-security-threat); "10 Biggest Threats to Human Existence," EcoWatch July 28, 2014 (https://www.ecowatch.com/10-biggest-threats-to-human-existence-1881939902.html).

[13] See Peffley and Hurwitz 2010, Bonilla-Silva 2014, Norton and Sommers 2011.

[14] See *Schuette v. Coalition to Defend Affirmative Action* (2014) and *Shelby County v. Holder* (2013). One of the facts disputed by the parties in *Shelby County* was the contemporary influence of racism

Gallup data show a remarkable division. In a 2008 national poll, 56% of Americans perceived racism to be widespread, while 42% disagreed. In 2016, the numbers were 61% to 38%, deeply divided even after the widely publicized police shootings and rise of the Black Lives Matter movement. While the influence of racism can take many forms, including lack of educational and job opportunities, restrictions from political power and voting rights, or psychological and physical threat, the focus of public discussion in recent years has shifted to criminal justice.

Questions about the facts of criminal justice are especially relevant to the discussion of DFPs because trials are perceived as searches for the truth. Determining facts is the very purpose of a criminal trial. They are systematic, ritualized, and public. Nonetheless, we often end up with no more accepted facts than when we began. One of the most notorious cases of a media trial with a deeply contested outcome was the O. J. Simpson case. For many Americans, the announcement of the verdict in 1995 may have been their first clear recognition of divided perceptions of reality among normal citizens. The twenty-year anniversary of the trial in 2015 inspired several popular documentaries and docudramas, which make much of the split-screen portrayal on television news of black and white audiences reacting to the verdict.[15]

Public trials of this nature can lay bare the divisions within American society. The shooting of Trayvon Martin in 2012 and the subsequent acquittal of George Zimmerman a year later did this in an unusually public way. A large sector of our society is convinced that Martin's death was murder and that a racist system allowed his murderer to go free. Another large group is convinced that Zimmerman committed no crime and that political pressures led to his unjust prosecution. A *Washington Post*–ABC News poll conducted the week after the trial asked, "Do you approve or disapprove of the jury's verdict last week finding Zimmerman not guilty in Martin's death?" Positive and negative responses were split 41% to 41%.[16]

---

in the southern states subject to restrictions under the 1965 Voting Rights Act, especially the role of racism in discouraging political participation by minorities. Chief Justice John Roberts was the topic of a PolitiFact report on the veracity of his comments on minority political participation (see "Was Chief Justice John Roberts Right About Voting Rates in Massachusetts, Mississippi," March 5, 2013).

[15] See *O.J.: Made in America* (2016) and *The People v. O.J. Simpson* (2016).

[16] The *Washington Post*–ABC News poll was conducted by telephone July 18–21, 2013, among a random national sample of 1,002 adults, including landline and cell phone respondents (3.5% margin of error; 18% had no opinion). The results are mirrored in a Pew Research Center poll that finds 39% "satisfied" with the verdict and 42% "dissatisfied" (http://www.people-press.org/2013/07/22/big-racial-divide-over-zimmerman-verdict).

It is hard to represent a more divided and polarized America. But when we take ideology and race into account, there is a clear imbalance: citizens who identified themselves as liberals were more likely to disapprove (57% to 22%), while conservatives were the reverse (34% disapproving and 52% approving). The numbers are even more dramatic when divided by race: 86% of blacks disapproved, while only 9% approved. Among whites the numbers were reversed, though not so dramatically: 51% approved and 31% disapproved. These polarized positions on the Martin–Zimmerman incident likely reveal not only different perceptions of the event but also different perceptions of the broader facts about race and racism in America.

After the Zimmerman verdict in 2013, the same *Washington Post–ABC News* poll asked, "Do you think blacks and other minorities receive equal treatment as whites in the criminal justice system or not?" A divided America responded 45% *Yes* and 50% *No*. This divide is not a new phenomenon. Stretching back several decades, perceptions were much the same. In 1988, the responses to the question were tied 43% to 43%, with some fluctuation up and down in between. The answer among blacks in 2013 was *No* (86% to 8%), while more whites saw the system as treating both races fairly (54% to 41%). These numbers have also remained similar for the last couple of decades. So the facts remain disputed, and the set of facts we perceive is a consequential starting point.

Sexual Orientation

Our third DFP is the origin of sexual orientation, which is divided between perceptions that individuals feel a stable kind of attraction from the time they are relatively young and perceptions that socialization and life events drive one's adult sexual orientation.[17] Perceptions of whether orientation is innate or experiential have been demonstrated to be one of the most powerful determinants of attitudes toward gay rights and have been tracked by the Gallup poll since 1977.[18] Figure 4.1 illustrates the steady change in perceptions during the 1980s and 1990s, from the dominant view in 1977 that sexual orientation is experiential (56%/13%) to relative parity of competing perceptions by around 2000. Perceptions showed remarkable stability around essentially equal shares from 2001 (39%/40%) to 2011 (42%/40%). Beginning around 2012, perceptions diverged again

---

[17] See Osmundson 2011, American Psychological Association n.d.
[18] See Haider-Markel and Joslyn 2008.

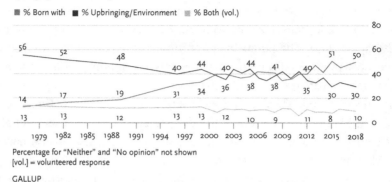

U.S Views on Origin of Being Gay or Lesbian

In your view, is being gay or lesbian–[something a person is born with (or) due to factors such us upbringing and environment]?

■ % Born with   ■ % Upbringing/Environment   ▨ % Both (vol.)

Percentage for "Neither" and "No opinion" not shown
[vol.] = volunteered response

GALLUP

FIGURE 4.1 Perceived Origins of Sexual Orientation

somewhat rapidly, moving to 50%/30% in favor of innate origins as of 2018.[19]

The division in public perception is mirrored in political debate. In the third presidential debate of 2004, the moderator Bob Schieffer asked President George W. Bush and Senator John Kerry, "Both of you are opposed to gay marriage, but to understand how you have come to that conclusion, I want to ask you a more basic question: Do you believe homosexuality is a choice?" This question makes an implicit assumption about the causal chain underlying many citizens' thinking: if homosexuality is innate, this is a strong argument for upholding gay rights. When we began collecting data in 2013—after the *Windsor* decision overruling the Defense of Marriage Act's definition of marriage as one man/one woman but before the *Obergefell* decision in 2015 that recognized the right of same-sex marriage throughout the United States—this DFP was at the core of American political debate. Perhaps in the post-*Obergefell* environment it has become less politically salient as well as less equally divided. On the other hand, gay rights continue to be contested, and the Supreme Court continues to hear challenges, such as the 2018 *Masterpiece Cakeshop* case on the clash of gay rights and religious rights, specifically whether a religious baker can be compelled by state anti-discrimination laws to make

[19] See http://news.gallup.com/poll/170753/americans-views-origins-homosexuality-remain-split. aspx (May 28, 2014) and http://news.gallup.com/poll/234941/say-nature-nurture-explains-sexual-orientation.aspx (May 24, 2018).

a wedding cake for a same-sex marriage.[20] We include the DFP of the origins of sexuality not only because of its importance for contemporary political debate but also because, like perceptions of racism, it extends our examination of DFPs into examples with broad social implications.

There are other DFPs we will analyze at different points in later chapters, including the influence of the national debt, the prevalence of false convictions, the dangers of vaccines, the rate of violent crime, and the effects of gun control, immigration, or raising the minimum wage— but the core analyses focus on these three dueling perceptions at the heart of American political debates.

Data and Initial Evidence

Our approach to examining DFPs is fundamentally empirical. We began commissioning surveys of citizen perceptions in 2013 and continued through 2017. Four separate national surveys over a five-year period provide a clear and detailed look at a range of DFPs and their relationships with other variables.

Most of the surveys were conducted by YouGov as part of the Cooperative Congressional Election Study (CCES) in 2013, 2014, and 2017.[21] The YouGov online panel combines quota and random probability sampling techniques to produce national samples that compare favorably in terms of their representativeness to samples collected using more traditional (telephone-based) methods. YouGov oversamples respondents from less common demographics (approximately 1,200 for each survey) and matches down to a sample of 1,000 that replicates the demographics of the United States for gender, age, race, education, ideology, and political interest. The 2016 survey was conducted by YouGov using the same

---

[20] In the 7/2 decision written by Justice Kennedy—author of the gay rights landmarks *Lawrence v. Texas* and *Obergefell v. Hodges*—the court overturned the ruling for the couple made by the Colorado Civil Rights Commission, on the grounds that the commission showed "a clear and impermissible hostility toward the sincere religious beliefs" of the baker in violation of the First Amendment. As of this writing, the court has not ruled on the core constitutional question of the tension between anti-discrimination laws and assertions of religious exceptions (in the absence of open government hostility to religion). Given this uncertain ruling in 2018, further public controversies and legal challenges will no doubt continue to arise.

[21] For details regarding the sampling methodology, see cces.gov.havard.edu. For a discussion of the CCES methods and matching procedures, see Ansolebehere and Rivers 2013 and Ansolabehere and Schaffner 2014. See Rivers 2009 and Yeager et al. 2011 for a good comparison of the pros and cons associated with telephone-based sampling techniques and different types of Internet-based techniques.

TABLE 4.1 National Surveys

DFPs	2013	2014	2016	2017
Climate	X	X	X	X
Racism	X	X	X	X
Sexuality	X	X	X	X
National debt (harmful?)				X
Vaccines (cause autism?)				X
False convictions (common?)				X
Undocumented immigration (takes jobs?)				X
Minimum wage (causes unemployment?)				X
Gun control (reduces mass shootings?)				X
Violent crime (going up?)				X

procedures, under the auspices of the UMass Lowell Center for Public Opinion.[22]

Table 4.1 displays the various fact perceptions that we measured on these surveys. The emphasis in the first three years was on perceptions of climate, racism, and sexuality. But in 2017, we were able to expand our instrument substantially, measuring several additional perceptions.

Our goal was to allow citizens to express their perception of a disputed fact across a range of certainty, indicating whether they understood a fact to be certainly true, probably true, probably false, or certainly false. For example, "Is this statement true or false? Global warming is occurring and is caused by human activity" [certainly true, probably true, probably false, certainly false]. In some iterations of the surveys, we presented half of the respondents with a statement from one direction ("The Earth is warming due to human activity") and the other half from the opposing direction ("The Earth may or may not be warming, but not due to human activity"), then combined the perceptions by reversing the responses to the second statement (i.e., a response that "The Earth is warming due to human activity" is *certainly true* is equivalent to a response that "The Earth may or may not be warming but not due to human activity" is *certainly false*). We employed slightly different wordings in different surveys, allowing for a

---

[22] Joshua J. Dyck and Francis Talty, 2016 UMass Lowell Faculty Research Poll. We also conducted several surveys using the *CALSPEAKS* Poll, a representative panel survey of Californians conducted by California State University's Institute for Social Research (for details, see Chapter 8). The results from those surveys are highly consistent with results from the national surveys, which we emphasize in most of the chapters that follow.

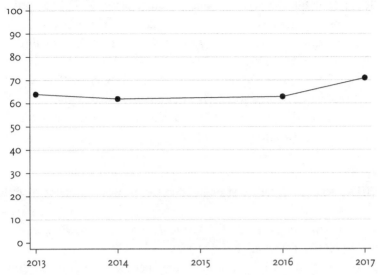

FIGURE 4.2 Perceptions That Anthropogenic Global Warming Is Real

robust test that does not rely on one specific phrasing.[23] Figures 4.2, 4.3, and 4.4 give a sense of the distribution of public perceptions during the 2013–2017 period.

Global Warming

2013: "Global warming is occurring and is caused by human activity."[24]
    Certainly True (32%), *Probably True* (32%), *Probably False* (17%), *Certainly False* (19%)

2014: "Global warming is just natural fluctuation and is not caused by human activity."
    Certainly True (14%), *Probably True* (23%), *Probably False* (29%), *Certainly False* (33%)

---

[23] See the appendix for a discussion of methodological choices in the survey measurement of fact perceptions, especially the questions regarding inclusion of a midpoint and the possibility of disingenuous survey responses.

[24] The measure of perceptions of climate change is a deliberately "double-barreled" question format. Survey research textbooks would caution against using such a measure because it simultaneously asks respondents two distinct questions: whether global warming is happening and, if so, whether human activity is causing it. In most cases, that would reduce the reliability of a measure. In this case, however, this double-barreled measure is the most straightforward way to capture the difference between people who believe that global warming is *both* real *and* anthropogenic and those who dispute either basis for dismissing anthropogenic climate change. Thus, in a single question, we were able to efficiently capture what we needed to capture.

2016: "The Earth is warming due to human activity." / "The Earth may or may not be warming but not due to human activity."
Certainly True (31%), *Probably True* (32%), *Probably False* (23%), *Certainly False* (14%)

2017: "The Earth is warming due to human activity." / "The Earth may or may not be warming but not due to human activity."
Certainly True (43%), *Probably True* (28%), *Probably False* (18%), *Certainly False* (12%)

Racism

2013: "Racism is still a strong influence on who succeeds or fails in America."
Certainly True (21%), *Probably True* (37%), *Probably False* (26%), *Certainly False* (16%)

2014: "Racism still prevents many people from succeeding in America."
Certainly True (30%), *Probably True* (33%), *Probably False* (23%), *Certainly False* (14%)

2016: "Racism often prevents minorities from being successful." / "Racism no longer has much influence over whether minorities are successful."

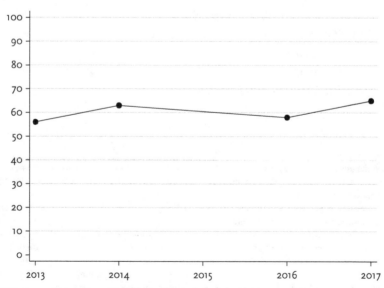

FIGURE 4.3 Perceptions That Racism Is Influential

Certainly True (28%), *Probably True* (30%), *Probably False* (27%), *Certainly False* (15%)

2017: "Racism often prevents racial/ethnic minorities from being successful." / "Racism no longer has much influence over whether racial/ethnic minorities are successful."
Certainly True (31%), *Probably True* (33%), *Probably False* (22%), *Certainly False* (14%)

Sexual Orientation

2013: "Homosexuality is a characteristic determined at birth."
Certainly True (24%), *Probably True* (33%), *Probably False* (20%), *Certainly False* (23%)

2014: "Sexual orientation is biologically determined."
Certainly True (22%), *Probably True* (41%), *Probably False* (22%), *Certainly False* (15%)

2016: "Sexual orientation is something people are born with." / "Sexual orientation is based on choice or experience, not genetics."
Certainly True (31%), *Probably True* (33%), *Probably False* (21%), *Certainly False* (16%)

2017: "People are born gay or straight." / "People are not necessarily born gay or straight."
Certainly True (29%), *Probably True* (33%), *Probably False* (17%), *Certainly False* (22%)

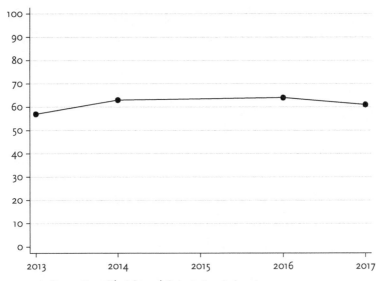

FIGURE 4.4 Perceptions That Sexual Orientation Is Innate

These data indicate that Americans are deeply polarized about perceptions of facts. Whether it is the existence of climate change, the prevalence of racism, or other politically influential states of affairs, we now find dueling accounts of empirical reality supported by different groups of citizens. What we are unsure of at this point is what causes those DFPs. That is our focus in Part II, to which we now turn.

II | Causes

5 | Your Facts or Mine?

THE PSYCHOLOGY OF FACT PERCEPTIONS

"The facts speak for themselves."

—*Lady Cora Crawley*

"Your facts or mine?"

—*Dowager Countess Violet Crawley*

"What is the difference?"

"Mine are the true facts."[1]

CHARLES DARWIN—THE GREAT ICON of scientific process over personal belief—claimed, "I have steadily endeavored to keep my mind free so as to give up any hypothesis, however much beloved (and I cannot resist forming one on every subject), as soon as facts are shown to be opposed to it."[2] If most people shared Darwin's claimed habit, this book would not be necessary. But we don't. Instead, we tend to do the reverse—to give up facts when our beloved values and allegiances are shown to oppose them.[3] We favor the prior and the personal over the different and distant.

In Part II of the book, we consider *why* people are so quick to assert that "mine are the true facts," even when they lack expertise to do so. In this chapter, we review the well-demonstrated psychological mechanisms that lead citizens toward perceiving only a specific set of facts, all the while

---

[1] *Downton Abbey*, season 6, episode 2.
[2] Darwin 1958, page 141.
[3] Even Darwin himself only claimed to have *endeavored* to follow evidence exclusively; he didn't claim to have succeeded.

believing in their sophisticated and unbiased appraisal. A constellation of reinforcing mechanisms adds up to citizens projecting their priors onto their perceptions.

We move on in Chapter 6 to a more specific focus on *core values*—deep understandings of right and wrong—as motivating factors. While we agree with many other researchers that partisan tribalism and the opinion leaders who manipulate it are important players, we argue that value projection plays a key role as well. We focus our theoretical discussion on the role of values because it has received relatively short shrift in the scholarly literature compared to the role of partisanship and because it has distinct consequences for whether dueling fact perceptions (DFPs) are more correctable or more entrenched. In Chapter 7, we describe a series of empirical studies comparing the predictive capacity of values to that of partisan tribalism as well as social identity consciousness and media propaganda. In Chapter 8, we take a step further, presenting and testing a theory of *intuitive epistemology* that seeks to illuminate how values shape perceptions by first shaping the *way people seek understanding.* Chapter 9 wraps up our consideration of causes by demonstrating the extent to which value conviction also drives perceptual *certainty.*

We begin this chapter on psychological mechanisms with the role of *personal knowledge* in perceiving a complex, uncertain, and value-laden reality.

Personal Knowledge

In many ways, this book is about *popular epistemology.* Most of the time that scholars speak of epistemology, the emphasis is on how we *should* proceed in determining which claims to knowledge are legitimate or illegitimate. But epistemology is also the study of how people really *do* gain their perceptions, or how they accept or reject claims to knowledge, rightly or wrongly. One such means is *eyesight*, one of the most trusted forms of personal knowledge.

The Dress Controversy

On an otherwise normal day in February 2015, "the dress" controversy became a national conversation on social media. It began with a posting on Tumblr that was quickly reposted on Buzzfeed:

What Colors Are This Dress?

There's a lot of debate on Tumblr about this right now, and we need to settle it.

This is important because I think I'm going insane.[4]

SWIKED (ORIGINAL POSTER): guys please help me—is this dress white and gold, or blue and black? Me and my friends can't agree and we are freaking the fuck out

LITTLEWOTSIT: So I just looked at this like, it's blue and black obviously and all my friends were like no it's blue and gold. Now I'm super confused, what is eyesight?

SWIKED: I see it as white and gold. My friend right here sees it as blue and black. I CANT HANDLE THIS

SNACKSANDHARTS: if that's not gold my entire life has been a lie

IJUSTLOVEYOUTUBERS: Okay, wtf. i just saw it as gold and white which was weird bc earlier it was blue and black so i thought maybe ye were fucking with me but i went to reblog and now its blue and black again?!1? I AM GOING TO CRY

KATZE-GETH-MEOW: My class just had a debate over this. Half sees black and blue, the other half sees gold and white. Someone please explain this . . .

SWIKED: SPREAD THIS UNTIL IT REACHES NASA WE MUST FIND ANSWERS

Within 24 hours, the BuzzFeed page had 28 million views, by far the most traffic in the history of the site to that time. Tumblr set a similar record. The phenomenon was discussed in the following two days on *Good Morning America*, CNN, *CBS News, Time, Slate*, the *Daily Mail*, and of course *The New York Times*. *The Washington Post* described it as a "drama that divided a planet." The *Today* show website described the divide as "two irrationally passionate camps." According to these media reports, face-to-face as well as Facebook discussions displayed a remarkable degree of certainty of perceptions and dismay at opposing ones.

As is often the case in American culture and politics, the late-night talk shows summarized the phenomenon in pithy terms. Jimmy Fallon's opening line on the *Tonight Show* the following day was, "Before we get

---

[4] http://www.buzzfeed.com/catesish/help-am-i-going-insane-its-definitely-blue#.ktgEVZ3ex (February 26, 2015, at 6:14 p.m.)

started, I wanted to ask your help with something for next week: Should I go with the blue and black tie, or the gold and white tie?" (he was of course holding up two identical ties). He concluded, "I apologize if I'm in a weird mood, because I just lost half of my friends over the color of a stupid dress." Jimmy Kimmel also addressed the controversy: "my wife and her mother got in a fight about it on Thursday night. The dress caused a lot of arguments over the weekend. . . . It splits pretty evenly between people who see it as gold and white, and people who are wrong. . . . My wife almost punched her mother in the face."

Various personalities from Kim Kardashian to a US senator weighed in on Twitter:

KIM KARDASHIAN: I see white & gold. Kanye sees black & blue, who is color blind?

NATE SILVER: The dress is cyan and magenta

ELLEN DEGENERES: From this day on, the world will be divided into two people. Blue & black, or white & gold.

CHRISTOPHER INGRAHAM (OF *The Washington Post*): Expect to see a spike in Google searches for "is my husband colorblind" and "divorce" after tonight

US SENATOR CHRIS MURPHY (D-CT): I know three things: 1) the ACA works; 2) climate change is real; 3) that dress is gold and white

Senator Murphy seems to be wrong about the dress, even while equating it with his other certainties like climate change. According to the manufacturer, as well as the published reports from those who have seen the dress in person, its colors are clearly blue and black. Only one specific photo—taken in particular lighting—is interpreted by many viewers in a different way. Judging by the available evidence, Senator Murphy is in the misguided majority: according to Buzzfeed polling, about two-thirds of viewers see the photo as white and gold rather than the correct blue and black.

It didn't take long for "the dress" controversy to enter scholarly debate. Daniel Drezner was perhaps the first to publish something on the connections between "the dress" and political science (the next day, February 27, in the *Washington Post*, "Theories of international politics and #TheDress"). Drezner concludes that the dress debate "shows that what look like objective facts are inevitably filtered through our own perceptions. . . . Now imagine that the question is about something more factually complex, like, oh, I don't know, whether Iran is pursuing a nuclear weapon or not. . . . It's possible to disagree about fundamental perceptions, and disagreement at that level is very, very difficult to reconcile."

One might ask why this particular phenomenon went viral in this way, inspiring this degree of intense feeling. Our answer is that Americans have started to become familiar with—and somewhat dismayed by—factual divides, both highly influential and relatively harmless, though the harmless ones are easier to discuss. We suspect that the vitriol inspired by "the dress," both joking and serious, has to do with an aspect of political epistemology we have yet to discuss: the role of personal knowledge.

"The dress" controversy offers an epistemological insight: *our trust in personal knowledge from our own senses often trumps external knowledge from other legitimate sources.* Those sources may be news media, scientific consensus, or university reports; but they are often no match for our own experiences. When someone disputes something we heard in school or on television, we may simply take note of the disagreement; but when someone disputes what we have personally observed, we are more likely to see them as stupid, crazy, or dishonest.

Some of the quotes from the original posting, as exaggerated as they seem given the utter silliness of the topic, provide interesting insights into the nature of personal knowledge. As "snacksandharts" phrases it, "if that's not gold my entire life has been a lie." Perhaps "snacks" (for short) meant that our own eyes should be the one thing that we can believe; if not, *anything* might be a lie.[5] Another poster on Tumblr ("littlewotsit") asks, "what is eyesight?" Perhaps she meant to ask, *Is eyesight an accurate means of knowing things? What epistemology can we trust if not eyesight?* The five senses may not be what they are cracked up to be as a source of knowledge. This is reminiscent of the important episode in Norse mythology discussed in Chapter 2, when Odin gave away an eye in order to gain deeper knowledge. Perhaps we should agree more with the Norse that what we see through the eyes is often false and, thus, that true understanding must be gained through other means, especially in the post-Photoshop world. The answer to the question "what is eyesight?" (read: our personal observations) may be *a limited and often misleading way to discern general states of affairs.* This contradicts most people's sense of certainty as it relates to their direct personal observation.

----

[5] This is reminiscent of the famous skit by Richard Pryor in which he says to his wife when she catches him with another woman, "Who you gonna believe, me or your lying eyes?" The original version of this line is attributed to the Marx Brothers in *Duck Soup*.

One of the reasons for the disparity between the known limitations of personal observations and our deep faith in them is the recognized psychological tendency to overvalue a limited number of personal experiences compared to a much larger number of observations made by others.[6] For example, if we (or a friend) own a particular make of car that has mechanical problems, this singular piece of personal evidence heavily influences our estimate of that car company, more so than several pieces of impersonal evidence from *Consumer Reports*. Even if we hear several positive reviews from external sources, they often do not count as strenuously as one personal experience.

The epistemological power of the personal is expressed clearly in Michael Polanyi's *Personal Knowledge*.[7] Though a renowned chemist, Polanyi argues that "complete objectivity as usually attributed to the exact sciences is a delusion and is in fact a false ideal."[8] He insists instead that personal knowledge (or what he calls *tacit* knowledge) is the foundation of our most trusted conclusions, as well as the wellspring of innovation. Tacit, or intensely individual and implicit, knowledge is gained through experience. It cannot be codified into intersubjective language than would allow it to be passed to others. One example is physical movements like riding a bike or swinging a bat, which we cannot explain verbally. Another is recognizing a face, which we can do accurately in an instant but cannot tell someone else how to do with nearly unlimited time. In Polanyi's view, we cannot, and *should not attempt to*, remove "the element of personal judgment" that is the foundation of our greatest trust.[9]

Personal knowledge creates trust to the extent that it can override other foundations of knowledge such as authoritative expertise or scientific consensus. A well-known example is the anti-vaccine movement, grounded in the belief that vaccinations cause autism, contrary to all established medical knowledge.[10] When challenged over her unscientific beliefs,

---

[6] See Tversky and Kahneman 1971. Overemphasizing personal evidence is a subset of the *availability heuristic* (see Kahneman and Tversky 1973, Kahneman et al. 1982). *Availability bias* refers to "the ease with which instances or occurrences can be brought to mind" (1974) which is likely to be increased by personal experience.

[7] Polanyi 1958. Michael Polanyi was the scientist turned philosopher of social science, not to be confused with his brother Karl Polanyi, the famous economic historian who wrote *The Great Transformation*.

[8] Ibid. 1958, page 18. His thesis predates Thomas Kuhn's more famous *Structure of Scientific Revolutions* and the turn toward sociological interpretations of scientific practice (see Kuhn 1962).

[9] Ibid.

[10] See *The New York Times*, "Minnesota Sees Largest Outbreak of Measles in Almost 30 Years," May 5, 2017; *The Washington Post*, "Anti-vaccine Activists Spark a State's Worst Measles Outbreak in Decades," May 5, 2017; see also Kirkland 2016.

Jenny McCarthy—one of the most famous and vocal leaders of the anti-vaccination movement—replied, "My science is named Evan, and he's at home. That's my science."[11]

On the other hand, while personal knowledge may be trusted and persuasive, it may seem to be limited when applied to *political* perceptions. Most political conflicts and issues deal with what Robert Abelson called *distal facts*, which are "only remotely experienced or not sensibly verifiable."[12] Unlike more proximal facts for which we can have personal knowledge, politics deals with unseen people and problems. However, even abstract problems and distant people may have close psychological connections by way of personal metaphor.

For example, the nature of human sexuality is something we may well believe we know from personal feeling or experience. We may have a deep-seated sense that we *know* how humans work, regardless of what the experts may say. Perceptions of the influence of racism may also be grounded heavily in personal knowledge rather than media or scholarly reports of general conditions. This may be especially true in regard to the different conclusions that are often reached by ethnic minorities and whites. We can easily conflate personal experiences with the state of affairs throughout America. For example, in 2015, when the Department of Justice released the report criticizing police practices in Ferguson, Missouri, one local resident responded, "I live in Ferguson so I knew this. We always knew what was going on."[13] Reactions to the Department of Justice report from other citizens with different life experiences were more skeptical, grounded in its contradictions of their own personal knowledge of race relations.

Even fact perceptions that may seem to be fully impersonal, such as the effects of the national debt, may be understood and processed in terms of a more personal fact, such as household budgets and individual debts. As some economists have pointed out, household debt and the national debt are quite distinct, leading to potential errors of perception. But that does not stop individuals from perceiving the complex and impersonal through the metaphor of something more simple and personal. Many perceptions of reality are inevitably influenced by the specific personal evidence that varies dramatically, rather than the broader evidence or aggregate data available to all of us.

---

[11] *Oprah Winfrey Show*, September 18, 2007.
[12] Abelson 1986.
[13] *The Washington Post*, March 3, 2015, "DOJ Report Renews Outrage in Ferguson."

We suspect the role of personal knowledge plays a strong role in perceptions—especially when we turn to the role of internal versus external influences in DFPs—but this concept alone does not tell us which personal perceptions we will have. What claims will we embrace or ignore? And when we have little personal connection, what do we trust as much as our own eyes? These questions bring us to the more specific facets of the psychology of factual perception, grounded in the combined workings of *cognitive psychology, social psychology*, and *motivated reasoning*.

The Confluence of Cognitive and Social Psychology

The unbiased observer "beholds nothing that is not there and the nothing that is," or so Wallace Stevens phrased it in his famous poem "The Snow Man."[14] A true observer does not imagine or project anything onto the scene—"beholds nothing that is not there"—and is willing to walk away empty-handed (noting only "the nothing that is"). Like Wallace, his friend George Santayana also wrote about epistemology. Perhaps Santayana's best-known saying is "the truth is cruel, but it can be loved, and it makes free those who have loved it."[15] Santayana thought most people failed at this and instead lived in epistemological chains. Perhaps the world is too cruel to see accurately, without intentional or unconscious blinders. The findings of both cognitive and social psychology converge on a similar conclusion.

Psychology has no unified paradigm or perspective but instead encompasses many different approaches (cognitive, social, developmental, personality, gestalt, and cross-cultural, to name a few, in addition to the several branches of clinical psychology). Cognitive psychology emphasizes information processing and concludes that humans are error-prone. Biases, heuristics, and flat out mistakes abound. Social psychology emphasizes the influences of other humans around us, or the effects of groups on individuals. One of the major conclusions is that we often make the mistake of attributing behavior to variations among individuals themselves rather than to the powerful effects of the group environment in which they operate (the fundamental attribution error, as social psychologists call it). Various aspects of conformity in response to social groups have been demonstrated in many different settings. To summarize

---

[14] *Harmonium, Poems by Wallace Stevens*. New York: Knopf, 1954.
[15] "Ideal Immortality" 1920.

the major conclusions of cognitive and social psychology, we are screw-ups and conformists. In many cases, our individual mistakes and group orientations may well lead in different directions, but in the case of contemporary fact perceptions they converge. As a general observation of human psychology, *when the known effects of cognitive and social psychology point in the same direction*, you can count on it occurring.

Cognitive Psychology

"When one side only of a story is heard and often repeated,
the human mind becomes impressed with it insensibly."

—*George Washington*[16]

Much of the academic recognition of systematic bias and error rather than accuracy and rationality can be traced to the pathbreaking (and Nobel prize–winning) work of Daniel Kahneman and Amos Tversky in the 1970s and 1980s.[17] The two psychologists popularized a vision of human processing distinct from the neoclassical economists' caricature of humans as rational agents who are highly informed, aware of the process of their decisions, and maximizing the goals they claim to be maximizing. Instead, Kahneman and Tversky demonstrated the real-world tendencies of humans toward cognitive biases such as the availability heuristic, base-rate neglect, and the asymmetric valuing of losses and gains (known as *prospect theory*). As George Washington argued, people do not always attend to and are not always persuaded by the best pieces of information available. Instead they engage in *selective cognitions* that add up to a highly selective view of the world.[18]

Scholars have identified several interrelated psychological mechanisms grounded in selective cognition:[19]

- Selective *attention* to evidence congruent with our predispositions
- Selective *acceptance* of congruent evidence (confirmation bias)

---

[16] Letter to Edmund Pendleton, January 22, 1795.
[17] See Michael Lewis' book on the long and productive friendship between Danny Kahneman and Amos Tversky (Lewis 2016); also Tversky and Kahneman 1971; Kahneman and Tversky 1979; Kahneman et al. 1982; and Kahneman 2011.
[18] See Shapiro and Bloch-Elkon 2008 for an excellent summary.
[19] We use the term *psychological mechanisms* to refer to identifiable causal paths believed to rely on common mental processes. Usually these mechanisms cannot be observed but have been suggested through experiments on reactions to stimuli. We can't be sure we are describing each mechanism exactly right and how independent each one is, as many seem to be interrelated and reinforcing. In our view, sometimes it is important to settle exactly which mechanism is operating or dominant but not when a host of mechanisms all lead in the same direction of perceptions being dependent on priors.

- Selective *skepticism* toward challenging evidence (disconfirmation bias)
- Selective *memory* of congruent information, and
- Selective *reinforcement* of the arguments that we hear ourselves make

Perhaps the most recognized forms of selective cognition are a confirmation bias in one direction (a tendency to accept information consistent with our priors) and disconfirmation bias in the other (a tendency to counterargue information inconsistent with our priors).[20] To put it another way, we tend to apply a low burden of proof when something accords with our prior beliefs and a high burden of proof when it does not; over time this leads to factual conclusions consistent with our priors, grounded in the dual mechanisms of uncritical acceptance and skeptical scrutiny.[21]

The selectivity also occurs *earlier* and *later* in the mental process. We don't just pay attention to all information equally in the first place; we pay greater attention to arguments that seem to affirm our prior beliefs and identities, from sources that we habitually trust. Several important studies have demonstrated the prevalence of selective exposure to information grounded in the known ideology or partisanship of the source (e.g., Fox News versus MSNBC or in social media bubbles), leading to greater exposure to some kinds of information than others.[22]

At the back end of the process, we do not remember everything equally but are more likely to remember information that jibes with our other beliefs. Those selective memories then appear to us to represent a larger amount of evidence supporting our side (that we can recall). And in the final stage of reasoning, in the act of discussing our views with others (and often arguing in favor of them), we then reinforce those views by repetition. By arguing against opposing views (and hearing ourselves do so persuasively, even if only to ourselves), we can become even more persuaded of our initial views after being presented with contradictory evidence. The

---

[20] See Ditto et al. 1998, Edwards and Smith 1996, Lord et al. 1979, Molden and Higgins 2005.

[21] See Gilovich 1991: "Information that is consistent with our pre-existing beliefs is often accepted at face value, whereas evidence that contradicts them is critically scrutinized and discounted" (page 50). "When we prefer to belief something, we may approach the relevant evidence by asking ourselves, 'what evidence is there to support this belief?' . . . Because it is almost always possible to uncover some supportive evidence, the asymmetrical way we frame the question makes us overly likely to become convinced of what we hope to be true" (page 81).

[22] Arceneaux and Johnson 2013, Arceneaux et al. 2013, Barker 2002, Frimer et al. 2017, Sears 2017, Spohr 2017.

arguments and evidence in favor of our position seem stronger and the opposition weaker; "if that's all they have," then we are reconfirmed in our initial positions.

But why? *Why are humans failing to rationally process information in an unbiased manner that leads to accurate perceptions?* An initial answer is the basic limitation on human effort. Psychologists from many perspectives agree that humans are cognitive misers, exerting only the amount of mental effort needed to reach a hasty conclusion, rather than examining, sorting out, and weighing the evidence fully each time we consider a question of fact. If we were not in large measure cognitive misers, we would be mentally overloaded to the point of collapse. This is especially the case when we are faced with tremendous amounts of information, much of which conflicts. In the contemporary environment of information overload, it is not possible or advisable to put maximum repetitive effort into each question of fact. We will instead be selective in all aspects of information processing.

These cognitive limits may set the stage for our dilemma, but they do not dictate *which* pieces of information we will selectively attend to, accept, reject, remember, and reinforce. Our prior beliefs and attachments provide that guidance; it is less effortful to gravitate toward the evidence, information, sources, and hence perceptions that we already hold. Similarity to prior inputs (coherence, as discussed in Chapter 2) provides an immediate guide to new processing. A path dependence or snowballing of prior beliefs would seem to be likely. Given limits to mental effort, that alone will lead us to assimilate the evidence congenial to our priors.[23] But there may be other motivations and psychological mechanisms operating as well, which brings us to the social side of psychology.

Social Psychology

"The desire for approbation is perhaps the most deeply seated instinct of civilized man."

—*Somerset Maugham*[24]

Maugham was not a social scientist but was nonetheless a keen observer of human psychology. *The Moon and Sixpence* was about his fascination with the only person he ever met who seemed to be immune from concern with

---

[23] Emotions like anger may increase this tendency (see Suhay and Erisen 2018).
[24] *The Moon and Sixpence*, page 67.

what other people thought of him (the painter Paul Gauguin). Maugham openly admitted he cared deeply what others thought of him, like most people do. This is the heart of the repetitive social psychology finding of deep conformity among humans.[25]

Some of the famous early social psychology experiments on conformity focused on *perceptions*, especially the Asch experiments of the 1950s.[26] When presented with questions about visual perception for which there were obvious answers—but prior to answering, *other* people had publicly given the clearly *incorrect* answer—participants in the studies were shockingly likely to also give the incorrect answer that conflicted with their own perceptions.

However, such social conformity may *not* be irrational. *Social proof* is the term for relying on the knowledge of others as a guide to our own conclusions.[27] This social epistemology is grounded in the following question: if our perceptions and those of several seemingly trustworthy people are different, is it more likely that *we are wrong* or that that *they are wrong*? Ordinary (non-hubristic) citizens do not typically assume that they are never the ones in error, and therefore they often bet on the group's perceptions over their own. However, note that this interpretation disputes the strong trust that most people place in their own observations. Personal knowledge tends to be quite powerful, and we would need a strong motive to discard it.

It is also quite possible (we think more likely) that conformity effects are driven by the desire to be accepted or thought well of by others, especially those who are in our close social groups. People may value these social connections more than they care about empirical accuracy. This motivation is likely framed in the negative as well as positive; the costs of social nonconformity may be quite high, especially in a polarized society.

Dan Kahan argues that conformist factual assertions have become "a marker of membership within identity-defining affinity groups," such that

> given the social meanings that factual positions on these issues convey,
> failing to adopt the stance that conveys who she is, whose side she is on,
> could have devastating consequences for her standing with others whose
> support is vital to her wellbeing, emotional and material. Under these

---

[25] Among many others, see Bentley 1908, Cohen 2003, Gerber et al. 2008, Sinclair 2012.
[26] Asch 1952, 1956.
[27] See Sherif 1935, see also Baron et al. 1996, Cialdini 2001.

conditions, it is a perfectly rational thing for one to attend to information in a manner that promotes beliefs that express her identity correctly, whether or not they are factually correct.[28]

Failing to express the right perceptions "could mark her as untrustworthy or stupid, and thus compromise her relationships with others."[29] For these social reasons, Lewandowsky et al. conclude that we live on "socially-defined epistemic islands."[30]

Motivations toward social conformity may lead to the same cognitive mechanisms of selectivity we discussed above (see p. 82):

- Selective *attention*: we watch Fox News or Stephen Colbert because it is expected within our group
- Selective *acceptance*: we apply a lower standard of evidence to the fact perceptions of our group
- Selective *skepticism*: we apply a higher standard of evidence to assertions opposing the perceptions of our group
- Selective *memory*: we remember more easily the evidence repeated by close associates
- Selective *reinforcement*: we discuss this evidence and our conclusions with members of our group

In this sense, the cognitive and social mechanisms may interact and reinforce each other. Whether this is best described as additive or multiplicative we don't know. When humans demonstrate that they tend to reach perceptions consistent with both their prior beliefs and their social groups, it can be difficult to determine which mechanism is dominant. Confirmation bias is sometimes referred to as "myside bias" (the cognitive influence) which is hard to distinguish from "ourside bias" (the social influence).

Motivated Reasoning

"Each sees in the world what is present in their heart."

—Goethe[31]

---

[28] Kahan 2016, pages 1, 13.
[29] Kahan 2013a, page 409.
[30] Lewandowsky et al. 2017, page 353.
[31] *Faust* 1808, Prelude 179.

As The Player says to Rosencrantz, "Audiences know what to expect, and that is all they are prepared to believe in."[32] When knowledge is uncertain, we may just shade our perceptions toward what we *want* to believe, which is the heart of motivated reasoning.[33] One way to understand the concept is that it is the confluence of the cognitive and social mechanisms discussed above, except motivated by desire rather than by simple error and bias. If we are guided, pushed, or pulled by motivations other than accuracy, then the human tendency to hold perceptions in line with priors will be even stronger than would be the case with mere error (Motivation + Error > Error alone).[34]

Democratic politics is of course a contest, so perhaps we should not be surprised that citizens bring to it "the psychology of the sports arena," as Philip Tetlock phrases it.[35] Another pioneer of moral psychology, Jonathan Haidt, famously said that "morality binds and blinds. It binds us into teams, but makes us go blind to objective reality."[36] One of the early studies of motivated reasoning was specifically about the sports arena, demonstrating the remarkable degree to which opposing sports fans (team partisans) literally see different things when watching the same sporting event.[37] Anyone who holds a long-standing team affiliation (or has been to a football game, either American or international) has seen the combination of cognitive and social effects on perceptions of events. We should not expect polarized politics to be any different. Or, rather, we should expect it to be worse.

Motivated reasoning has been defined as "the tendency of individuals to unconsciously conform their assessment of information to some goal *collateral* to determining its *truth*," such that "individuals are *opportunistically*

---

[32] *Rosencrantz and Guildenstern Are Dead*, act III, scene i. One of the jokes of *Hamlet* is that no ones seems able to keep straight which of the two friends is which; even the characters themselves seem to be confused sometimes. Factual uncertainty prevails.

[33] See Kunda 1990 for the original formulation; also Ditto et al. 1998, Edwards and Smith 1996, Molden and Higgins 2005. Liu and Ditto 2012 describe motivated reasoning as "post hoc reasoning processes that shape descriptive beliefs" (page 317). See Kahan 2016 for a summary and the argument that motivated reasoning is the core psychological mechanism behind DFPs. Scholars have shown that motivated reasoning applies to a broad range of political perceptions, including candidate evaluations and policy preferences (e.g., Bolsen et al. 2014, Redlawsk 2002, Redlawsk et al. 2010, Schaffner and Roche 2017, Taber and Lodge 2006, 2013, Taber et al. 2009). For a dissenting perspective on motivated reasoning, see Friedman 2012 and 2018, arguing that informational cascades may lead to similar spirals of conviction, without recourse to psychological explanations relying on non-rational or non-accurate motivations.

[34] Or maybe Motivation × Error.

[35] Tetlock 2005, page 232.

[36] Haidt 2012, page 311.

[37] Hastorf and Cantril 1954.

adjusting the weight they assign evidence to conform it to their political identities."[38] Likewise, Flynn, Nyhan, and Reifler emphasize that reasoning is motivated when we "seek to reach conclusions that reinforce existing loyalties rather than ones that objective observers would deem 'correct.'"[39] The key point is *alternative motivation rather than mere error*. Motivation toward accuracy or truth would lead us to consider all available evidence and to apply the same burden of proof even-handedly. If perception is motivated by other goals, there is more to blame than errors under time constraints.

An important facet of the motivated reasoning paradigm is that we are largely *unaware* of our alternative motivations, perceiving ourselves to be unbiased. One illustration can be found in a national poll conducted right before Trump's inauguration: 84% of respondents were concerned that fake news was hurting the country, but 79% were confident that they could tell real news from fake news.[40] In other words, Americans have heard that fake news is a problem, but they tend to see fake news stories as the ones that dispute what they already believe to be the case, unaware that their own perceptions might be a part of the problem.[41]

Even if we are not aware of the motivation, this does not mean all of the mechanisms through which motivated reasoning is effective are likewise beneath consciousness. One of the standard ways of thinking of cognitive psychology is a division between system 1 and system 2 thinking, also known as unconscious and conscious, peripheral and systematic processing. The first is unaware and mentally miserly, relying on rules of thumb, shortcuts, or other heuristics, while the second is aware and effortful (though not necessarily more accurate).[42] Kahan argues that motivated reasoning appears not only in the realm of system 1 automatic processing alone but also in system 2: "High numeracy—a quantitative reasoning proficiency that strongly predicts the disposition to use System 2 processing—also magnifies politically motivated reasoning." He finds "a progressive increase in political polarization as individuals of opposing outlooks become even more proficient in critical reasoning."[43] In other

---

[38] Kahan 2016, pages 2, 9.

[39] Flynn et al. 2017, page 133.

[40] FoxNews poll January 15–18, 2017, 1,006 registered voters, ±3% margin of error. "How concerned are you that fake news is hurting the country?" (Very 61%, Somewhat 23%, Not very 7%, Not at all 8%); "How confident are you that you can tell real news from fake news?" (Very 42%, Somewhat 37%, Not very 11%, Not at all 8%).

[41] See Silverman 2016, Allcott and Gentzkow 2017, Lazer et al. 2018.

[42] See Kahneman 2011, Barker and Hansen 2005, Barker 2018.

[43] Kahan 2016, page 12.

words, people employ their greater cognitive skills to bolster motivated reasoning and match priors to predispositions.

If the interrelated effects of cognitive and social psychology are increased by political sophistication, this suggests a supporting motivation. Greater cognitive abilities could conceivably be employed to *decrease* the use of selective cognitions in favor of deeper consideration and accuracy, or they could be used to *increase* the focus on selective cognitions, deepening bias. Similarly, greater knowledge could be used to replace the social conformity pressures, or it could be employed to more accurately match our social positions to the fact perceptions that reinforce them. Given that political sophistication leads toward the second options, motivated reasoning seems to supply the impetus.

What is this unaware, multisystem motivator? Kahan argues that the most likely motivation is "the formation of beliefs that maintain a person's connection to and status within an identity-defining affinity group whose members are united by shared values."[44] This represents a combination of social conformity and belief congruence, especially of political values. As Frank Lutz (the conservative pollster) phrases it, "We don't collect news to inform us. We collect news to affirm us."[45] This view also combines both belief congruence (affirmation of our current views) and social conformity (affirmation of our group status).

The motivation may be to simply maintain current beliefs, avoiding dissonance or self-doubt.[46] Some studies have found that assuaging the ego through affirmation immediately prior to factual correction allows opposing information to be accepted more easily.[47] In this sense, the psychological mechanisms we have been discussing may be *protective* cognitions rather than merely *selective* cognitions. Robert Abelson expressed this idea in the important essay "Beliefs Are Like Possessions."[48] Because we think of beliefs as possessions (we "acquire" them, "hold," "cherish," or "abandon" them like physical items), the other psychologies of possession may also apply (such as the *endowment effect*, the tendency to ascribe greater value to something after we own it.) We often assume that *we* own our beliefs, but they may well own *us*. Abelson argues that just as we hold closely to our possessions (and protect them from fire and flood), we also protect our beliefs from challenge and change.

---

[44] Ibid., page 2.
[45] Scherer 2012.
[46] See, for example, Festinger 1957.
[47] See Lewandowsky et al. 2012, Sherman and Cohen 2006.
[48] Abelson 1986.

Any cognition may have a motivation behind it; the question is *which* motivation. (In this sense, motivated reasoning is sometimes referred to as *politically* motivated reasoning or *directionally* motivated reasoning, making the specific motivation more clear.[49]) While some cognitions may just happen by themselves through automatic processes, many are likely motivated by *something*. It is clear that there are several possible motivations, each of which may be dominant at any one time, including empirical accuracy, belief coherence, and social acceptance. The concept of motivated reasoning is simply highlighting the motivations toward belief and acceptance rather than toward accuracy.

It seems likely that empirical accuracy will be a strong motivation when the payoff or result of the effort is money or avoiding injury, that social acceptance will be a strong motivation when the belief or behavior affects social status, and that belief congruence will be influential when the belief in question is deeply held or closely connected to our self-perception. So what does this suggest about DFPs like those pertaining to climate change, racism, or sexuality? The personal payoff in terms of money or health for most dueling facts seems *low*; social acceptance regarding the facts our groups take seriously seems *high*; and belief congruence for the facts that are closely connected to our core values also seems *high*. One could argue that the wrong understanding of climate change could hurt one's personal survival, but that is a long-run proposition. It also assumes that people believe that their personal stance will influence government policy. The more immediate concern is what their social contacts will think of them and what they think of themselves. For perceptions of political facts, *the social motivations and belief motivations seem likely to be dominant over accuracy motivations.*

The Mercier Thesis: "Reasoning Is for Arguing"

One more aspect of the recent research on motivated reasoning deserves a mention. Hugo Mercier and his coauthors offer an important argument about the human urge to communicate for *presentation value rather than truth value.*[50] The Mercier thesis can be summarized as "reasoning is for

---

[49] See especially Kahan 2016, what he refers to as the "politically motivated reasoning paradigm," and Flynn et al. 2017: "Directionally motivated reasoning leads people to seek out information that reinforces their preferences (i.e., confirmation bias), counterargue information that contradicts their preferences (i.e., disconfirmation bias), and view proattitudinal information as more convincing than counterattitudinal information (i.e., prior attitude effect)" (page 132) (i.e., motivated reasoning ratchets up cognitive biases).

[50] See Mercier and Sperber 2011 and 2017 for the best discussion of these ideas.

arguing": "we produce reasons in order to justify our thoughts and actions to others and to produce arguments to convince others to think and act as we suggest."[51] In this view, the primary goal of reason (and often perception) is not *accuracy* but *acceptance*.

Mercier grounds this argument in evolutionary psychology. It is unclear to scholars why reason evolved (and in humans alone) and why it is so flawed as a mechanism for accurate perception. Mercier argues that reason is a fundamentally social construct—"first and foremost a social competence"—driven by the evolution of a social animal more dependent on the support of the group for survival and procreation than on individual talents.[52] In the long hunter–gatherer period of human existence (when most of our evolution took place), what was more likely to keep people alive and allow them to mate: (a) perceiving and communicating facts accurately or (b) gaining higher social status in the clan that protected them from dangers? Mercier's point is that (b) was at the evolutionary core and endowed humans with the tendency to communicate in a conformist fashion that endeared them to the group.[53] Hence, reasoning is social, and the generation of *trust* is the core issue: given that we are presenting ourselves and our arguments in the best (not always accurate) light and know that others are doing the same thing, judging trust *of others* is the problem and gaining trust *from others* is the goal.[54]

The same motivation applies to perception as well as reason (gathering as well as presenting arguments). Human perception has evolved toward efficiency in finding *arguments*, not reality. "Skilled arguers" in particular "are not after the truth but after arguments supporting their views."[55] This process would result predictably in confirmation bias, which is dysfunctional if we are looking for the truth but quite functional if we are focusing

---

[51] Mercier and Sperber 2017, page 7.

[52] Ibid., page 11.

[53] "The primary function for which [reason] evolved is the production and evaluation of arguments in communication" (Mercier and Sperber 2011, page 58). Or, as a colleague phrased it, "You mean he thinks humans are more motivated to convince people to have sex with them than to get things right? Yeah, I'll buy it."

[54] "When we listen to others, what we want is honest information. When we speak to others, it is often in our interest to mislead them, not necessarily through straightforward lies but by at least distorting, omitting, or exaggerating information so as to better influence them in their opinions and in their actions. When we listen to others, then, we should trust wisely and sometimes distrust. . . . If we distrusted others only when they don't deserve our trust, things would be for the best. Often, however, we withhold our trust out of prudence, not because we know that others are untrustworthy but because we are not sure that we can trust them." (Mercier and Sperber 2017, pages 8–9). Sperber et al. 2010 refer to this as "epistemic vigilance."

[55] Mercier and Sperber 2011, page 57.

our limited mental efforts on our ability to persuade others (and hence have higher social status).[56]

This thesis is similar to Harry Frankfurt's argument about the prevalence of bullshit (discussed in Chapter 2). Mercier does not cite Frankfurt in the 2011 article or the 2017 book, but we think these ideas are deeply connected: reasoning is motivated by social approval over factual accuracy, and people express a great deal of bullshit, defined as assertions designed for their social value (impressiveness) rather than their knowledge value (accuracy). Stephen Colbert would agree; "truthiness" is also related to those two concepts. Rather than following the motto *esse quam videri* ("to be rather than seem to be," the motto of Appalachian State University, the University of Tampa, Berklee College of Music, and of course the Boy's Latin School of Maryland), we are often motivated to employ instead Colbert's reverse motto inscribed beneath the fireplace in his studio, *videri quam esse* (to seem to be rather than to be).

If the Mercier thesis holds water, many supposed errors in perception may not be errors at all but are instead simply serving a different purpose from factual accuracy: social status. To summarize Mercier's contribution to this discussion, the answer to the question posed above (see "Cognitive Psychology," p. 83)—*why are humans failing to rationally process information in an unbiased manner that leads to accurate perceptions?*—is quite possibly that they are not trying to. They have other motivations that lead them in other predictable directions.

Conclusion

Several strands of the psychology of perception—personal knowledge, selective cognitions, social conformity, and motivated reasoning— converge on the expectation that citizens will project their priors onto their perceptions. The power of personal knowledge suggests that perceptions will rely heavily on our individual experiences framed by our individual pattern of core beliefs and social interactions, rather than dispassionate evidence provided by impersonal experts. Cognitive psychology argues that DFPs are driven by a multitude of non-rational failures of attempted accuracy grounded in selective perception and processing. Social psychology argues that impulses (both aware and unaware) toward group

---

[56] Arguing in front of others and feeling a sense of social accountability also lead to bolstering and overconfidence (Tetlock 1985, Lerner and Tetlock 1999).

belonging will predictably shift citizens away from empirical accuracy. And motivated reasoning wraps up these perspectives with a neat psychological bow, adding that the seeming mistakes we make may not really be mistakes because they are serving different motivations. We are persuaded that the evidence suggests the full range of cognitive, social, and motivated reasoning effects are taking place, encompassing a range of psychological foundations. Our position is that these psychological mechanisms are overlapping and reinforcing (like the various facets of political polarization); they are very difficult to parse out, so it is not clear which process is dominant under what conditions. But it doesn't matter as long we concede that at least *one or more of these mechanisms is connecting priors to perceptions* in an unconscious manner that opposes accuracy.

The psychology of perceptions, as we have presented it so far, has been relatively uncontroversial. Even the most rational perspectives concede that perceptions are dependent on priors to some degree. The real question is about *which priors*. Do the psychological mechanisms described in this chapter point to *environmental factors*, such as party leadership and media, as the source of DFPs, as many scholars argue? Or do these mechanisms suggest that internal processes such as the projection of core values and social identities also play an important role?

If DFPs are entirely or even mostly a product of the external environment, then we may be able to correct misperceptions through education, fact-checking, or other reforms. On the other hand, if a big part of the story is ordinary individuals projecting their divided values, then misperceptions likely cannot be corrected through known mechanisms. In the next few chapters, we make the theoretical and empirical case for value projection, and thus for the durability of DFPs in the American public square.

6 | The Psychology of Fact Perceptions II
VALUE PROJECTION

"Do unto others as you would have them do unto you"

—*Luke 6:31*

A sadist and a masochist walk into a bar.

"Hurt me!" says the masochist.

The sadist stares at him and says, "No."

A<small>N ASSUMPTION UNDERLYING THE FIRST</small> quotation is that human preferences are essentially similar, while the anecdote beneath suggests that preferences are quite different. We suggest that beliefs about the highest human goals are often more different than alike, which is to say that *values are pluralistic*. Our thesis is that competing core values are one of the strongest influences on fact perceptions. The combined mechanisms of personal knowledge, selective cognitions, social conformity, and motivated reasoning discussed in the previous chapter all contribute to the *projection of preferred values onto perceived facts*.

Values

Isaiah Berlin describes values as "not means to ends but ultimate ends, ends in themselves."[1] These ends can be thought of as the *backstops* of our arguments. If we ask someone to explain a political position and then press

---

[1] Berlin 1991, page 10.

him or her to justify that justification and continue in this fashion, the point at which he can go no further is a core value.[2]

Psychological definitions of values stress their role as motivators: "a conception of the desirable"; "the dominating force in life"; "an enduring belief that a specific mode of conduct or end-state of existence is personally or socially preferable."[3] Another important facet of values is their abstract character as "trans-situational goals" and "abstract trans-situational guides."[4] Some of the major political science researchers on values— Stanley Feldman, Paul Goren, Jon Hurwitz and Mark Peffley, William Jacoby, Robert Lane, and Phil Tetlock—have emphasized the abstract nature of values as "personal statements regarding the individual's priorities" or "general conceptions about the desirable and undesirable end-states of human life" or "an abstract belief about a desirable end state or mode of conduct that transcends different situations, motivates political evaluation, and can be ordered in terms of relative importance."[5] The consensus view seems to be that values are *standing judgments of better or worse priorities* or, in more psychological terms, *trans-situational evaluative predispositions*. In common language, they are *deep understandings of what is right and wrong*.[6]

The evidence for the role of values as a key component of belief systems—distinct from ideologies or partisan affiliation—was originally grounded in qualitative studies.[7] The same findings have been confirmed by survey research that documents the strong relation between values and political judgments of many kinds.[8] What this collective evidence

---

[2] "Values are backstops of belief systems. When we press people to justify their political preferences, all inquiry ultimately terminates in values that people find it ridiculous to justify any further" (Tetlock et al. 1996, page 26).

[3] Kluckhohn 1951; Allport 1961; Rokeach 1973.

[4] Schwartz 1992, Rohan 2000. Rohan highlights an important distinction between values as organizing principles and attitudes as evaluations of specific objects, such as policy proposals: "I propose that the term *attitude* is used only for evaluations of specific entities. The term *values* can then be reserved for discussions of abstract trans-situational guides" (Rohan 2000, page 258).

[5] Hurwitz and Peffley 1987, Jacoby 2006, Goren 2005.

[6] Values are distinct from self-interest as "beliefs about what is right and what is wrong, not what's in it for me" (Kinder 1998).

[7] See Hochschild 1981, McCloskey and Zaller 1984. In 1962 Robert Lane published an influential but mistitled book, *Political Ideology*, in which he argued that the public has value orientations in abundance, even if they are not well articulated and do not map directly onto a Left/Right ideological spectrum.

[8] The state of political science knowledge regarding values can be summarized that they differ from other ideational constructs (Rohan 2000); that the mass public employs them (Lane 1962); that they are organized in hierarchies (Peffley and Hurwitz 1985); that they are the basis of policy attitudes (Peffley and Hurwitz 1985, Hurwitz and Peffley 1987) and candidate evaluations (Feldman 1988); that we can identify some of the central value conflicts in American politics (McCloskey and Zaller 1984,

demonstrates most clearly is that political judgments are constrained by core values. All of this is in line with what Converse wrote in 1964 about the constraint of belief systems: "Often such constraint is quasi-logically argued on the basis of an appeal to some superordinate value or posture toward man and society."[9]

Another powerful component of belief systems is political ideology along the Left/Right spectrum, but ideology tends to be limited to the relatively small subset of citizens who are highly politically engaged.[10] Conservatism and progressivism have become more attached to partisan politics and issue positions than they were in the past, but ideology remains the province of a relatively small part of the population—especially politicians, party leaders, and activists.[11] A larger proportion of citizens hold a partisan affiliation, but the content of that attachment may vary as partisan leaders shift positions. By contrast, almost all citizens hold stable and entrenched values. Though often unarticulated and unexamined, these predispositions are at the core of their beliefs. While ideology and partisanship are powerful constructs for those who hold them, values may be more core and more common, and therefore deeply influential.

Value Conflict

"Conflicts between ends equally ultimate and sacred, but irreconcilable within the breast of even a single human being, or between different men or groups, can lead to tragic and unavoidable collisions."

—Isaiah Berlin[12]

Value conflict can be seen as the inevitable product of the condition that some values are incompatible with others. This condition and its role as a source of conflict are explained most clearly by Isaiah Berlin in his *Four*

Feldman 1988, Feldman and Steenbergen 2001); and that value conflict is central to political judgment (Feldman and Steenbergen 2001, Jacoby 2006, Tetlock 1986, Tetlock et al. 1996).

[9] Converse 1964, page 7.

[10] See Converse 1964 for the earliest description of the innocence of ideology among American citizens and Kinder and Kalmoe 2017 for the latest.

[11] See Noel 2014. Very recent surveys do show a marked increase in the percentage of citizens (now as much as 25%) who hold consistently liberal or conservative positions across various issue realms (e.g., Pew Research Center 2014).

[12] Berlin 1969, page 102.

Essays on Liberty and *The Crooked Timber of Humanity*. These works provide the philosophical basis for value pluralism: "it is what I should describe as pluralism—that is, the conception that there are many different ends that men may seek and still be fully rational, fully men."[13] But values are not only multiple; some are inherently in conflict with others: "what is clear is that values clash" as "some among the Great Goods cannot live together." Hence "in the end, men choose between ultimate values."[14] For any given political value there is a competing one, and most often a directly opposed value—individualism versus collectivism, militarism versus pacifism, etc. To the degree to which we favor one, we automatically and inevitably oppose the other.

When Isaiah Berlin introduced the term *value pluralism* to political science discussion, he also observed that some thinkers resist the idea that human ends are multiple and contradictory. (Walter Lippmann also mentions this in *The Phantom Public*). Why resist this observation? Perhaps because it suggests that people have non-rational attachments that reasoned evidence cannot overcome (as the saying goes, you can't reason someone out of a position they didn't reason into[15]) or perhaps because value conflict also suggests the permanence of difference and discord, which many thinkers hesitate to recognize.[16]

---

[13] Berlin 1991, page 11. See also Jon Elster (1983) *Sour Grapes* on the "plurality of ultimate values" (page 38), and Joseph Schumpeter: "ultimate values—or conceptions of what life and society should be—are beyond the range of mere logic. They may be bridged by compromise in some cases but not in others" (1942, page 251).

[14] Berlin 1991, pages 12, 13, 171.

[15] Often attributed to Jonathan Swift: "Reasoning will never make a man correct an ill opinion, which by reasoning he never acquired" (*Letter to a Young Clergyman*, 1720).

[16] See Fiorina et al. 2005 and Friedman 2018. The usual approach to disputing the existence of value conflict in contemporary America is to demonstrate goals that Americans *do* agree upon (effective national defense, good healthcare, quality education) and stop with the observation that we do in fact agree. However, agreement on *some* things does not at all preclude disagreement on *other* things. This approach ignores the many important ends on which we radically disagree. Moreover, even seeming agreements on "good healthcare" elide the underlying situation that we define "good" very differently depending on whether our values indicate that *more equal* but potentially *lower-quality* treatment paid for through higher taxes is or is not preferable to *less equal* but potentially *higher-quality* treatment paid for by individuals. One value orientation sees the first option as "good," while the second value orientation sees the second as "good," even as both agree on the goal of "good healthcare." Another reason disputes over values (ends as well as means) tend to dominate democratic conflict is the inevitable limitations of budgets. As soon as two or more shared ends are considered, the question becomes *which is more important* and hence deserving of funding (job creation versus environmental protection versus national security, etc.). Each of these goals considered alone might be understood in terms of competing means, but limited budgets force us to prioritize competing ends. For a more detailed discussion of the dominance of value conflict in democratic politics, see Marietta 2010.

The evidence from the last several years of national survey data is clear about the depth of value conflict among American citizens. In our surveys in 2013 and 2014, we focused on two of the core value conflicts that influence contemporary politics.[17]

Collectivism–Individualism: the degree to which a citizen prioritizes social responsibility versus personal responsibility as a public virtue.[18]

Humanism–Theism: the degree to which an individual prioritizes reliance on secular scientific knowledge versus reliance on traditional religious faith for guidance.

The first value conflict has been shown to influence a wide range of American political attitudes,[19] and the latter lies at the heart of the "culture wars."[20]

In broadest terms, the distinction between individualism and collectivism involves whether individuals view their primary responsibility to be toward themselves and their families compared to the broader social community. On the one side, many Americans have a strong inclination toward personal responsibility and individual decision-making, which many trace to the frontier mentality. But the American frontier experience was not only about rugged individualism. It also required group efforts and mutual protection in order to survive and thrive. Not only did the individual have duties to the group, but the group took responsibility for the weaker members. The collectivist perspective stresses the claims that individuals can legitimately make for help from the rest of us, especially in hard times. Collectivism is about not only economic inclusion but also other forms of inclusion toward groups who have been excluded from economic and social success. In this sense, collectivism is a broader value emphasizing equality in several dimensions. This value divide influences

---

[17] See Feldman 2013 for a good overview.
[18] This value is sometimes conceptualized as *egalitarianism* versus individualism (emphasizing equality of outcome) or *humanitarianism* versus individualism (emphasizing the desire to help others). Another word sometimes employed is *communitarianism*, essentially a synonym for collectivism (both emphasizing the aspect of group decision-making for collective benefits rather than individual decision-making for individual benefits). See Feldman and Zaller 1992, Feldman and Steenbergen 2001, Marietta 2011.
[19] Feldman 1983, Kerlinger 1984, Kahan and Braman 2006, Schwartz and Bilsky 1990, Schwartz 1992.
[20] See Barker and Carman 2012, Hunter 1991, Layman 2001, Layman and Carsey 2002, Marietta and Barker 2007, White 2002; for a somewhat similar conceptualization, see Kahan et al. 2012 and Nisbet and Markowitz 2014.

political debate across a wide range of issues regarding economic redistribution, government regulation, healthcare, taxation, the welfare state, affirmative action, and racial justice.

Humanism versus theism centers on whether citizens appeal to a traditional and transcendent source of moral authority or to human reason about moral issues. It is not at heart a question of whether one *is* nominally religious but whether one *thinks* in a traditionally religious fashion about morals. James Davison Hunter refers to this value division as centering on reactions to *moral absolutism*, or the belief that judgments of right and wrong are clear and trans-situational, or whether they are gray and vary with circumstances ("*X* is wrong, which is well-established" or "whether *X* is wrong depends on the situation, which I must judge"). Is the world black and white in a way we can discern if we learn from tradition, or are there many shades of gray?[21] This value dimension may be one of the most influential because it is attached to strong emotions and has ramifications that are easy to understand. It is an umbrella for a large number of political debates that have moral dimensions.

We followed the measurement approach of asking survey respondents, "What is more important for society?" and prompting them with four-point response scales that are balanced at the poles by the two values in conflict, phrased in common language that is accessible to ordinary citizens.[22] Collectivism–individualism is balanced between "cooperation and helping others" and "self-reliance and personal responsibility." Humanism–theism is balanced between "scientific knowledge" and "religious faith." Figures 6.1 and 6.2 illustrate the results for 2013 (the 2014 data are essentially identical).[23]

In regard to each of these core values, American citizens demonstrate dramatic divisions, with nothing approaching a consensus. There are many other important value conflicts in contemporary American politics as well, but these are two of the central divisions. One could

---

[21] Note that they word *gray/grey* can be spelled either way; it is one of the unusual words in contemporary English with fully ambiguous spelling, reflecting its definition. (If it were *wrong* for gray to also be spelled grey, that would be oddly contradictory.)

[22] For a similar empirical approach employing these measures, see Barker and Carman 2012, Marietta and Barker 2007.

[23] 2013: strong collectivist 22%, collectivist 29%, individualist 23%, strong individualist 26%; 2014: 21%, 28%, 29%, 22%, respectively. In 2013 the dichotomous break was 51%/49%; in 2014, 49%/51%. In regard to humanism–theism, 2013: 29%/22%/23%/26%; 2014: 30%/22%/23%/25%; dichotomous, in 2013 51%/49%, and in 2014 52%/48%.

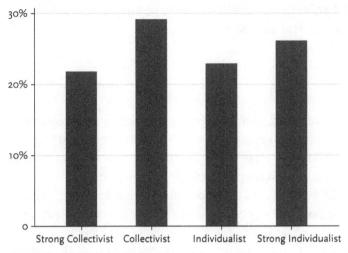

FIGURE 6.1 Collectivism–Individualism Among Americans, 2013

object that this is just one means of measuring values; aside from directly political values, there are other conceptions and measurements (*personal* values, as described by Shalom Schwartz, and *moral* values or moral foundations, as described by Jonathan Haidt). In the analyses to follow, we will employ all three of these distinct conceptualizations and measures—political, personal, and moral values—each of which yields the same results: *values are projected onto fact perceptions, any way you conceptualize them.*

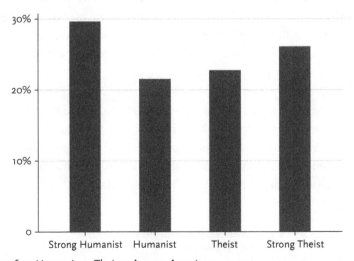

FIGURE 6.2 Humanism–Theism Among Americans, 2013

Value Projection: Motivated Reasoning and the Somewhat Moral Fallacy

"Isn't it pretty to think so?"

—*Ernest Hemingway, The Sun Also Rises*

Facts are often uncertain, while our core beliefs tend to be more clear. The values of our social groups, on which we rely for support and well-being, are also relatively clear to us. The mechanisms of motivated reasoning discussed in the last chapter work through these two channels: motivation to maintain our beliefs and motivation to maintain our social standing. Violating our values or the values of our group has high psychic and personal costs, while perceiving some facts over others is an available and less personally costly choice (at least in the short run). Hence our core hypothesis: *citizens tend to project their values onto their perceptions of fact.*

Philosophers have long discussed the prevalence of the moral fallacy, or the unintentional and unaware conflation of facts and values. This is deeply related to the venerable (but shaky and porous) fact/value dichotomy discussed in Chapter 2. As we discussed then, the divide between facts and values is honored more in the breach, as Shakespeare put it.[24] Rather than maintaining a principled division, the moral fallacy leads people to substitute *what ought to be* for *what is*; we project what we *want* onto what we *observe*, such that empirical observations are faulty in a normative direction. The natural fallacy is the opposite, when we assume that what occurs naturally in the world must be a good thing, such that moral conclusions are faulty in an empirical direction.[25] At first it might seem that the same person would not commit both fallacies, but unfortunately we can commit the moral fallacy when we focus on empirical judgment and the natural fallacy when we focus on moral judgments, such that the two tendencies cyclically reinforce each other.

In the previous chapter on the more mainstream psychology of perception, we discussed the specific mechanisms that aid and abet this process: the cognitive psychology mechanisms of selective cognitions (attention, acceptance, skepticism, memory, and reinforcement), the social psychology mechanisms of multifaceted conformity, and the influential role of personal knowledge. Motivated reasoning ratchets up all of

---

[24] "It is a custom more honored in the breach than the observance." *Hamlet* act I, scene iv.

[25] Many writers use the older terms *moralistic* and *naturalistic* fallacy. See Moore 1903, Singer 1981, Curry 2006.

these effects and works through any of these mechanisms. Reasoning is motivated by values, both ours and those of our group.

But is this the moral fallacy? Do we want to see that our values already control the world? Or do we want to see that the world demands that our values have more control? In other words, are we biased toward seeing a world *already in tune* with our values or one *in need of the application* of our values? Perhaps value projection is not the moral fallacy, per se, but only a somewhat moral fallacy. The full moral fallacy would mean we tended to see how our values *already exist* in the world, which is not exactly what people do.

Lippmann argued that "we submit the shadows of things to the desires of the mind"; what is clear and obvious might escape our moral projections, but what is somewhat unclear—in shadow—inevitably is shaped by our desires.[26] But what do we desire? Do we see what we want to *be* or see what we want to *see*? The first implies that we will see the world already in accord with our values. (Egalitarians would see equality.) The second implies that we will see the world screaming out for the application of our values that have not yet come to fruition. (Egalitarians will see inequality that needs to be addressed.)

We expect that the projection of values is motivated more by what we want to *see* than by what we want things to *be*. In other words, we do not project our values onto perceptions as if they were already in existence; value projection is not prospective. Instead we project what our values suggest we should see if our values were important, which is often the things that our values suggest should change. Value projection aggrandizes the *importance* of our values more than the existing *power* of our values. People do not necessarily want to see a world already reflecting their desired end state. If that were the case, people would have no use for their political values (or need for a political agenda or political participation); perceiving an already perfect world would deflate rather than increase the importance of their values. Instead they perceive a world ready to enact their preferences for change rather than a world in which their preferences for change have already arrived.

Value projection is likely to occur in a negative as well as a positive sense because we are also motivated by what we do *not* want to see. We

---

[26] Lippmann 1927, page 155. "Pictures of the world are drawn from things half heard and of things half seen; they deal with shadows of things unsteadily, and submit unconsciously to the desires of the mind" (page 153). "Rationally, the facts are neutral to all our views of right and wrong. Actually, our canons determine greatly what we shall perceive and how" (Lippmann 1925, page 79).

want to see things that are laudatory to our values, and we want to avoid recognizing things that suggest clear criticisms of our values.

Projecting values accurately onto perceived facts requires some sense of the political situation or some degree of political knowledge. But only a small amount of political savvy seems to be needed to do it to some degree, allowing ordinary people to *project the political meaning of their values onto their perceptions of facts*. For example, egalitarians—who want *greater equality*—would not tend to see equality already existing; they see the need for *greater equality*. Equality may be what they want to *be* in the world but not what they want to *see* in the world. The same is the case for individualists, who would want to see individualism as effective (and needed) more than already existing. Egalitarians will also be reluctant to recognize observations that challenge the need for, or efficacy of, greater equality, while individualists will tend to ignore observations that raise criticisms of greater self-reliance in society.

With this in mind, we suspect that the values of collectivism–individualism and humanism–theism predict dueling fact perceptions (DFPs) in clear patterns. It is important to note that these two values are empirically quite distinct from each other. Their correlations are only .10 in the 2013 measures and .09 in 2014.[27] As such, we expect these value conflicts to behave differently with respect to fact perceptions, depending on the perceived fact in question. This will serve as something of a discriminant validity test of the value projection mechanism. That is, if value cleavages predict DFPs only when theory clearly suggests that they should, and not otherwise, then we can have greater confidence that the measures are validly capturing what they are supposed to, rather than serving as proxies for some other dynamic.

Collectivism–Individualism and Specific DFPs

Climate change is a collective problem requiring a collective solution. Hence, collectivists should be more inclined to see such a problem and to endorse the solutions that increase the role of this value. It is important to see that if collectivists wanted to see their core value as *already effective*, they would come to the opposite conclusion; but they are more

---

[27] Both values are also distinct from ideology and party identification (PID). The correlations of collectivism–individualism in 2013 and 2014 are .42/.41 with PID and .32/.36 with ideology. For humanism–theism, the correlations are .33/.29 with PID and .41/.44 with ideology. (PID and ideology are more highly correlated together at .59/.63.)

likely to see their beliefs as *needed*. The collectivist or egalitarian is also likely to be more attuned to the environmental inequalities presented by climate threats to poor and disadvantaged communities. Individualists, on the other hand, would be less inclined than collectivists to acknowledge climate change. If we focus on individual actions and responsibilities as the core virtues, a lone individual should not be accountable for a problem she did not create. Moreover, individualists do not want to be told that higher taxes and greater government interventions are necessary to combat climate change, to limit the consumption and pollution causing it, or that free markets have created and failed to contain the problem. If global warming is real and human activity is responsible, it means that the individual actions within the free market have failed to prevent problems and that greater government regulation is needed, which individualists resist but collectivists welcome.

For individualists to perceive racism as an enduringly powerful determinant of success, they would have to acknowledge the limitations of self-reliance and accept that social conditions account for differences in achievement, which individualists do not want to do. Hence, we expect that individualists are more likely to perceive racism as no longer a meaningful impediment to personal success in America. Collectivists, by contrast, are more sensitive to evidence of unequal treatment suffered by minorities. So, if racism were no longer impactful, collectivists would have to admit that existing efforts designed to combat it could be softened or even eliminated, which would lower the importance of their values.

On the other hand, we do *not* recognize a clear theoretical connection between collectivism–individualism and perceptions regarding the origins of sexuality.

Humanism–Theism and Specific DFPs

In regard to sexuality, theists should be more likely than humanists to view homosexuality as a socially conditioned choice because many of them consider it sinful and non-conducive to child-rearing (and therefore "unnatural"). Disobedience to biblical authority or natural law is seen as a mistaken free-will choice. Moreover, in a degraded world, the value that is needed is more theism, rather than more rewriting of the rules by human desires. Humanists, on the other hand, who tend to be less encumbered by such doctrines, should be more likely to see this question from the perspective of sexual minorities, who often speak about having been aware of their sexuality for as long as they can remember. What does the world need

TABLE 6.1 Hypothesized Relations of Values to DFPs

Individualism:	Climate change is *not* real
	Racism is *not* influential
	No relation to sexual orientation
Theism:	Climate change is *not* real
	No relation to racism
	Sexual orientation is *not* innate

in this case? It needs more humanist attention to the voices of oppressed humans.

As for climate change perceptions, theists believe that God is in control, not humans, so if the planet is warming, it is part of God's unfolding plan and is thus not *ultimately* attributable to human behavior.[28] Theists also tend to be less enamored of human secular scientists as knowers of truth, so they are less inclined to trust the scientific consensus on this subject. Humanists, on the other hand, are much more inclined to trust the findings of human-led science, as well as to accept the idea that humans are responsible for changes in the world. Humanists are more inclined to see the need for human actions grounded in our ability to alter reality; just as we got ourselves into this, humanism is needed to get us out.

However, we see no compelling theoretical connection between humanism–theism and perceptions of racism.

Each of these expectations is illustrated in Table 6.1.

Conclusion

The last two chapters presented a broad and multifaceted rendition of the psychology of fact perception. To summarize the several mechanisms that we suggest are operating and reinforcing each other, we can take an example of the value of humanism–theism as it relates to perceptions of the origins of sexual orientation. Imagine a hypothetical citizen who embraces the value of theism. In our view, she would likely conclude that sexual orientation is experiential rather than innate because of the combined and interactive effects of personal knowledge, selective cognitions, social conformity, and motivated reasoning, all leading to value projection.

---

[28] See Barker and Bearce 2014.

Feelings of personal knowledge are likely to be high in regard to sexual attraction. She is likely not only to have personal experience in how this aspect of humanity functions but also to have personally witnessed many individual circumstances. Something this inherently personal is likely to inspire trust in our personal knowledge and lead to projection of those feelings and experiences onto others.

With theistic values as a guide, her cognitions are likely to be selective in that direction. She will tend to pay greater attention to media reports or Internet stories from more theism-friendly sources, which are more likely to report on suggestions that sexual orientation evolves due to circumstances. She is more likely to accept such reports after applying a lower standard of evidence to the ones that sound plausible to her. She is more likely to selectively counterargue the stories she does hear that suggest that sexual orientation is innate, applying a higher and more skeptical standard to those reports. If these reports come from secular scientists or universities that she believes to be hostile to religious faith, the information is easier to discount as biased. When the topic comes to mind, she is more likely to remember the evidence in favor of the experiential position. And when the topic is discussed, expressing her views and what she has heard to support them is likely to reinforce those beliefs in her mind.

Those discussions are likely to take place within her social groups comprised of individuals who hold similar values and have undergone similar cognitive processes. She is more likely to care about the opinions held by others in her church congregation and her neighborhood (and about the opinions they hold of *her*). After hearing their views, social proof may tell her what is likely to be true, and social conformity may well encourage her to refrain from publicly disputing the views of the seeming majority (of those who count).

All of these effects may be subtle, or they may be directionally motivated by theism and hence more powerful. What a theist would prefer to observe are the empirical conditions that demand more of that value in society—that sexuality is a choice or a reaction to events, suggesting the need for personal decisions and social organizations grounded in greater theism. Motivations to aggrandize core values, maintain important social connections, and perceive the facts that reinforce each of them will ratchet up the effects of selective cognition and social conformity. The mechanisms of cognitive and social psychology, especially when motivated by values, will lead toward predictable perceptions.

We also think a couple of other important things are going on, which solidify the projection of values onto DFPs (described in Chapters 8 and

9). But one doesn't have to be convinced of those arguments (about how values carry epistemology or how sacred values lead to sacred facts) in order to see the influence of value projection. Considering only the accepted psychology of perception alone, one can see the clear path from values to facts. With all of this in mind, the next chapter undertakes the core empirical tests of the role of values in fact perceptions, while also accounting for the influence of partisan tribalism, opinion leadership, and social group consciousness.

7 | Polarized Leaders Versus Polarized Values

> "The best way to reach truth is to examine things as they really are,
> and not to steer by *fancies which we have worked up for ourselves*
> or *have been taught by others to imagine*."
>
> —*John Locke*[1]

> "What each man does is based not on direct and certain knowledge,
> but on pictures *made by himself* or *given to him*."
>
> —*Walter Lippmann*[2]

L OCKE IN 1690 AND LIPPMANN in 1925 lay out two alternatives about the origins of political perceptions: they are the product of internal beliefs that we project onto the outside world, or they are the products of external influences that others provide for us. They might be "fancies which we have worked up for ourselves" or ones we "have been taught by others to imagine." They may be pictures a citizen "made by himself" or ones "given to him." One of the central questions about the origins of dueling facts is whether they are the product of opinion leadership by elites or value projection by citizens themselves.

The previous chapters lay out the psychological case for value projection. This chapter takes an extensive empirical look at the capacity of citizens' core values to predict fact perceptions, relative to the role of partisan leadership. In a secondary way, we are also interested in the role of social identity consciousness, especially race and gender identities, as well as the role of media propagandists. We start from the presumption that

---

[1] Locke 1690, book II, chapter xi.15 (italics added).
[2] Lippmann 1922, page 16 (italics added).

party leadership, social identities, and media propaganda are all important predictors of dueling fact perceptions (DFPs), but we posit that core values also contribute in powerful ways that have particular democratic significance.

Partisan Leadership and Value Projection

The idea that partisan leadership undergirds DFPs has many advocates and long origins. As the authors of *The American Voter* put it way back in 1960, "party identification raises a perceptual screen through which the individual tends to see what is favorable to his partisan orientation. The stronger the party bond, the more exaggerated the process of selection and perceptual distortion will be."[3] In other words, partisanship—an internalized group affinity, independent of values or policy preferences—is akin to supporting a sports team, and sports fans readily change their perceptions about players, playing styles, rules, penalties, and pretty much everything else when the team changes. They do so in part to protect their tribal identity and in part because they are motivated to believe information endorsed by a trusted source.[4] So party leaders (through the media and otherwise) promulgate strategically advantageous understandings of reality and bring citizens' perceptions along with them.

The process of partisan leadership has three essential components: (1) citizens' psychological attachment to the team, (2) team leaders' incentives to bend the truth to their strategic ends, and (3) citizens' exposure to the leaders' pronouncements—in and through the media. Accordingly, partisans may be more susceptible to factual politicization than nonpartisans, but politically *attentive* partisans should be particularly susceptible. And those who get most of their information from overtly partisan or ideological media outlets should be even more susceptible.[5] This notion of elite influence over citizen points of view, broadly defined, is very well established empirically.[6]

---

[3] Campbell et al. 1960, page 133. For empirical accounts of the partisan leadership approach, see Bartels 2002, Bullock et al. 2015, Gaines et al. 2007, Gerber and Huber 2010, Hochschild and Einstein 2015, Jerit and Barabas 2012.

[4] See, for example, Campbell et al. 1960, Green et al. 2002, Lewis-Beck et al. 2008.

[5] See Barker 1998, 2002, Barker and Knight 2000, Barker and Lawrence 2006, Baum 2002, 2005, Baum and Groeling 2008, Brewer and Cao 2006, Flaxman et al. 2016, Jamieson and Capella 2010, Levendusky 2013; but see Arceneaux and Johnson 2013.

[6] See, for example, Chong and Druckman 2011, Lupia and McCubbins 1998, Nicholson 2011, 2012.

Party identity and the leadership dynamics that manipulate it are, without a doubt, important parts of the DFP story. Our question is whether they are the only ones. As we discussed in Chapter 6, we argue that citizens are motivated to accept information that accords with their prior value commitments, independent of their partisan attachments and irrespective of what party leaders might do or say.[7] It is less like mindless fandom and more like sincere faith: it is not content-neutral, and it does not depend on opinion leadership (though it can certainly be enhanced by it). So, for example, if a citizen believes that sexual orientation is a "lifestyle choice" rather than an innate characteristic, it is not because the GOP presidential nominee or Sean Hannity has insinuated as much but rather because she is a committed theist who cannot conceive of a world in which such nontraditional lifestyles could be natural.[8] Her values can be primed by Hannity, and their role can be thereby enhanced by his endorsement; but they do not *depend* on it in the way that partisanship does. Consequently, her perception is not likely to change if Hannity or the party change its mind.

In Chapters 5 and 6, we argued that the psychological mechanisms relating to personal knowledge, cognitive psychology, social psychology, and motivated reasoning all intertwine and reinforce the projection of core values onto fact perceptions. But these combined mechanisms *also reinforce the role of partisan leadership*. The selective cognitions described in Chapter 5 could magnify and entrench the views of a citizen's political party (as well as reinforce the observations congruent with individual values). Social conformity could reinforce a partisan leader's assertions (as well as reinforce the values of the partisan group). When a partisan identity is related to a specific fact perception, personal knowledge could reinforce that observation (as well as reinforce individual perceptions shaped by personal values). And motivated reasoning could be directed toward conformity to the party's views (as well as toward aggrandizing one's own values and maintaining consistency between beliefs and perceptions). In some senses, the recognized psychology reinforces value

---

[7] Also see Wells et al. 2009; Reedy et al. 2014.

[8] Of course, party leadership and core value projection are surely not mutually exclusive. For one thing, latent values can also be primed by external sources, including partisan media propagandists (e.g., Barker 2002). And core values—at least the way political scientists have traditionally measured them as overtly political statements—are interwoven with partisan or other identities (see Goren 2005, Goren et al. 2009). Value statements can also serve to signal virtue to fellow tribal members, thereby cementing in-group status. This is why we take great care in the analyses we describe to (a) use various value measurement strategies, including those that distinguish them from policy attitudes to as great an extent as possible, and (b) fully account for partisan and other identities, in our attempt to clarify the independent role of values as DFP motivators.

projection (especially the more cognitive side), but in other senses, the same mechanisms could *also* reinforce partisan leadership (especially the more social aspect).

So people *do* tend to conform to their partisan group and to the messages from its leaders, but *they do so more when the group's values are the same as their own* and *when the group's perceptions make sense to them because of these similarities of values.* Values account for *which* factual perceptions the group will embrace. In other words, it is the *content* of group membership—shared values—that drives much of the role of group influence. The partisan facts argument emphasizes the more *external* mechanisms of opinion leadership and partisan media messaging; in this view, citizens are *led* to partisan fact perceptions. Our argument emphasizes the *internal* mechanisms originating in citizens themselves, grounded in their prior beliefs that influence the choice of media and shape group identity as well as derive from it. Recognizing the internal mechanism is important not only because it completes the causal story but because *the polarization of values is enough to create dueling facts* and *enough to maintain them,* even if the external forces change direction or improve in the future.

To summarize things so far, the partisan facts account describes an external mechanism grounded in the political environment, whereas the value projection account describes an internal mechanism created by citizens' own deeply held beliefs. In the partisan facts telling, party leaders (through the media and otherwise) promulgate strategically advantageous understandings of reality and drag citizens along with them, while in the value projection telling, divided value systems produce divided fact perceptions because top-down leadership is not necessary if bottom-up values are powerful enough for people to project them onto their fact perceptions.

The relative external or internal origins of DFPs speak to their durability as a defining feature of contemporary politics. If party leaders or media propagandists drive DFPs and values are minimally influential, then DFPs could wane if those leaders were to see strategic benefits in tempering their messaging. But if core values play consistent and substantial roles in the DFP story—irrespective of what party leaders or their media minions might say—then DFPs will almost certainly persist.

For example, if party leaders could be motivated to pursue median-voter strategies rather than base-mobilization strategies (which could in theory be facilitated by changes to the nominating or congressional redistricting institutions), they could be likewise motivated to embrace majoritarian fact perceptions. Such changes to the official party line "from the top" could very well encourage party loyalists to follow suit. In much the same way, if market forces were to encourage mass media to reject *narrowcasting* as a business model (crafting a message in an attempt to capture a particular slice of audience share rather than appealing to a broad audience), they would be incentivized to reprioritize objective truth-telling. Either or both of these changes could be achieved through certain institutional reforms (in theory at least). And if they were, DFPs could slowly depolarize. By contrast, if internal value projection drives DFPs to a substantial degree, then any potential changes to strategic messaging by partisan elites and their media consorts would probably fall on deaf ears. And that would mean that DFPs (and their negative democratic consequences) would likely endure, no matter what reformers might do. What is more, when civic educators succeed at waking up a mostly lethargic citizenry, DFPs spread more rapidly.[9] The only cure would be to encourage citizens to care *less* about the issues affecting their country and their lives—something that few civic educators or democratic reformers want to hear.

Social Identity and Social Identity Consciousness

Of course, partisanship and values are not the only factors that might shape perceptions of reality. Just as partisan tribalism can drive people to protect their identities by adopting the factual beliefs of the tribe, the same is likely to be true with respect to social group attachments. We are talking not only about simple differences in biologically and socially constructed traits such as gender, race, and ethnicity but also about differences in *the degree to which those traits are important to one's psychological sense of identity* (and therefore the degree to which one feels a sense of solidarity toward others who share those traits). "Group consciousness" of this nature is a fundamental shaper of attitudes and vote choices,[10] so it stands to reason that such social affinities would also motivate perceptions of reality, particularly (or perhaps exclusively) with respect to factual disputes that are highly racialized or sexualized. However, unlike partisan identity—which is a lot like fandom in that it is deeply felt but not necessarily rooted

---

[9] This would represent a variant of the democratic paradox identified by Diana Mutz (2006), who demonstrated that participatory democracy and deliberative democracy are empirically incompatible.
[10] For general treatments of the role of social identity, see Lazarsfeld et al. 1944, Berelson et al. 1954, Campbell et al. 1960, Achen and Bartels 2016. For treatments of social group consciousness, see Gurin 1985, Broman et al. 1988, Demo and Hughes 1990.

in anything rational or substantive in many cases[11]—social identities *are* rational and substantive. That is, while race and gender identities are socially constructed in part,[12] they are also partially rooted in uniquely shared experiences and points of view that have nothing to do with the perspectives of group leaders.

While these identity and group consciousness dynamics are surely important, we do not spend as much theoretical or empirical energy assessing their influence because we suspect that the number of DFPs that are deeply influenced by social identity consciousness (independent of that which is entangled in partisanship) is much narrower than those that are influenced by core values or by partisan leadership. For example, we expect that one's perception of whether racism continues to drive many economic and criminal justice outcomes has a lot to do with whether one is black or white and the experiences that one has had as a result. We also imagine that such racial identity affects perceptions of the frequency of false convictions. However, we see less theoretical justification to anticipate that racial or ethnic identity would drive many DFPs that do not have clear racial undertones. The same is true for gender identity and identity consciousness. But to the extent that social identities do indeed motivate DFPs, in addition to values and independent of partisanship, it would provide that much more reason for pessimism with respect to DFP permanence— because social identities, like values, are not as easily manipulated as partisan ones are.

Partisan Media

Another hypothesis argues that DFPs are the product of partisan media exposure. In this view, it is not values or identities or even party leaders that are the core causes of DFPs, but instead the endorsements, exhortations, and manipulations of leaders in popular media, such as Sean Hannity, Rush Limbaugh, and Rachel Maddow. This argument is more often made regarding the Right side of American politics, often described as

---

[11] The ideologies that correspond to partisan identities are obviously substantive and meaningful, but that is not partisanship (and ideologies are partially a byproduct of values). Pure partisanship, as conceptualized by Campbell et al. 1960, is psychological attachment to a team, rooted in early socialization.

[12] This is not to say that social identity consciousness is not enhanced by external events (e.g., high-profile cases of legal injustice, such as the Rodney King and O. J. Simpson trials) or charismatic group leaders (e.g., Malcolm X, George Wallace, Gloria Steinem, Donald Trump). It clearly is. So such group consciousness is not an entirely internal mechanism. But it is more of one than partisan consciousness is.

the conservative "echo chamber."[13] On the other hand, consumption of partisan media may be the product of self-selection by existing partisans, and hence the additional influence of listening to Hannity may have little influence.[14] With the blending of news reporting with opinion journalism in contemporary media, it is easy to consume reinforcing information exclusively.[15] Given this debate, it is important to test empirically if partisan media consumption is strongly related to DFPs and whether we still find independent effects of values and party leadership when ideological media consumption is taken into account. On the continuum from internal to external influences, while values are the most internal influence, partisan media leadership is the most external.

In the remainder of this chapter, we describe our attempts to sort out the relative capacity of value projection, party leadership, and (to a lesser extent) social identity consciousness and partisan media to account for DFPs. Our primary focus is to observe the degree to which values in particular reveal a consistently strong capacity to account for DFPs—independent of partisanship, ideology, social identities, news media, or any external leadership dynamics.

Empirical Tests

As we discussed in Chapter 4, we commissioned several separate studies to test our propositions about the role of value projection. In the remainder of the chapter, we present analyses of four years' worth of nationally representative survey data from YouGov—both as part of the Cooperative Congressional Election Study (2013, 2014, 2017) and independent of it (2016). The 2017 data enabled us to assess the extent to which patterns observed in the age of Obama and divided government continue to hold in the era of Trump and unified Republican control.

Some other scholarship has identified values as important DFP determinants, but those studies have suffered under (a) restricted samples,[16] (b) esoteric fact perceptions as the focus of their investigations,[17] or (c) the

---

[13] Barker 2002, Morris 2005, Jamieson and Capella 2010, Levendusky 2013, Hopkins and Ladd 2014, Martin and Yurukoglu 2017, Martin and McCrain 2018.

[14] See Arcenaux and Johnson 2013.

[15] Barker 2002, Prior 2007, Baum and Groeling 2008.

[16] See Wells et al. 2009; Reedy et al. 2014.

[17] Specifically, they have focused either on low-salience fact disputes in the context of state ballot initiatives (Wells et al. 2009; Reedy et al. 2014) or "risk perceptions" associated with pursuing one or another policy option (e.g., Kahan and Braman 2006, Kahan 2013a, 2016).

tendency to conflate—conceptually and empirically—value projection, partisanship, and social identity consciousness as DFP mechanisms.[18] To our knowledge, no other examinations of DFP motivators have (1) focused as intently on isolating the independent predictive capacity of values versus other motivators, (2) gathered as much national data (across as many years), (3) examined as wide a range of DFPs, (4) operationalized values in as many different ways, or (5) constructed models that erect as many hurdles to identifying independent value effects as we do here.

Using the 2013–2017 data, in each of the studies we conducted a series of binary probit regression analyses, looking at the degree to which differences in (a) value priorities, (b) partisan identities, (c) exposure to partisan messaging, and—in 2017—(d) social identity consciousness predict increases or decreases in the probability of believing something to be true or false.[19]

The Factual Disputes in Question

In our 2013–2016 studies, we focused on understanding the three DFPs that we described in Chapter 4: climate (in 2017, 71% believed that "the Earth is warming due to human activity"), racism (65% believed "racism often prevents racial/ethnic minorities from being successful"), and sexuality (61% believed that "people are born gay or straight"). However, in 2017 we were able to analyze seven additional fact perceptions, which we will describe in more detail—(1) the national debt will cause economic harm, (2) vaccines cause autism, (3) false convictions are common, (4) increases in the minimum wage lower employment, (5) undocumented immigrants take jobs, (6) gun control reduces mass shootings, and (7) violent crime is increasing—for a total of ten DFPs across a broad range of political domains.

Measuring Partisan Identity and External Party Leadership

The partisan leadership story is layered and conditional. It depends on people who have a psychological attachment to their party becoming aware of party leaders' perspectives on the facts and reflexively adopting

---

[18] Kahan and Braman 2006, Kahan 2013a, 2016.

[19] To reiterate, the original measures were four-point scales (0 = certainly false; 1 = probably false; 2 = probably true; 3 = certainly true). But in this chapter, we use the dichotomous scales to simplify presentation of results. The results obtained using the full scales (and ordinal probit regression models) produce very similar substantive and statistical results to those we report in this chapter.

them as their own. Thus, this theoretical account does not apply to non-partisans, and it does not really apply to the politically inattentive either (inattentive partisans do surely pick up some cues, but if they are uninterested in politics, they are also probably less protective of their partisan identities and thus less inclined to use those cues to decide what is true). Therefore, to capture these layers, the partisan leadership story is told in successive models. First, we included a traditional measure of party identification (PID) in the model to get a simplistic view of its predictive capacity.[20] Next, we created an interaction term that multiplied PID by news attentiveness[21] and included all three variables in the model simultaneously.[22] If our theoretical account is accurate, PID will not typically reveal much predictive capacity among the inattentive but will spike among the attentive.[23]

Measuring Value Projection

To maximize the reliability of our measures—and thus the internal and external validity of our research design—we employed three different strategies. In 2013 and 2014, we followed the measurement approach described in Chapter 6, following the standard approach of political scientists by focusing on values that are overtly "political." In 2016, we shifted course, following the *personal values* strategy pioneered by Shalom Schwartz and his colleagues. And in 2017 we changed course again,

---

[20] Seven-point branching scale: "Generally speaking, do you think of yourself as a Democrat [Would you call yourself a strong Democrat or a not very strong Democrat?], Republican [same follow-up], Independent [Do you think of yourself as closer to the Democratic or the Republican Party?], Other."
[21] Four-point scale: "Some people seem to follow what's going on in government and public affairs most of the time, whether there's an election going on or not. Others aren't that interested. Would you say you follow what's going on in government and public affairs 'hardly at all,' 'only now and then,' 'some of the time,' or 'most of the time'." Because the significant variance was between those who claim to follow "most of the time" and those who follow any lesser amount, we simplified this variable into a dichotomy.
[22] In analyzing and describing interaction effects, we follow the procedures outlined in Brambor et al. 2006 and Berry et al. 2012.
[23] In other analyses (the results of which we do not present out of space considerations and compassion for the reader), we pursued additional *party leadership* measurement strategies. One created a three-way interaction term of PID, news attentiveness, and partisan news consumption. Another (in the 2017 studies only) replaced news attentiveness in the interaction with a measure of how embarrassed or proud one feels when thinking of other people who share the same partisan identity (0 = consistently embarrassed; 3 = consistently proud). None of these alternate measurement strategies enable party leadership to predict DFPs as well as the approach we focus on here. As such, none of the alternative strategies provide as stringent a test of the independent predictive capacity of value projection. In other words, what we discuss is the most expansive presentation of party leadership's distinct predictive role and the most conservative presentation of value projection's distinct predictive role, which is why we have chosen to emphasize these results.

following the *moral foundations* framework championed by Jonathan Haidt and his colleagues. Numerous empirical studies have validated both of these latter approaches.[24]

In 2013–2014, we focused on collectivism–individualism (measured as "cooperation and helping others" versus "self-reliance and personal responsibility") and humanism–theism ("scientific knowledge" versus "religious faith").[25] We asked respondents to indicate the extent to which they thought one or the other value was "more important for society" (on four-point scales; 0 = strongly prefer cooperation/scientific knowledge; 3 = strongly prefer individualism/religious faith).

As a means of comparing "apples to apples" with respect to value projection and partisanship as determinants of DFPs, we also created interaction terms that multiply each value by the same news attentiveness item that we multiplied with PID to create the party leadership variable. This allows us to empirically evaluate our claim that value projection, unlike partisan leadership, is more of an internal mechanism. In successive analyses, we enter one or another of these "value leadership" measures into the equation, to observe the degree to which the value projection effects depend on external leadership, relative to that associated with PID.

To summarize the specific hypotheses laid out in Chapter 6 (see Table 6.1), we expect collectivists to be more likely than individualists to believe that climate change is real and anthropogenic and that racism still prevents racial minorities from being successful, but we do not expect the two groups to view sexuality differently. We expect humanists to be more likely than theists to believe that sexuality is innate and that the climate is warming, but we see no reason to expect the two groups to perceive the prevalence of racism differently. Furthermore, while we anticipate that news attentiveness may enhance these relationships, we also expect them to remain significant even among those who do not pay regular attention to public affairs—which we expect to stand in contrast to what we observe about the role of PID.

---

[24] See Lindeman and Verkasalo 2005, Schwartz and Bilsky 1990, Schwartz 1992, Schwartz and Boehnke 2004, Schwartz et al. 2001, Graham et al. 2009, Haidt 2012.

[25] In 2013, to further establish robustness, we also included an alternative—and broader—cultural value dimension: openness–traditionalism. Rather than being so closely tied to religiosity, openness–traditionalism encompasses a broader conceptualization of the American culture wars. To measure it, we asked respondents to consider the competing values in everyday language of "traditional roles for gender and family versus openness to new arrangements" and to indicate (on the same four-point scale) which of the two is "more important for society" (0 = strongly prefer openness and 3 = strongly prefer traditional roles). The findings using this measure strongly resemble those we report here.

Measuring Social Identities and Group Consciousness

In 2013–2016, the best we could do to account for the influence of social identities was to include measures of gender and race (along with age, income, and education).[26] However, in 2017, we were able to add measures of gender and racial–ethnic identity consciousness to the models. Specifically, the survey asked, "When you think about most other people who share your ethnic (gender) identity, how much pride or embarrassment do you feel?" (0 = consistently embarrassed; 1 = mostly embarrassed but sometimes proud; 2 = sometimes embarrassed but mostly proud; 3 = consistently proud; mean = 2.014; standard deviation = .77). After converting the responses to a 0–1 scale, we created interaction terms that multiplied the ethnic pride measure by a simple race measure (0 = white; 1 = non-white) and the gender pride variable by gender (0 = male; 1 = female; mean = 2.14; standard deviation = .75).

Accounting for Ideology

In all of our analyses and across all years, we controlled for the influence of *ideological identification* more broadly,[27] even though such identification is itself in part a byproduct of the way people prioritize their values and cluster them.[28] We did this in order to make the value constructs "swim upstream" if they were to demonstrate independent predictive capacity, meaning that the associations we observe are likely understated (as is the predictive capacity associated with PID).

We recoded all of the independent variables from their natural scales to 0–1 (with decimal points in between), to reveal the minimum-to-maximum effects associated with the variables and to ease interpretation of results.[29]

---

[26] Race: 0 = white; 1 = non-white (means: 2013 = .27; 2016 = .20; 2017 = .35; standard deviations: 2013 = .45; 2016 = .40; 2017 = .48); gender: 0 = male; 1 = female (means: 2013 = .53; 2016 = .58; 2017 = .59. standard deviations: 2013 = .50; 2016 = .49; 2017 = .49); age: 18–88 (means: 2013 = 48.08; 2016 = 47.19; 2017 = 48.57; standard deviations: 2013 = 17.20; 2016 = 16.58; 2017 = 17.18); income: 0 = <$10,000; 12 = >$200,000 (means: 2013 = 4.80; 2016 = 4.84; 2017 = 4.79; standard deviations: 2013 = 3.03; 2016 = 3.08; 2017 = 3.24); education: 0 = <high school; 5 = graduate degree. (means: 2013 = 3.44; 2016 = 2.29; 2017 = 2.52. standard deviations: 2013 = 1.44; 2016 = 1.47; 2017 = 1.47).
[27] 0 = "very liberal"; 4 = "very conservative" (means: 2013 = 2.02; 2016 = 2.03; 2017 = 2.01; standard deviations: 2013 = 1.10; 2016 = 1.07; 2017 = 1.18).
[28] Barker and Tinnick 2006, Graham et al. 2009, Jost et al. 2009, Pjurko et al. 2011.
[29] In keeping with the Cooperative Congressional Election Study's sampling strategy, we clustered standard errors by congressional district. Given the presence of interaction terms in the model, we calculated those standard errors using the delta method (see Ai and Norton 2003). We also employed Scott Long's procedure to convert probit coefficients to changes in predicted probabilities (Long and Freese 2014).

2013 Data

Starting with our 2013 data, Table 7.1 displays differences between respondents in terms of their likelihood of perceiving (1) climate change as real and anthropogenic, (2) racism as a strong influence on success, and (3) sexual orientation as innate rather than conditioned. To simplify presentation, the table combines results from a few different models: (a) one that included the simple measures of both values and PID but no interactions,

TABLE 7.1 Value Projection, Partisan Leadership, and DFPs (2013)

	HUMAN-DRIVEN CLIMATE CHANGE IS REAL	RACISM IS INFLUENTIAL	SEXUAL ORIENTATION IS INNATE
Simple model			
Collectivism–Individualism	−.24 ***	−.23 ***	−.06
Humanism–Theism	−.06 †	−.08 *	−.34 ***
PID (GOP high)	−.26 ***	−.27 ***	−.10
Interactive models			
Collectivism–Individualism (inattentive)	−.11 **	−.17 ***	−.08
Collectivism–Individualism (attentive)	−.38 ***	−.32 ***	−.10
Humanism–Theism (inattentive)	−.01	.04	−.29 ***
Humanism–Theism (attentive)	−.12 *	−.17 ***	−.36 ***
PID (inattentive)	−.07	−.10	−.13
PID (attentive)	−.46 ***	−.43 ***	.07
Controls (from simple model)			
Ideology (con high)	−.31 ***	−.30 ***	−.31 ***
Non-white	.06 †	.10 ***	−.13 ***
Female	.07 ***	.01	.08 **
Education	.04	−.02	−.03
Age	−.01	.03	.07
Income	.04	−.05	.14 ***
N	876	879	879

Analyses are binary probit regressions. Coefficients are percentage-point differences in the probability of perceiving the DFP to be true, associated with minimum-to-maximum differences in the independent variable in question. For example, individualists are 24 percentage points less likely than collectivists to perceive climate change to be real and anthropogenic.

Shaded cells represent statistically significant relationships.

$^{†}p < .10$, $^{*}p < .05$, $^{**}p < .01$, $^{***}p < .001$.

(b) one that added the party leadership interaction (PID * news attentiveness), (c) one that removed the party leadership interaction and added just the first value interaction (collectivism–individualism * news attentiveness), and (d) one with just humanism–theism * news attentiveness.[30]

Simple Results

Looking first at the results from the simpler models (with no interactions), we see that value projection is significantly associated with fact perceptions across the board, even after parsing out the influence of party leadership, ideology, and a host of other potentially confounding variables. Strong individualists are 24 percentage points less likely than strong collectivists to perceive climate change as real and anthropogenic and 23 percentage points less likely to perceive racism as an enduringly powerful determinant of social outcomes. Both of these relationships are statistically significant at the 99% confidence level (at least).

The magnitude of these effects is broadly comparable to that of PID (before taking into account the leadership aspects through media attention). Strong Republicans are 26 percentage points less likely to perceive that climate change is caused by humans (if it is real at all) and 27 percentage points less likely to believe that racism determines success or failure. The small differences between the effects associated with collectivism–individualism and PID are not statistically significant.

As for the predictive capacity of humanism–theism, strong theists are 34 percentage points less likely to perceive sexual preference as innate, relative to strong humanists. This relationship is much larger than the corresponding relationship between PID and perceptions of sexuality ($p <$ .05). Perception of sexual orientation is one of the interesting cases in which PID is not a statistically significant predictor of that DFP, while a specific core value very much is. Humanism–theism is also associated with climate perceptions, though this relationship is weaker than many of the others (only 6 percentage points and $p < .10$). Strong theists are also 8 percentage points less likely to perceive racism as an enduringly

---

[30] We estimated these conditional effects separately, rather than all at once, because the same measure of news attentiveness was part of all three leadership interactions, complicating the interpretation of each.

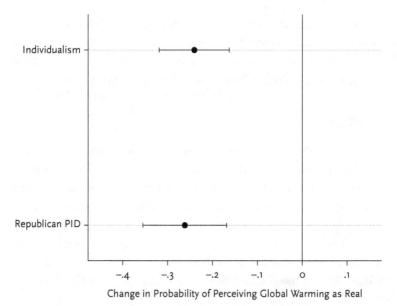

FIGURE 7.1 Individualism, PID, and Perceptions of Climate Change
NOTE: Bars represent 95% confidence intervals.

powerful determinant, which we did not anticipate.[31] We want to emphasize that these findings have emerged not only after accounting for the role of party identification but after accounting for the role of broad ideological identification as well.

Figures 7.1 and 7.2 illustrate the key relationships for perceptions of climate change and sexuality. In regard to perceptions of anthropogenic global warming, the core value of collectivism–individualism is as influential as partisan identity, while humanism–theism also has a small independent influence. For sexual orientation, humanism–theism is powerfully related to perceptions, while PID is not a driving force.

Effects Conditioned by News Attentiveness

Looking at the second block of results in Table 7.1, we see that most of these effects spike rather dramatically among those who follow public affairs most of the time, relative to those who do not.[32] The important thing to notice, though, is that *the predictive capacity of PID is strongly*

---

[31] This relationship does not appear in the 2014 analysis, which conforms to expectations (see the appendix); this is the only respect in which the relationships between values and DFPs differ in 2013 and 2014.
[32] We calculated these effects using the methods described in Brambor et al. 2006, Berry et al. 2012.

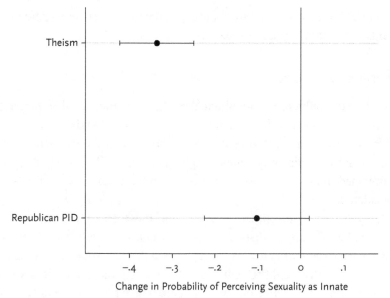

FIGURE 7.2 Theism, PID, and Perceptions of Sexual Orientation
NOTE: Bars represent 95% confidence intervals.

conditioned by news attentiveness, while that of values is not. This observation supports our argument that partisan-driven fact perceptions are largely an external process, and thus amenable to change, whereas value-driven fact perceptions contain a substantial component that has nothing to do with external influence, meaning that they are likely to be much more durable.

Social Identities

When it comes to social identity, we do not think too much can be said by using simple demographic indicators to capture such potential relationships. However, it is worth noting that, not surprisingly, non-whites were 10 percentage points more likely than whites to view racism as powerfully consequential (independent of the racial differences that are captured in PID). This relationship might be enhanced among those who possess a genuine sense of racial consciousness, something we examine with the 2017 data. Non-whites were also about 6 percentage points more likely to believe that humans are responsible for climate change and 13 percentage points less likely to believe that sexuality is innate.[33] Women are also less likely than

---

[33] The relationship with perceptions of climate was unexpected but not entirely surprising given that

men to be climate skeptics, by about 7 percentage points, and 8 percentage points more likely to believe sexuality is innate.

Conservative Media

To gauge the influence of ideological media exposure, we also included a conservative media variable (1 = FoxNews or political talk radio as one's primary news source; 0 = other) to see how much independent predictive capacity media propaganda might have, as well as whether values maintained their predictive capacity when partisan media effects are considered.[34]

Only in regard to climate change—the most prominent and perhaps most widely discussed disputed fact—did conservative media consumption have a strong influence on perceptions, as well as somewhat lessen the influence of values and PID. Citizens who reported that their primary news source was a conservative one were 17 percentage points less likely to perceive climate change as being real ($p < .001$). In that model, the influence of collectivism–individualism fell from 24 percentage points to 18 and PID from 26 to 21 percentage points, bringing values, PID, and partisan media to relative parity of influence. In regard to perceptions of racism, partisan media consumption had an 8 percentage-point relationship ($p < .05$), while the role of values and PID remained constant at a substantially higher degree of influence. Conservative media consumption had no statistically significant relationship with perceptions of sexuality, and the strong connection to theism was unaffected.

Out of sympathy for the reader, we have relegated presentation of the 2014 results to the appendix. The results confirm the same patterns and expectations, with one exception: the relationship between humanism–theism and perceptions of racism does not appear, conforming to our original hypotheses.

Table 7.2 summarizes the observed relationships between specific values and DFPs so far, relative to our expectations. All of the expectations

---

non-whites tend to live in areas that are disproportionately affected by environmental problems. The environmental racism literature is expansive. For a starting point, see Pulido (2000).

[34] "What is your primary media source when it comes to information about politics and current events?"—1) talk radio; 2) National Public Radio; 3) a major national newspaper; 4) a local or hometown newspaper; 5) CBS, ABC, or NBC nightly news; 6) Fox News channel; 7) MSNBC; 8) CNN; 9) online sources of traditional media sources; 10) blogs; 11) something else. Including talk radio along with FoxNews as conservative media yields stronger effects than FoxNews alone, grounded in the dominance of that medium by conservative voices (see Barker 2002).

TABLE 7.2 Hypothesized Relations of Values to DFPs

		2013	2014
Individualism:	Climate change is *not* real	Supported	Supported
	Racism is *not* influential	Supported	Supported
	No relation to sexual orientation	Supported	Supported
Theism:	Climate change is *not* real	Supported	Supported
	No relation to racism	Significant Relationship	Supported
	Sexual orientation *not* innate	Supported	Supported

are supported, aside from the singular case in 2013 in which an unexpected relationship appears. But *all of the predicted value relationships manifested in both 2013 and 2014*, illustrating the ability of values to differentiate among DFPs, accounting for which beliefs result in which perceptions.

2016 Data

Up until now, we have been conceptualizing values as essentially *political*: evaluative predispositions toward competing social ends. Other lines of thinking about values have conceptualized them as priorities across the whole spectrum of *personal* goals. As Joseph Schumpeter defined values in *Capitalism, Socialism, and Democracy*, they are "conceptions of what life and society should be," encompassing both personal and political aspirations.[35] While *political* values may be more directly connected to perceptions of political facts, the influence of values on fact is even more noteworthy if *personal* values have a similar influence. In 2016, to assess reliability and robustness, we altered the measurement strategy to employ the approach of gauging basic human values pioneered by Shalom Schwartz and colleagues, which has been validated in numerous empirical studies.[36] Previous research has shown that when it comes to structuring political attitudes, the predominant Schwartz values are *self-transcendence* and *conservation*.[37] Each of these constructs combines other, lower-order

---

[35] Schumpeter 1942, page 251.

[36] Lindeman and Verkasalo 2005, Schwartz and Bilsky 1990, Schwartz 1992, Schwartz and Boehnke 2004, Schwartz et al. 2001.

[37] Goren et al. 2016. In alternate models, we also included the other two Schwartz summary value measures—self-enhancement and openness—as a foil. Following Goren et al., we expected these

values: self-transcendence merges *universalism* (being tolerant, under-standing of others, and broad-minded) and *benevolence* (being helpful and forgiving). Conservation combines *tradition* (respect for traditions, accepting customs), *conformity* (politeness, honoring family members, not upsetting others), and *security* (stability, safety for loved ones).

The specific measures start with the following question: "Please indi-cate how important each of these values are to you, as guiding principles in your life." The survey then presents the brief descriptions of each value (for example, "stability, safety for loved ones" for security). Respondents indicated how important the value is to him or her on a five-point scale (0 = not at all important; 5 = supremely important). From these, we created measures of self-transcendence and conservation that range from 0 to 1.[38]

Both self-transcendence and conservation are broader value constructs than collectivism–individualism and humanism–theism, and previous scholarship has shown them to be more comprehensively predictive of attitudes. In regard to fact perceptions, we can expect these values to have similarly broader influences. That is, we do not expect the effects asso-ciated with one or another value to differentiate in the same way that we did when we were looking at collectivism–individualism or humanism–theism. Thus, we expect that self-transcendence values are associated with believing that climate change is real and anthropogenic, that racism is powerful, and that sexual orientation is innate. By contrast, we expect that conservation values are associated with believing the opposite to be true in each case.

These models measure party leadership in the same way we described earlier and include all of the same control variables (measured the same way). As we discuss the findings from 2016 and 2017, we focus on models including simple (non-interactive) value projection measures but interac-tive party leadership measures, based on our findings in 2013 and 2014 that partisan fact perceptions are largely dependent upon external leader-ship but that value-based fact perceptions are not.

Table 7.3 displays the results of the 2016 analyses. As the table illustrates, the different approach to the measurement of values does not

---

other value measures to reveal null results, which they did. These null results, in the face of the sub-stantive results associated with self-transcendence and conservation, provide valuable suggestive evidence of discriminant validity for our findings.

[38] Self-transcendence encompasses benevolence and universalism (Cronbach's alpha = .74), so the raw score ranges from 0 to 10 (mean = 8.18; standard deviation = 1.97); conservation combines tra-dition, conformity, and security (Cronbach's alpha = .78), so it ranges from 0 to 15 (mean = 12.08; standard deviation = 2.91); both recoded to 0–1.

TABLE 7.3 Value Projection, Partisan Leadership, and DFPs (2016)

PREDICTORS	CLIMATE	RACISM	SEXUALITY
Self-transcendence	.27	.25	.14
Conservation	−.17	−.15	−.16
PID (inattentive)	−.07	−.10	−.13
PID (attentive)	−.47	−.44	−.08
Ideology (con high)	−.40	−.40	−.39
Non-white	−.01	.08	−.04
Female	.04	.02	.02
N	946	946	941

Shaded cells represent statistically significant relationships ($p < .05$). Analyses are binary probit regressions. Coefficients are percentage-point differences in the probability of believing the DFP is true, associated with minimum-to-maximum differences in the independent variable in question. For example, those who support self-transcendence values are 27 percentage points more likely than those who oppose them to believe that climate change is real and anthropogenic. The models also include controls for age, family income, and education; but space constraints preclude their inclusion here.

significantly alter the results. The same patterns that we observed in the 2013 and 2014 data hold here as well. Specifically, citizens who hold self-transcendence values are 27 percentage points more likely than those who do not to believe that climate change is real and anthropogenic, 25 percentage points more likely to believe that racism is still a powerful determinant of outcomes, and 14 percentage points more likely to believe sexual preference is innate. Likewise, those who endorse conservation values are 17 percentage points more likely than those who do not to be climate change skeptics, 15 percentage points more likely to perceive racism as no longer consequential, and 16 percentage points more likely to believe that sexual preference is socially conditioned. Again, these patterns stand out even after accounting for the influence of ideological identification more generally.

Party leadership is, again, very predictive as well, *but only when news attentiveness is high*. And not surprisingly, non-whites were a little more likely than whites to perceive racism as powerful (8 percentage points), but neither race nor gender were independently predictive of anything else. So when it comes to social identity, so far, the effects appear to be limited in range and much smaller than those attributable to value projection, party leadership, or ideological identification. However, we expect the relationships we observe to be stronger in the 2017 data when we are able to employ a richer operationalization of social identity *consciousness* rather than just identity itself.

2017 Data

Our 2017 data collection offered the opportunity to conduct the broadest and most stringent test of our hypotheses yet. First, by using Haidt's *moral foundations* measures, we were able to capture the variance in value perspectives grounded in a third perspective: *moral values*, as opposed to political or personal values. Second, by expanding the number of factual disputes from three to ten, we were able to dramatically enhance the scope of our inquiry and address the concern that patterns we observed in previous years were a byproduct of those specific fact disputes. Finally, by including measures of racial/ethnic identity consciousness in our models, we were able to not only broaden our overall understanding of what drives DFPs but also address the concern that values are a byproduct of social identity.

In Haidt's original formulation in *The Righteous Mind*, he describes a set of specific value foundations: care, fairness, sanctity, loyalty, and authority. Political liberals tend to uphold care as a core value, while political conservatives tend to focus on sanctity, loyalty, and authority. Fairness comes in two styles—focused on equality and focused on proportionality—the first being favored by the Left and the second by the Right.[39] If we separate fairness into its two aspects, the moral foundations framework includes six values: care, fairness (equality), fairness (proportionality), loyalty, sanctity, and authority. As such, this framework offers our most inclusive operationalization of value orientations.

We measured each of the moral values by asking respondents to indicate the extent to which they agreed or disagreed (0 = strongly disagree; 3 = strongly agree) with a series of statements:

1) *Care*: "Compassion for those who are suffering is the most crucial virtue" (mean = 2.22; standard deviation = .73)

---

[39] "Everyone cares about fairness, but there are two major kinds. On the left, fairness often implies equality, but on the right it means proportionality—people should be rewarded in proportion to what they contribute, even if that guarantees unequal outcomes" (Haidt 2012, pages 160–161).

2) *Equality:* "When the government makes laws, the number one principle should be ensuring that everyone is treated fairly" (mean = 2.45; standard deviation = .72)

3) *Proportionality:* "A fair and just society makes sure that those who break the rules get what they deserve" (mean = 1.68; standard deviation = .90)

4) *Loyalty:* "People should be loyal to their own" (mean = 1.49; standard deviation = .93)

5) *Sanctity:* "Some behaviors are sick and should be illegal, even if no one is getting hurt" (mean = 1.77; standard deviation = .96)

6) *Authority:* "People don't have enough respect for authority anymore" (mean = 2.05; standard deviation = .93)

Care and equality values are the moral foundations of ideological liberalism. We expect care ("compassion for those who are suffering") to predict perceptions that climate change is real, that racism is influential, and that sexuality is innate. A concern for suffering should lead citizens to be more attuned to the claims of minorities, LGBT citizens, and Mother Nature. Those factual conditions also demand more care; these perceptions are what call for more application of the value, emphasizing its importance. Equality ("ensuring that everyone is treated fairly") should predict the perceptions that climate change, the influence of racism, and innate sexuality are all real because greater equality of treatment is called for in each of these cases.

The remaining values provide the moral foundations for ideological conservatism, reflecting the observation that contemporary conservatism has more distinct moral dimensions than does liberalism. Accordingly, we expect the ability of each foundation to predict fact perceptions to be more varied. We expect that proportionality ("a fair and just society makes sure that those who break the rules get what they deserve") may play a large role because championing discipline, personal responsibility, and punitiveness may be the consistent glue that informs American conservatism—across economic, cultural and foreign-policy dimensions.[40] Such eagerness to enforce personal responsibility should lead one to perceive racism as inconsequential (individual responsibility is what is needed) but may have no influence on climate or sexuality.

---

[40] See Barker and Tinnick 2006, Marietta 2011.

As for sanctity, we expect that those who agree that "some behaviors are sick and should be illegal, even if no one is getting hurt" tend to believe that sexuality is conditioned. The belief that moral sanctity is a virtue suggests that human choices predominate and that an emphasis on moral choice is needed in contemporary society. That belief tends to be reinforced in the social groups that view traditional gender and sexual identities as natural and important for social stability. The opposing perception—that sexual orientation is innate—would suggest that behavior is less of a choice, which would lessen the importance of sanctity as a value. In regard to perceptions of climate or racism, we do not necessarily envision a connection to this value priority.

When it comes to authority, we expect those who agree that "people don't have enough respect for authority anymore" to take a sympathetic view toward traditional commandments and social arrangements (and the facts that support them); hence, they should see sexuality as conditioned rather than innate.

Finally, we expect loyalty ("people should be loyal to their own") to be the least predictive of Haidt's moral foundations because we would guess it is highly conditional upon social identity. That is, if a loyalist is white, that loyalism might lead to very different fact perceptions than if she is black. In regard to climate, racism, or sexuality, we would not expect a relationship.

Simple Results

First, maintaining consistency with previous years and allowing direct comparisons with those analyses, we begin by observing the results without considering the influence of the new racial/ethnic identity consciousness measures and just with respect to the three DFPs that we have emphasized so far: climate, racism, and sexuality. As Table 7.4 reveals, the general story in 2017 is the same as it was in 2016, 2014, and 2013.

We see that those who prioritize care were about 11 percentage points more likely to affirm climate change and humankind's role in it than those who do not, 39 percentage points more likely to believe that racism shapes success, and 17 percentage points more likely to believe that sexuality is innate—all of which are consistent with our expectations. The other liberal value in the model, equality, is less predictive, overall, but not irrelevant: those who prioritize it were 17 percentage points more likely than those who do not to affirm climate change, but they were no more or less likely to view racism as powerful or sexuality as innate. Unlike the effects

TABLE 7.4 Value Projection, Partisan Leadership, and DFPs (2017)

PREDICTORS	CLIMATE	RACISM	SEXUALITY
Care	**.11**	**.39**	**.17**
Equality	**.17**	.01	.04
Proportionality	.04	**−.12**	.06
Sanctity	.05	−.01	**−.12**
Authority	**−.14**	−.05	**−.18**
Loyalty	−.02	.04	.02
PID (inattentive)	**−.26**	**−.14**	−.11
PID (attentive)	**−.32**	**−.33**	**−.18**
Ideology (con high)	**−.32**	**−.26**	**−.41**
Non-white	**.07**	**.08**	**−.17**
Female	**.10**	**.05**	**.08**
N	957	962	961

Shaded cells represent statistically significant relationships ($p < .05$). Analyses are
binary probit regressions. Coefficients are percentage-point differences in the probability
of believing the DFP is true, associated with minimum-to-maximum differences in
the independent variable in question. For example, those who support care values are
11 percentage points more likely than those who oppose them to believe that climate
change is real and anthropogenic. The models also include controls for age, family
income, and education; but space constraints preclude their inclusion here.

associated with care, which ran the board across the three DFPs, the independent effects associated with equality fail to materialize in regard to two
(racism and sexuality).

However, on the conservative side, those who value proportionality
were 12 percentage points less likely to perceive racism as determinative
of success (but had no significant relationship with perceptions of climate
or sexuality, as anticipated), and those who value sanctity were 12 percentage points less likely to perceive sexuality as innate (and again had no
connection to perceptions of the other DFPs). Citizens who value authority
were likewise 14 percentage points less likely to believe in climate change
and 18 percentage points less likely to view sexuality as innate. And loyalty was not predictive of any of these three fact disputes, all as expected.[41]

Consistent with the findings from 2013, 2014, and 2016, partisanship is
highly predictive as well but mostly among those who pay close attention to

---

[41] It is worth mentioning that, consistent with what we observed in the models from earlier years,
in alternative specifications in which we multiplied value orientations by news attentiveness, we
observed that the predictive ability of these values is enhanced by, but not dependent on, such
attentiveness.

politics and public affairs. Ideology also displays large independent effects, and identities (race and gender) reveal smaller but consistent effects.

Overall, while these results do not conform perfectly with our expectations with respect to every hypothesized linkage between moral values and fact perceptions (equality underperforms), they are very consistent with our broad argument that value projection is both powerful *and* independent of partisanship, ideology, or other confounding factors—a finding that is enhanced by the observation that different values predict differentially.

Considering the Role of Social Identity Consciousness

As Table 7.5 displays, the social identity consciousness variables produce important patterns that were not as clear in the previous analyses. Among non-whites, those with a strong sense of ethnic pride are 25 percentage points more likely than whites to believe that racism is consequential

TABLE 7.5 Value Projection, Partisan Leadership, Identity Consciousness, and DFPs (2017)

PREDICTORS	CLIMATE	RACISM	SEXUALITY
Care	**.10**	**.37**	**.16**
Equality	**.17**	.01	.04
Proportionality	.06	**−.12**	.06
Sanctity	.05	−.01	**−.12**
Authority	**−.13**	−.02	**−.19**
Loyalty	.01	.05	.03
PID (inattentive)	**−.23**	**−.12**	−.10
PID (attentive)	**−.32**	**−.30**	**−.17**
Ideology (con high)	**−.31**	**−.21**	**−.41**
Non-white (abashed)	**−.22**	**−.24**	**−.18**
Non-white (proud)	−.01	**.25**	**−.17**
Female (abashed)	−.04	.12	−.06
Female (proud)	**.15**	.04	**.13**
N	957	962	961

Shaded cells represent statistically significant relationships ($p < .05$). Analyses are binary probit regressions. Coefficients are percentage-point differences in the probability of believing the DFP is true, associated with minimum-to-maximum differences in the independent variable in question. For example, those who identify as non-white *and* are proud of that identity are 25 percentage points more likely than whites to believe that racism is consequential. The models also include controls for age, family income, and education; but space constraints preclude their inclusion here.

(compared to an 8 percentage-point relationship with non-white identity alone, illustrated in Table 7.4). However, non-whites who lack ethnic pride tend to perceive much less racism, seeing things pretty much like whites do.

As for gender identity and consciousness, women who lack gender consciousness do not perceive reality any differently from men. However, *proud* women are 15 percentage points more likely than men to affirm climate change, and they are 13 percentage points more likely to believe that sexuality is innate.

Notably, though, the results of the analyses incorporating measures of identity consciousness are nearly identical regarding both the value projection effects and the party leadership effects. Hence, there is no reason to believe that social identity consciousness dilutes the role of party leadership or value projection as important motivators of DFPs.

Analyzing Additional DFPs

So far, liberal readers might look at these results and feel relatively satisfied. One interpretation of them is that those who (a) identify as conservative or Republicans, (b) hold conservative values, or (c) attend to conservative media are more likely to be misinformed regarding climate change, the power of racism, and the origins of sexuality. After all, the preponderance of evidence and academic endorsement on each of these disputes would support such an interpretation. For this reason, it is important to broaden our tests to include DFPs for which the best available evidence and institutional support are not clearly on one side of the divide. Specifically, we analyzed perceptions of whether (1) the national debt will cause economic harm, (2) vaccines cause autism, (3) false convictions are common, (4) increases to the minimum wage lower employment, (5) undocumented immigrants take jobs from American citizens, (6) gun control reduces mass shootings, and (7) violent crime is increasing, for a total of ten DFPs across a broad range of political domains. Vaccines are similar to climate change in the sense that there is broad scientific consensus about the answer (they do not cause autism), but the evidence with respect to the others is much less conclusive.

For each of these DFPs, we again asked respondents to "indicate whether each of the following statements is true or false" (certainly true, probably true, probably false, certainly false); half of the sample was given a statement from one perspective and the other half from the opposite perspective (with those answers reversed to provide one unified scale).

National debt: "Large amounts of national debt, like the US currently
has, eventually cause great harm to a nation's economy" ("Large
amounts of national debt, like the US currently has, do not necessarily cause great harm to a nation's economy") (85% perceive the
debt to be harmful). Unlike climate change, it is not the *existence* of
the debt that is at issue but its *consequences*.[42] Some see the debt as
likely to have tremendous negative effects on the economy as well as
on national security, while others see the debt as promoting economic
stimulus, infrastructure improvements, and greater equality of access
to healthcare and education, all of which contribute to economic productivity. One of the prominent voices on the unworried side of the
factual debate is Paul Krugman, Nobel Prize–winning economist and
columnist for *The New York Times*, who describes "the wrongheaded,
ill-informed obsession with debt" as the "triumph of ideology over
evidence," connected to "our postmodern, fact-free politics."[43] One
of the most prominent debt hawks in the public sphere is Paul Ryan,
Republican vice presidential candidate in 2012 and Speaker of the
House of Representatives 2015–2018. In 2013, Ryan warned that "the
debt will weigh down our country like an anchor."[44] The core factual
dispute is whether the national debt is likely to lead to harms in the future or whether the debt is a manageable thing about which we should
not be worried. This DFP is unusual in the sense that the mass public
is not truly polarized, with the great majority of citizens perceiving
the debt to be harmful; however, this is not the tenor among elites,
many of whom argue the opposing view that the national debt is not a
concern or even has positive aspects.

Vaccines: "Vaccines may be a cause of autism" ("Vaccines do not cause
autism") (26% perceive vaccines to be a potential cause). Contrary to
all of the available scientific evidence, the belief that vaccines cause
autism has proven to be remarkably persistent. Many prominent ce-
lebrity supporters as well as movement activists continue to promote
this perception.

---

[42] See the controversy between Reinhart and Rogoff (2010, Reinhart et al. 2012) and their critics
(especially Herndon et al. 2013) over the economic influence of debt-to-gross domestic product
ratios above 90%. For a non-academic summary illustrating the difficulty in sorting out a definitive
conclusion, see Cassidy 2013.

[43] See Krugman 2012, 2015, emphasizing "the fact that federal debt isn't at all like a mortgage. . . .
First, families have to pay back their debt. Governments don't—all they need to do is ensure that
debt grows more slowly than their tax base. . . . Second, an over-borrowed family owes money to
someone else; U.S. debt is, to a large extent, money we owe to ourselves" (Krugman 2012).

[44] Conservative Political Action Conference speech March 15, 2013.

False convictions: "False convictions of innocent people are extremely rare" ("False convictions of innocent people occur frequently") (62% perceive false conviction to be common). The current controversy over the prevalence of false convictions suggests an indictment or exoneration of our criminal justice system.[45] The conflict may reflect the popularity of *Making a Murderer* and *Serial*, two cultural phenomena arguing that false convictions are prevalent, often due to police misconduct. It may also reflect the rise of the Innocence Project and the large number of exonerations in recent decades. One of the best-known examples of a post-DNA test exoneration is the Central Park Five, who were convicted in 1990 of the rape of the Central Park jogger and freed in 2002 after the confession (and DNA match) of a convicted rapist currently in prison. Many citizens believe in their innocence, while others believe they are guilty (along with the confessed perpetrator) of the crime to which they confessed. One of the most prominent proponents of their guilt is Donald Trump. A 2014 article in the *Proceedings of the National Academy of Sciences* argues that "in the past few decades a surge of hundreds of exonerations of innocent criminal defendants has drawn attention to the problem of erroneous conviction. . . . All the same, the most basic empirical question about false convictions remains unanswered: How common are these miscarriages of justice?"[46]

Minimum wage: "Increasing the minimum wage usually results in less employment" ("Increasing the minimum wage does not usually result in less employment") (45% perceive that minimum wage increases lower employment). Economists have long argued about the theory and evidence of the influence of minimum wage laws. Noted economists David Card and Alan Krueger published a famous paper in 1994 arguing that, contrary to many years of accepted economic theory, raising the minimum wage did *not* lower employment in low-wage industries. This argument was met with several rebuttals, but no consensus emerged among economists.[47] More recently, a pair of dueling studies came to opposite conclusions about the recent increase in the minimum wage in Seattle from $9.47 to $11 per hour in 2015 and to $13 per hour in 2016. One paper argues

---

[45] See *Time* special edition "Innocent: The Fight Against Wrongful Convictions," May 19, 2017. See also Godsey 2017.

[46] Gross et al. 2014, page 7230. They estimate that among death row convicts alone, at least 4% would be exonerated if their cases were fully re-examined over time.

[47] See especially Neumark and Wascher 2007, responding to Card and Krueger 1994.

that the change brought about a reduction of low-wage employment, while the other says it did not.[48] No agreement is likely to arrive any time soon.

Immigration: "Undocumented Latino immigrants take jobs from working class Americans" ("Undocumented Latino immigrants do not take jobs from working class Americans") (48% agreed that immigrants take jobs). The specific ways in which immigrant workers do or do not compete with native-born Americans for low-wage employment are deeply disputed among economists.[49]

Gun control: "When countries enact gun control laws nationwide, mass shootings tend to go down" ("When countries enact gun control laws nationwide, mass shootings do not tend to go down") (57% perceive that gun control lowers mass shootings). The debate about the effects of gun possession and concealed carry laws on crime and death rates has a combative history, long before the more recent political responses to mass shootings. Perhaps the best-known work arguing for positive effects of gun ownership is *More Guns, Less Crime*,[50] which inspired many responses and refutations.[51]

Crime: "Violent crime is going up in the United States" ("Violent crime is not going up in the United States") (66% perceive crime to be rising). While violent crime as a whole has been in decline since the early 1990s, it has also risen in specific cities in recent years, which gives the opposite impression.[52]

We can hypothesize which of the moral values will predict perceptions of these DFPs, which vary across a broad range of political domains. *Care* should predict perceptions that false convictions are frequent, minimum wage increases do not reduce employment, undocumented immigrants do not take jobs, and gun control diminishes mass shootings. We do not, however, necessarily expect this value to predict perceptions of debt or crime. Likewise for vaccines, as compassion for others as a core value could suggest the need for vaccines to protect us as well as the need to protect us from vaccines; either perception could be motivated by care.

We think *Equality* should predict perceptions that the national debt is not harmful (because a harmful debt would militate against greater

---

[48] Jardim et al. 2017, Cengiz et al. 2017.
[49] See Blau and Mackie 2017, Schuck 2017.
[50] Lott 1998.
[51] See, for example, Hemenway 2006, Dezhbakhsh and Rubin 1998, Duggan 2000.
[52] See PolitiFact December 4, 2017, "Violent crime is up some, but still well off historical highs."

government spending and other actions needed to create greater equality), that false convictions are common, that raising minimum wages does not lead to falling employment, and that immigration does not lower employment. We see less reason for it to be connected to vaccines, guns, or crime.

Proportionality (conservative fairness) is likely connected to seeing the debt as consequential, false convictions as rare, the minimum wage as causing unemployment, undocumented immigration as hurtful, and crime as rising. The connections to vaccines and guns are less clear to us.

Sanctity seems likely to lead to perceptions that the debt is calamitous (it is a violation of control and proper rules), that vaccines are harmful, that undocumented immigrants take jobs, and that crime is on the rise. Sanctity seems less connected to false convictions, wages, and guns.

Authority should lead to perceptions that the debt is harmful, false convictions are rare (the judicial authority is correct), undocumented immigrants take jobs (they are violating the law), gun control is ineffective, and surely that violent crime is going up.

Loyalty we think will have few connections, perhaps just that false convictions are rare (criminals have committed violations of loyalty to society and we should be loyal to the system that judges them).

Table 7.6 displays the 2017 results, following the same steps. Because the presence of the social identity consciousness measures provides the most information, we focus our discussion on the results from these fully specified models.

Value projection reveals itself to be the most consistent predictor of these seven perceptions of facts. Compared to PID and ideology, which fail to predict some of the DFPs, at least two distinct moral values are related to each perceived fact. The individual values clearly differ as to which perceptions they predict—further validating the legitimacy of the findings. Specifically, the care foundation independently and significantly predicted three of the four we hypothesized (convictions, immigration, and guns). Equality predicted two out of four accurately (convictions and wages). Proportionality predicted four out of five (convictions, wages, immigration, and crime). Sanctity predicted four out of four (debt, vaccines, immigration, and crime). Loyalty predicted false convictions as anticipated. And authority strongly predicted perceptions of the debt, convictions, minimum wage effects, guns, and crime. Overall, nineteen out of the twenty-three hypothesized relationships were confirmed (a rate of 83%). Partisan identity, on the other hand, predicted only three out of the seven DFPs among the politically attentive and only one (guns) among the inattentive.

TABLE 7.6 Value Projection, Partisan Leadership, Identity Consciousness, and DFPs (2017)

PREDICTORS	DEBT BAD	VACCINES HARMFUL	FALSE CONVICTIONS COMMON	MINIMUM WAGE HURTS	IMMIGRANTS TAKE JOBS	GUN CONTROL WORKS	CRIME UP
Care	-.04	-.02	.11	-.04	-.22	.09	-.05
Equality	.09	-.16	.22	-.25	-.11	.13	-.07
Proportionality	.03	.13	-.13	.16	.26	.05	.22
Sanctity	.13	.12	.02	.05	.10	.05	.13
Authority	.09	.10	-.11	.11	.24	-.22	.26
Loyalty	-.10	.03	-.08	.01	.06	.04	.07
PID (inattentive)	.00	.07	-.05	.08	.09	-.22	.01
PID (attentive)	.10	.06	-.11	.30	.19	-.42	.05
Ideology (con high)	.04	.07	-.06	.28	.17	-.34	.02
Non-white (abashed)	-.03	.17	-.18	.02	.15	-.07	.08
Non-white (proud)	.02	.10	.18	.00	-.19	.00	.01
Female (abashed)	.11	.00	-.02	.05	.02	-.02	.01
Female (proud)	.01	-.04	.00	-.04	-.02	.06	.16
N	963	956	976	958	972	966	969

Shaded cells represent statistically significant relationships ($p < .05$). Analyses are binary probit regressions. Coefficients are percentage-point differences in the probability of believing the dispute is true that are associated with minimum-to-maximum differences in the independent variable in question. For example, those who prioritize care values are 22 percentage points less likely than those who oppose them to believe that undocumented immigrants take jobs from citizens. The models also include controls for age, family income, education, and church attendance; but space constraints preclude their inclusion here.

In sum, the predictive strength of value projection is generally comparable and often stronger than that of party leadership or ideological identification, and it is more consistent. There is not a single fact dispute for which value projection is not a significant predictor; the same cannot be said for either partisan leadership or ideology.

As for social identities, again, ethnic minorities and women who lack consciousness of that identity tend to perceive reality in a way that is more consistent with conservative values and Republican Party identification. However, identity consciousness among non-whites is associated with perceiving racism as consequential, false convictions as common, and that undocumented immigrants do not take jobs from American citizens but nothing else. Identity consciousness among women, meanwhile, is associated with believing that climate change is real and anthropogenic and that violent crime is rising.[53] The limited predictive capacity of identity, restricted to only a few DFPs, is not surprising given that many factual disputes do not have clear racial or gender connections.

Conclusion

Across a range of perceived realities, over several years, employing different measures, it appears that values are independently predictive of perceptions. The value projection mechanism is indeed value-specific; rather than just a projection of more generalized ideological affect or partisan identity, specific values are related to specific fact perceptions in predictable ways. This is the case regardless of whether we conceptualize values as political, personal, or moral constructs, and it is true even after accounting for partisan identity, gender and racial identity consciousness, external leadership (including exposure to partisan media), ideology, and demographics. Social identity consciousness appears to motivate fact perceptions as well but across a narrower range of disputes. While partisanship is a strong and consistent predictor of fact perceptions, it is typically dependent upon external leadership to achieve that influence—in a way that is not true of values. These findings argue for a more long-term and pessimistic view of DFPs than we might have if identities or external leadership told the entire story.

---

[53] Perceptions of crime are particularly interesting because gender consciousness leads toward the perception of rising crime associated with *conservative* values, perhaps because women approaching the question of crime through a female perspective are more attuned to the threat of violence (most often committed by men and often directed toward women).

8 | A Theory of Intuitive Epistemology

"Men would rather believe than know."

—E. O. Wilson[1]

"On any longer view, man is only fitfully committed to the rational—to thinking, seeing, hearing, knowing. Believing is what he is really proud of."

—Martin Amis[2]

E PISTEMOLOGY—THE STUDY AND PRACTICE of knowledge claims— often poses the question, *How do we know?* Perhaps it would more usefully phrase the question, *How do* you *know?* This chapter argues that implicit foundations of knowledge vary systematically among citizens, creating disparate perceptions of reality. In the last chapter, we discussed the origins of dueling fact perceptions (DFPs) in divided values. In this chapter, we dive deeper into how that occurs, offering an insight into the origins of fact perceptions that explains how preferred values are projected onto perceived facts. We provide a theory of intuitive epistemology and describe the results of an empirical study examining how different value priorities lead to distinct habitual questions, which in turn drive fact perceptions. If applied epistemology varies systematically among citizens (in a predictable fashion grounded in competing value systems), this will create opposing perceptions of reality.

Epistemology, as it is usually understood, has two parts, one of which is underappreciated. The aspect emphasized in an ordinary political science class is how questions are answered: which means of gathering evidence, which means of analyzing data, which interpretation of results? The more

---

[1] Wilson 1975, page 285.
[2] Amis 2002.

neglected aspect is how we decide which questions to ask. Epistemology encompasses the selection as well as assessment of questions; what is asked can be as important as how it is answered.

It is reasonable to expect a trained expert (or perhaps even an ordinary citizen) to rise above her ideological and social biases when she *analyzes* data, but doing so when it comes to determining what to study in the first place is a much more daunting assignment. When it comes to decisions about what to spend time assessing, there is no doubt that ordinary people and experts alike are guided by their values. We care about certain things more than other things, and we make little attempt to hide it. As August Comte phrased it in the early days of social science, "It is for the heart to suggest our problems, it is for the intellect to solve them."[3]

With that in mind, the epistemological issue that arrives earlier in the search for knowledge—*what questions draw our attention?*—is the focus of our argument in this chapter.

Intuitive Epistemology

> "Cultural influences have set up the assumptions about the mind,
> the body, and the universe with which we begin;
> pose the questions we ask; influence the facts we seek."
>
> —*Gunnar Myrdal*[4]

Some observations come to us by brute force without our volition: major political events, news flashes, the naked guy running past on the street. Another large group of observations we must choose to seek out. About the non-volitional observations, we may choose to look for more detail, as we do for some political events, or we may seek nothing further (which is likely the case with the naked guy). So some questions we choose to ask and others not. But *there has to be a question*, and which question we ask greatly influences the facts we are likely to observe.

It is one thing to observe that humans vary in "the facts we seek," as Myrdal phrased it, but another to understand how exactly that occurs. In the 1998 volume *The Future of Fact* (discussed in Chapter 2), one of the contributions by philosophy faculty argues that people have a "will to truth."[5] From a starting point similar to our own (and Plato's in the

---

[3] Comte 1848, page 13.
[4] Myrdal 1944, page 92.
[5] Lichtenberg 1998, pages 43–68.

cave)—"ignorance of facts is sometimes curable, sometimes not"—Lichtenberg argues that people really do pursue empirical accuracy above other goals: "compelled by our natures to seek understanding, we experience a will to truth."[6] This is a strong statement with little empirical backing, that such a will is stronger than the will to believe or the will to belong or other human motivations. Belief and acceptance are powerful motivators, and while the accuracy goal may lead people in the same direction, attachments to different beliefs and to different groups will guide people toward their own poles.

Moreover, people may be motivated to perceive the facts that will help them win arguments. In Chapter 5, we discussed the Mercier thesis that the human motivation to be *persuasive* (or impressive or even entertaining) dominates the human motivation to be *correct*. Because our immediate incentive is standing within our group, we may experience more payoff for persuasion than for accuracy. To the degree that the Mercier thesis is accurate, individual epistemology may lean far from accuracy and toward the collection of arguments and information that advance the persuasiveness of our position (especially after we have made it known). The idea that most people most of the time are motivated more by empirical accuracy than by other considerations may be wishful thinking. When accuracy conflicts with morals or with acceptance or with aspirations to influence, the more powerful motivator is not at all clear.

Philip Tetlock offers a perspective opposed to the assumptions that epistemology is focused on accuracy alone and that it is standardized among humans.[7] He suggests that practical epistemology has functionalist foundations far beyond accuracy: epistemology in the wild is more teleological than open-ended, more ends-driven than value-neutral. This suggests that individuals display a range of distinct directional goals and possible intuitive methods. Tetlock's core proposition is that individuals hold distinct frameworks for discerning political knowledge. Citizens perceive things differently not merely because their desires and standards of evidence are different (as motivated reasoning suggests) but more fundamentally *because their motivating questions are different*.

In contrast to the frequent assumption in social science that people are "intuitive scientists" who attempt to maximize empirical accuracy or that they approximate "the intuitive economist whose primary goal in life is to maximize subjective expected utility," Tetlock suggested a series of

---

[6] Ibid., pages 48–9.
[7] See Tetlock 1991, further developed in Goldberg et al. 1999, Tetlock 2002.

alternative metaphors for understanding practical epistemology. The first is that, rather than scientists or economists, people can be described more accurately as *intuitive politicians*, whose dominant goal is being accepted by their group: "People are in a fundamental sense politicians who depend on the good will of the constituencies to whom they are accountable."[8] Most people quickly and "quite correctly, view opinion conformity as a reliable means of gaining the approval and respect of others."[9] At one end of a possible spectrum would be "schemers who actively seek out information about the expectations of others, carefully calculate the impact of their decisions, anticipate potential objections, and craft accounts to pre-empt these objections."[10] At the other end of that spectrum would be people deeply committed to expressing the truth without regard to the social cost. We could describe the poles of the continuum as *Machiavellian manipulators* versus *philosopher saints*. Tetlock suggests that a midrange on the continuum is most likely most of the time. The reader will have to decide where most people are on that spectrum in their experience, but we have known few at the saintly extreme, who are not at all influenced by the social environment and its deep incentives. We suggest that most of the time people are at least as strongly motivated to be popular as to be correct.[11]

The metaphor of the intuitive politician takes us away from the idealist view of scientific epistemology, but it does not give us specific guidance on the direction people will lean. The intuitive politician may attempt to mirror the views of her most important social group, but this insight provides no specific guidance without knowing which group that is and what those perceptions are. Tetlock's next metaphor offers a more specific direction: the *intuitive prosecutor*. This epistemology seeks out norm violations, identifying transgressions of accepted rules, boundaries, or

---

[8] Tetlock 1991, page 473. Tetlock's approach is compatible with Mercier's but distinct in the sense that Mercier focuses on the incentive to establish a higher position within a group through being considered clever, witty, amusing, or likeable—the respect or leadership that can draw friends or sexual partners—while Tetlock is focused on the incentive to be merely accepted as a member of the group. Hence, Tetlock is explaining a broader range of people (all group members, who have an incentive to conform), while Mercier is explaining the likely smaller number of group members who engage in argumentation as a means of advancing their standing (who have an incentive to impress as well as conform).

[9] Ibid., page 461.

[10] Ibid., page 456.

[11] It is worth noting that even those who think they are never Machiavellian manipulators and always philosopher saints may still think very much like their group simply through socialization. People may share the values (and epistemology) of their group, with no pretense involved. Philosopher saints can be conformist in outcome while saintly in process.

limits. Intuitive prosecutors demonstrate a low threshold for affixing blame and imposing penalties, in order to "uphold the social order."[12] This epistemological goal provides more specific predictions of what the people who follow it will seek and observe. However, we still do not know which individuals will follow which intuitive method.

Tetlock's essential insight is that people differ in their epistemological foundations. We build on this insight to suggest that the range of possible intuitive methods may be value-driven, matching specific core values to specific habitual questions. In other words, *value systems carry intuitive epistemology*. If we have knowledge of a person's values, we may also have insight into their intuitive method, grounded in which questions they will ask more quickly and more often.

In the last chapter, we discussed values within three different frameworks—political values, Schwartz's personal values, and Haidt's moral values—demonstrating that each of these value conceptions is strongly predictive of polarized fact perceptions. Each could also be connected to its own intuitive approach to epistemology. Rather than flesh out and test the full range of value conceptions, we focus here on Haidt's moral values—care, fairness as equality, fairness as proportionality, sanctity, loyalty, and authority—as an example of how values may carry epistemology.

If each of these core moral values carries an intuitive method—*a compelling question habitually asked when looking at the political world*—what might those questions be? Ben Franklin famously advised people to "keep your eyes wide open before marriage, half shut afterward." In Franklin's view, it is best to observe as many flaws in a possible spouse before *making* a marriage decision (in order to avoid marrying the wrong person) and then to observe as few flaws as possible in order to *maintain* a marriage decision. In some realms, we may resist seeing things that upset us—such as our parents' sexual behavior or unethical actions by someone we admire—but in politics people seem to be on the lookout for what transgresses their values or offends their sensibilities. Voters often vote *against* rather than *for*. Hence, we propose that habitual questions may be framed more negatively than positively. Table 8.1 displays our first cut at the intuitive methods that would be paired with each of the Haidt moral values, grounded in a core question each kind of practical epistemologist in the wild would tend to pose.

---

[12] Goldberg et al. 1999, page 790.

TABLE 8.1 Intuitive Epistemology

MORAL VALUE	INTUITIVE METHOD	CORE QUESTION
None (value-neutral)	Scientist	Are we being given misleading information?
Care	Caregiver	Are people being harmed?
Equality	Crusader	Are people being discriminated against?
Proportionality	Umpire	Are people cheating or taking more than they deserve?
Sanctity	Purist	Are people committing indecent acts or degrading something sacred?
Loyalty	Loyalist	Are people being disloyal to us?
Authority	Constable	Are people dishonoring cherished traditions or proper authorities?

Citizens with no dominant value orientation would be intuitive scientists—pure independent observers, free of bias, and value-neutral. As Darwin phrased it, "a scientific man ought to have no wishes, no affections, a mere heart of stone." Their question is about the accurate empirical facts of the situation or, to frame it in the negative, *Are we being given misleading information?* As much as we doubt it, it is *possible* that ordinary citizens tend to be first and foremost intuitive scientists, so we have to allow for this possibility.

We are much more sanguine about the influence of the six value-driven epistemologies. The liberal caregiver epistemology, associated with the care/harm moral foundation, is concerned foremost with, *Are people being harmed?* Fairness focused on equality leads to the crusader intuitive method, inquiring *Are people being discriminated against?* The alternative form of fairness from the conservative side—proportionality—leads to a different question: *Are people cheating or taking more than they deserve?* Purists want to know if "people are committing indecent acts," loyalists if "people are being disloyal to us," and constables if "people are dishonoring cherished traditions or proper authorities."

There is an important overlap between the Haidt and Tetlock conceptions: the intuitive prosecutor—Tetlock's broad category of seekers of norm violations—comprises aspects of the umpire, purist, loyalist, and constable epistemologies. In a sense, the prosecutor is all of the conservative methods combined, vigilantly watching for norm violations across the spectrum of fairness, sanctity, loyalty, and authority (think of the Javert character in *Les Misérables*). However, we think there are meaningful differences between these different breeds of watchdogs, so we break the prosecutor down into component parts grounded in distinct motivating values.

If the Haidt conception of moral foundations describes a relatively comprehensive and accurate system of values (which we think it does) and the matching intuitive methods are the habitual questions asked by each group of intuitive epistemologists (as we suggest they are), then this creates a testable system of the role of intuitive epistemology.

An Empirical Look at Intuitive Epistemology

To test this concept, we designed a study to gauge the "go-to" question individual citizens ask when looking at the political world. Surely people can be primed and framed into shifting from one intuitive method to another or, in Tetlock's phrase, from one "functionalist metaphor" to a different one. But if intuitive epistemology has a long-term impact, it is because people do not shift across the spectrum randomly or with equal frequency for each person. The "habits of the eyes," as Lippmann phrased it, are indeed habits; one can be distracted from them, but they reappear more often than other behaviors.

For this study, we employed the *CALSPEAKS* panel, a longitudinal survey of a sample of California residents.[13] While our previous studies of dueling fact perceptions employed national samples to gauge the proportion and influence of DFPs nationwide, we are focused here more on mechanism and process than strict representativeness (as is frequently the case in political psychology studies). A local sample—even one shifted toward the more liberal and demographically diverse population of California—will reveal the underlying psychological mechanisms, regardless of whether its local demographics differ somewhat from the national patterns.

---

[13] *CALSPEAKS* is administered by the Institute for Social Research at California State University-Sacramento. The panel employs random stratified sampling (by five California regions), drawing its sample from the population of residential addresses included in the US Postal Service file. Administrators augmented the *CALSPEAKS* panel during the initial wave of recruitment (August 2015) with a quota sample in order to achieve representativeness through post-stratification weighting. To account for the difference across sample respondents in the way they were initially recruited into the panel, our models cluster random errors by recruitment type. Technical details regarding sampling, panel management, weighting, and sample characteristics can be observed at http://www.csus.edu/isr/calspeaks.

In a survey conducted in June 2017, we gauged respondents' moral foundations[14] and a range of fact perceptions. Later in the survey (to avoid contamination of the value and factual measures) we posed the core question of the study:

Please imagine that a factual controversy relating to an important public policy issue is being discussed widely in the news. As you try to figure out what to believe, what would be the most important things you would consider? From the list below, please RANK THE THREE MOST IMPORTANT considerations, as far as you are concerned (most important = 1, second most = 2, third most = 3). [the order of options below were randomly rotated]

Does it appear that the information about this controversy is misleading?
[SCIENTIST]
Does it appear that people are being harmed?
[CAREGIVER]
Does it appear that people are being taken advantage of or discriminated against?
[CRUSADER]
Does it appear that people are cheating or taking more than they deserve?
[UMPIRE]
Does it appear that people are committing indecent acts or degrading something sacred?
[PURIST]
Does it appear that people are being disloyal to us?
[LOYALIST]
Does it appear that people are dishonoring cherished traditions or proper authorities?
[CONSTABLE]

---

[14] The Haidt moral value measures employ the following wording: "Please read the following statements and indicate your agreement or disagreement: [Strongly Agree, Somewhat Agree, Somewhat Disagree, Strongly Disagree]

'Compassion for those who are suffering is the most crucial virtue'
'When the government makes laws, the number one principle should be ensuring that everyone is treated fairly'
'A fair and just society makes sure that those who break the rules get what they deserve'
'Some behaviors are sick and should be illegal, even if no one is getting hurt'
'People should be loyal to their own'
'People don't have enough respect for authority anymore'"

This is a novel approach to gauging a range of possible intuitive methods. If intuitive epistemology exists as we have described, then the various methods are unaware and unconsidered constructs that cannot be measured easily. The goal of this empirical approach is to invoke a situation in which the individual may look for further information, but it is important that the factual dispute at issue is vague because a specific problem could trigger certain questions more than others. The question about "a factual controversy relating to an important public policy issue" could apply to any given situation that may come along.

This survey question is a difficult one for respondents to answer, and it represents a taxing cognitive load to sort through seven options. We suspect that even citizens with a dominant intuitive method may not identify the question that matches it as their first choice. For this reason, we also included a second and third choice out of the seven possibilities. We then dichotomized this measure for each intuitive approach, identified as either one of citizens' priorities (the top three out of seven) or in the bottom set that did not gain their attention. Priming or distraction could take an epistemology out of first place among the seven options, but it is likely to remain in the top three if it is indeed habitual, identifying their "go-to" question (or questions) when looking at the political world. It is also possible that individuals have more than one epistemology to which they tend to adhere, so this measurement approach serves several purposes.

The dichotomized dependent variable also allows us to employ a statistical analysis that is one of the easiest to understand and illustrate. The full statistical results (from a set of binary probit regressions of each intuitive method against moral values and a range of control variables including gender, race, education, income, and age) are available in the appendix. The figures in this chapter illustrate the changes in the likelihood of identifying each intuitive method associated with each of the moral values independently (holding the other moral values and control variables constant). The figures answer the question, *As moral values differ among citizens (for example, from low to high on the sanctity scale), how much does that alter the likelihood of expressing a specific intuitive method?*

The answer is that in three out of six intuitive methods, the predicted relationships emerge. In regard to crusader, purist, and loyalist epistemology, the strongest predictor (more so than party identity [PID]) is the associated moral value. Moving from the lowest to highest range of fairness (equality) is associated with a 27% increase in the likelihood of expressing the crusader intuitive epistemology. For the purist epistemology, the percentage change associated with its underlying moral value (sanctity) is 20%; for loyalist epistemology and the loyalty moral value, it is 19%.

Figure 8.1 illustrates all six moral values in order of the strength of their connection to crusader epistemology (privileging the core question, *Does it appear that people are being taken advantage of or discriminated against?*). As hypothesized, the strongest predictor of crusader epistemology is equality-based fairness. Care is also a positive predictor (21% more likely), while sanctity is a negative predictor (18% less likely). Loyalty, authority, and proportionality-based fairness (the conservative version) are not significant predictors. (The results in the figures are illustrated with a 90% confidence interval represented by the horizontal brackets; if the brackets fall outside of the zero line, we can be at least 90% confident that the effect is real [distinct from zero], while results for which the zero line falls well within the brackets should be considered just random fluctuations.) The final variable illustrated in each of the figures is PID (illustrated from strong Democratic to strong Republican affiliation). In the current political culture, PID is almost always a powerful predictor of attitudes and behavior, but crusader epistemology is at least as strongly related to fairness (27% moving from low to high) as PID (–23% moving from strong Democrat to strong Republican).

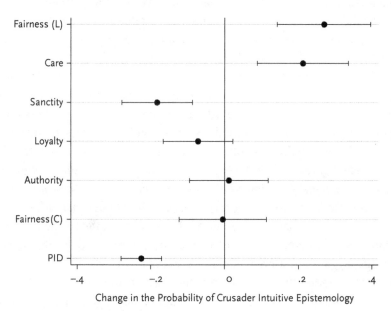

Change in the Probability of Crusader Intuitive Epistemology

FIGURE 8.1 Values and Crusader Intuitive Epistemology

NOTE: Bars represent 90% confidence intervals.

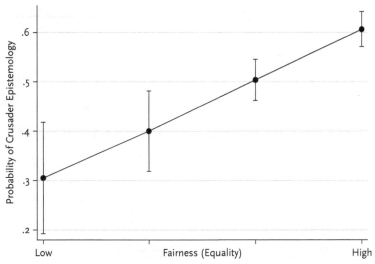

FIGURE 8.2 Fairness and Crusader Intuitive Epistemology
NOTE: Bars represent 95% confidence intervals.

Figure 8.2 focuses just on the strongest predictor of crusader epistemology—fairness (equality)—as it rises across citizens. At the lowest levels of the liberal conception of fairness, citizens are unlikely to hold crusader epistemology, but this rises to 60% likely at the highest level of regard for fairness.

Figures 8.3 and 8.4 illustrate the analysis for purist and loyalist intuitive epistemology. Purists, who look for violations of decency, are statistically associated only with the moral value of sanctity. Republican party affiliation also predicts this epistemology but to a weaker degree (7% compared to 20%). Loyalist epistemology is predicted by the loyalty value (19%) as well as by sanctity (11%). PID also has a connection but a relatively small one (5%).

It is important to note that one of the confirmed patterns is with a liberal epistemology (crusader) and the other two are on the conservative side (purist and loyalist), suggesting that moral values are associated with epistemological approaches on both sides of the ideological spectrum.

Intuitive scientist epistemology—favoring no specific goal-directed question but simply seeking to know if information is misleading—is *not* positively associated with specific values (as predicted) except for loyalty in a *negative* direction (see appendix Table A8.1). None of the moral values positively predicts a scientist approach, but loyalty is associated with *not* questioning whether provided information is

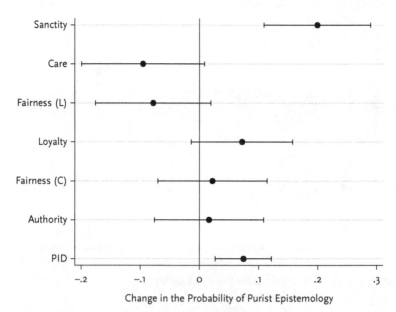

FIGURE 8.3 Values and Purist Intuitive Epistemology

NOTE: Bars represent 90% confidence intervals.

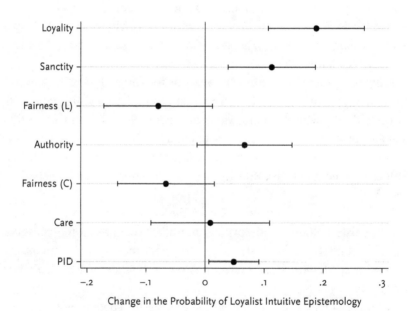

FIGURE 8.4 Values and Loyalist Intuitive Epistemology

NOTE: Bars represent 90% confidence intervals.

TABLE 8.2 Summary of Findings

INTUITIVE EPISTEMOLOGY	HYPOTHESIZED STRONGEST PREDICTOR	RESULTS
Scientist	No moral value	Supported
Caregiver	Care	*Proportional fairness is strongest predictor*
Crusader	Fairness (equality)	Supported
Umpire	Fairness (proportionality)	*Equal fairness is strongest predictor*
Purist	Sanctity	Supported
Loyalist	Loyalty	Supported
Constable	Authority	*Sanctity is strongest predictor*

faulty. Age and education are also strong predictors, with younger and more educated people more likely to question misleading information. Interestingly, Republican citizens seem to be *more* likely to be intuitive scientists, possibly because Republicans are more likely in the current environment to question the veracity of news reports and distrust mainstream media.

Table 8.2 summarizes the findings so far.

Intuitive Epistemology and Fact Perceptions

The origins of intuitive epistemology are important because we assume that the questions that people habitually ask lead to different perceptions of facts, which does indeed seem to be the case. We conducted a separate analysis treating the intuitive methods as independent variables predicting fact perceptions (both variables with dichotomized measures, looking at whether the presence of the intuitive method changed the likelihood that each DFP was perceived to be real). In regard to climate change, we expect the caregiver intuitive approach (focused on identifying harms) to predict perceptions that climate change is real. For racism, we expect crusader epistemology (looking out for fairness understood as equality) to predict perceptions that racism is influential. As for sexuality, we would expect crusaders to see it as innate.[15]

---

[15] "Is this statement true or false?" [Certainly True, Probably True, Probably False, Certainly False] [random ½ sample for each version, combined to one variable] *Climate*: "The Earth is warming due to human activity"/"The Earth may or may not be warming but not due to human activity." *Racism*: "Racism often prevents minorities from being successful"/"Racism no longer has much

TABLE 8.3 Predictions of DFPs and Intuitive Epistemology

FACT PERCEPTION	HYPOTHESIZED INFLUENCE OF INTUITIVE EPISTEMOLOGY	FINDING
Climate change	Caregiver → real	Supported
Racism	Crusader → influential	Supported
Sexual orientation	Crusader → innate	Supported
National debt	Umpire → dangerous	Supported
Terrorism	Loyalist → increasing	Supported
False convictions	Crusader → common	Supported
Vaccines	Purist → dangerous	Supported

We also added a few other DFPs, to allow for a broader range of epistemological connections: *national debt, terrorism, false convictions*, and *vaccines*.[16] We expect (1) the umpire epistemology to predict perceptions that the national debt is dangerous, (2) the loyalist epistemology to predict perceptions that terrorism is a prominent danger, (3) the crusader epistemology to predict perceptions of prevalent false convictions, and (4) the purist epistemology to predict perceptions that vaccines cause autism.

These patterns are exactly what we find (see Table 8.3). The intuitive methods raise the likelihood of each of these perceptions in the predicted ways, ranging from 8% to 16% (full results can be found in the appendix). One the other hand, intuitive scientists are not significantly likely to perceive any of the DFPs differently.

Among the core three DFPs we have been examining, the single strongest influence of epistemology pertains to perceptions of racism, which Figure 8.5 illustrates. As predicted, citizens employing the crusader intuitive approach—focused on alertness to injustice—were 14% more likely to perceive racism as prevalent. Loyalist epistemology—focused on identifying disloyalty toward the group—was associated with a 9% *lower* likelihood of the same perception. This is an interesting case in which

---

influence over whether Americans are successful." *Sexuality*: "Sexual orientation is something people are born with"/"Sexual orientation is based on choice or experience, not genetics."

[16] *Debt*: "The national debt (the amount owed by the American government) is likely in the future to cripple economic growth and national security"/"The national debt (the amount owed by the American government) is manageable and will not cause large problems in the future." *Terrorism*: "Terrorist attacks inspired by radical Islam are a substantial threat to Americans"/"Terrorist attacks inspired by radical Islam are not a substantial threat to Americans." *False convictions*: "False convictions of innocent people are very rare"/"False convictions of innocent people occur frequently." *Vaccines*: "Vaccines cause autism"/"Vaccines do not cause autism."

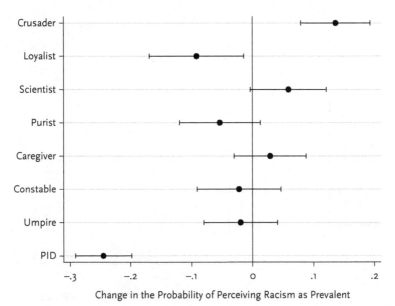

FIGURE 8.5 Intuitive Epistemology and Perceptions of Racism

NOTE: Bars represent 90% confidence intervals.

competing intuitive epistemology (crusaders versus loyalists) combine to move perceptions in opposite directions, creating a 23% greater likelihood of opposing perceptions of racism.

Figure 8.6 illustrates the results for perceptions of terrorism, which showed one of the strongest influences of the relevant intuitive method (13% change in likelihood of perceptions, comparable to PID at 15%).

As illustrated in Figure 8.7, crusaders are about 8% more likely to believe false convictions to be prevalent. Loyalists, on the other hand, are 8% more likely to have the opposing perception that false convictions are rare. For each of the DFPs, none of the other intuitive methods have bearing on perceptions.

Beyond PID

As a final note, though several of the DFPs are associated clearly with PID, one in particular is not: the perceived dangers of vaccination.[17] One of the important aspects of that controversy is how decidedly the scientific

---

[17] See the discussion in Chapter 5 regarding personal knowledge and perceptions of vaccines and autism.

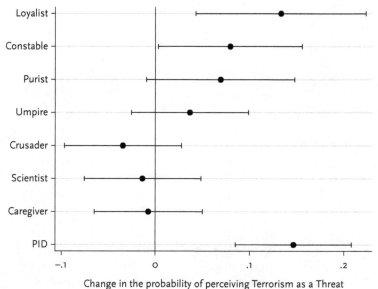

Change in the probability of perceiving Terrorism as a Threat

FIGURE 8.6 Intuitive Epistemology and Perceptions of Terrorism

NOTE: Bars represent 90% confidence intervals.

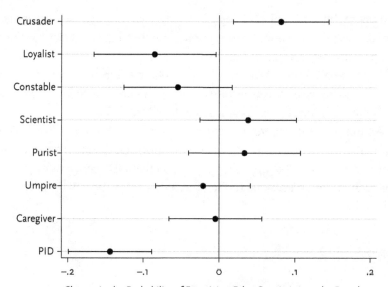

Change in the Probability of Perceiving False Convictions to be Prevalent

FIGURE 8.7 Intuitive Epistemology and Perceptions of False Convictions

NOTE: Bars represent 90% confidence intervals.

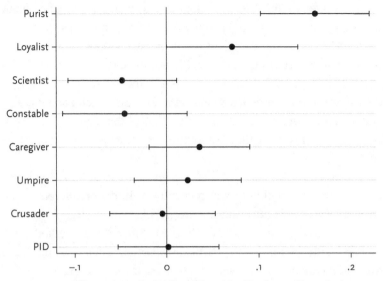

FIGURE 8.8 Intuitive Epistemology and Perceptions That Vaccines Cause Autism
NOTE: Bars represent 90% confidence intervals.

community and the available evidence support not only the safety but the positive social consequences of vaccination (and the sometimes dire consequences when herd immunity fails, as illustrated by the measles outbreaks in places where vaccination levels have fallen). Another fascinating aspect is that perceptions of vaccines are *not* associated with partisanship: Democrats or Republicans are no more likely to embrace the non-demonstrated view that vaccines cause autism. What was once thought to be a movement by the Left (more associated with hippies and Hollywood) has been embraced by elements of the Right as well.[18] If partisanship is not driving this divided fact perception, what is?

As illustrated in Figure 8.8, the answer seems to be purist intuitive epistemology. Purists are 16% more likely (the strongest association in the study) to perceive that vaccines cause autism. Heightened awareness to indecent acts or the degradation of the sacred leads to the perception that doctors are wrong (or lying) about the dangers of vaccines. Loyalist epistemology also leads in the same direction (though less powerfully and only at the .10 level of statistical significance). Again, this seems to be associated with seeking evidence of those who are betraying us, in this

---

[18] See Uscinski and Parent 2014.

case the medical establishment of doctors and pharmaceutical companies. One might think it would be an epistemology more associated with liberalism—such as the caregiver focus on harm—that would lead to the anti-vaccination perspective, but that is not the case. The purist and, to a lesser extent, loyalist intuitive methods are the stronger driving factors, and both are often associated with conservatives, which accounts for the negative perceptions of vaccines on that side of the ideological spectrum. PID, in and of itself, bears absolutely no relationship to perceptions of vaccines.[19]

Polarized perceptions of vaccines are an example of how PID is not always a viable explanation of fact perceptions. In the broader sense, if the origins of DFPs were only a unidimensional ideology or PID, this would not account for the wide variation of values and value-laden methods that are associated with specific DFPs. Partisanship often remains an independent factor, but the divergent belief systems *below* the umbrella construction of partisanship show variation across DFPs. These sub-ideological or sub-partisan belief systems play a crucial role in understanding the origins of DFPs.

Conclusion: Values Carry Epistemology

Knowing is hard; believing is easy. This observation alone may explain much of the dueling facts phenomenon. As Lippmann phrased it, "The environment is complex. Man's political capacity is simple."[20] We may resist Lippmann's conclusions and see citizens as having greater capacities when it comes to facts. But all of the forgoing suggests that in reality our grasp of facts is weak. We are more likely to achieve coherence with our prior beliefs than to reach correspondence with accurate empirical observations.

The mechanism by which this occurs is a trickier matter. We suggest that in addition to the several psychologies of perception discussed in the previous chapters, Tetlock's concept of intuitive epistemology plays a strong role. Value systems carry intuitive epistemology. Values serve many functions, and in this sense a value is not merely a predisposition for what we would like to exist but also a predisposition for how we discern its existence.

---

[19] This finding comports with the analysis of the 2017 national data illustrated in Table 7.6.
[20] Lippmann 1927, page 68.

9 | The Roots of Certainty

SACRED VALUES AND SACRED FACTS

"Whoever says he is 100 percent right is a fanatic,
a thug, and the worst kind of rascal."

—Czeslaw Milosz, The Captive Mind

"If everything isn't black and white, I say why the hell not?"

—John Wayne

A FINAL ASPECT OF THE EPISTEMOLOGY of fact perceptions is *certainty*. As William James phrased it, "to know is one thing, and to know for certain that we know is another."[1] How do citizens come to the view that they are *sure* that something is the case, rather than just holding a working impression that they are willing to change and update? This particular aspect of practical epistemology—*how do we know to be certain?*—may be even more psychologically driven, rather than truly empirically framed, than simple questions of knowledge.

So far, our argument has revolved around core values and perceptions of facts: *preferred values shape perceived facts*. This occurs through several psychological pathways, culminating in value projection. The process is compounded by intuitive epistemologies, which are associated with specific values and lead citizens to ask different questions and hence perceive different facts in response. Our final point is about the connection between a specific kind of fact perception (certainty) and a specific kind of value (sacred or absolute). One of the great surprises about dueling fact perceptions (DFPs) is how resistant they can be to correction or new

---

[1] Williams James 1896. James was one of the founders of American academic psychology in the early 1900s, when, like many fields, it was as much philosophy as empiricism. James was also a proponent of pragmatist epistemology, as described in Chapter 2.

information. Attempting to correct factual claims can actually provoke recipients to dig in their heels, in a backfire or boomerang effect.[2] And even when it appears that a misperception has been corrected, deep-seated "belief echoes" can endure.[3] But this is not universally the case; some perceptions are changeable in response to new information.[4] We suspect that not all perceptions are held equally. Some are certain, and some are merely suspected. But what is the origin of certainty?

There are not only different kinds of fact perceptions but also different kinds of values. Sacred or absolute values are a subset of core beliefs that defy the usual expectation that value conflicts can be resolved by compromise.[5] They are held as moral absolutes that resist trade-offs with other values or dilution by practical considerations. For the holder of a sacred value, to compromise is to reveal moral weakness (to ourselves but perhaps more importantly to others in our core social groups). We suspect that some of the resistance of fact perceptions to change—their apparent sacredness to some people—is due to their association with absolute values. Sacred values lead to sacred facts.

An Overabundance of Certainty?

The scientific mindset teaches us that certainty should be an oddity. We should be open to correction and embrace new findings that change perceptions and conclusions. We should always be willing to abandon our current views when new information warrants it. Darwin and Popper (among others) certainly taught this (though Thomas Kuhn [among others] pointed out that even the scientific community often fails to adapt as quickly as it should when holding onto previous paradigms).[6] Perhaps

---

[2] Nyhan and Reifler 2010, 2015c, Flynn et al. 2017, Pluviano et al. 2017. But see Guess and Coppock 2017.

[3] Thorson 2016. See also Skurnik et al. 2005 on the "illusion of truth" created by cognitive attention.

[4] Haglin 2017, Wood and Porter 2019, Hopkins et al. forthcoming.

[5] See Tetlock et al. 1996, Fiske and Tetlock 1997, Tetlock 2003. See also Baron and Leshner 2000, Baron and Spranca 1997, Ritov and Baron 1999, Marietta 2008, 2009, 2012.

[6] Darwin 1958, Popper 1935, Kuhn 1962. Popper seems to agree with Stephen J. Gould that "The factual correction of error may be the most sublime event in intellectual life, the ultimate sign of our necessary obedience to a larger reality and our inability to construct the world according to our desires" (Gould 1993, page 452, quoted in Hardin 2009, page 9). Popper commands self-criticism and self-falsification, which is a high standard to expect to occur in the real world; operationally, it more likely means attempted falsification of our views by others and of others' views by us. It suggests an *adversarial* epistemology more than a *self-critical* one. The metaphor is more a public trial than a private introspection. One of the problems with adversarial epistemology is that both sides can lose. Each side can sow doubt about the other, leading individual citizens to reject both. If both sides are damaged, individuals are effectively free to believe whatever they want.

TABLE 9.1 The Frequency of Certainty in Fact
Perceptions: Climate, Racism, and Sexuality

	2013	2017
All 3 certain	11%	21%
2 certain	26%	27%
1 certain	33%	29%
None certain	30%	24%

even more important than a willingness to *change* views is a slowness to *form* them. Scientific methods teach us that knowledge is hard won and often lacking; on many things we simply do not have enough available data to draw a conclusion and should admit a lack of knowledge. As they say, the three little words that people do not say enough are not "I love you" but "I don't know."

But this slowness to conclude and openness to change is *not* how ordinary people operate. To quote William James again, "the greatest empiricists among us are only empiricists on reflection; when left to their instincts, they dogmatize like infallible popes."[7] How much certainty is there in the American public about dueling facts? To proceed empirically rather than dogmatically, our method of assessing DFPs allows us to look directly at the question of certainty. Our measurement technique asks citizens whether a specific DFP is "certainly false," "probably false," "probably true," or "certainly true." A scientific approach among the public might lead to a preponderance of *probable* responses, unless citizens were faced with overwhelming evidence with very little legitimate opposition. This characterizes some DFPs, but many have strong evidence and theory on both sides. So how much certainty do Americans hold? The answer, displayed in Table 9.1 is *a lot*.

More Americans think of *most* of these three DFPs as certain than *none* of them as certain. And if the comparisons of the 2013 and 2017 data are indicative, certainty seems to be rising. The percentage of Americans who see at least two out of the three DFPs as certain was 37% in 2013 and 48% in 2017.[8] Clearly, John Wayne's penchant toward certainty—quoted at the beginning of the chapter—is as American as westerns. Contemporary

[7] James 1896.
[8] The difference in levels of certainty between 2013 and 2017 is statistically significant at the .01 level.

fact perceptions are more *Henry V* and less *Hamlet*, though perhaps they should be the other way around, especially if Oliver Wendell Holmes is correct that "certainty generally is an illusion."[9]

The human tendency toward overcertainty is clearly a broad pattern, far beyond DFPs. In *How We Know What Isn't So*, Gilovich summarizes the psychological literature's view that "one of the most documented findings in psychology is that the average person purports to believe extremely flattering things about him or herself—beliefs that do not stand up to objective analysis."[10] We know empirically that people chronically overestimate the accuracy of their beliefs.[11] In one of the foundational studies of the dueling facts phenomenon, James Kuklinski and his coauthors found that those who held the *least* accurate political beliefs expressed the *most* confidence in them.[12] And even among experts, overconfidence seems to be endemic.[13]

Sacred Values, Sacred Facts

The *certain* category of fact perceptions is matched by an *absolute* category of values. For any given value dimension, citizens can vary along a spectrum of internal value conflict, from ambivalence to absolutism. In this sense, internal value conflict is the opposite of sacredness; high internal value conflict allows for negotiability, while the lack of internal value conflict allows absolute belief. Sacredness is the sense in which some things are inviolable, such that it is offensive to weigh them against other considerations or perhaps even to question their validity.[14] *A sacred*

---

[9] Holmes 1897.

[10] Gilovich 1991, page 77.

[11] Fischhoff et al. 1977, Griffin and Tversky 1992.

[12] Kuklinski et al. 2000.

[13] See Tetlock 2005, Taleb 2007. Also recall the confidence with which nearly every political scientist in the United States predicted victory for Hillary Clinton in the 2016 presidential election.

[14] *Sacred* in the sense discussed here does not mean holy; it means absolute, which is often, but not exclusively, religious. The more closely a value is tied to religion, the more easily it is accorded sacred status. But it is important to note that while many sacred values are clearly religious, many are not. Sociologists such as Berger, Durkheim, and Eliade describe the defining feature of the sacred as inviolability, which makes a sacred political position unquestionable and its opposition unconscionable. The sacred is something set apart for special reverence. In Durkheim's phrase, sacred things are "set apart and forbidden" ([1912] 1995, page 44); for Berger "the sacred is apprehended as 'sticking out' from the normal routines of everyday life" (1967, pages 15–26). In Eliade's language, it is "the manifestation of something of a wholly different order" (1957, page 11). Durkheim famously argues that all human societies divide their mental worlds into two distinct realms of the sacred and non-sacred ([1912] 1995). The second is open to normal discussion and negotiation, but the first is inviolable.

value is a principle that is held to be absolute, resisting trade-offs with other values.

One of the core facets of sacredness is the setting of boundaries.[15] What is sacred is what establishes a limit to thought or behavior. Hence, sacred rhetoric entails the language of limits—one must not mention this; this kind of relationship is improper; this cannot be allowed; one *must* do this; one must *not* do that. Cultural relativism and value pluralism to the contrary, sacred thinking holds that some things are just not acceptable—delineating the boundaries of the sacred.[16] The abrogation of sacred boundaries, either religious or secular, is not only offensive but also a potential source of political motivation.

Sacred boundaries may limit certain thoughts from consideration or at least impose high costs to one's morality or decency if one does consider them.[17] In this sense, sacred values may influence not only behavior but also perception. Sacredness may be related to the *denial of sacrilege*, or the refusal to admit the existence of things that should not be the case. This could be termed *sacred blindness*, or an extension of the moral fallacy to the *denial* of observations.[18] Resistance to recognizing offensive realities could be described as cultivated ignorance for the sake of not having to think unpleasant thoughts or for the sake of not having to face unpleasant social reactions. The boundaries of the sacred may have an interesting breadth, extending from action to contemplation to observation.

The influences of sacred values are likely to be both cognitive and social. To question certain facts in our minds may also be to question the importance of our commitments to certain values. In Chapter 2, we discussed the inevitable interconnection of empirical and normative considerations, even when we do not want them to intermingle. Try as we might to maintain the philosophical distinction, their conflation in common language works against us (as Putnam explained) and the "demandingness" (as Maslow described it) of facts toward values and values toward facts is hard to exclude from our minds. And some fact perceptions may be more

---

[15] See Marietta 2012, pages 30–32.

[16] See James Davison Hunter's definition in *The Culture Wars*: "the 'sacred' is that which communities love and revere as nothing else. The 'sacred' expresses that which is non-negotiable and defines the limits of what they will tolerate" (1991, page 322).

[17] See Tetlock et al. 2000 for evidence of the social and internal sanctions imposed in response to transgressions against sacred values, including sanctions for just *considering* such transgressions (the mere contemplation effect).

[18] See Marietta 2012, page 32. See also Michael Walzer on symbolic thought: "symbolic systems set (rough) limits to thought, supporting certain ideas, making others inconceivable" (Walzer 1967, page 196).

deeply defining of group identity than others. If so, the propensity to reject challenging information is likely related to group identity.[19] To the degree that we seek to maintain fealty and avoid estrangement from identity groups, resistance to uncomfortable facts related to sacred boundaries is perfectly rational, as well as psychologically driven.[20]

Both aspects may add up to Lee McIntyre's observation in *Respecting Truth* that "we may outright refuse to believe something that conflicts with beliefs that we find sacred."[21] We suspect that this selective denial of disconfirming information and certainty of fact perception is driven by the extremity of values, such that citizens who hold sacred value commitments will be more certain about their fact perceptions.

Analysis

In our surveys, we do not have explicit measures of absolute values, but extremity of values is a close substitute. Thus, to test our hypothesis, we replicated the Chapter 7 estimation of the relationship between values and fact perceptions, with one difference: we *folded* the DFP and value scales such that they reflect certainty of fact perceptions and extremity of values—in either direction.[22] If anything, this is an overly careful measure of sacred values, likely to underestimate their role and influence (i.e., if strong values predict certainty of perceptions, sacred values will surely do so).

We also folded the party identification and ideology variables in the models, in order to gauge the comparative effects of extremity of these beliefs.

Table 9.2 presents the results using the 2013 data. Citizens with extreme value positions on collectivism versus individualism or humanism versus theism were distinctly more likely to hold certain perceptions of all three of the DFPs.[23] Value extremity consistently displays the

---

[19] Magnetic resonance imaging evidence suggests that exposure to politically contradictory beliefs activates brain regions associated with self-representation; see Kaplan et al. 2016.

[20] Binning et al. 2015, Chaiken and Maheswaran 1994.

[21] McIntyre 2015, page 6. See also Liu and Ditto 2012, who find that "the tendency to recruit facts in support of moral positions is likely to be most pronounced in individuals with strong moral convictions" (page 322). Also See McIntyre 2018.

[22] We coded "certainly true" or "certainly false" as 1 and "probably true" or "probably false" as 0 and the most extreme category of each value in either direction as 1 and the lesser value commitments as 0.

[23] These analyses cannot definitively sort out the question of endogeneity—could it be that the influence is the reverse; certainty of fact perceptions is driving extremity of values? If this were the case, then specific fact perceptions—climate, racism, sexuality—are influencing broad core values. For example, certainty about sexual orientation being innate or experiential is driving the sacredness

TABLE 9.2 Certainty of Fact Perceptions and Extremity of Beliefs (2013)

	CLIMATE	RACISM	SEXUALITY
Extremity of beliefs			
Strong collectivism–individualism[a]	.10 ***	.12 ***	.04
Strong humanism–theism	.11 ***	.07 **	.13 ***
Strong PID	.04	.00	.05 *
Strong ideology	.07 *	.06 *	.04
Control variables			
White	−.04	−.10 **	−.06 *
Female	.01	.03	.07 **
Family income	.10 †	.03	.01
Education	.11 †	−.08	.03
Age	−.05	−.07 †	−.10
News interest	.13 ***	.16 ***	.10 ***
N	873	882	882

Analyses are binary probit regressions. Results are average changes in the probability of the perception that the DFP is *certain* ("certainly true" or "certainly false" compared to "probably true" or "probably false") associated with a full range change in the independent variable. For example, the increase in the probability of being certain about global warming associated with extremity of collectivism or individualism is 10%.

Shaded cells represent statistically significant relationships.
$^†p < .10$, $*p < .05$, $**p < .01$, $***p < .001$.

[a]Folded scale: 1 = strong individualist or strong communitarian, 0 otherwise. The same applies to humanism–theism. PID is also folded, as is ideology.

stronger relationship compared to extremity of party identity (PID) or ideology. Partisan extremity is surprisingly weak. Extremity of ideology plays an independent role but not as strongly or consistently as values. Comparing the strongest value relationship to ideology for each DFP, climate is .10 to .07, racism .12 to .06, and sexuality .13 to non-significant.

Figure 9.1 displays the relationships regarding racism more clearly. The evidence suggests that absolutism regarding facts is driven by absolutism regarding values; sacred values create sacred facts.

---

of humanism–theism as a core value. There may be some back-feeding or reinforcing effects, but it seems unlikely that all of the causal influence goes from facts to values rather than from values to facts.

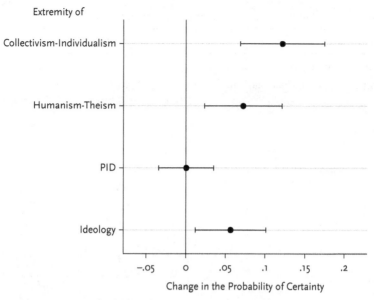

FIGURE 9.1 Extremity of Beliefs and Certainty Regarding Racism
NOTE: Bars represent 95% confidence intervals.

2017 Data and Moral Values

For a broader test of the connections between sacred values and certain facts, we can examine the 2017 data, which incorporate a larger range of DFPs and a larger number of values. Table 9.3 illustrates ten separate probit regression analyses of the full range of certain perceptions against the extremity of moral values (including the competing influence of extreme PID and ideology).

As the table displays, the extremity of moral values is clearly connected to the certainty of fact perceptions. For the Care moral value, sacredness is connected to certainty in eight out of ten cases, ranging from a 7% to a 15% increase in the probability of certainty. The other liberal value (equality) has a connection to certainty in four out of ten cases. As for the conservative moral foundations, extremity of proportionality increases the probability of certainty for eight of the ten DFPs. Sanctity, loyalty, and authority demonstrate connections to a smaller number but with equal or greater force. Partisan intensity, on the other hand, is related to certainty in only two cases (racism and sexuality). And when it comes to perceptions of the national debt, extreme partisan identity is *negatively*

TABLE 9.3 Certainty of Fact Perceptions and Extremity of Beliefs (2017)

EXTREMITY OF	CLIMATE	RACE	SEX	DEBT BAD	VACCINES HARMFUL	FALSE CONVICTIONS COMMON	MINIMUM WAGE HURTS	IMMIGRANTS TAKE JOBS	GUN CONTROL WORKS	CRIME UP
Care[a]	.15	.09	.09	.03	.07	.09	.02	.09	.10	.09
Equality	.06	.06	.06	.06	.06	.08	.00	.06	.04	.04
Proportionality	.05	.15	.11	.09	.07	.03	.10	.12	.11	.07
Sanctity	–.02	.04	.05	.06	.04	.08	.03	.02	.05	.04
Loyalty	.09	.09	.05	–.11	.09	.12	.05	.07	.06	.05
Authority	–.05	.03	.04	.12	–.05	.02	.12	.08	.02	.17
PID	.00	.08	.08	–.18	.07	.02	.07	–.02	.00	–.01
Ideology	.19	.19	.13	.06	.06	–.02	.08	.05	.26	.00

Analyses are binary probit regressions. Results are average changes in the probability of the perception that the DFP is *certain* ("certainly true" or "certainly false" compared to "probably true" or "probably false") associated with a full range change in the independent variable. For example, the increase in the probability of being certain about global warming associated with extremity of the care value in either direction is 15%. The models also include controls for race, gender, age, family income, education, and news interest; but space constraints preclude their inclusion here.

Shaded cells represent statistically significant relationships ($p < .05$).

[a]All values are folded scales (1 = strong belief, 0 otherwise). PID is also folded, as is ideology. Moral values are measured by reaction (0 = strongly disagree; 3 = strongly agree) with the following statements. *Care*: "Compassion for those who are suffering is the most crucial virtue" (mean = 2.22; standard deviation = .73); *Equality*: "When the government makes laws, the number one principle should be ensuring that everyone is treated fairly" (mean = 2.45; standard deviation = .72); *Proportionality*: "A fair and just society makes sure that those who break the rules get what they deserve" (mean = 1.68; standard deviation = .90); *Loyalty*: "People should be loyal to their own" (mean = 1.49; standard deviation = .93); *Sanctity*: "Some behaviors are sick and should be illegal, even if no one is getting hurt" (mean = 1.77; standard deviation = .96); *Authority*: "People don't have enough respect for authority anymore" (mean = 2.05; standard deviation = .93).

related to certainty, suggesting that partisanship may increase cross-cutting influences in some cases.

Perhaps the clearest way to illustrate the connection between sacred values and certain perceptions is to look at the aggregate effects across the full range of DFPs in 2017. We created an index of certainty encompassing the ten different fact perceptions (from 0 to 10 certain perceptions; mean = 4.12, standard deviation = 2.46). In that analysis—illustrated in Figure 9.2—the extremity of values is associated with greater total certainty for *all* of the moral values ($p < .01$ or more in each case). Extremity of the care and proportionality moral foundations is related to holding almost one more DFP certain, out of ten (.83 and .94, respectively). For equality, the average increase in the number of DFPs held as certain is .49. For sanctity, it is .39, loyalty is .76, and authority is .46. Ideology also has a consistent relationship: extremity of liberalism or conservatism is related to a .99 increase in the average number of certain DFPs ($p = .001$). However, the same is not the case for PID. There is no statistically significant relationship between extremity of PID and DFP certainty in the aggregate (regression coefficient = .11, $p = .58$).

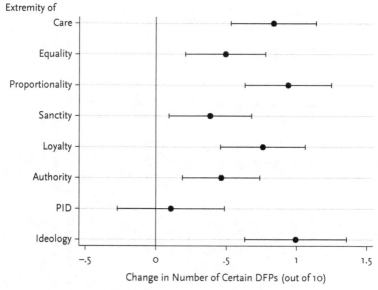

FIGURE 9.2 Extremity of Beliefs and Aggregate Certainty
NOTE: Bars represent 95% confidence intervals.

Conclusion: The Entrenched Causes of Dueling Fact Perceptions

Disputed fact perceptions are one thing, but *certain* ones have a different character. When we are certain, protective cognitions become stronger. The several mechanisms of selective cognition (attention, acceptance, skepticism, memory, and reinforcement) likely intensify. The recognition of certainty among our social contacts amplifies the mechanisms of social psychology that encourage conformity to the group's perceptions. If we are motivated to maintain existing perceptions, the same motivations toward our certain ones can only be more powerful.

This chapter concludes our discussion of the origins of DFPs. Our core arguments revolve around the psychology of value projection. Many intertwined psychological influences, from cognitive psychology, social psychology, and motivated reasoning, all combine to influence perceptions of facts in the same direction: toward those suggested by our core values (Chapters 5 and 6). The empirical evidence across several years of national surveys, gauging values in different ways, in regard to a broad range of DFPs, suggests that values are projected onto facts, as much as or more than partisan leadership influences perceptions (Chapter 7). The role of value projection may be guided by an even more deep-seated influence: the intuitive epistemology that frames the questions we ask even before we begin to seek answers (Chapter 8). And the certainty of perceptions may be driven by the sacredness of values (Chapter 9). All of this suggests that DFPs are driven by the core beliefs of ordinary citizens and will be resistant to change. DFPs—especially certain ones—are less likely to allow for compromise and deliberation and more likely to lead to incivility toward those who see things differently. The next sections of the book turn to those negative consequences and unlikely correctives.

III | Consequences

10 | The Democratic Consequences of Dueling Facts

"Even a seemingly slight distortion of the truth can have dangerous effects."

—*Pope Francis*[1]

"Without a common set of facts, it becomes nearly impossible to have a meaningful debate about important policies."

—*The Rand Corporation*[2]

"Without some common baseline of facts . . . we're going to keep talking past each other."

—*Barack Obama*[3]

T HE POPE AND THE RAND Corporation do not always agree, but on the negative consequences of dueling fact perceptions (DFPs) they do. The outgoing president also was clear in his farewell speech that he believes the dissipation of facts held in common is a serious emerging problem. What does it mean for a democratic society if its citizens hold contradictory perceptions of the realities at the heart of their political debates? We would like to divide our thoughts into the *clear* and the *controversial* consequences.

---

[1] "Fake News and Journalism for Peace," Message of His Holiness Pope Francis for World Communications Day, January 24, 2018.
[2] Kavanagh and Rich 2018, page xvi.
[3] Farewell Speech, January 10, 2017. In a Facebook post on June 16, 2018, Obama included *Truth Decay* by Kavanagh and Rich on his summer reading list.

Clear Consequences

DFPs clearly lead to a series of unfortunate democratic events: greater *public ignorance*, more entrenched *policy gridlock*, and the failure of *deliberation*.

Public Ignorance

Perhaps the clearest consequence is the effect on citizen competence, limiting the ability of normal voters to understand the state of affairs accurately and determine in an effective way which policies or candidates to support. Many scholars have decried the broad lack of political knowledge in the American public.[4] But as much of the scholarship we reviewed in Chapter 3 makes clear, the only thing worse than low information may be mistaken information. Confident misperceptions may be a grave dilemma for democratic decision-making. With the demise of consensus perceptions of influential realities, public knowledge has moved to a potentially more problematic phase beyond mere ignorance.

Poor (or No) Policy Decisions

Another clear consequence is policy gridlock: if democratic decision-makers cannot agree on the facts, productive debate is nearly impossible. With no agreement on basic realities, we have little chance of a consensus on which national problems need to be solved, let alone how to address them. In other words, without agreement on *where we are*, deciding collectively *where we ought to go* is practically impossible. As Glenn Kessler—the fact checker of *The Washington Post*—phrased it in 2012, "If the two sides cannot even agree on the basic facts, then it becomes difficult to understand how they ever could reach agreement on the key issues that face the nation."[5]

A related consequence is surely poor policy outcomes. Even if decision-makers can make decisions, those decisions may well be informed by dicey

---

[4] See Converse 1964, Achen and Bartels 2016, Lupia and McCubbins 1998, Delli Carpini and Keeter 1996, Lupia 2016. Among many pithy statements regarding Americans and political knowledge, two of our favorites are that there is "not more than a chemical trace" of policy knowledge in the electorate (Miller and Stokes 1963) and that "the mass of absolutely illiterate, of feeble-minded, grossly neurotic, undernourished and frustrated individuals, is very considerable, much more considerable there is reason to think than we generally suppose" (Lippmann 1922, page 48).

[5] Kessler 2012.

interpretations of facts that draw no consensus agreement. Lewandowsky et al. make the broad argument that "a functioning democracy relies on a well-informed public."[6] Hochschild and Einstein state it more specifically: "We believe, along with Thomas Jefferson and his many successors, that if ordinary people had more knowledge of states of affairs and a more accurate understanding of provable causal relationships, and if they used that knowledge and understanding, they would on balance make better political and policy choices and their polity would function more fairly and effectively."[7] Collective action—and, perhaps as importantly, collective action that is perceived by both sides of the ideological and partisan divide as legitimate—depends on collective perceptions of facts.

The Impossibility of Democratic Deliberation

Aside from self-interested political participation, we also hope that citizens and leaders will listen to each other and weigh opposing views—in a word, deliberate. Grounded in the work of Jürgen Habermas, the deliberative democracy tradition argues that the form as well as content of civic engagement matter.[8] Deliberative theorists emphasize the importance of *reciprocity*, or the norm of employing reasoning that is mutually justifiable and facts that are mutually acceptable.[9] Under these circumstances, the governing factor is in Habermas' famous phrase "the forceless force of the better argument"; however, no argument is likely to be accepted by both sides when they disagree about basic facts.

The participatory and deliberative approaches to democracy are often seen as espousing compatible virtues, as both advocate greater civic engagement.[10] However, recent empirical work demonstrates that

---

[6] Lewandowsky et al. 2017, page 353.

[7] Hochschild and Einstein 2015, page 37.

[8] See Habermas 1984, 1996. Other major works in this tradition include Dryzek 1990 and Fishkin 1991.

[9] On reciprocity, see especially Gutmann and Thompson 1996 and Benhabib 2002. Political theorists such as Amy Gutmann, Dennis Thompson, and Seyla Benhabib argue that the prevalence of essential value conflict is a major challenge for productive deliberation. Gutmann and Thompson argue that fundamental value conflict can be overcome through deliberation, but Benhabib is not as sanguine on this point.

[10] As distinct from the deliberative approach, advocates of participatory democracy emphasize the value of direct political action among all sectors of society, even those whose certain or absolutist views may not allow for deliberation at all; the seminal works in this tradition include Pateman 1970 and Barber 1984. An important distinction between the participatory and deliberative traditions is that participatory democrats expect citizens to have recognized interests and fully formed opinions, while deliberative democrats emphasize the willingness to engage in discussion, rethink views, and find a consensus.

the two are in important senses antithetical. Deliberation discourages participation because it increases ambivalence and forces citizens to reveal political positions that can exact social costs. On the other side of the coin, greater participation also discourages deliberation because engaged citizens become more politically extreme and committed, limiting their own and others' consideration of alternatives. An excellent discussion of these tensions can be found in Diana Mutz's *Hearing the Other Side*.[11] As Mutz argues, people often value social harmony more than political expression, leading increased exposure to deliberation to decrease participation. When political discussion focuses on disputes over *facts as well as principles*, we can expect even less real deliberation and even more decline in willingness to continue to participate.

To summarize the clear consequences, in a political environment characterized by DFPs and struggles by elites and masses alike to grasp their implications, we are likely to suffer from a lack of accurate knowledge among citizens, a lack of agreement on public problems and their solutions, and a lack of true deliberation.

Controversial Consequences

Further democratic consequences of DFPs are possible, even likely; but they are not necessarily established by the known evidence and theory. Some are even a bit speculative, including rising perceptions of *mental illness*, higher barriers to *scandal*, and divided perceptions of specific *events*.

Perceptions of Mental Illness

"I do believe the president is mentally unstable."

—*Ruben Gallego, Democratic Congressman from Arizona*

CNN, January 27, 2017

"What I think is really mentally unstable is people that don't see the positive impact that this President is having on the country."

—*Sarah Sanders, White House Press Secretary*

FoxNews, January 5, 2018

One of the core definitions of insanity is perceiving something that is not there—a giant rabbit, a dog telling you to commit crimes—or, on the other

---

[11] Mutz 2006.

hand, refusing to perceive what clearly *is* there. Any of the DFPs we have been examining can be framed in one of these ways, from either perspective.[12] Hence, the public debates about disputed realities can be expected to cause accusations not only of stupidity or lying but also of mental illness. This has surely been the case regarding President Trump. In a different time, one might assume that he would be insulated from such suspicions due to his status as a high-profile real estate mogul and entertainer (among other things). But not now.[13] Many psychologists have argued publicly for the removal of the Goldwater rule (the American Psychiatric Association's guideline to not diagnose political figures from a distance, first put in place when some psychologists suggested in 1964 that Barry Goldwater was clinically insane).[14] If we cannot agree on what is real, we cannot agree on who is sane.

Scandal Is Dying

Dueling facts may be contributing to another contemporary phenomenon: political scandal seems to be dying. In *Democracy for Realists*, Achen and Bartels argue that one of the benefits of even poorly functioning democracy is the incentive to avoid scandal, or "violating consensual ethical norms"; thus "no president will strangle a kitten on the White House lawn" and "taking bribes will generally be punished."[15] However, as partisan polarization takes hold, the possibility of scandal recedes. The logic of this hypothesis is grounded in the nature of scandal: wrongdoing is only scandalous if it leads members of the perpetrator's own party to abandon him or her. If partisanship trumps impropriety, then scandal is toothless.

The first time we took note of this was after the infamous election of Marion Barry. One of us was living in Washington, DC in 1994 when Barry won his comeback election for a fourth term as mayor after his arrest, conviction, and six-month jail term for smoking crack. His campaign slogan was, "He may not be perfect, but he's perfect for D.C.," though

---

[12] Foucault famously argued that the power to define reality and hence who was crazy (and belonged in a mental institution) was a very powerful thing indeed (see Foucault 1977). Without descending too far into Foucault (who might have been crazy himself, but that doesn't mean he wasn't right), another thinker in the same time period, Huey Newton, famously defined power as "the ability to define phenomena" (Hilliard and Weise 2002, page 227).

[13] See, among many examples, "The Madness of King Donald," *New York Magazine*, February 10, 2017; "Is Trump Making America Mentally Ill?" *Washington Post*, June 13, 2017; "Trump Defends His Sanity Amid Questions About His Mental State," CNN January 7, 2018; "What Trump's Speech Says About His Mental Fitness," *The New York Times*, February 6, 2018.

[14] See Lee 2017.

[15] Achen and Bartels 2016, page 318.

his informal slogan was "Get over it." *The Washington Post* endorsed his Republican opponent, not on policy but on personal grounds. Many citizens in DC and throughout the nation were shocked that the scandal did not prevent his election. But if a partisan voting bloc is so devoted to its perceptions that no event or information can change its resolve, then political scandal is essentially impossible.

At the time, this was mainly a phenomenon of specific examples of local politics in which the partisan vote was ironclad, but the same phenomenon seems to be growing nationally, with partisans less and less likely to abandon their leaders regardless of circumstance. During the 2016 campaign, Trump famously commented that he could shoot someone in the middle of Fifth Avenue, and his supporters would still vote for him. This is, of course, an exaggeration but maybe not too much of one. We wonder how much evidence of what sort of wrongdoing would be required in the current day for partisans to abandon their champions. We suspect that scandal is dying. Dueling facts shot it on Fifth Avenue.

Divided Perceptions of Events

"Nowhere is the contingency of fact more apparent, or more strenuously denied, than in the management of the past."

—*Michael Herzfeld*[16]

Perceptions of historical events likely share many of the same qualities as contemporary DFPs—except they may be even more polarized. While contemporary factual conditions often provide a great deal of legitimate and relevant evidence, for historical events—even of the recent past—the evidence may be even more tenuous and easily dismissed, opening the door more widely to the projection of priors rather than the application of evidence.

Historical DFPs include the Alger Hiss/Whitaker Chambers case and the Clarence Thomas/Anita Hill affair. Perceptions of these events were highly divided at their time and remain deeply disputed for those Americans who have personal memory or historical knowledge of them. The Hiss controversy of the late 1940s—was he a communist spy or not?— was a long-standing dividing point between liberals and conservatives, representing the larger debates over the threat of espionage from Soviet Russia and the legitimacy of the red scare tactics of Joseph McCarthy and

---

[16] Herzfeld 1998, page 78.

Richard Nixon.[17] The controversy during the Supreme Court confirmation of Clarence Thomas in 1991—was Anita Hill telling the truth about being sexually harassed, or was Thomas telling the truth that it was a politically motivated lie (in his phrase a "high-tech lynching")?—still evokes deep, certain, and disputed beliefs, representing the larger debates over sexual harassment in the workplace.[18] As controversial and influential as each of these factual disputes was at its time, Americans are notoriously forgetful or unaware of historical events. They are DFPs for those who know about them, but this may be a small subset of the public.

Unlike the older historical DFPs, more recent events are widely known and openly disputed. These include the Trayvon Martin and Michael Brown shootings. Perceptions of individual incidents of police race killings—which include Freddie Gray in Baltimore, Eric Garner in Staten Island, Philando Castile in Minnesota, and many others—may mirror the larger factual divide over the degree of racism and its influence in society. In that sense, perceptions of these events may reflect the same dynamics that influence other DFPs, rather than a neutral consideration of the evidence in each specific case.

To examine the relationships between priors and perceptions of specific events—at least in the limited sense of perceptions of one of the violent events that sparked the Black Lives Matter movement—we included a question about the Trayvon Martin killing within the 2013 Cooperative Congressional Election Study. The Zimmerman trial had concluded with a not guilty verdict in July 2013, four months before the survey was fielded. Our goal was to look at the degree to which perceptions of this specific event reveal similar patterns to the broader DFPs we have been examining. Table 10.1 and Figure 10.1 display the relationships among values, party affiliation, and approval or disapproval of the verdict.

---

[17] See, for example, Moynihan 1998: "Belief in the guilt or innocence of Alger Hiss became a defining issue in American intellectual life." The public debate reflected epistemology as well as ideology—whom do you trust, the patrician Harvard Law graduate and former Supreme Court clerk endorsed by the secretary of state or the common man who hid evidence of his communist days in a pumpkin on his own farm? Elitism versus populism deeply influenced perceptions of this DFP (see Chapter 12).

[18] See the 2013 documentary *Anita* and the 2016 HBO movie *Confirmation*. The Christine Ford–Brett Kavanaugh controversy took place while this book was in press. As of late 2018—after the first and second round of Senate hearings—the public is aware of a clear accusation of sexual assault and a clear denial of wrongdoing, with little additional information but tremendous amounts of elite signaling regarding values, identities, and partisanship. Under these conditions, our evidence and theory predicts tremendous polarization of factual perceptions, accompanied by unwarranted certainty and disdain for those who hold opposing perceptions, which is exactly what seems to have occurred. A Rasmussen survey from 27-30 September 2018 (the final hearing took place on 27 September), indicated that 38% of likely voters believed Ford was telling the truth and 39% believed Kavanaugh (Rasmussen 2018). An NPR/PBS/Marist poll conducted 1 October found 45% believed Ford and 33% Kavanaugh. Democrats believed Ford 76% to 5% and Republicans the reverse, 8% to 76%.

TABLE 10.1 Perceptions of the Trayvon Martin Incident (2013)

	APPROVE ZIMMERMAN VERDICT[a]
Collectivism–Individualism	.29 ***
Humanism–Theism	.06
Party identification (GOP high)	.32 ***
Ideology (con high)	.24 **
Non-white	−.19 ***
Female	−.11 ***
N	986

Results are average changes in the probability of approval of the Zimmerman innocent verdict (1 = approve [48%]; 0 = disapprove [52%]) associated with a full range change in the independent variable. For example, the probability of approving of the not guilty verdict associated with moving from strong collectivism to strong individualism increases on average by 29 percentage points. The models also include controls for age, education, and family income; but space constraints preclude their inclusion here.
Shaded cells represent statistically significant relationships.
**$p < .01$, ***$p < .001$.
[a]"Last summer the trial of George Zimmerman resulted in a Not Guilty verdict in the death of Trayvon Martin. Do you approve or disapprove of the jury's verdict?" (strongly approve [16%], approve [32%], disapprove [26%], strongly disapprove [26%]).

Partisanship played a strong role in perceptions of the accuracy of the Zimmerman verdict. Strong Republicans were 32 percentage points more likely than strong Democrats to see Zimmerman as innocent. As we have seen in earlier analyses, this effect is very much reliant on partisan leadership through media attention (*attentive* Republican partisans were 48 percentage points more likely than Democrats to approve of the verdict, while politically inattentive ones demonstrated only a 17 percentage-point difference). Race clearly plays a strong independent role as well. But even controlling for these effects, perceptions of this event are deeply related to the value of collectivism versus individualism, with individualists being 29 percentage points more likely to approve of the verdict. Humanism–theism, on the other hand, had no relationship with perceptions of the incident, similar to the previous findings with regard to perceptions of racism (see Chapter 7). Non-whites were 10, 11, and 8 percentage points (in 2013, 2014, and 2016) more likely to perceive racism to be influential but 19 percentage points more likely to disapprove of the Zimmerman

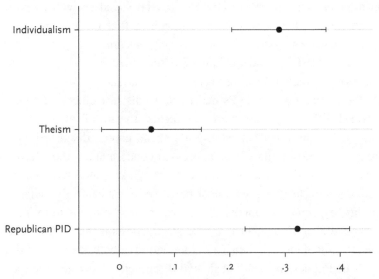

FIGURE 10.1 Values, PID, and Perceptions of the Trayvon Martin Incident

NOTE: Bars represent 95% confidence intervals.

verdict. It seems that the role of values and identity may be the same or even stronger when it comes to perceptions of events compared to perceptions of broader social facts.

Social Consequences

"The opponent has always to be explained, and the last explanation that we ever look for is that he sees a different set of facts. Such an explanation we avoid, because it saps the very foundation of our own assurance that we have seen life steadily and seen it whole."

—*Walter Lippmann*[19]

"It used to be that Americans could disagree over politics and still go out and have a drink. Not anymore. Nowadays, if you disagree, one of you isn't just wrong. One of you is a bad person. And who wants to go drinking with a bad person?"

—*Ruben Navarrette Jr.*[20]

---

[19] Lippman 1922, page 82.
[20] CNN, October 18, 2012.

The broader consequences of DFPs may be social as well as political. Or perhaps the better way of phrasing it is that the *broader political consequences may occur through social mechanisms*. What we have in mind are distrust and disdain of other citizens who hold opposing perceptions of reality, leading to spiraling polarization.

If the recognition of DFPs causes us to distrust others who perceive the world differently, then we move further toward all of the ills of declining cohesion, communication, and social capital discussed by many scholars. Several scholars have expressed concern about the rise in rude, disrespectful, and hostile public commentary associated with the current polarization.[21] Disagreements over perceived facts can only increase this incivility, especially if opposing perceptions lead citizens to think others are insincere or insane. One of the strong proponents of the continual public testing of factual claims as a foundation of both science and democracy, Karl Popper, argued that factual disagreement is often seen as "the work of powers conspiring to keep us in ignorance, to poison our minds by filling them with falsehood, and to blind our eyes so that they cannot see the manifest truth." If this is the case, then "only the most depraved wickedness can refuse to see the manifest truth."[22] Seeing others in this light will inevitably poison how citizens interact with each other.

In this sense, divided perceptions of reality may be a cause as well as a consequence of polarization. The recognition of factual disputes may alienate and divide citizens further, creating a vicious downward spiral in which political polarization leads toward divided perceptions of reality, and those divided perceptions lead toward greater polarization.

While the directly *democratic consequences* of DFPs—public ignorance, policy gridlock, decreased deliberation—are relatively clear and the more *speculative consequences*—the perception of mental illness, practical impossibility of scandal, and divided perceptions of events—are potentially important but less clear, the *social consequences* we believe are worth a longer examination. The following chapter takes a closer look at how DFPs shape personal interactions. This is a broad social influence, which loops back toward consequences for American democracy.

---

[21] Incivility goes beyond disagreement or criticism to name-calling, derision, insults, character assassination, mockery, vulgarity, and disruption of others' speech. See Herbst 2010, Jamieson 1992, Mutz 2007, 2015, Mutz and Reeves 2005, and Sobieraj and Berry 2013.

[22] Popper 1963 page 7, 8. Quoted in Friedman 2015.

11 | Disdain and Disengagement

THE SOCIAL AND PROFESSIONAL CONSEQUENCES OF DUELING FACT PERCEPTIONS

"He who denies either my moral judgments or my version of the facts
is to me perverse, alien, dangerous."

—*Walter Lippmann*[1]

W HAT HAPPENS WHEN ORDINARY CITIZENS are faced with others
who hold contrary perceptions of reality? While differences of
opinion on policy or party are one thing, disputes over reality
may well be another. The studies in this chapter examine the social and
professional consequences of dueling fact perceptions (DFPs). Through a
series of novel experiments, we take a look at how citizens react to peers
whom they perceive to be factually misguided. We assess the degree to
which such perceptions of wrongheadedness lead to *affective polarization*, or the growing emotional distaste that liberals and conservatives feel
toward each other.[2] To that end, we examine not only expressions of hostility but also social shunning—which eliminates opportunities to "hear
the other side" and the possibilities for real deliberation.[3]

We consider how this process may play out through social media. Other
scholars have observed that social media may facilitate affective polarization because of the virtual distance between communicants and the echo

---

[1] Lippmann 1922, page 22.
[2] See Jamieson 1992, Mutz and Reeves 2005, Iyengar et al. 2012, Sobieraj and Berry 2013, Iyengar
and Westwood 2014, Herbst 2010, Webster and Abramowitz 2017, Mason 2018.
[3] See especially Mutz 2006.

chamber dynamics that social media algorithms perpetuate.[4] But to our knowledge, no one else has focused on how factual disagreements on social media may affect broader social and political dynamics.

Social and Professional Disdain

The workplace may be one of the last remaining spaces in which Americans regularly interact with fellow citizens across the political spectrum and are expected to maintain decorum.[5] However, in recent years, several studies have demonstrated various ways that political differences increasingly damage what used to be thought of as largely apolitical social interactions.[6] *Factual disagreement*, specifically, might play a particular role in poisoning our relationships. As we see it, people can tolerate their colleagues/acquaintances who may hail from the opposite side of the partisan aisle in the same way that we can work alongside a Ravens (Steelers) fan; we may mutter under our breath or rib each other while waiting for the microwave, but we can at least work together on a project without too much discomfort—at least so long as the other person seems honest and keeps her ideas to herself when she's in the breakroom.

By contrast, when we see someone proudly propagating what we consider to be a blatant and obvious falsehood on social media, we can feel gobsmacked. For someone to say *that*, we often conclude, he must be either stupid or devious (not to mention obnoxious). And such conclusions about that person's mental capacity or character may lead us to avoid that person at lunch or on collaborative projects. Put simply, we can "agree to disagree" on a lot of things, but the prospect of working closely with someone whom we consider to be proudly ignorant—or, worse yet, a bit shady—may be more than many of us can stomach.

The "proudly" aspect to the perceived ignorance might be especially rousing of other people's scorn, which is one reason why we have chosen to study this dynamic within the context of social media provocations. Because of the interpersonal distance afforded by virtual communication, many people feel liberated to broadcast perspectives on social media that

---

[4] See Azzimonti and Fernandes 2017, Vaccari et al. 2016, Epstein and Robertson 2017. But see Lee et al. 2014 and Boxell et al. 2017. For an overview of the relationship between social media and misinformation, see Guess et al. 2018b.

[5] See Mutz and Mondak 2006.

[6] See Chen and Rohla 2018, Gift and Gift 2015, Hersh and Goldenberg 2016, Huber and Malhotra 2017, Iyengar et al. 2018, McConnell et al. 2018, Nicholson et al. 2016, Wintoki and Xi 2017.

they would be more reluctant to share in person. And for better or worse, social media have become central to the way huge swaths of Americans maintain social relationships and manage professional networks. Hence, if factual disputes are going to weaken workplace harmony, they are perhaps likely to do so through social media, which makes it a good context in which to analyze these relationships.

All of this leads to the following hypotheses:

H₁: Exposure to factual disagreement on Twitter predicts negative affect toward the source

H₂: Exposure to factual disagreement on Twitter predicts socio-professional shunning of the source

A Twitter Experiment

To test these hypotheses, we fielded a series of randomized, controlled survey experiments (in February 2016 and August 2017), using the population-based *CALSPEAKS* panel of Californians.[7] The February 2016 survey interviewed 742 respondents, and the August 2017 survey interviewed 815 respondents.

Fact Perceptions

The February 2016 experiment began by asking respondents the same questions about fact perceptions of climate change and racism as in our national surveys described in earlier chapters:

Please indicate the degree to which you believe each statement below is true or false:
- The Earth is warming due to human activity/The Earth may or may not be warming, but not due to human activity
- Racism still has powerful influence over whether people succeed/Racism no longer has much influence over whether people succeed

---

[7] *CALSPEAKS* is administered by the Institute for Social Research at California State University-Sacramento. See details in Chapter 8, note 13, page 145.

To broaden the generalizability of our tests, the August 2017 experiment replaced the climate and racism items with ones pertaining to the minimum wage, immigration, and free trade:

- The unbiased evidence shows that raising the minimum wage would help low-skill workers overall, even if some workers face fewer hours or layoffs as a result/The unbiased evidence shows that raising the minimum wage hurts low-skill workers overall because workers commonly face fewer hours or layoffs as a result
- The unbiased evidence shows that undocumented immigrants enhance the economy, overall/The unbiased evidence shows that undocumented immigrants hurt the economy, overall
- The unbiased evidence shows that free trade agreements with countries like Mexico and China take jobs away from blue-collar Americans/The unbiased evidence shows that free trade agreements with countries like Mexico and China do not take jobs away from blue-collar Americans[8]

We carefully chose these particular factual disputes in order to see if it makes a difference whether the scientific and social scientific evidence is one-sided. The scientific consensus surrounding climate change (whether it exists and whether humans are responsible) is well known, and social scientists largely agree that racism endures as a powerful social determinant.[9] By contrast, economists debate the consequences associated with minimum wage increases, immigration, and free trade, at least in regard to their impacts on employment and the economy more generally.[10]

Experimental Treatments

After survey respondents indicated the degree to which they believed the factual assertions to be true or false, they responded to several unrelated

---

[8] We measured the responses to each of these statements on a five-point scale (0 = "Certainly True"; 1 = "Probably True"; 2 = "Not Sure"; 3 = "Probably False"; 4 = "Certainly False"). We then merged and recoded responses from the different (liberal vs. conservative) frames into a single response set, using higher values to indicate liberal fact perceptions. The means/standard errors for these four variables are as follows: climate change = 2.81/.08; racism = 2.54/.07; minimum wage = 1.92/.07; free trade = 1.75/.06.

[9] See, for example, Peffley and Hurwitz 2010, Bonilla-Silva 2014, Norton and Sommers 2011.

[10] See Jardim et al. 2017, Cengiz et al. 2018, Blau and Mackie 2017, Schuck 2017.

questions that served to distract them before moving to the heart of the study. Each experiment began with the following instructions:

Imagine you can choose a work partner for a long-term project that will require a lot of interaction. One of your options is Bob Stratford, a guy at work you haven't met. A snapshot of his Twitter page appears below. Please examine it for a few moments and think about whether you want to work with him.

We then randomly exposed participants to one of several hypothetical Twitter feeds, all of which included two innocuous tweets (references to the Beatles and the television show *Downton Abbey* in 2016 and to the Beatles and a muffin recipe in 2017). The critical experimental manipulation involved randomly sandwiching one of the following factual assertions in between the other two tweets:

- Why are there still so many climate change deniers? Very frustrating.
- Why do people go along with the climate change crowd? There has been no global warming for about 15 years now.
- Why do people continue to deny that institutionalized racism still plagues this country? Why can't we just admit it?
- Why do people try to blame racism for everything? Sure there is some racism left, but not enough to keep minorities from succeeding.

An example of the 2016 treatments appears in Figure 11.1.

In 2017, the randomized tweet was one of the following factual assertions:

- The facts are now clear: raising the minimum wage to $15 hurts working people by reducing their hours and income. Why are we doing this?
- The facts are now clear: raising the minimum wage to $15 helps working people. Why aren't we doing this everywhere in the country?
- The facts are clear: studies show that illegal immigration provides needed workers and helps the US economy
- The facts are clear: studies show that illegal immigration takes jobs from low-skill workers and hurts the US economy
- The facts are clear: studies show that trade deals with Mexico and China take jobs from Americans
- The facts are clear: studies show that trade deals with Mexico and China benefit Americans

FIGURE 11.1 2016 Hypothetical Twitter Feed

An example of the 2017 Twitter feed appears in Figure 11.2. We also randomly exposed one-fifth of the respondents to a control condition that did not include a factual assertion.

Socio-Professional Disdain

To measure social–professional ostracism, we then asked, "To what degree would you favor/oppose working with Mr. Stratford?" (0 = strongly favor; 3 = strongly oppose).[11]

The final step was to create measures of respondents' appraisals of Bob's intellectual capacity and integrity. The surveys presented respondents with

---

[11] The means and standard errors associated with these variables (post-weighting) are as follows: 2016 = 1.27/.05; 2017 = 1.79/.04. The questions measuring social and workplace shunning preceded the questions assessing Bob's intellect and integrity.

Bob Stratford @bobstratford1 · 1m

"The facts are now clear: raising the minimum wage to $15 hurts working people by reducing their hours and income. Why are we doing this?"

⟲ Bob Stratford Retweeted

Modern Recipes @ModernRecipes · Jul 15

Please RT #recipes #food #cooking #delicious #cook #recipe Sausage, Egg, and Cheese Hash Brown Muffins bit.ly/2ulCZyA

FIGURE 11.2 2017 Hypothetical Twitter Feed

the following question: "Based on what you have seen, how well do you think each of the following words describe his personality traits?"

	Not at all well	Not very well	Fairly well	Very well
Stupid				
Shady				

From this, we created two variables to capture each assessment, with responses ranging from zero ("Not at all well") to three ("Very well").[12]

---

[12] The means and standard errors associated with these variables (post-weighting) are as follows: (1) stupid_2016 = .73/.04; (2) shady_2016 = .70/.04; (3) stupid_2017 = .64/.05; (4) shady_2017 = .61/.05.

Statistical Analysis

To get a picture of the polarizing effects of factual disagreement on Twitter, we conducted a series of binary probit regression analyses.[13] We predicted each of our dependent variables (seeing Bob as "stupid," seeing him as "shady," and being willing to work with him) with (a) individuals' perceptions regarding the disputes in question (climate change and racism in 2016; minimum wage, immigration, and free trade in 2017), (b) exposure (or not) to the various experimental treatments (Bob affirming/denying climate change or affirming/denying the power of racism in 2016; Bob making positive/negative claims regarding consequences of minimum wage increases, undocumented immigration, or free trade in 2017), and (c) interaction terms that multiply the individuals' perceptions by each of the relevant treatments (e.g., multiplying respondent perceptions of climate change by exposure to Bob affirming it and by exposure to Bob denying it and so on).

In so doing, we were able to calculate the relative probabilities of holding Bob in contempt (expressed either through character judgments and intent to shun) across four categories of agreement/disagreement for each factual dispute. For example, we were able to compare those who (1) agreed with Bob's claim that climate change is real, (2) agreed with him that it is not real, (3) disagreed with his claim that it is real, and (4) disagreed with his claim that it is not real. The same is true with regard to perceptions of racism, the minimum wage, immigration, and free trade.

Importantly, we controlled for party identification in all models, in order to distinguish (to some extent) the affectively polarizing effects of *factual* disputes from those of *partisan* tribalism.[14] Finally, we also controlled for gender, race, age, family income, and education.[15]

---

[13] To perform these binary probit estimations, we first dichotomized each of the dependent variables such that positive appraisals of Bob equal "1" and negative appraisals equal "0." We had originally estimated ordinal logistic regression models, to take advantage of the fuller range of variance in each variable; but post-estimation tests revealed that those models violated the proportional odds assumptions associated with such models. The results of those models were very similar, substantively and statistically, to what we report here. As a further test of robustness, we also estimated each regression using the multinomial probit estimator, which also produced very similar results. We report the binary probit results here because they are much easier to interpret and require much less space to describe.

[14] 0 = strong Democrats, 1 = Democrats and Independents who lean Democratic; 2 = Independents who do not lean toward either party; 3 = Republicans and Independents who lean Republican; 4 = strong Republicans.

[15] Gender: 1 = female; race: 1 = non-white; age: 1 = 18–25, 2 = 26–34, 3 = 35–49, 4 = 50–64, 5 = 65 and older; income: 1 = <$15k, 2 = $15.01–$30k, 3 = $30.01–$50k, 4 = $50.01k–$75k,

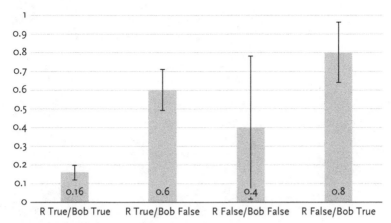

FIGURE 11.3 Probability of Rating Bob "Stupid" (Climate Change)

NOTE: Bars represent 95% confidence intervals.

Results

In order to maximize clarity in the presentation, we rely on a series of bar charts, beginning with the results for climate change (tables of the full regression results can be found in the appendix).

Climate Change (Affect): As Figure 11.3 illustrates, among respondents who believe in climate change (R True), seeing Bob deny it (Bob False) was associated with a 44 percentage-point increase in the probability of judging him to be "stupid" (.16 when Bob affirms climate change, .60 when he denies it; $p < .05$). Among those who deny climate change (R False), seeing Bob affirm it (Bob True) predicts a similarly large increase in the probability of viewing him negatively (.4 to .8); but the confidence intervals around these latter estimates are very large, meaning that the increase is not statistically significant and cannot be considered reliable.

As for perceptions of Bob's integrity, Figure 11.4 reveals a similar pattern. Among climate affirmers, seeing Bob deny rather than affirm it predicts a 56 percentage-point increase in the probability of seeing him

---

5 = $75.01k–$100k, 6 = $100.01k–$150k, 7 = $150.01k–$200k, 8 = >$200k; education: 1 = <high school graduate, 2 = high school graduate, 3 = some college, 4 = baccalaureate degree, 5 = postgraduate degree. We clustered the Huber-White (a.k.a. "robust") standard errors by the different methods that *CALSPEAKS* used to recruit the panel from which the sample was drawn, and we included post-stratification sampling weights to enhance representativeness. As with nearly all contemporaneous survey samples, regardless of mode or sampling method, the raw data underrepresent Latinos, Millennials, men, and those with low levels of educational attainment. Weighting details to account for these factors are observable at www.csus.edu/isr/Calspeaks.

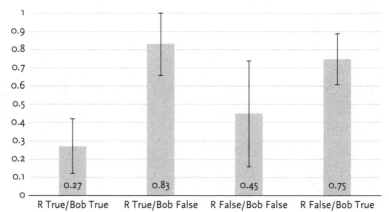

FIGURE 11.4 Probability of Rating Bob "Shady" (Climate Change)

as "shady" (.27 to .83, $p < .05$). On the other side of the ledger—among deniers—seeing Bob affirm climate change prompts a 30 percentage-point increase in the probability of judging him as deceptive. But again, this latter relationship is not statistically significant.

Climate Change (Ostracism): Now to the central question: do such negative feelings translate into social and professional ostracism? When it comes to *working* with Bob, Figure 11.5 shows that among climate deniers the difference between those who saw Bob agree with them versus disagree with them was again not statistically significant. However, consistent with the previous results among affirmers, seeing Bob's skeptical tweet led to a 36 percentage-point drop in willingness to work alongside him (.88 to .52, $p < .05$).

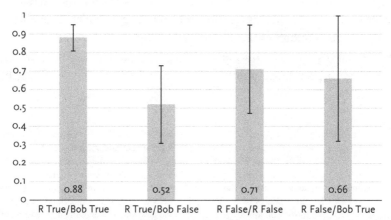

FIGURE 11.5 Probability of Willingness to Work with Bob (Climate Change)

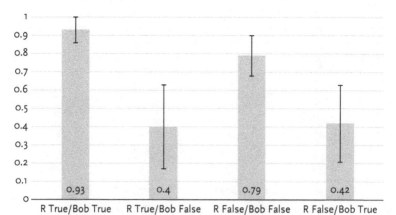

FIGURE 11.6 Probability of Willingness to Work with Bob (Racism)

When it comes to the perception of climate change, seeing a hypothetical colleague make what one considers to be a false empirical claim on Twitter seems to dilute regard for that colleague more times than not. Does the pattern hold with respect to different fact disputes? For the rest of the chapter, we focus on the core variable of respondents' interest in working with Bob—given that the patterns are similar in each case with respect to their perceptions of his intellect and character.

Racism: Looking now at Figure 11.6, we see that the pattern holds (and then some) when it comes to perceptions of racism's influence: among believers, seeing Bob deny its influence seems to make people about 53 percentage points less likely to want to work with him ($p < .05$)—a 17 percentage-point increase from what it had been when the dispute was climate change. And this time, the effects are more symmetrical: among deniers, seeing Bob affirm racism's influence makes people 37 percentage points less likely to say they would work with him ($p < .05$).

To summarize the findings so far, we see that factual disagreement is associated with significant disdain toward hypothetical co-workers. It is important to remember that these relationships emerge *while controlling for the influence of partisan disagreement*. Interestingly, the effects are stronger and more consistent among those whose perceptions are consistent with liberal points of view. They are also stronger and more symmetrical when the dispute in question has to do with the "easy" issue of race compared to the "hard" issue of climate change.[16] This difference

---

[16] In other words, it is easier for people to form an opinion (or, in this case, a perception) about racial issues because people experience them directly and feel them "in their gut." See Carmines

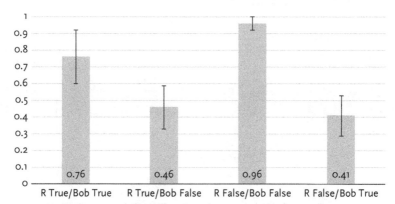

FIGURE 11.7 Probability of Willingness to Work with Bob (Minimum Wage)

might be a coincidence, or it could have something to do with the fact that by now most Americans are aware that there is something very close to a *scientific* consensus when it comes to climate change (whether they believe the scientists or not), whereas citizens are much less likely to be aware that there is a similar consensus among social scientists when it comes to racism's influence.

Next, we discuss the results from the 2017 experiments focusing on perceptions of the economic consequences of minimum wage increases, undocumented immigration, and free trade.

Minimum Wage: As Figure 11.7 illustrates, the same pattern emerges. Among those who believe that minimum wage increases hurt employment (R True, the conservative position), seeing Bob disagree (Bob False) is associated with a 30 percentage-point drop in willingness to work with him; and this time it does barely achieve statistical significance. But again, disagreement prompts greater disdain among those with liberal perceptions: for those who perceive that minimum wage increases do not harm employment, seeing Bob claim the opposite predicted a 55 percentage-point drop in willingness to collaborate with him (.96 to .41, $p < .05$).

Immigration: Now we turn to the results for perceptions of whether undocumented immigration helps or hurts the economy. Figure 11.8 tells a familiar story: among those who believe that immigration *hurts* the economy (the conservative perspective), seeing Bob disagree predicted a

and Stimson 1980. See also Egan and Mullin 2017 summarizing US public opinion on climate change: "In contrast to many other issues, people's understanding of the problem relies on expert opinion more than their own personal experiences" (page 211).

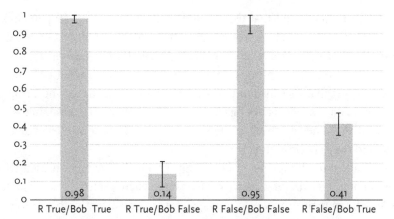

FIGURE 11.8 Probability of Willingness to Work with Bob (Immigration)

54 percentage-point drop in willingness to work with him (.95 to .41, $p <$ .05). But among those who believe that it *helps* the economy, seeing him disagree predicts a whopping 84 percentage-point drop (.98 to .14, $p <$ .05). And, as we have said before, these effects are on top of that which can be attributed to partisan disagreement.

Free Trade: Figure 11.9 displays the results for our final experiment, on the free trade dispute. We are a broken record at this point: among those who believed that trade deals with countries like Mexico and China take jobs away from Americans, seeing Bob claim the opposite produced a 49 percentage-point (.74 to .25) drop in willingness to work with him. And among those who believe that such trade deals *help* Americans, the effect is nothing short of shocking: seeing Bob disagree with them on Twitter

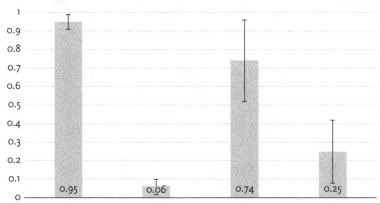

FIGURE 11.9 Probability of Willingness to Work with Bob (Free Trade)

reduced the likelihood that they would work with him by 89 percentage points (.95 to .06). These results are our most noteworthy yet because *differences in perceptions as they relate to free trade cross-cut the traditional party line.* Accordingly, these results provide the most convincing evidence yet that the disdain that people feel toward those who disagree with them on the facts is not just another way of expressing disdain toward those of the other partisan or ideological tribe. They are independent of that, and they are profound.

Overall, three things stand out about the results we have presented in this chapter thus far. First, as we have observed across all five fact disputes, those who perceive the world in ways that are consistent with ideological liberalism tend to express greater disdain toward those who disagree with them. Second, the disagreement prompts deeper disdain (on both sides of the aisle) when it is gut-level or "easy" in the Carmines and Stimson sense—as race and immigration are, while climate change and the minimum wage are not. Third, the effects tend to be stronger in the 2017 data than they were in the 2016 data. There are a few potential explanations for this, including differences in the specific factual disputes. Another possible explanation is that factual polarization and distrust of those who see things differently have intensified in the Trump era.

Political Disengagement

So far we have been focusing on the personal disdain and social disengagement that result from the recognition of DFPs. A related question is how factual disputes influence broader forms of political engagement and participation. Is there an effect on *macro*-engagement in citizen politics as well as *micro*-engagement with specific individuals? One of the unresolved debates in the scholarly literature on political polarization is whether it is associated with rising or declining political engagement. On the positive side, a Pew Research Study released in June 2014 reports that greater antagonism toward opposing partisans is associated with greater political participation.[17] Republicans who view the Democratic Party as "very unfavorable" rather than only "mostly unfavorable" were 18% more likely to say they always voted and 11% more likely to report having contributed money to political groups. Democrats demonstrated similar but smaller effects: 12% for voting and 8% for contributions. This hypothesized

---

[17] Pew Research Center 2014.

connection between polarization and participation is supported by several other empirical studies.[18] However, some studies have demonstrated a negative effect on political engagement, especially in depressing voter turnout.[19] The divide over fact perceptions as a specific form of polarization has yet to be empirically examined for its effects on political participation. Do dueling perceptions of reality contribute to lesser or greater citizen engagement? Are citizens disgusted and dispirited or energized and engaged by the conflict over facts?

This question becomes even more interesting if we consider *who* might be dispirited or engaged. Exposure to factual pontificating may affect different types of citizens differently—turning off moderates while mobilizing ideologues.[20] Recognition of factual disputes may strike ideologues as an even greater reason to engage in politics, while moderates may be more likely to be discouraged by conflict even over the prevailing facts.[21] If so, the result would be an electorate that is skewed toward the extremes, deepening political polarization.

At the culmination of the 2016 experiment, we asked participants whether they were likely to engage in the political activities that tend to enjoy relatively high rates of participation, like voting or discussing politics with others.[22] We wanted to see if exposure to statements that highlight factual disagreement—compared to statements that highlight partisan disagreement—would diminish the likelihood of common forms of political engagement. To that end, we created two dichotomous outcome variables: (1) whether a citizen intended to share political opinions with others and (2) whether a citizen planned to vote in *both* upcoming elections or not (we lumped those who planned to vote in only one election together with those who planned to vote in zero elections in order to create a variable with greater variance—since most people indicate an intention to vote in general elections).

The experimental treatment in this case is exposure to *any* of the four fact-claim tweets (affirming climate change or denying it, affirming the influence of racism or denying it). The control group comprised respondents

---

[18] See Abramowitz and Saunders 2008, Hetherington 2008, and Levendusky 2010.
[19] See Rogowski 2014.
[20] See Abramowitz 2011.
[21] See Ulbig and Funk 1999, Boudreau 2013.
[22] "Please tell us how likely you are to participate in each of the following political activities this election year": "share your political opinions with people you know well," "vote in the primary elections in June," and "vote in the general elections in November" (very likely [4]; somewhat likely; somewhat unlikely; very unlikely [1]).

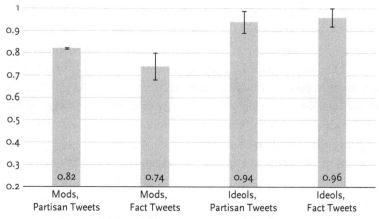

FIGURE 11.10 Exposure to Fact-Claims and Willingness to Share Opinions, Conditioned by Ideological Intensity

who received partisan tweets (pro-Democrat or pro-Republican). To test the hypothesis that exposure to fact-claims mobilizes ideologues while demobilizing moderates, we included independent variables that reflect (1) the experimental treatment versus control (exposure to any of Bob's fact statements vs. exposure to one of his partisan statements), (2) a folded ideology measure (0 = moderates; 1 = liberals/conservatives; 2 = strong liberals/strong conservatives), and (3) an interaction term that multiplied the folded ideology variable by the experimental treatment variable. We also controlled for respondent beliefs regarding both climate change and racism's influence (to account for the possibility that one side of the factual divide may be more motivated than the other).[23] Finally, as we have throughout this book, we included controls for race, gender, age, income, education, and party identity.

As Figures 11.10 and 11.11 highlight, the evidence supports our hypothesis that factual argumentation skews the electorate toward extremism. Moderates ("Mods") who were exposed to any of Bob Stratford's fact-claim tweets were 8 percentage points *less* likely to anticipate sharing their political opinions ($p < .01$) than moderates who saw his partisan tweets. Moderates were also 14 percentage points *less* likely to say they were going to vote in both the primary and general elections ($p < .05$).

By contrast, strong ideologues ("Ideols") reacted in the opposite fashion. With respect to the propensity to share opinions, there was no

---

[23] The results do not differ in any meaningful way, regardless of whether we include these additional control variables in our models.

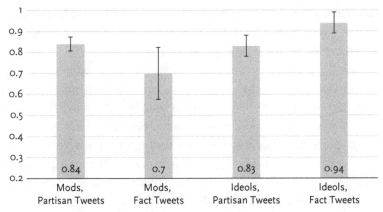

FIGURE 11.11 Exposure to Fact-Claims and Plans to Vote, Conditioned by Ideological Intensity

discernable effect because ideologues were 94% likely to intend to express their opinions after viewing the partisan tweets (and had little room to manifest a significantly higher effect when viewing the factual tweets). But when it comes to voting, ideologues were 11 percentage points *more* likely to say they were going to vote consistently when exposed to the fact-claims rather than partisan messages.

Unfortunately for the state of civil society, the more moderate citizens are the ones more likely to retreat from political engagement in the face of dueling facts, while those with strong ideologies feel more strongly motivated. The net result is to leave the field to the ideologues, fostering further polarization.

Conclusion

> "A world-known-in-common is part of the moral fabric of ordinary social interaction."
>
> —*Steven Shapin, A Social History of Truth*[24]

The consequences of DFPs are social as well as political. Our core finding is that disputed facts drive a retreat from civil engagement, or as Shapin phrased it, "ordinary social interaction." Citizens are less willing to even work with those who dispute their perceptions of facts. Political moderates get so turned off by seeing argument over facts that they retreat from

---

[24] Shapin 1994.

politics altogether, while ideologues mobilize. When ordinary citizens encounter others who believe different facts, the results are disdain and disengagement—both personally and politically.

We see this play out in the context of social media, which has become a normal means through which Americans evaluate each other. The role of social media in affective polarization has been broadly conjectured but not carefully assessed, especially when disputes center on facts. Social media may be no place for deliberation, or the meaningful consideration of others' perspectives and re-evaluation of our own, rather than the presentation and hardening of prior positions. The reciprocity that deliberative theorists prize—the mutual respect for each other's legitimate arguments—is not evident in our studies. Instead, the recognition of factual disagreement leads directly to perceptions of greater stupidity and less virtue.

Of course, these studies are burdened by a few limitations. First, our sample was restricted to Californians. Although California is a large state with tremendous ethnic, socioeconomic, geographic, and partisan diversity and although sampling was stratified and weighted to reflect that diversity, this was not a national sample. Nevertheless, we believe the dynamics of reactions to contrary facts by citizens in other states are likely to be very similar to those of Californians. Second, it is important to reiterate that our Twitter experiment is a facsimile. Until researchers examine *actual* disdain and ostracism as a function of *actual* social media behavior, we will have some concern that the artificiality of our "laboratory" may have affected the strength of the relationships we observe (though it is not clear whether such artificiality would serve to magnify or weaken those relationships).

While others have argued persuasively that DFPs have negative political ramifications, we add that there are negative social influences as well. But the social ramifications of disdain and disengagement also contribute to negative democratic consequences. The recognition of factual disputes alienates and divides citizens further, creating a vicious downward spiral in which political polarization leads toward divided perceptions of reality, and those divided perceptions lead toward greater polarization.

IV |Correctives

12 | Political Knowledge and Fractured Perceptions

EDUCATION IS NOT THE ANSWER

"The underlying causes of faulty reasoning and erroneous beliefs will never be eliminated."

—*Thomas Gilovich, How We Know What Isn't So*[1]

"Why do we believe in the authority of any fact, given that few of us are in a position to verify most of them?"

—*Francis Fukuyama, "The Emergence of a Post-Fact World"*[2]

OUR PESSIMISM ABOUT THE CORRECTION of dueling fact perceptions (DFPs) began with our evidence about their causes. If the causes were only external—partisan leadership or ideological media—DFPs could be more easily influenced. But the internal nature of DFPs—created by value projection as much as by external influences—suggests that they are entrenched and here to stay. The multifaceted and overlapping psychological mechanisms that create and maintain the close connection between core values and fact perceptions are very unlikely to lift of their own accord or in response to political or social reforms.

However, possible corrections should be identified and discussed.[3] One is greater education, and another is fact-checking. This chapter examines the first, while the next two chapters discuss the second. For readers who hope that we can educate ourselves out of the predicaments described in this book, this chapter will provide no comfort.

---

[1] Gilovich 1991, page 186.
[2] Fukuyama 2017.
[3] See Born 2017 and Kavanagh and Rich 2018 for detailed overviews.

Overview

In the headnote above, Fukuyama—a well-known optimist—wonders why we should trust authorities who tell us about facts, when we cannot verify the facts ourselves? He immediately answers his own (non-rhetorical) question: "The reason is that there are impartial institutions tasked with producing factual information that we trust." A common rejoinder in the current day is, "Really, are there?" Many citizens question whether these authorities on facts—news media and universities—are truly impartial and trustworthy. Other scholars of fact perceptions and misperceptions have expressed some degree of confidence that universities and media can establish and maintain consensus facts.[4] We are more pessimistic because of the widespread and growing distrust of these institutions.

Our understanding of the role of education and knowledge in the formation of DFPs is grounded in the broader context of divided perceptions of facts: *a multifaceted realignment of authority*. Unlike realignments of partisanship or demographics, the realignment of authority is characterized by dissipating trust in previously authoritative sources of consensus knowledge and rising reliance on disparate sources of information. Trust in knowledge-creating institutions is being replaced by greater trust in personal knowledge coherent with prior beliefs. There are several aspects of this story to discuss, some of which reinforce what others have said before and some of which we offer as new facets to be considered:

1) As others have pointed out before us, political knowledge and education are *not* employed by ordinary citizens to reach consensus perceptions of facts; *they are employed to reinforce perceptions grounded in priors* (as we have argued, via value projection and partisanship leadership). Our survey evidence reaches the same conclusion.

2) The ineffectiveness of political knowledge and education is tied to public perceptions of the institutions that have been entrusted

---

[4] Hochschild and Einstein: "we remain cautiously optimistic that education and the repetition of brute facts can spur the active use of knowledge" (2015, page 149). Lewandowsky et al. see much of the post-truth landscape as the result of strategic actors and hence correctable: "we do not consider the current situation intractable. We suggest that post-truth misinformation has arguably been designed and used as a smokescreen to divert attention from strategic political actions or challenges . . . post-truth politics—much like climate denial—can be identified as a rational strategy that is deployed in pursuit of political objectives. One implication of this view is that post-truth politics may cease when its effectiveness is curtailed" (2017, page 360).

to communicate knowledge (news media) and produce knowledge (universities). Many scholars and citizens would prefer to see education as an answer. *We offer a potential reason why education is not effective: distrust of universities.* Part of the story of the realignment of trust is the decline of the institutional authority of university knowledge, grounded in changing perceptions of university faculty.

The Role of Political Knowledge and Education

What is an effective corrective to DFPs? Is political knowledge? Is education? Greater political knowledge is perhaps the more direct potential pathway: more knowledge could lead to more accurate and consensus fact perceptions. But there are reasons to expect that political knowledge may not bring exclusively positive effects. The most noted studies on the role of political knowledge in our democracy have decried its chronic absence among citizens.[5] And when knowledge of politics *is* present, it tends to come with other features—stronger ideology, partisanship, or value certainty—which may foster the projection of priors onto perceptions. Education, on the other hand, is distinct from raw political knowledge. It is believed to inculcate not only specific pieces of information but also certain positive qualities of mind: a habit of questioning, skills in applying evidence, and a willingness to rethink positions. As well as producing greater knowledge, education is supposed to foster the ability and desire to seek out and evaluate new claims to knowledge.

One of the repeated claims throughout American history is that knowledge and education improve society. George Washington wrote that "Knowledge is in every Country the surest basis of public happiness."[6] Benjamin Franklin thought not only that greater knowledge led toward understanding of sickness and health (as we described in Chapter 2) but that "The good Education of Youth has been esteemed by wise Men in all Ages, as the surest Foundation of the Happiness both of private Families and of Commonwealths."[7] Probably the most noted advocate of education was Thomas Jefferson, founder of the University of Virginia, who argued that if we "Educate and inform the whole mass of the people, enable them to see that it is their interest to preserve peace and order, they will preserve

---

[5] Delli Carpini and Keeter 1996, Lupia 2016.
[6] "From George Washington to the United States Senate and House of Representatives," January 8, 1790.
[7] *Proposals Relating to the Education of Youth in Pennsylvania,* 1749.

it, and it requires no very high degree of education to convince them of this. They are the only sure reliance for the preservation of our liberty."[8]

In the Progressive Era, John Dewey's argument in *Democracy and Education* (1916)—that a democratic form of public education was the bedrock of democratic government—became the mantra of many university departments of education. More recently, a US senator gave a floor speech entitled "Why Education Is Essential to Our Democracy."[9] This endorsement of the link between education and democracy reflects the dominant academic view stemming from prominent studies such as Seymour Martin Lipset's famous 1959 study of the foundations of democracy or the Almond and Verba emphasis on the "civic culture" in 1963, which concluded that "the man with limited education is a different political actor from the man who has achieved a higher level of education."[10] From the time of Almond and Verba to now, education has been seen as an obvious driver of political participation as well as the backbone of support for civil liberties and civil rights.[11]

The importance of education to democracy is a truism in the sense that everyone assumes it is the case without much discussion. Odd word, *truism*, which refers to something so obviously true that it needs no justification, though the power of that assumption may allow the reality of any truism to degrade without many people noticing. The accuracy of the *education strengthens democracy* truism may depend on factors like *trust* in educational institutions. Without trust in universities, higher education may simply allow individual citizens to strengthen the connections from their values to their perceptions of facts. The broad agreement that education improves democracy and democracy improves education may need to be tempered by the newer recognition that education does not always work in this way in the current environment. If university students distrust the *content* of their education and gain only *skills* in argumentation, then educated citizens are more likely to perceive facts as their values dictate, bolstered by greater cognitive abilities.

---

[8] Letter to Uriah Forrest, December 31, 1787.

[9] Michael Bennet (D. Colorado), February 6, 2017.

[10] Lipset 1959, Almond and Verba 1963, page 315.

[11] As Donald Green and his coauthors phrase it, "For more than a half-century, research on tolerance has documented the powerful correlation between education and support for civil liberties. . . . Using a variety of measurement strategies, researchers have consistently found that willingness to extend civil liberties to unpopular target groups increases with formal education" (Green et al. 2011, page 463). See also Galston 2001, Gimpel et al. 2003, Campbell 2006.

Political Knowledge

Truisms still require testing. The weight of the empirical evidence suggests that politically knowledgeable and sophisticated citizens tend to hold more polarized fact perceptions.[12] They are also more resistant to fact-checking.[13] Other studies similarly suggest that knowledge reinforces existing biases.[14] Our data confirm that greater political knowledge tends to accentuate rather than defeat the close connections between values and perceptions.

Our 2014 national survey incorporated a five-question battery of political knowledge. Two questions are standards in similar scales: "Do you happen to know which party currently has the most members in the House of Representatives [the Senate] in Washington?" The next three questions are designed to be more difficult: "What job or political office is held by John Boehner [David Cameron] [John Roberts]?" Following a relatively broad interpretation of accurate answers (counting responses in the ballpark such as "Republican boss," "leader of England," or "Supreme Court judge") yields an evenly dispersed six-point scale of political knowledge from zero to five.[15]

When we add this variable to the analysis of the three core DFPs (regressing perceptions against values, party identity [PID], ideology, demographic variables; as in Table 7.1 but adding political knowledge), it has essentially no effects. The relationship between greater political knowledge (the influence of the full range from 0 to 5 on the knowledge scale) and perceptions of climate change is .01 ($p = .79$). For perceptions of racism it is $-.03$ ($p = .57$) and for sexuality, $-.05$ ($p = .22$). For none of the three DFPs does rising political knowledge have a statistically significant influence on which fact is perceived.

It may be entirely possible, however, that political knowledge is employed by some people to increase the likelihood of one perception and by other people to solidify the *opposite* perception. Greater political knowledge clearly does not lead to consensus, but it may be employed to project

---

[12] See Hofstetter and Barker 1999, Nalder 2010, Joslyn and Haider-Markel 2014, Reedy et al. 2014, Sides 2015, Nyhan and Reifler 2016, Kahan et al. 2017. As Flynn et al. summarize it, "directionally motivated reasoning occurs most often with people who have relatively high levels of political knowledge" (2017, page 136).

[13] See Nyhan et al. 2013, Nyhan and Reifler 2016.

[14] See Gauchat 2015: "Only for scientifically sophisticated respondents, those 1.5 standard units above the mean, is conservative political ideology associated with less favorable views towards science's authority."

[15] Mean = 2.33, alpha = .84; 5 = 22%, 4 = 11%, 3 = 12%, 2 = 12%, 1 = 17%, 0 = 26%.

priors more accurately. When we interact political knowledge with core values, this is exactly what we find. Table 12.1 illustrates the interactive effects of greater knowledge.

The pattern of the interactions is clear: when knowledge is higher, the relationship between values and perceptions tends to be the same or stronger. The one exception is humanism–theism as a predictor of perceptions of climate change. In this case, citizens higher in political knowledge lose the relationship between theism and the denial of climate change. However, for the three other value/DFP combinations with strong relationships in the aggregate, that connection is maintained when political knowledge rises. This is especially the case for perceptions of racism; the relationship between individualism and seeing racism as no longer influential is much stronger among more politically knowledgeable citizens. So do citizens employ political knowledge to seek out legitimate evidence and arrive at consensus facts or to seek out and confirm the fact perceptions aligned with their values? The evidence leans toward the second.

Education

> "Education for freedom must begin by stating facts and enunciating values, and must go on to develop appropriate techniques for realizing the values and for combating those who, for whatever reason, choose to ignore the facts or deny the values."
>
> —*Aldous Huxley*[16]

One could argue that political knowledge could be expected to aid in value projection; after all, specific knowledge of politics may well be gathered while cheerleading for your side. Gaining details that bolster one's predispositions may easily reinforce the tendency to project priors onto perceptions. And even if greater knowledge *were* effective in creating consensus perceptions, we have few levers with which to encourage greater political sophistication among citizens. Political scientists have bemoaned the low levels of civics knowledge in the mass public for several decades, but there is little evidence that the situation has improved.[17] The real target for reform is education. Greater funding for public education and greater access to its resources is a much more realistic proposal than simply

---

[16] *Brave New World Revisited*, page 321.
[17] See Delli Carpini and Keeter 1996, Lupia 2016.

TABLE 12.1 The Interactions of Values and Knowledge (2014)

VALUE PROJECTION AND KNOWLEDGE	CLIMATE CHANGE IS REAL	RACISM IS INFLUENTIAL	SEXUAL ORIENTATION IS INNATE
Collectivism–Individualism			
When knowledge high	–.18 ***	–.30 ***	.06
When knowledge low	–.16 **	–.14 *	.02
Humanism–Theism			
When knowledge high	–.07	–.07	–.26 ***
When knowledge low	–.17 ***	–.07	–.30 ***

Analyses are binary probit regressions. Results are average changes in the probability of perceptions that the DFP is true associated with a full range change in the independent variable. For example, the probability of believing global warming is true associated with moving from strong collectivism to strong individualism when knowledge is high declines on average by 18%. Control variables are not displayed.

Shaded cells represent statistically significant relationships.
$*p < .05, **p < .01, ***p < .001$.

calling for citizens to pay closer attention to politics (for the thousandth time). Moreover, education is a process as well as an end. Greater education instills the skills, practice, and desire to seek out legitimate information and weigh its validity, which could lead to the lessening of DFPs and a rise in consensus fact perceptions.

However, looking back to the analysis in Chapter 7, education—like political knowledge—is not predictive of the facts we believe (see Table 7.1). Levels of education have no statistically significant relationship with perceptions of climate, racism, or sexuality. The same is the case in 2014 as well as 2016 and 2017. Simply put, education alone does not help.

What about the interaction of education and value projection? Does increasing education lessen the propensity to match preferred values to perceived facts? Table 12.2 illustrates the interactions of education and values in the perceptions of facts in the 2014 data (to use the same year as the political knowledge analysis in Table 12.1).

Here, the influence of education is clear—but not the way the reformers would like: citizens employ education to project prior beliefs onto perceptions more accurately. This includes the connection between collectivism–individualism and climate change or racism as well as humanism–theism and climate change or sexual orientation. *All* of the relationships between values and perceptions are stronger among the more

TABLE 12.2 The Interactions of Values and Education (2014)

VALUE PROJECTION AND EDUCATION	CLIMATE CHANGE IS REAL	RACISM IS INFLUENTIAL	SEXUAL ORIENTATION IS INNATE
Collectivism–Individualism			
When education high	**–.18** *	**–.31** **	–.03
When education low	–.15	–.11	.09
Humanism–Theism			
When education high	**–.15** **	–.07	**–.30** ***
When education low	–.12	.01	**–.24** ***

Analyses are binary probit regressions. Results are average changes in the probability of perceptions that the DFP is true associated with a full range change in the independent variable. For example, the probability of believing global warming is true associated with moving from strong collectivism to strong individualism among highly educated citizens declines on average by 18%.

Shaded cells represent statistically significant relationships.
*p < .05, **p < .01, ***p < .001.

educated.[18] The greater skills in gathering and evaluating evidence are employed not to seek out the same legitimate information that would lead to greater consensus but instead to find, accept, and remember confirming information and to reject disconfirming data more effectively than citizens with lesser degrees of education can do.

Figure 12.1 illustrates the distinction between citizens with only a high school diploma or less and those with at least a two-year college degree (the top half of the distribution) as they pertain to the relationship between collectivism–individualism and perceptions of racism. While citizens in the lower half of educational achievement do project their values onto this fact perception to some degree, citizens in the upper half do it much more powerfully.

Our data analyses confirm what other scholars have noted before: political knowledge and education are employed not to seek out more legitimate factual accounts that might lead to consensus perceptions of fact but instead to cement the strong connections between priors and perceptions, in this case core values and perceived facts. The hopeful pathway of education is unlikely to bear fruit, regardless of the best intentions of

---

[18] Haider-Markel and Joslyn 2018 similarly find that higher levels of education are associated with greater employment of stereotypes.

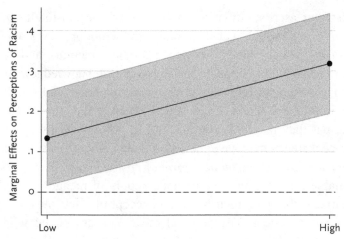

FIGURE 12.1 The Interactions of Collectivism–Individualism and Education in Perceptions of Racism (2014)

NOTE: The figure illustrates the marginal effect of collectivism–individualism (with .95 confidence bands) on fact perceptions at low and high levels of education (high = 2-year degree or more). Effects are for a full movement along the value scale (strong collectivist to strong individualist).

educators and reformers. The remainder of this chapter explores one of the core reasons we think this is that case: *distrust of universities*.

Anti-Elitism and Populism

> "We only know what we're told . . . and for all we know it isn't even true."
>
> —*Rosencrantz & Guildenstern Are Dead, Act II*

Before looking at some provocative data on perceptions of universities, it is important to discuss the context of distrust. A famous perspective on Americans is that they lack regard for intellectualism and especially for intellectuals themselves. Richard Hofstadter's 1962 *Anti-Intellectualism in American Life* is a classic for good reason: it criticizes the disrespect for intellectual elites even as it realizes that popular democracy almost inevitably creates this tendency. Hofstadter's most noted claim is that "respect for intellect and its functions is important to the culture and health of any society, and that in ours this respect has often been notably lacking."[19]

---

[19] Hofstadter 1962, page 20.

Hofstadter ascribes three origins to American anti-intellectualism: *evangelicalism* (which values morals and emotions over intellect), *pragmatism* (which values experience over abstraction), and *political equality* (which values popular opinion over elite knowledge). His view is that the American impulses to disregard expertise and intellectuals (and therefore universities) have always been at the core of American culture, but they may also rise and fall in power over time. We think three recent trends may have increased their influence: *rising data, declining trust*, and *populism as a form of epistemology*. The oversupply of available information plus the undersupply of recognized authority leads citizens throw up their hands and accept the facts most congenial to their value system. The political movement associated with these trends could be described as populism, which has also risen and fallen in American history. Currently it seems to be enjoying an influential rebirth.

Rising Data

"Life is short and information endless"

—*Aldous Huxley*[20]

The overabundance of information may breed ignorance. This counter-intuitive (and possibly counter-Enlightenment) concept was breached in *Dialectic of Enlightenment*, the great post–World War II work on modern epistemology, or why Enlightenment methods of knowledge can lead to misguided and even barbaric outcomes. In Horkheimer and Adorno's view, the Enlightenment both seeks and fears the truth: "the cause of the Enlightenment's relapse into mythology is to be sought not so much in the nationalist, pagan, or other modern mythologies concocted specifically to cause such a relapse as in the fear of truth which petrifies enlightenment itself."[21] In short, Enlightenment knowledge is a psychological burden easily dodged with Enlightenment methods, which allow for selective attention and specious counterargument. Information that is both too much and too untrustworthy leads to the entrenchment of prior beliefs and confidence in personal knowledge: "The flood of precise information makes people smarter and more stupid at once."[22]

---

[20] Preface to *Brave New World Revisited*, page 235.
[21] Horkheimer and Ardono 1947, page xvi.
[22] Ibid., page xvii.

The knowledge explosion of recent times—and greater immediate access to it via the Internet—may have had this effect. The plethora of information, not the paucity of it, is the problem; too much to sort through, with too much contradiction and too little guidance. Jeffrey Friedman in *Power Without Knowledge* argues that the contemporary problem is "inadequate interpretations of too much information. . . . A 'blooming, buzzing confusion' indicates an overabundance of data, not a dearth of them. We need to interpret because we need to screen out most information if any of it is to become coherent. Only after sifting the oversupply of information down to a manageable sample can it be interpreted as indicative of the need for a specific political action."[23] The problem is too much data and too little trust in traditional authorities to sort it out for us.

Declining Trust

The multifaceted decline in trust in recent years spans government, social institutions, religious institutions, corporations, and many other groups. Whether generalized or specific, trust has fallen, including trust in the institutions charged with creating and distributing knowledge. A recent study of disputed facts by Jennifer Kavanagh and Michael Rich of the Rand Corporation concludes that "confidence in major institutions, such as government, newspapers, and television news—organizations that used to be primary sources of factual information—has dropped sharply over the past 20 years."[24]

The institutions that produce and disseminate knowledge are not immune to alterations in trust and may even be especially vulnerable because they end up reporting on their own failures. Some of the prominent academic failures that have hurt the reputation of science and social science in recent years were roundly criticized by academics themselves, including the Wakefield falsified study of vaccines and autism (published in the *Lancet* and later withdrawn, along with Wakefield's license to practice medicine), the Lacour falsified study on attitudes toward gay rights (published in *Science* and later withdrawn), and the Bellesiles falsified study of gun ownership in the colonial era (awarded the Bancroft Prize in history, which was later withdrawn).

---

[23] Friedman 2019, page 86 manuscript.
[24] Kavanagh and Rich 2018, page 33.

Similarly, the high-profile failings within journalism were roundly condemned and made known by journalists: Dan Rather (fired from CBS, as discussed in Chapter 1), Brian Williams (fired from NBC in 2015 for embellishing his experience), Stephen Glass (fired from the *New Republic* in 1998 for fabricating stories), and Jayson Blair (resigned under pressure from *The New York Times* in 2003 after fabricating stories, which the *Times* described as "a low point in the 152-year history of the newspaper").[25] Perhaps the best-known recent example of misreporting is the *Rolling Stone* story on the alleged University of Virginia fraternity rape case, later found to be fraudulent and the result of extraordinary lapses of normal journalistic procedures. A report commissioned by *Rolling Stone* and conducted by the Columbia Graduate School of Journalism concluded that the magazine failed to engage in "basic, even routine journalistic practice" to verify details of the story. Again, this was widely reported in *The New York Times*.[26] The publisher of *Rolling Stone* argued that it represented an isolated episode and that the reporter responsible would continue to write for the magazine, prompting criticism from other media outlets, such as CNN's headline, "No One fired at Rolling Stone. *Really?*" and Politico's tweet, "What would *Rolling Stone* in its heyday write about an institution that screwed up unbelievably, damaged people's lives, but punished no one?"[27]

Gallup data show a distinct decline in media trust over the past decade. Between 1997 and 2003, trust in media was stable (53% in 1997, 54% in 2003). By 2016, the Gallup figure was down to 32%. Aside from the well-reported incidents of academic and media misconduct, the decline in trust may also be related to the perceived politicization of media outlets, with some clearly on the Right and others on the Left, which are not trusted by opposing partisans. As Les Moonves phrased it at a political fundraising event in 2006, "partisanship is very much a part of journalism now."[28]

The Gallup report of 32% of Americans who expressed trust in media in 2016 is really divided between 51% of Democrats and only 14% of Republicans.[29] A similar partisan divide characterizes trust in

---

[25] Barry et al. 2003: "A staff reporter for *The New York Times* committed frequent acts of journalistic fraud while covering significant news events in recent months, an investigation by *Times* journalists has found. The widespread fabrication and plagiarism represent a profound betrayal of trust."
[26] Smaiya 2015. See also Farhi and Shapiro 2015.
[27] Stelter 2015; John Bresnahan, Twitter, April 5, 2015.
[28] Abcarian and Hannessey 2012.
[29] In one of the most recent studies of the demographics of American journalists, Weaver et al. 2018 find that the proportion of journalists who are registered Republicans declined from 25.7% in 1971 (a ratio of 1:1.4 Republican to Democrat) to 18.0% in 2002 (1:2.0) to just 7.1% in 2013 (1:4.0).

academia.[30] Gallup reported in 2017 that while 56% of self-identified Democrats expressed confidence in colleges and universities, only 33% of Republicans did so.[31] Among Republicans who expressed low confidence, the most cited reason was "too liberal/political" (32%), while Democrats on the low confidence side only cited that reason 1% of the time, instead focusing on "too expensive" as the reason for their lack of confidence (36%). Similarly, a 2017 Pew study reported that the proportion of Democrats who say that colleges and universities "have a positive effect on the way things are going in this country" is 72%, slightly up from 65% in 2010.[32] Republicans, on the other hand, have declined in positive perceptions of academia from 58% in 2010 to just 36% in 2017. For the first time in Pew's polling history, a minority of Republicans reported a positive assessment of the influence of universities on American life. This view is as prevalent among Republicans with postgraduate degrees (only 35% positive) as among those with only high school diplomas or less (37%).[33]

The decline of trust in knowledge-creating and knowledge-disseminating institutions has a grave influence on perceptions of facts. In Chapter 1, we discussed the deep importance of trust in the origins of perceptions of reality. Many political realities offer us little personal access— maneuverings in the capital, conditions across the globe, the experiences of others, subtle forces that influence society outside of our observation—so we must trust reports from what we believe to be legitimate sources of knowledge about these unseen but influential facts. In regard to scientific knowledge, we must trust scientists. Russell Hardin writes that "much of even scientific knowledge depends on testimony, rather than on direct investigation."[34] And this is clearly the case for nonscientists, for whom "much of our knowledge has this structure—it depends on reliance on some authority. Only rarely do we genuinely investigate for ourselves."[35] Hardin also points out that this trust in experts is more necessary than foolish: "There

---

[30] And distrust of other institutions as well. For an excellent treatment of how the decline in trust has affected American politics, see Hetherington and Rudolph 2015. See also Motta 2017.

[31] Gallup, August 16, 2017, "Why Are Republicans Down on Higher Ed?" The question format was, "Please tell us how much confidence you, yourself, have in colleges and universities—a great deal, quite a lot, some, or very little?" Democrats: 56% a great deal or quite a lot; Republicans: 33%.

[32] Pew Research Center 2017.

[33] The margin of error for the sample of 2,504 Americans is ±2.3% (for Republicans alone ±3.5%), which puts this level of difference between educational groups within the margin of error of the sample.

[34] Hardin 2009, page 4.

[35] Ibid., page 11.

is a compelling sense in which it is useful to us to rely on the authority of others, because it enables us to make better choices for ourselves than we would if we had to rely only on what truths we had demonstrated in some way entirely to ourselves. It is thus deeply in our interest to rely on others."[36]

Trust in external experts is necessary in regard to knowing many political facts as well. Dan Kahan observes that "citizens aren't in a position to figure out through personal investigation whether the death penalty deters, gun control undermines public safety, commerce threatens the environment, et cetera. They have to take the word of those whom they trust on issues of what sorts of empirical claims, and what sorts of data supporting such claims, are credible. The people they trust, naturally, are the ones who share their values."[37] Those they trust the most for guidance may or may not be scientists: "For many citizens, men and women in white lab coats speak with less authority than (mostly) men and women in black frocks."[38] Farhad Manjoo concludes his book *True Enough* with a word about trust being at the heart of the contemporary dilemma of disputed facts: "you're not just deciding a reality; you're also deciding to trust that reality—which means deciding to distrust the others. . . . Choosing means trusting some people and distrusting others. Choose wisely."[39]

Trust is a precondition of shared facts, which rely on the reports of others and hence trust in their reliability. But trust in academia as a source of knowledge and in media as disseminators of knowledge is dramatically lower than it once was. The gatekeeping function of traditional media has been replaced by a broad array of opposing sources. In that sense, perhaps trust does not really *decline*; instead, it may merely *shift*.

Populism as Epistemology

If universities and news media are not considered trustworthy sources of knowledge, what replaces them? American populism has always been difficult to define with precision, either in the past or in the Trump era.[40]

---

[36] Ibid., page 13.

[37] Kahan and Braman 2006, page 149. "Again (for the umpteenth time), ordinary citizens aren't in a position to determine for themselves whether this or that scientific study of the impact of gun control laws, of the deterrent effect of the death penalty, of the threat posed by global warming, et cetera, is sound" (page 165).

[38] Ibid., page 165.

[39] Manjoo 2008, page 230.

[40] See Oliver and Rahn 2016: "Populism is a promiscuous term used to describe a diverse set of political movements around the world. . . . At its core, populism is a type of political rhetoric that pits a virtuous 'people' against nefarious parasitic elites who seek to undermine the rightful sovereignty

Populist appeals often focus on economic culprits (not just hard times but bad actors), nationalism, and anti-elitism as interwoven strands of rhetoric.[41] Our best definition of the current American populism centers on the epistemology of facts: the view that the beliefs and perceptions of normal citizens are the correct ones. What middle America thinks is good and true is what is really good and true. In economic terms, that puts populists in opposition to both the very poor and the very rich, who are simply not like regular folk.[42] Populism upholds the beliefs of ordinary people rather than extraordinary people. If the perceptions of normal folk are correct, then the views of the hypereducated are surely suspect. Academia and media are the province of advanced degrees, while populists are often holders of high school educations and public university degrees, who tend to see people with leafy residue or PhDs as educated fools, many of whom have never held real jobs. In this sense, populism is about epistemology. Who do you trust?[43] Who is right about factual disputes? The populist answer is always normal folk, not faculty, not career politicians, and certainly not experts.[44]

---

of the common folk . . . for populists, the good is found in the common wisdom of the people rather than the pretensions of the expert" (page 190).

[41] There is also an element of populism that emphasizes the evil or selfish intent of elites to exploit the public, which seems to manifest in support for conspiracy theories (see Hofstadter 1964, Uscinski and Parent 2014). An *Economist*/YouGov national poll (December 17–20, 2016) illustrates the extent of popular belief in conspiracies: "Vaccines have been shown to cause autism": definitely true 8%; probably true 23%; "The U.S. government helped plan the attacks of 9/11": definitely true 7%; probably true 18%; "Russia tampered with vote tallies in order to get Donald Trump elected President": definitely true 11%; probably true 26%; "Millions of illegal votes were cast in the election": definitely true 11%; probably true 35%.

[42] One nineteenth-century president summarized the populism of his era: "If the rabble were lopped off at one end and the aristocrats at the other, all would be well with the country." This was Andrew Johnson, not Andrew Jackson (Trump's ideal president). In regard to Trump's populist appeal, it is important to not be fooled by him being an aristocrat. He identifies against elites, and his supporters accept this. That is not so odd: George W. Bush did not fight in his generation's war (unlike his war-hero father), but people accepted him as a militarist patriot; FDR was an aristocrat (often referred to as a "class traitor" by other aristocrats) but was accepted as an advocate for the poor. To be clear, it is not money that populists dislike (they would like to have it themselves); it is elitism. The television show *Frasier* hit this note perfectly, long before the age of Trump. The title character and his brother Niles were foodies (one of the egregious traits of elites from the perspective of populists). In one episode they discovered fast food, which they had never eaten. It was delicious. But they hated themselves for it. Niles suddenly discovers the answer: "You've embraced the peasant cuisine of Italy and France, why shun the peasants in our own backyard?" It is worth remembering that Trump eats fast food often and publicly.

[43] If the reader is thinking, "That should be *whom* do you trust," the populist answer is probably not you.

[44] Trump stated this very clearly in a *Wall Street Journal* op-ed during the campaign: "On every major issue affecting this country, the people are right and the elites are wrong. The elites are wrong

A recent book inspired by the Trump era clearly announces *The Death of Expertise*. Tom Nichols explains in the preface that "we live in a society that works because of a division of labor, a system designed to relieve each of us from having to know about everything. Pilots fly airplanes, lawyers file lawsuits, doctors prescribe medication."[45] The opening of the book seems to communicate a faith in experts; our national problem is a lack of respect for expertise and those who offer it. The book first places blame on citizens, but then it slowly shifts to the real target: experts themselves. Nichols describes some of the prominent cases of failed expertise, such as the consensus mis-prediction by foreign-policy experts of the collapse of the Soviet Union and the consensus mis-prediction by public opinion and polling scholars of the 2016 election. Experts themselves may have something to answer for in the death of expertise, an aspect of our public conversation that populists are primed to seize upon. The public errors of experts and depletion of the respect given to expertise allow for their replacement by the epistemology of populism: the lionizing of ordinary folk and their perceptions.

In sum, information and trust have gone in opposite directions: information has exploded, while trust in authority has declined. This leaves citizens in a vacuum, into which they project their values. Populism has encouraged this embrace of personal knowledge and disregard of university knowledge. These three contextual factors—in addition to all of the psychological mechanisms discussed in previous chapters—have contributed to the falling trust in universities.

The University as Authority

"First, the university is located in a permanent position of social influence.
Its educational function makes it indispensable and automatically
makes it a crucial institution in the formation of social attitudes. Second,
in an unbelievably complicated world, it is the central institution for
organizing, evaluating, and transmitting knowledge."

—*Port Huron Statement, 1962*

---

on taxes, on the size of government, on trade, on immigration, on foreign policy. Why should we trust the people who have made every wrong decision?" ("Let Me Ask America a Question," April 14, 2016). On the influence of distrust in government and support of Donald Trump (as well as Bernie Sanders), see Dyck et al. 2018.

[45] Nichols 2017, page ix.

"The usual appeal to education can bring only disappointment."

—*Walter Lippmann*[46]

"The University of Google is where I got my degree from."

—*Jenny McCarthy*[47]

As the headnotes suggest, (1) universities have traditionally been seen as the key institution responsible for legitimating knowledge (especially by those on the Left, for example, the Students for a Democratic Society in the 1960s who wrote the Port Huron Statement), (2) others have seen this institution as overrated, and (3) to a growing extent the authority of that institution is being replaced.

Anna Kirkland (one of the foremost scholars of the vaccine controversies) writes that "we cannot learn this lesson too many times: scientific evidence, no matter how clear it seems to be to the people who produce it and vouch for it, does not have magical power to change minds."[48] To paraphrase John Wayne (quoted in Chapter 9), it seems important to ask "Why the hell not?" Chris Mooney—no fan of such resistance to academic expertise—suggests in *The Washington Post* that conservatives are "likely to be aware that the scientific community is a very politically liberal place, overall—far more liberal than the American public. And knowing this, in turn, they're inclined to distrust it."[49] He cites a 2009 Pew survey, which reports that while 20% of the public identified as "liberal," 52% of scientists did so; 37% of the public identified as "conservative," while only 9% of scientists.[50]

In *Asymmetric Politics*, Matt Grossmann and David Hopkins offer a clear summary of the ideological state of our knowledge institutions: "Academia and the news media, two of the social institutions traditionally responsible for creating and spreading information, are both disproportionately populated by liberals and Democrats."[51] They conclude that "Any analysis of conservative suspicions of science and the media should thus begin with the acknowledgement that the right's perception of these professions

---

[46] Lippmann, 1927, page 17.

[47] Oprah Winfrey Show, 2007.

[48] Kirkland 2016, page 196.

[49] March 2, 2015.

[50] http://www.people-press.org/2009/07/09/public-praises-science-scientists-fault-public-media/.

[51] Grossmann and Hopkins 2016, page 133. "Through some combination of conservatives' interest in other careers, active discrimination against conservative scholars, and the self-reinforcing process produced by academia's early reputation for liberalism, universities became disproportionately populated by liberals and have long inspired distrust from the conservative movement" (page 134). See the full discussion in Chapter 4.

as disproportionately occupied by liberals is no illusion." How much that situation influences the scholarly conclusions of the university is a more open question. Grossmann and Hopkins argue that "it is likely that the collective left-leaning orientation of academics influences their intellectual output, even if implicitly and unconsciously."[52]

In *Respecting Truth*, Lee McIntyre offers a similar set of observations: "It is unfortunately true that a good deal of social science today is unreliable, due to its infection by political ideology. Even in universities, in some fields there is no clear line between 'research' and political advocacy," due to the university's "widespread infection with ideology."[53]

Dan Kahan takes a more nuanced view of the likely role of ideology within universities: "Not only do scientists—like everyone else—have cultural identities. They are also highly proficient in the forms of System 2 information processing known to magnify politically motivated reasoning. Logically, then, it might seem to follow that scientists' factual beliefs about contested social risks are likely skewed by the stake they have in conforming information to the positions associated with their cultural groups."[54]

To summarize, university faculty do not hold a balance of liberal and conservative views, and citizens are likely well aware of this, which likely has ramifications for how they perceive university knowledge.

Trust in the University

We commissioned a survey through YouGov in 2014 to examine the nature and correlates of trust in universities.[55] This evidence allows us to quantify the trust that Americans hold in the knowledge produced by universities as well as to explore the potential origins of mistrust. The results suggest a remarkably high degree of distrust, strongly tied to political ideology. Simply put, conservatives do not have confidence in universities, quite possibly because they perceive them to be run disproportionally by liberals.

---

[52] Ibid., page 137 for both quotes.
[53] McIntyre 2015, pages 135, 122.
[54] Kahan 2016, page 17.
[55] The survey was conducted by YouGov in April of 2014, sponsored by the Center for Public Opinion at UMass Lowell. The survey employed the same procedures as the previous studies, employing a national stratified sample of 1,000 respondents. (YouGov interviewed an oversample of respondents [1,172 in April 2014], who were then matched down to a sample of 1,000 to produce the final data set. The respondents were matched to a sampling frame replicating the US population on gender, age, race, education, PID, ideology, and political interest.)

The core question addressed levels of trust:

Professors at American universities often present new evidence relating to important national topics like global warming or the prevalence of racism. When you hear of university research of this nature, how believable do you think it is?
It is almost certainly correct
It is probably correct
It is probably wrong
It is almost certainly wrong

Only 13% believed that the assertions made by university researchers were almost certainly correct. Another 62% believed them to be probably correct. But 21% saw such research as *probably wrong* and 9% *almost certainly wrong*. Nearly as many people see university pronouncements as almost certainly *wrong* (9%) as those who see them as almost certainly *correct* (13%).

Perhaps the more striking story is illustrated in Table 12.3. The difference between self-identified Democrats and Republicans is remarkable. While only 10% of Democrats are distrustful of university knowledge, a full 59% of Republicans see university assertions as likely to be wrong. The same pattern holds true for self-identified liberals and conservatives (only 7% of liberals see university knowledge as likely to be wrong, while 55% of conservatives do). Distrust of universities is essentially a conservative and Republican phenomenon.

A later question asked respondents about their perceptions of the ideological makeup of university faculty:

Consider your impressions of the political ideology of American college professors, whether they tend to be conservatives or liberals. If you had to guess, what percentage of college professors would you say are liberals, are conservatives, or are something else?
_____ % liberals
_____ % conservatives
_____ % something else
(Your answer should total to 100%)

The results displayed in Table 12.4 again show a remarkable partisan split. Americans as a whole see liberal faculty outnumbering conservatives by 2 to 1 (57% to 29%). But Democrats see a smaller advantage to the

TABLE 12.3 Trust in University Knowledge

	ALL RESPONDENTS	DEMOCRATS	REPUBLICANS	LIBERALS	CONSERVATIVES
University knowledge correct	**70%**	**90%**	**41%**	**93%**	**45%**
"Almost Certainly Correct"	13%	19%	4%	24%	6%
"Probably Correct"	57%	71%	37%	69%	39%
University knowledge wrong	**30%**	**10%**	**59%**	**7%**	**55%**
"Probably Wrong"	21%	7%	42%	5%	35%
"Almost Certainly Wrong"	9%	3%	17%	2%	20%

TABLE 12.4 Perceptions of College Faculty (2014)

	ALL RESPONDENTS	DEMOCRATS	REPUBLICANS	BEST AVAILABLE EVIDENCE
Perceived percentage of faculty who are liberal	57%	50%	70%	66%
Perceived percentage of faculty who are conservative	29%	35%	21%	16%
Average ratio of liberal to conservative faculty	2.0 to 1	1.4 to 1	3.3 to 1	4.8 to 1

liberal side (50% liberal to 35% conservative, or a ratio of 1.4 to 1). Republicans, on the other hand, perceive faculty to be about 70% liberal to only 21% conservative, or a dominance of 3.3 to 1.

We can compare these public perceptions to the best available evidence from scholarly studies of university faculty. Three recent studies—grounded in national surveys of university faculty conducted in 1999, 2006, and 2011—provide estimates of the ratio of liberal to conservative professors: 4.8 to 1, 4.9 to 1, and 4.8 to 1.[56] Taking these results as the best available evidence of the actual situation, the perceptions reported in the recent surveys suggest that Americans as a whole *underestimate* the degree of liberal political leanings among university faculty. While it may not be surprising that Democrats underestimate the preponderance of liberal faculty, the more surprising result is that *even Republicans* underestimate the true situation, perceiving conservative faculty to be more common than they truly are.

So is there a connection between distrust of the university and perceptions of its ideological balance? To test this proposition in the most straightforward way, we can examine the relationships among these

---

[56] These figures are grounded in three recent studies of academic ideology: Rothman et al. 2005, Hurtado et al. 2011, and Gross and Simmons 2014, averaging the results of these three studies. Rothman et al. (employing 1999 data) report 72% liberal and 15% conservative faculty (4.8:1), Hurtado et al. (employing 2011 data) report 63% liberal and 13% conservative (4.8:1), and Gross and Simmons (grounded in a 2006 survey) find 44% liberal and 9% conservative (4.9:1). The three studies converge on the same result, a ratio of around 4.8:1. Gross and Simmons find a larger differential among social science faculty (58% to 5%, or 11.6:1).

TABLE 12.5 Correlates of Distrust in University Knowledge

PID (GOP high)	**.36** ***
Perceived ratio: liberal to conservative faculty (liberal high)	**.29** ***
Age[a]	**.13** ***
Gender (male)	**.09** ***
Religiosity[b]	**.14** ***
Income	**−.15** *
Education	**−.13** **
Political knowledge[c]	.03
N	901

Binary probit regression. Results are percentage-point changes in the probability of perceptions that university knowledge is wrong, associated with a full range change in the independent variable. For example, the probability of believing university knowledge is wrong increases on average 36 percentage points moving from strong Democrat to strong Republican. Shaded cells represent statistically significant relationships.
$*p < .05, **p < .01, ***p < .001$.
[a]19–95, mean = 48; grouped into six categories: 1 = <30, 2 = 30–39, 3 = 40–49, 4 = 50–59, 5 = 60–69, 6 = 70+; recoded 0–1). Older people are more likely to believe the university is wrong.
[b]Pew *religious importance* (4-point scale: not at all important, not too important, somewhat important, very important; recoded to 0–1); other ways of conceptualizing religiosity (church attendance, frequency of prayer) have lesser effects.
[c]Same six-point knowledge scale as in the previous analysis; 5 = 19%, 4 = 17%, 3 = 16%, 2 = 15%, 1 = 17%, 0 = 16%.

variables, controlling for other possible influences. Table 12.5 illustrates a regression analyses of distrust in the university as the dependent variable.

The most powerful independent variable is PID: strong Republicans are 36% more likely than strong Democrats to perceive university knowledge to be wrong. The second most powerful influence is the perceived ideology of faculty. The perceptions of the ratio of liberal to conservative professors were broken down into five categories:

1) <1 (more conservative than liberal) 15%
2) 1.0 (even balance) 20%
3) >1.0–2.0 (small liberal advantage) 21%
4) >2.0–6.0 (strong liberal advantage) 24%
5) >6.0 (very strong liberal advantage) 21%

Category 4 is the most empirically accurate perception according to the academic studies. So about 24% of the public had it right, while 21% overestimated and 56% underestimated. Citizens in the highest category were 29% more likely to perceive university knowledge to be wrong than

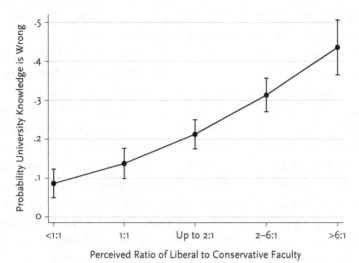

FIGURE 12.2 Perceived Ideology and Trust in University Knowledge

NOTE: Bars represent 95% confidence intervals.

those in the lowest group (those who perceived a *conservative* advantage among faculty).

Figure 12.2 provides a more detailed look at the influence of perceptions of faculty ideology. The 24% of the sample who perceived the ratio of Democratic to Republican professors to be between 2.0 and 6.0 (the most accurate category) were 18% more likely to distrust academic knowledge claims than those who perceived the ratio to be even (1:1) and 23% more likely than the 15% of the sample who perceived the balance of faculty to favor conservatives.

Some demographic variables also have an influence on trust in universities: older people and men are *more* likely to register distrust. Religiosity also has a strong influence: those who say that religion is very important in their lives are 14% more likely to express distrust than those who say religion is not at all important. But the effects of religiosity never rise near the level of partisanship or the perceived ideology of faculty, suggesting that religiosity seems to be a secondary explanation to the larger ideological factors. Education itself does have a positive effect on the perceived accuracy of university knowledge but not nearly as strong an effect as perceptions of academic ideology.

An analysis of this sort, with these types of survey data, cannot demonstrate conclusively what is causing what. We can't be sure that distrust in the university is driven by perceptions of its faculty. Partisanship and ideology (or underlying core values) may have a strong influence through other pathways. What is clear is that *partisan identity, perceptions of the ideology of faculty, and distrust of university knowledge are all strongly interconnected*. A likely causal connection that explains the attitude of Republicans and conservatives toward universities is how they see the ideology of faculty. If universities are populated by opposing partisans and controlled by the opposing ideology, why would conservatives trust the knowledge they assert, any more than liberals or Democrats would trust assertions of an institution run by conservatives? Scholars often argue that their ideology does not affect their conclusions—that their training and methods overcome any ideological bias—but fewer and fewer Americans are likely to believe this interpretation of scholarly purity in our current era of political polarization. Distrust of partisan motives and of the opposing ideology seems to be the tenor of the times, and it should be no surprise that this extends to perceptions of universities.

In this sense it may be important to distinguish between *distrust of science as a method of knowledge generation* and *distrust of the university as a group of people practicing it*. Conservatives could distrust both scientists *and* science or trust science but distrust scientists (especially social scientists). In a study of public trust in science over the past four decades, Gordon Gauchat argues that "the credibility of scientific knowledge is tied to cultural perceptions about its political neutrality and objectivity" and demonstrates a clear relationship between political conservatism and lack of trust in scientists.[57] But he does not distinguish between these two possible sources of distrust—the methods and the practitioners, science and scientists—concluding that "this study points to a growing political polarization of science, even though the source of this polarization remains empirically underdetermined."[58] Chris Mooney argues that the source of conservative distrust is clearly rejection of science as a method.[59] Our analyses suggest the opposite: that the rejection of the practitioners as opposed to the practice plays a large role. The perceived ideology of the university contributes to its rejection.

---

[57] Gauchat 2012, page 168. This study is grounded in General Social Survey data from 1974 to 2010. The key question of the analysis focuses on trust in people (scientists) rather than trust in the method (science): "I am going to name some institutions in this country. As far as the people running these institutions are concerned, would you say you have a great deal of confidence, only some confidence, or hardly any confidence at all in them [the Scientific Community]?" 1974–2010 aggregate responses: "a great deal" 40.8%, "only some" 46.2%, "hardly any" 6.6%, "don't know" or refused 6.5%. Republicans and Independents, as well as conservatives and moderates, show a decline in confidence compared to Democrats and liberals from the 1970s to 2010.
[58] Ibid., page 184.
[59] Mooney 2005, 2012.

A final ironic note can be found in the survey evidence: because Republicans actually *underestimate* the degree to which liberal professors outnumber conservative ones, their rejection of university knowledge might be *even greater if citizens accurately perceived the true degree of ideological imbalance on campus.*

The Realignment of Authority: Trust, Knowledge, and Democracy

"We are in the midst of a civilization-warping crisis of public trust."

—*Senator Ben Sasse (R Nebraska), March 4, 2017, Twitter*

"Trust me, I'm a doctor"

—*Slogan for Dr. Pepper*

"I'm not a doctor, but I play one on TV."

—*Vicks cough syrup commercial, circa 1984*

This chapter addressed a potential corrective to DFPs: greater political knowledge and formal education. However, the empirical evidence suggests that this possible corrective is not effective; greater knowledge and education are employed to cement the connection from values to perceptions rather than to move citizens toward consensus perceptions of facts. This represents the contemporary paradox of knowledge and democracy. The simple proposition that education or knowledge improves Democracy is problematic. Sophistication is brought to bear not in order to update perceptions but instead to apply priors to perceptions more effectively.

But why have the relationships among knowledge, education, and democracy soured? We have argued earlier that the core cause is the psychological strength of value projection. In this chapter, we added that the two traditional sources of consensus facts—universities as the source of knowledge and media as the disseminators of knowledge—have lost credibility and trust. The loss of trust in universities is a phenomenon of the Right: liberals continue to trust university knowledge, but conservatives no longer do. Our analyses suggest that distrust not only comes from the Right but targets the institutions controlled by the Left. As we demonstrated above, this seems to be driven by the Left-shift of university faculty or, more accurately, the recognition of that shift. The dominance of liberal faculty is a real phenomenon—even more so than most conservatives realize, according to our data—which suggests that the conservative distrust of academia is a long-term problem. When the other side runs the evidence factory, it is unlikely you will trust the evidence.

The fracturing of consensus authority is one source of the fracturing of facts. The rejection by some groups of citizens of both media and academia as sources of knowledge can be described as a *realignment of authority*. Unlike previous realignments of partisanship or issue positions, the realignment of authority is grounded in shifting trust in previous consensus institutions of knowledge creation and dissemination. Knowledge and democracy can be intimately connected but only through trust; without trust in the equation, democracy is unmoored from the positive influence of education and from the authority of consensus facts.

13 | Let Facts Be Submitted to a Candid World

FACT-CHECKING AS A POTENTIAL SOLUTION

"The history of the present King of Great Britain is a history of repeated injuries and usurpations, all having in direct object the establishment of an absolute Tyranny over these States. To prove this, let Facts be submitted to a candid world."

—*Declaration of Independence, 1776*

AFTER ITS SOARING WORDS ON the nature and origins of rights, the Declaration of Independence moves to an empirical argument about the justifications for the break with England. Jefferson does not hold the "history of repeated injuries and usurpations" to be self-evident; instead, he insists that "to prove this, *let facts be submitted to a candid world.*" This statement assumes that (a) what the document is reporting are facts and (b) a legitimate listener ("a candid world") will accept them. What if the declaration's assertions were fact-checked? Several of the "facts" submitted do sound a bit dodgy. In addition to the better-known discussion of taxation without representation, there are these charges against King George:

He has abdicated Government here, by declaring us out of his Protection and waging War against us.

He has plundered our seas, ravaged our Coasts, burnt our towns, and destroyed the lives of our people.

He is at this time transporting large Armies of foreign Mercenaries to compleat the works of death, desolation and tyranny, already begun with circumstances of Cruelty & perfidy scarcely paralleled in the most barbarous ages, and totally unworthy of the Head of a civilized nation.

A fact checker might note that the violence committed by the British Crown was not even close to the violence (or cruelty and perfidy) committed in earlier "barbarous" ages (see Steven Pinker's book on the remarkable decline of violence in the modern world).[1] Moreover, the charge of burning towns and destroying the lives of Americans is clearly exaggerated. Would such corrections have been accepted? Are corrections accepted now in our current politics?

Fact-checking is often suggested as a potential corrective for dueling facts. In *Do Facts Matter?* Jennifer Hochschild and Katherine Einstein write that fact-checking may be one way to improve the public's understanding of politicized realities. They describe FactCheck.org in particular as "sober and informative, focused on correctly depicting states of affairs." But they also sound a note of caution about the reliability of the industry: "who will fact-check the fact-checkers? . . . It is easy to see how even a citizen who is seeking knowledge could get caught in a reverberating hall of mirrors."[2] So is fact-checking clearly useful or inherently flawed as an aid to discerning reality?

In this and the following chapter, we examine the nature and influence of fact-checking as a possible solution. This chapter focuses on the method and process of fact-checking—its underlying epistemology—in which there are clear flaws that limit its legitimacy and persuasion. Chapter 14 discusses a direct test of citizens' reactions to fact-checks that dispute their inclinations. In both philosophical foundation and practical application, these studies suggest that fact-checking will not be a successful corrective to dueling facts. We conclude that unfortunately (and regardless of the great effort and resources currently being put into the industry) fact-checking is not likely to be effective.

The Efficacy of Fact-Checking

> "It might, however, be a good thing if there were competent tribunals, preferably not official ones, where charges of untruthfulness and unfairness in the general news could be sifted."
>
> —*Walter Lippmann*[3]

---

[1] Pinker 2011.
[2] Hochschild and Einstein 2015, pages 158, 159.
[3] Lippmann 1922, page 209.

Lippmann once suggested that something akin to contemporary fact-checking institutions should be developed, but he also suspected that such institutions would not be effective. Fact checkers are fighting against two dominant problems in how normal citizens react to their reporting: (1) the multifaceted psychological mechanisms of resistance to opposing information (which are especially strong among more educated and politically knowledgeable citizens) and (2) the perception that fact checkers are ideological partisans who do not provide legitimate information (which is also especially strong among more educated and politically knowledgeable citizens). A Rasmussen poll from September 2016 illustrates the problem of trust: "Do you trust media fact-checking of candidates' comments, or do you think news organizations skew the facts to help candidates they support?" Only 29% expressed trust in fact-checking.[4]

Regardless of these difficulties, professional fact checkers seem to hold a deep belief that positive effects will appear.[5] Political science, communication, and especially journalism faculty have also given a great deal of support and encouragement to the fact-checking enterprise. Perhaps the strongest advocate is Kathleen Hall Jamieson of the Annenberg School at the University of Pennsylvania and cofounder of FactCheck.org along with Brooks Jackson. Her essay "Implications of the Demise of 'Fact' in Political Discourse" was awarded the 2016 Henry Allen Moe Prize from the American Philosophical Society. She argues that the "erosion of the credibility of knowledge-certifying institutions" has degraded their ability "to anchor presuppositions and arbitrate competing claims."[6] This problem has been created by "the undermining tactic alleging that the knowledge-certifying institutions have been corrupted by peer pressure, ideological bias, and self-interest," allowing political actors to "question the impartiality of fact-checking institutions."[7] Disagreements with these institutions

---

[4] http://www.rasmussenreports.com/public_content/politics/general_politics/september_2016/voters_donot_trust_media_fact_checking.

[5] Brooks Jackson in 2011: "I think that it's good what we do, I'm glad to see there's more of it. I take it on faith that doing more of it will have a positive effect on democracy. I would love some evidence that it's true. If you have any that it's not, I'm not going to pay any attention to it" (quoted in Graves 2016, p. 182).

[6] Jamieson 2015, pages 72, 73.

[7] Ibid., pages 71, 72.

constitute "conjurers' wiles," "palatable deceptions," and "attacks on knowledge-certifying institutions."[8]

Journalism researchers such as Michelle Amazeen and Lucas Graves also argue in favor of the legitimacy and positive influence of the fact-checking enterprise.[9] Graves' 2016 book on the industry (*Deciding What's True*) is a full-throated endorsement of the procedures of fact-checking.[10] In the popular press, fact-checking seems to enjoy the same assumptions of efficacy. For example, Michael Shermer—prolific science author, perhaps most known for *Why People Believe Weird Things* (1997) and *The Believing Brain* (2011)—extolled the virtues of "today's fact-checking ethic" in his column for *Scientific American* in 2018: "even as pundits pronounced the end of veracity and politicians played loose with the truth, the competitive marketplace of ideas stepped up with a new tool of the Internet age: real-time fact-checking."[11]

Recent empirical studies have demonstrated that fact-checking may indeed have important political influences, such as moderating whether citizens believe claims made in negative advertising and encouraging politicians to refrain from making unsubstantiated claims.[12] Other recent studies also suggest that fact-checking the statements made during a campaign can influence how voters perceive the truthfulness of competing politicians, though this doesn't tend to alter their vote choices.[13]

However, several strands of research have suggested that fact-checking faces meaningful limitations on its influence over citizens' perceptions of facts. The majority of studies indicate that citizens seem to resist fact-checking messages that oppose their factual beliefs, especially if the appeals clash with their ideological or partisan leanings.[14] Perhaps more

---

[8] Ibid., pages 66, 69.

[9] Amazeen 2013, 2015, 2016, Graves 2013a, 2013b, 2016, 2017.

[10] "It may be worth saying outright that I am sympathetic to the broad fact-checking project" (Graves 2016, page 20), though he also admits that "the most serious and sustained critique of this brand of journalism is that it discounts the value-laden nature of political discourse by trying to offer decisive factual conclusions about subjective questions of opinion or ideology" (2017, page 519).

[11] Shermer 2018.

[12] Fridkin et al. 2015, Nyhan and Reifler 2015a and 2015b.

[13] See Nyhan and Reifler 2016, Nyhan et al. 2017, Wintersieck 2017.

[14] For a meta-analysis and summary, see Chan et al. 2017; see also Garrett et al. 2013, Jarman 2016a 2016b, Lewandowsky et al. 2017, Nieminen and Rapeli 2019, Young et al. 2017. "This body of research has converged on the conclusion that corrections are rarely fully effective: that is, despite being corrected, and despite acknowledging the correction, people by and large continue to rely at least partially on information they know to be false" (Lewandowsky et al. 2017, page 354).

interesting are the findings that attempts at correction may induce *greater* confidence (the backfire effect) and that even apparent corrections may mask the persistence of prior beliefs, what Emily Thorson refers to as "belief echoes."[15]

In one of the most critical assessments of the fact-checking enterprise, Joseph Uscinski describes several core flaws, including unclear selection criteria of facts to be checked (when is a claim suspicious enough to warrant a rating?), inconsistent aggregation or disaggregation of factual claims (does one false part of a broader statement make the statement false or mostly true?), and the treatment of unverifiable claims (such as complex causal mechanisms or especially future predictions) as verifiable facts to be checked.[16]

Uscinski and Ryden Butler describe the main problem with "the naïve political epistemology at work in the fact-checking branch of journalism" as "the tacit presupposition that there cannot be genuine political debate about facts." They suggest two possibilities: (a) "one can compare statements about politics, policy, society, economics, history, and so on—the subject matter of political debate—to 'the facts' so as to determine whether a statement about these topics is a lie" or (b) "the subject matter of politics is often complex, ambiguous, and open to a variety of conflicting interpretations, even when empirical claims are being made." They side with option (b) on the grounds that "the methods of social science are not firmly enough grounded in objective reality to make a consensus of experts a reliable barometer of truth."[17] Uscinski's point is not merely that citizens resist fact-checking for *bad* reasons but that they may do so for *good* reasons as well.

---

[15] Nyhan and Reifler 2010, Thorson 2016. But see Guess and Coppock 2017.

[16] As James Kuklinski points out, "The factual evidence that would be most helpful to citizens when they are evaluating policy options—the future consequences of each option—does not exist. . . . There is one common and important situation where knowing 'the facts' is impossible: when policy makers are debating policy options and making predictions about the consequences of each option" (2007, pages 2, 3).

[17] Uscinski and Butler 2013, pages 162, 165, 172; see also Uscinski 2015. RealClearPolitics instituted a new feature called Fact Check Review in April 2018, devoted to "checking the fact checkers." One of their goals is to "evaluate each claim to determine whether it is a statement of fact that can be definitively proven true or false, as opposed to rhetorical hyperbole or outright opinion that falls outside the true purview of fact-checking" (Leetaru 2018). As of June 2018, RealClearPolitics rates the major fact checkers as checking opinions rather than facts 12% of the time at FactCheck.org, 15% at PolitiFact, and 25% of the time at *The Washington Post*.

The Rise of Institutional Fact-Checking

The fact-check industry came to prominence within a brief period of time between the invasion of Iraq and the election of Barack Obama. Although fact-checking as an aspect of journalism is not entirely new—and has long been a basic element of all legitimate reporting—the new enterprises focus on this subset of journalistic practice. The first major online fact-checking institution was FactCheck.org, launched in December of 2003 by Kathleen Hall Jamieson and journalist Brooks Jackson, sponsored by the Annenberg Public Policy Center at the University of Pennsylvania. According to Jackson and Jamieson in their book *unSpun: Finding Facts in a World of Disinformation*, the site was "designed to be a consumer advocate for voters."[18] Four years later, in 2007, the two other major sites were founded: PolitiFact at the *St. Petersburg Times* (which became the *Tampa Bay Times* in 2012) under the direction of Bill Adair (their Washington, DC bureau chief, now a professor of journalism at Duke) and The Fact Checker at the *Washington Post* by Michael Dobbs (taken over by Glenn Kessler four years later in 2011).

Dobbs ties the emergence of the industry to Ronald Reagan's "startling assertions that turned out to be completely erroneous."[19] Reagan's election year of 1980 was also the year CNN began airing as the first twenty-four-hour news station. FOX News was founded sixteen years later in 1996, beginning the era of openly partisan television news. (MSNBC began operation the same year but was not clearly partisan until some time later, slowly shifting to the progressive side with the arrival of Chris Matthews in 1999, Keith Olbermann in 2005, and Rachel Maddow in 2008.) Dobbs argues that the final impetus for fact-checking as an independent aspect of journalism was the lack of media investigation—from either side of the partisan divide—into the Bush administration claims for the justifications of the Iraq War:

> In suggesting a "Fact Checker" feature to the editors of *The Washington Post* in the summer of 2007, I was motivated in large part by a sense that Washington reporting has strayed from the truth-seeking tradition. . . . The problem was particularly acute in coverage of the run-up to the war in Iraq in 2002–2003 . . . when *The Post* and other leading newspapers failed to seriously challenge the White House line on weapons of mass destruction.[20]

---

[18] Jackson and Jamieson 2007, ix.
[19] Dobbs 2012, p. 4
[20] Ibid., page 3.

After the ideological polarization of American politics, after the rise of partisan television news, after the election of George W. Bush and the invasion of Iraq, the fact-check industry arose rapidly between 2003 and 2007.

According to a 2015 study, the three major fact checkers accounted for over three-quarters of the fact-checks published between 2003 and 2012.[21] While they share core similarities as part of the same movement within journalism, the three fact checkers also display important differences. FactCheck.org has academic as well as journalistic roots, while PolitiFact and The Fact Checker are firmly within professional journalism. In terms of the format of reporting, FactCheck.org insists on providing long-form narratives, while PolitiFact and The Fact Checker provide ratings of factual statements along scales they have devised.[22] Both also print assessments of statements that are true as well as false, while FactCheck.org only reports on false statements. (See Table 13.1) These institutional differences may or may not influence their reliability or persuasiveness, though it suggests the need for a closer look at the collective epistemology of fact-checking.

The Epistemology of Fact-Checking

In 2014, Glenn Kessler (*The Washington Post's* Fact Checker) confidently asserted in *Foreign Affairs* that "Political fact-checking has thus become an essential component of independent journalism in a democratic society. It teaches both politicians and voters that there is something called ground truth—facts that are not in dispute and can create a base level of knowledge for evaluating statements made by government officials and opposition figures."[23] Kessler's optimism matches Brooks Jackson's in the earlier quote; both leaders of the fact-checking movement are sure that the new institutions are working, regardless of the lack of evidence that the fact checkers' attempt to provide consensus fact perceptions—"ground truth"—is accepted by the public. There is considerable evidence that ordinary citizens do *not* trust fact checkers. Perhaps a better first question is whether it is clear that citizens *should* trust fact checkers.

---

[21] Wintersieck and Fridkin 2015.

[22] "Rating statements with devices such as 'truth-o-meters' or 'Pinocchios' are popular with readers, and successful attention-grabbers. But such ratings are by their nature subjective—the difference between one or two 'Pinocchios' is a matter of personal judgment, and debatable. Some statements are clearly true, and some provably false, but there's no agreed method for determining the precise degree of mendacity in any statement that falls somewhere in between" (Brooks Jackson, FactCheck.org, December 21, 2012).

[23] Kessler 2014.

TABLE 13.1 Fact-Checking Institutional Differences

	FACTCHECK.ORG	POLITIFACT	THE FACT CHECKER
Professional origin	Academic/journalistic	Journalistic	Journalistic
Format	Narrative only	Scale + narrative	Scale + narrative
True/false balance	False only	False and true	False and true

Addressing this question requires a focus on two foundational concerns of epistemology: *how do fact checkers determine their questions?* and *how do they determine their answers?* Amazeen identifies these same two epistemological questions in a paper for the New America Foundation: "deciding which claims to check and which evidence to consider are two difficult areas to negotiate."[24] The importance of the first question has to do with selection bias. Because fact checkers represent themselves as neutral arbiters of truth versus fiction in the service of accurate citizen engagement in politics, what they choose to examine for truth and falsity is no small matter for their perceived legitimacy.

So how do the fact checkers pick the specific factual assertions that they examine? Each of the fact checkers offers a summary of its practice on its website. The least informative is the one provided by FactCheck.org: "We monitor the factual accuracy of what is said by major U.S. political players in the form of TV ads, debates, speeches, interviews and news releases. Our goal is to apply the best practices of both journalism and scholarship, and to increase public knowledge and understanding." This description provides little information about their processes of selection or assessment.

The Fact Checker has a somewhat more extensive discussion:

The purpose of this Web site, and an accompanying column in the Sunday print edition of *The Washington Post*, is to "truth squad" the statements of political figures *regarding issues of great importance*, be they national, international or local. As a presidential election approaches, we will increasingly focus on statements made in the heat of the presidential contest. But we will not be limited to political charges or countercharges. *We will seek to explain difficult issues*, provide missing context and provide analysis and explanation of various "code words" used by politicians, diplomats and others to obscure or shade the truth. (Italics added)

---

[24] Amazeen 2013, page 2.

This is followed by a section entitled "A Few Basic Principles" (italics added):

- This is a fact-checking operation, not an opinion-checking operation. We are interested only in verifiable facts, though on occasion we may examine the roots of political rhetoric.
- *We will focus our attention and resources on the issues that are most important to voters.* We cannot nitpick every detail of every speech.
- We will stick to the facts of the issue under examination and are unmoved by ad hominem attacks. The identity or political ties of the person or organization making a charge is irrelevant: all that matters is whether their facts are accurate or inaccurate.
- *We will adopt a "reasonable man" standard for reaching conclusions.* We do not demand 100 percent proof.
- We will strive to be dispassionate and non-partisan, drawing attention to inaccurate statements on both left and right.

The two italicized sentences are The Fact Checker's statements of the core epistemological concerns of selection and assessment. In regard to selection, he focuses on what he perceives to be most important to voters. This is a highly subjective standard, but Kessler argues that he indeed allows readers to guide the selection of many topics: "I would say about 30 to 40 percent of the fact checks are reader generated. . . . Reader input is very important because there is no way I can possibly hear or see everything. It also lets me know what is on people's minds."[25]

The most extensive and detailed discussion of method is the one by Bill Adair entitled "The Principles of PolitiFact" (November 1, 2013 edition). The first subsection of the document is "Choosing claims to check":

Because we can't possibly check all claims, we select the most newsworthy and significant ones. In deciding which statement to check, we ask ourselves these questions:
- Is the statement rooted in a fact that is verifiable? We don't check opinions, and we recognize that in the world of speechmaking and political rhetoric, there is license for hyperbole.
- Is the statement leaving a particular impression that may be misleading?

---

[25] Email correspondence with Kessler, March 7, 2014.

- Is the statement significant? We avoid minor "gotchas" on claims that obviously represent a slip of the tongue.
- Is the statement likely to be passed on and repeated by others?
- Would a typical person hear or read the statement and wonder: Is that true?

This builds upon Kessler's focus on importance (is the statement significant? will it likely be repeated?) and adds a concern with whether the statement sounds fishy. Adair clarified this last concern in a post on May 29, 2013: "We select statements to fact-check based on our news judgment—whether a statement is timely, provocative, whether it's been repeated and whether readers would wonder if it is true." Kessler also endorses this approach: "Obviously I will pursue it if it looks suspect."[26]

Grounded in his participant observation of the fact-checking process at PolitiFact and FactCheck.org, Graves claims that selection is based on "news sense," which reduces to the expert judgment acquired by years working in journalism.[27] Bill Adair phrases it, "We are journalists, not social scientists. We select statements to fact-check based on our news judgment."[28] However, it is important to remember, as Adair pointed out, that he, Jackson, and Kessler are experienced journalists rather than social scientists. Their assessment of what is important and questionable may or may not be shared among themselves, with the public, or with scholars of politics.

Another aspect of claim selection is a focus on falsity, reflected in the scales employed by two of the major fact checkers: *the more false, the higher the rating*.[29] The Fact Checker opts for a well-known cultural trope for dishonesty (Pinocchio). The more false the statement, the more Pinocchios it is awarded, up to four (for "Whoppers"). The gold standard is a Geppetto Checkmark, named for the truthful woodcarver who created the deceitful puppet. PolitiFact prefers its creation of a Truth-O-Meter, a scientific-looking box with a needle that runs from "True" to "False." A statement so false as to make "a ridiculous claim" sets the box aflame with a "Pants on Fire" rating, another cultural trope referring to the popular children's taunt.

---

[26] Email correspondence March 2014.

[27] Graves 2016, chapter 3.

[28] Ibid., page 88.

[29] Graves also endorses the fact checkers' claims that they pursue stories that sound suspicious: "The focus on falsehood colors the selection process from the beginning. 'We look for things that don't sound right,' Brooks Jackson has explained" (Ibid., page 93).

FactCheck.org is even more focused on false reports, to the exclusion of any mention of accuracy. It differs from the other two major fact checkers in *only reporting falsehoods*. Graves explains the FactCheck.org rationale: "If a reporter knows or if research shows that a budget statistic is accurate, for instance, the work stops there. . . . More than once I heard this explained as a matter of resources—to write up an analysis of truthful claims would leave less time to debunk the false ones."[30]

The focus on falsity is the opposite of social science approaches to knowledge grounded in statistical inference. It is quite different to assume falsehood and report when truth is found than to assume truth and report when falsehood is found. Statistical methods take the first approach: they assume that the world is full of lies (randomness, spurious relationships) and look for the exceptions of truths (nonrandom patterns, from which we can draw inferences). If we accept the epistemological basis of falsification, then even those contingent truths are quite possibly lies, and we should discard them willingly if new evidence demands it.[31] Pointing out lies is shooting fish in a data barrel, while identifying possible truths is the hard part. If the mainstream political science approach to method is accurate (randomness and lies are common, while real patterns and truth are rare), the implication is that fact checkers have a broad range of possible lies to identify, from which they pick only a small subset to examine. The fact checkers must by necessity reduce all of the many lies to a small number on which to focus each week (and for PolitiFact, one special "lie of the year" chosen from the many possible candidates for such a distinction). Under these conditions, fact checkers are likely to demonstrate meaningful selection bias in the realities they choose to assess.

When we turn from *selection* to *assessment*, the more difficult problems of epistemology and method appear. In regard to how they determine the truth or falsity of a statement, Kessler (The Fact Checker) maintains that he will "adopt a 'reasonable man' standard for reaching conclusions." When asked in correspondence if he employs "a standard path or a methodology to determine facts" he responded, "No. I keep reporting till I get the answer. Sometimes it takes days, sometimes it is very quick." Adair at PolitiFact identifies their "Process for Truth-O-Meter Rulings": "A writer researches the claim and writes the Truth-O-Meter article with a recommended ruling. After the article is edited, it is reviewed by a panel

---

[30] Ibid., page 93.
[31] See Popper 1935.

of at least three editors that determines the Truth-O-Meter ruling."[32] None of the three fact checkers identify any specific means of assessing or weighing the evidence with which they evaluate a claim under investigation, instead relying on journalistic judgment. The only clear standard is PolitiFact's process of employing a panel of editors to determine the final score on the Truth-O-Meter. But this procedure still relies on subjective expertise rather than intersubjective method. To the extent that PolitiFact imposes a higher standard than the other fact checkers, the standard is "our judgment" rather than "my judgment."

In the broader sense, perhaps a key difference in how journalism faculty interpret fact-checking and how we as political science faculty interpret the institution lies in the willingness to accept journalists' assertions of their own professional aspirations toward truth-finding to the exclusion of other motives. As political science scholars, it seems odd to take at face value the assertions of institutional actors who hold their own incentives for power and prestige. One perspective assumes that journalists hold professional training and ethics that insulate them from other human motives. Another perspective is open to the possibility that fact-checking affords the fact checkers the power to be right, to act as judges, to tell politicians they are wrong. Assertions of institutional authority can be partly about power, like many other political phenomena.

The Question of Ideological Bias

There is no dispute that the fact checkers award a higher percentage of false ratings to Republicans.[33] This can be interpreted in two ways: Republicans lie more or fact checkers are biased in a liberal direction, choosing to evaluate conservatives more often and rating them negatively more often. Empirically, those two things cannot be differentiated easily. So for ordinary citizens as well as scholars it comes down to trust: do we trust the journalistic professionals to make legitimate analyses or distrust their ability to make unbiased evaluations? This problem regarding perceptions of fact-checking mirrors the larger problem regarding dueling facts: normal

---

[32] See Graves 2016 for a more in-depth description of the process of the editorial panel, described among PolitiFact workers as the "star chamber" (pages 150-154). The book emphasizes the consensus that is achieved: "Most star chamber sessions last just ten or fifteen minutes and involve little controversy; of the more than twenty-five I observed, only a handful proved at all contentious. . . . In roughly 90 percent of cases, the writer's original ruling survives the process, I heard" (pages 150, 153).

[33] See Ostermeier 2011, Farnsworth and Lichter 2016.

citizens are faced with contradictory presentations, without the ability to sort them out accurately, so they default to the authorities they trust or simply maintain their own prior beliefs.

In the conclusion of *Deciding What's True*, Graves addresses the contradiction openly: "Two possible explanations exist for statistics inclined so dramatically against one party. One interpretation . . . was that PolitiFact must be biased in choosing claims to check. . . . The other explanation, of course, was that the results revealed an *actual* bias in political behavior."[34] Graves disagrees that there is an impasse; the evidence produced by fact checkers demonstrates that Republicans lie more: "It is impossible not to notice that the signal cases, mentioned over and over in articles and at conferences about fact-checking, come mainly from the Republican side."[35]

A core contradiction of fact-checking—being in the political arena but claiming to be out—is clear in the fact checkers' disingenuous statements about this debate. PolitiFact claims to "rate the factual accuracy of specific claims; we do not seek to measure which party tells more falsehoods."[36] The fact checkers claim to take no position on partisan veracity but also claim that their fact-checks in the aggregate are accurate, which would clearly indicate that Republicans lie more. But they deny that they are saying that. This is an untenable position from professionals intent on maintaining their own status as truth tellers (fact checkers reject false equivalence in principle but embrace it in the specific question of partisan lying; readers are free to draw the clear conclusion, but the fact checkers will not say it directly, even as they claim to reveal the truth fearlessly). As Graves phrases it, "they refuse to talk about the largest conclusions to be drawn from a decade of fact-checking in the United States: Republicans distort the truth more often and more severely than Democrats." Graves urges them to abandon this position: "If one party distorts the discourse more, why not focus on it?"[37] The answer is that the industry can only choose between encouraging accusations of partisanship or accusations of dodging the question; so far they prefer the latter.

Regardless of the accusations of ideological bias, media criticisms of fact-checking have come from both Left and Right. Critics from the Left include Paul Krugman, Rachel Maddow ("PolitiFact, you are ruining it for everyone"), and the *Huffington Post*, notably in an article entitled "PolitiFact Has Decided That a Totally True Thing Is the Lie of the Year

---

[34] Graves 2016, page 219, italics in original.
[35] Ibid., page 217.
[36] PolitiFact, May 29, 2013
[37] Graves 2016, pages 16, 224.

for Some Reason." Critics from the right include Mark Hemingway of the *Weekly Standard*: "If the stated goal seems simple enough—providing an impartial referee to help readers sort out acrimonious and hyperbolic political disputes—in practice PolitiFact does nothing of the sort. . . . At the most basic level, the media's new 'fact checkers' remain obdurately unwilling to let opinions simply be opinions." Ben Smith of *Politico* concluded in May of 2010 that "most political disputes are too nuanced to fit the 'fact check' framework."[38]

An Empirical Look at the Consistency of Fact-Checking

While we have no external gold standard of truth to apply to the fact checkers' assertions about reality (they claim to *be* that gold standard), we *can* test their consistency: if they contradict each other, we can conclude that their collective wisdom is suspect. We see this as a minimum standard for legitimacy: *Do the major fact checkers ask the same questions and offer the same answers regarding the major disputed realities of our time?*

We conducted and published just such an analysis while researching this book.[39] In order to create a test of the guidance offered by the three major fact checkers, we examined the assessments published across a two-year period, from January 1, 2012, to December 31, 2013 (which includes the 2012 presidential campaign). We focused on three disputed realities: whether anthropogenic climate change exists or is an unfounded assertion, whether racism is a declining force in American society or is still influential (or growing) in power, and whether the national debt is growing to a dangerous degree or remaining at a manageable level that will not cause major economic harm. Totaling up all of the statements in regard to each of these three disputed realities allowed us to examine the fact checkers' *selections* and *assessments*: do they examine the same facts, and do they reach the same conclusions about their truth or falsehood?

To summarize the results of that study regarding the selection of claims to check, there are clear differences in epistemological focus among the major fact checkers. The disputed fact of the influence of racism is one of the largest distinctions. PolitiFact chose to evaluate several assertions on the influence of racism, including statements by Jimmy Carter, John Lewis,

---

[38] Krugman 2011, Linkins 2011, Hemingway 2011, Smith 2010. Smith and Glenn Kessler (The Fact Checker) had a public disagreement the following year over Kessler's fact-checking (and dispute) of *Politico*'s reporting of a comment alleged to have been made by Vice President Joe Biden.
[39] See Marietta et al. 2015 for full details of the study.

Jesse Jackson, Cory Booker, Eric Holder, John Roberts, leaders of the NAACP, and several members of Congress. We believe this comports with the importance of the topic as well as the clear dispute among American citizens about the influence of racism in contemporary society. However, The Fact Checker and FactCheck.org do not agree with PolitiFact about the relevance of this topic, declining to evaluate any of the statements examined by PolitiFact or any of the other many statements about race and racism in our politics during the two years of the study. This is a striking omission given the importance of the topic to American politics.

When it comes to climate change, we begin to see distinctions in the two sides of a given factual dispute that are evaluated. Both kinds of assertions—suggesting that climate change is real and that it is false—were examined by PolitiFact. The Fact Checker and FactCheck.org, on the other hand, only fact-checked assertions *opposing* the reality of climate change. Assertions supporting its reality were not checked, suggesting that those two fact checkers did not see those assertions as questionable to most readers. What all three fact checkers agreed upon is that the assertions suggesting that climate change is not real are false.

Finally, the national debt is mutually seen as an important topic, but the fact checkers again disagree on which kinds of statements to question. PolitiFact sees assertions that the national debt is growing and problematic to be questionable and in need of fact-checking; however, the many statements asserting the opposite are not assessed at nearly the same rate, suggesting that they sound to the fact checkers at PolitiFact to be true on the face. The Fact Checker and FactCheck.org disagreed with this approach, questioning both kinds of assertions. Fact checkers exercise a large amount of subjectivity not only in which disputed realities to evaluate but also in which kind of positive or negative assertions to check or ignore. In sum, the three major fact checkers display substantial differences in the disputed facts that they address.[40]

---

[40] These findings have drawn the criticism that we should expect different media outlets to cover different topics. However, the distinctions in coverage among the three major fact checkers are not akin to the minor variations among mainstream media outlets. Three major newspapers may have a different front-page headline on a given day but still cover roughly the same topics over the course of the week. The differences found in this study span a two-year period, over which temporary differences in emphasis should even out. A second criticism is that the differences may be accounted for by economies of coverage within the industry, if different fact checkers intentionally avoid ground already covered by their competitors. This is not supported by other scholarship on the fact-check industry. One of Graves' conclusions from his participant observation was that the elite fact checkers have no professional concerns that discourage examination of the same facts: "fact-checks run regardless of whether another news outlet or fact-checker has already covered the same ground" (Graves 2016, page 96). "A tremendous amount of overlap exists in the claims checked by FactCheck.org, PolitiFact, and The Fact Checker, who frequently cite one another in their published

Perhaps the core question of the study is whether the fact checkers provide the same evaluations of contested facts. While the three major fact checkers differ in their rating techniques, the ratings provided by PolitiFact and The Fact Checker can be compared directly by placing the Truth-O-Meters and Pinocchios on the same 5-point scale, with 1 indicating true and 5 indicating false. This approach condenses the PolitiFact 6-point scale to The Fact Checker 5-point scale by counting both "Pants on Fire" and "False" ratings as equivalent to 4 Pinocchios.[41] Table 13.2 illustrates the comparisons and the exact descriptions of the ratings employed by each fact checker.

The best window into potentially conflicting evaluations may be the unusual cases when the fact checkers evaluate precisely the same statements. While the three major fact checkers often consider the same general states of affairs, they rarely focus on the exact same quotation by one politician. There are only three cases in this study of the same explicit statement being evaluated by different fact checkers. All three relate to the national debt, one of the topics most subject to verification with data that are mutually accepted as legitimate.

The first example is a statement made by Senator Dick Durbin on ABC's Sunday news show *This Week* in November of 2012: "Social Security does not add one penny to our debt, not a penny." This assertion drew attention from fact checkers but did not draw agreement about its veracity. FactCheck.org described it as a blatant falsehood (November 28, 2012): "Sen. Richard Durbin says that, 'Social Security does not add one penny to our debt.' That's false. It was wrong 21 months ago, when Durbin said it once before, and it's even more off the mark now." The discussion cites reports from the Congressional Budget Office to conclude, "It's true that Social Security is 'a separate funded operation,' primarily through payroll taxes and income taxes on benefits. But tax revenues no longer cover the cost of Social Security benefits. As a result, Social Security is adding to the debt." However, The Fact Checker of the *Washington Post* disagreed: "We do not think this line is a slamdunk falsehood, as some believe [linking to the FactCheck.org review], but it is certainly worth revisiting." After a discussion of the mechanics of the Social Security

---

articles. 'That's the nature [of fact-checking],' Kessler has explained. 'It doesn't really matter that they've done it before and I haven't' " (page 98).

[41] This accords with Kessler's interpretation of their comparison: "This is how I view it: Geppetto = true, One Pinocchio = mostly true, Two Pinocchios = half true, Three Pinocchios = mostly false, Four Pinocchios = false/Pants on Fire" (Kessler email correspondence, March 24, 2014).

TABLE 13.2 Fact Checker Equivalent Ratings

RATING	POLITIFACT	THE FACT CHECKER
5	"Pants On Fire"/"False" The statement is not accurate and makes a ridiculous claim./The statement is not accurate.	🐷 🐷 🐷 🐷 Whoppers.
4	"Mostly False" The statement contains an element of truth but ignores critical facts that would give a different impression.	🐷 🐷 🐷 Significant factual error and/or obvious contradictions.
3	"Half True" The statement is partially accurate but leaves out important details or takes things out of context.	🐷 🐷 Significant omissions and/or exaggerations. Some factual error may be involved but not necessarily. A politician can create a false, misleading impression by playing with words and using legalistic language that means little to ordinary people.
2	"Mostly True" The statement is accurate but needs clarification or additional information.	🐷 Some shading of the facts. Selective telling of the truth. Some omissions and exaggerations, but no outright falsehoods.
1	"True" The statement is accurate, and there's nothing significant missing.	✔️ Statements and claims that contain "the truth, the whole truth, and nothing but the truth" will be recognized with our prized Geppetto checkmark.

fund—also citing the Congressional Budget Office—The Fact Checker awarded just one Pinocchio (equivalent to PolitiFact's "Mostly True"), contradicting FactCheck.org's assessment.

The second instance is Jay Carney's statement that the rate of increase in federal spending under Obama has been lower than all of his predecessors since Eisenhower. In May of 2012, The Fact Checker rated this statement as three Pinocchios (false), while PolitiFact said it was mostly true.[42] The third case was President Obama's statement that deficits are falling at the fastest rate in sixty years. In July 2013 PolitiFact rated

---

[42] To be clear about this particular disagreement, PolitiFact evaluated the blog post itself; The Fact Checker evaluated Jay Carney's quotation of that blog post, a slight distinction regarding the same factual assertion grounded in the same source.

this statement true. FactCheck.org described it as false. These overlapping fact-checks resulted in disagreements representing all three combinations of fact checkers: FactCheck.org and The Fact Checker disagreed on the first one, The Fact Checker and PolitiFact disagreed on the second one, and PolitiFact and FactCheck.org disagreed on the third. These are clear disparities of perceived realities among the professional fact checkers when evaluating precisely the same statements.

However, one-to-one comparisons of this nature are rarely possible given the fact checkers' propensity to choose different specific quotes from the vast field of statements made by political leaders. The only means of comparison is to examine the same broad assertions—such as the existence of anthropogenic climate change—made by different speakers but addressing the same general point. While the fact checkers do not examine the same quotes at the same time, they do examine the same general assertions over a longer period of time, providing a database of evaluations for citizens to peruse. If a citizen were to consult a fact checker over a substantial period of time looking for an understanding of climate change or the national debt, what is the general impression created by the reports of one fact checker versus the reports of a different fact checker?

The good news is that about one disputed fact—climate change—they agree. The bad news is that they disagree about the national debt. PolitiFact finds that assertions that the debt has negative consequences are generally false, while The Fact Checker finds that these kinds of assertions are generally true.[43] If a confused citizen were to turn to FactCheck.org, he would find that its reports give an impression closer to the more positive evaluation of the status of the national debt endorsed by PolitiFact, rather than the more negative assessment by The Fact Checker.

To summarize the comparative epistemologies of the fact checkers, in regard to questions asked, the three fact checkers disagreed about which disputed facts should be examined. As for the answers offered, they agreed on one disputed reality (climate change) and disagreed on another (national debt). Fact-checking seems to allow for meaningful differences in the realities assessed as well as in the conclusions reached. This suggests that for the engaged citizen attempting to sort out the disputed realities of the current political environment, consulting fact checkers will not

---

[43] PolitiFact evaluations of assertions that the national debt has negative consequences were given an average rating of 3.3 on the 1–5 scale (on the false side), while The Fact Checker awarded an average rating of 2.3 (on the true side), a statistically significant difference. See Marietta et al. 2015 for details.

necessarily be of great service in determining which version of competing realities to endorse.

The Fact Checker's definition of two Pinocchios includes "significant omissions and/or exaggerations." Our analysis suggests that fact-check journalism leads to significant omissions of some questions by some institutions. The Fact Checker's definition of three Pinocchios includes "significant factual errors and/or obvious contradictions." For the fact checkers to dispute each other's findings about the nature of the national debt is a clear contradiction. This suggests an overall rating for the fact-check industry of two or three Pinocchios. Other scholars might see the selection bias and contradictory findings as leading toward a somewhat more negative rating, while others may contend that journalistic standards decrease it to a mere one Pinocchio. But we conclude that the major fact-checking institutions do not deserve a Geppetto checkmark in regard to sorting out the disputed realities of contemporary American politics.

Conclusion

The professional fact-checking of political realities seems to be enjoying a boom in productivity and reputation. Many scholars have been optimistic that these new institutions would be able to solve or at least aid the dilemma of dueling facts. Optimism aside, the question that remains is how useful these institutions are in aiding citizens to navigate the politics of disputed realities. When it comes to campaigns and politicians, fact-checking seems to have some positive effects on the behavior of elected officials and on citizens' evaluations of their veracity. But in regard to the broader disputed facts of contemporary politics, the epistemology of fact-checking seems to falter. If the epistemology of fact-checking is flawed and its conclusions lack consensus, this suggests that citizens have reasons for distrust.

This conclusion allows us to see the politics of fact-checking in a more realistic and less deferential way. But this doesn't tell us how citizens do in fact react when fact checkers contradict their beliefs. For that we need to focus on a more direct test of the influence of fact-checking, discussed in the following chapter.

14 | Citizen Reponses to Fact-Checking

WITH KIM L. NALDER AND DANIELLE JOESTEN MARTIN[1]

"There is an inherent difficulty about using the method
of reason to deal with an unreasoning world."

—*Walter Lippmann*[2]

I F FACT-CHECKING IS TO HAVE a positive influence, citizens must trust
it. Both Left and Right must regard fact checkers as a legitimate source
of accurate facts, especially when faced with offerings of "alternative
facts" and fake news (whether distributed by humans or by bots, whether
over Facebook or traditional media sources).[3] But do citizens trust fact-
checkers to guide them, or do they fall prey to all of the psychological
mechanisms discussed in earlier chapters, leading them to dismiss the
fact-checks that dispute their priors, only embracing those that tell them
what they already believe?

No shortage of scholars and public figures have expressed optimism
that such high-profile "truth detectors" might slow the rise of dueling fact
perceptions.[4] But evidence of fact-checking's efficacy is mixed, at best.[5]
Indeed, some have suggested that bringing facts to a culture war might be
like bringing a knife to a gunfight.[6]

----

[1] Kim L. Nalder is professor of political science, executive director of the *CALSPEAKS* poll, and
director of the Project for an Informed Electorate at California State University, Sacramento; and
Danielle Joesten Martin is assistant professor of political science at California State University,
Sacramento.
[2] Lippmann 1922, page 259.
[3] We understand "fake news" as fabricated stories emerging from non-reputable sources.
[4] See Jackson and Jamieson 2007, Amazeen 2015, Graves 2016, Wintersieck and Fridkin 2015.
[5] Garrett et al. 2013, Jarman 2016a, 2016b, Young et al. 2017, Suhay and Garretson 2018. For a meta-
analysis and summary, see Chan et al. 2017. Guess et al. 2018a find almost no overlap between the
consumers of fake news and the consumers of fact-checks during the 2016 presidential campaign.
[6] See Jarrett 2016.

But might certain contextual and individual characteristics mitigate the popular tendency to resist such fact-checking? Specifically, do people respond differently to fact-checks of candidates who share their partisan identity compared to fact-checks that target the "other side"? And does fact-checking work better on Democrats than Republicans? Given widespread distrust of traditional purveyors of information (mainstream media, academia, and the scientific community), especially among Republicans and conservatives, to what extent does such populism and anti-elitism drive fact-checking resistance?[7] If the answer is "substantially," might greater educational attainment mitigate such resistance? These questions are important because if greater education or respect for intellectuals can temper resistance to fact-checking, then there may be some hope of slowing the advance of factual division, perhaps through expanded civic education or other reforms.

In this chapter, we examine the manner and extent to which fact-checking about a candidate (in this case, Hillary Clinton) can influence perceptions of the fact checkers themselves, as well as attitudes about the candidate. We then explore the extent to which those effects are conditioned by (a) interpartisan versus intrapartisan candidate comparisons (Clinton vs. Donald Trump compared to Clinton vs. Bernie Sanders), (b) the party identification of the recipient of the fact-check (Republicans vs. Democrats), (c) populism, and (d) education.

The Conditioning Roles of Populism and Education

One reason fact-checking might fall on deaf ears is the public's pervasive distrust of experts and intellectuals. This aspect of populism enjoys a long tradition in the United States, and it has picked up speed in recent years—especially among conservatives and Republicans (see Chapter 12).[8] This is easy to understand; people who consider "eggheads" to be arrogant, out of touch, and lacking in common sense are quick to push back when they perceive the eggheads and their egghcaded institutions to be telling them that they are ignorant.[9]

---

[7] See Hofstadter 1964, Rigney 1991, Lecklider 2013.

[8] Hofstadter 1964, Rigney 1991, Lecklider 2013, Fingerhut 2017.

[9] The term *populism* is similar to what other scholars have termed *anti-intellectualism* (e.g., Hofstadter 1964), but we prefer the former because it does not carry as much pejorative spin.

If populism does indeed motivate resistance to fact-checking correctives, then it is easy to imagine that greater education (and association with academic institutions) might motivate acceptance of fact-checking.[10]

However, as we discussed at length in Chapter 12, the weight of the evidence suggests that the opposite may be true. Researchers have not yet concluded that education, in particular, is associated with resistance to fact-checking; but they have observed that political knowledge is.[11] Perhaps the benefits of formal education (in contrast to knowledge of politics) encourage citizens to accept the assertions of fact checkers. On the other hand, instead of using their advanced critical thinking skills to arrive at more accurate judgments of objective truth, highly knowledgeable persons might marshal those skills to construct stronger defenses of their standing beliefs. After all, we know that education is associated with intellectual hauteur, which prompts assurance that one's standing beliefs are correct, making it easier to reject information that calls those beliefs into question.

The Case of the 2016 Democratic Nomination Contest

The 2016 presidential nomination contest between Hillary Clinton and Bernie Sanders is an ideal lens through which to evaluate voters' receptiveness to non-partisan fact checkers, especially as it pertains to potential partisan asymmetries.[12] In May of that year, attitudes toward candidate Clinton—perceptions of her honesty, in particular—were extremely polarized and not just along partisan lines. That is, negative affect toward Clinton among Sanders supporters was comparable to that among Republicans, which is remarkable given Clinton's long-standing status as a pariah to those on the Right.[13] Thus, by exposing Clinton's opponents (on both Right and Left) to a PolitiFact infographic that contradicted the "crooked Hillary" narrative, we are able to evaluate the relative willingness of Republicans and Democrats to update their perceptions of her. We were also able to analyze differences in fact-checking resistance *within* as

---

[10] Jamieson 2015, Helfand 2016.

[11] See Nyhan et al. 2013, Nyhan and Reifler 2016.

[12] While Hillary Clinton was the front runner for the Democratic nomination, Senator Bernie Sanders presented a remarkably strong challenge from her ideological left, collecting 43% of the primary votes (to Clinton's 55%). This was all the more remarkable because Sanders had always run as an Independent since his election to the House of Representatives in 1990 and then the Senate in 2007.

[13] See Buchanan 2016, Carpentier 2016.

well as across parties, by comparing Sanders supporters' evaluations of Clinton relative to Sanders and Donald Trump, respectively.[14]

Using the *CALSPEAKS* panel, we administered a randomized controlled survey experiment to a representative sample of Californians just a couple of weeks before the state's Democratic primary contest (May 23–30, 2016).[15]

To observe differences in candidate support prior to the experimental treatment, we first measured Democrats' and Independents' vote intentions.[16] Armed with this contextual information (and after measuring a battery of policy preferences as a distraction), we exposed respondents to the experimental treatment, beginning with the following statement: "Nonpartisan fact-checking organizations like PolitiFact rate controversial candidate statements for truthfulness." Then, to one *randomized half of the sample*, we followed that statement with "Each presidential candidate's current average PolitiFact truthfulness score is placed on the scale below" (see Figure 14.1).

We had compiled the information in the graphic from the PolitiFact website in early May. PolitiFact offers summary reports on specific political figures prominently on its website, which they call a "PolitiFact scorecard."[17] We calculated an average truthfulness score for each candidate based on the sum of each type of statement (True, Mostly True, Half True, Mostly False, False, or Pants on Fire), with True scored highest and Pants on Fire scored lowest, divided by the total number of statements

---

[14] It may be more accurate to say that we were able to analyze inter-*ideological* versus intra-*ideological* candidate comparisons, given that Senator Sanders is not technically a Democrat, even though he was competing for the Democratic presidential nomination.

[15] $N = 748$. See the discussion in Chapter 8 for details of the *CALSPEAKS* panel.

[16] 0 = Sanders, 1 = undecided/other, 2 = Clinton; mean = 1.0, standard deviation = .85. We did not measure Republicans' primary candidate preferences because Republicans could not vote in the Democratic primary and the Republican nomination was effectively decided by that point.

[17] At PolitiFact.com see the running header for "People," which has pull-downs for specific individuals including Donald Trump, Mike Pence, and Barack Obama (during the 2016 campaign these included Hillary Clinton and Bernie Sanders). See also "Comparing Hillary Clinton, Donald Trump on the Truth-O-Meter" (http://www.politifact.com/truth-o-meter/lists/people/comparing-hillary-clinton-donald-trump-truth-o-met). These summary reports are often referenced by news media; see for example William Davies, *The New York Times*, August 24, 2016: "PolitiFact has found that about 70 percent of Donald Trump's factual statements actually fall into the categories of 'mostly false,' 'false,' and 'pants on fire' untruth." This is something of a mischaracterization as PolitiFact does not claim to sample *all* of the factual statements made by a candidate but only fact-checks the statements that they already suspect of falsehood; hence, PolitiFact is not suggesting that 70% of Trump's statements are lies but only 70% of the ones they checked because they sounded fishy. Similarly, Hillary Clinton's comparable rating is 26%, which is much lower than Trump's but does *not* suggest that she lied a quarter of the time she spoke. This kind of media reporting illustrates the reliance on the PolitiFact scorecards in major media outlets as well as the misinterpretation of their meaning.

Average Truthfulness Score

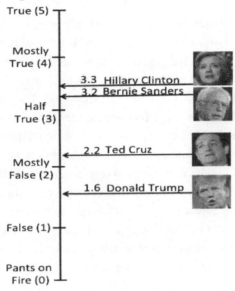

FIGURE 14.1 PolitiFact Graphic

rated by PolitiFact. Higher scores indicate that a candidate has a more truthful record.

We then asked all respondents (regardless of whether they had seen the graphic), "In your view, how reliable are these sorts of ratings?" (0 = very unreliable; 3 = very reliable).

Next, we asked, "In your view, how honest are each of the following candidates?" A table appeared below the question, with three rows ("Sanders," "Clinton," and "Trump," in randomized order across respondents) and five columns ("Very Dishonest," "Somewhat Dishonest," "Neutral," "Somewhat Honest," and "Very Honest"). We coded each on a scale ranging from 0 ("Very Dishonest") to 4 ("Very Honest"). We deliberately used this question format—with all three candidates appearing in the same question—to encourage respondents to evaluate the candidates in comparative terms, given that the PolitiFact graphic had used such a format. Respondents tended to view Sanders as honest, on balance (mean = 2.6), and as considerably more honest than either Clinton or Trump. They viewed Clinton as a little more honest than Trump ($p < .001$), but the mean assessment of both Clinton and Trump fell on the dishonest side of the scale (1.54 and 1.24, respectively).

Hypotheses

Our core hypotheses focus on whether exposure to the PolitiFact image affects perceptions of (1) the candidates' relative honesty and (2) the fact checkers' reliability. We also wanted to see how those reactions might differ among Sanders supporters ($n = 154$), Clinton supporters ($n = 166$), undecideds ($n = 111$), or Republicans ($n = 191$).[18]

More precisely, we were focused on the degree to which exposure to the graphic might alter perceptions of *Clinton*, relative to her opponents, because she was the candidate whose reputation for dishonesty the graphic contradicted and who therefore stood to potentially benefit the most from people being exposed to the graphic. After all, other surveys revealed that Trump was already widely perceived as dishonest, and the graphic just provided confirmatory evidence of that.[19] Similarly, we know from other sources that Sanders was widely perceived as honest, and again, the graphic did nothing to dispel that notion.[20] Clinton, on the other hand, had been carrying a reputation for dishonesty—whether deserved or not— for twenty-five years, and the ubiquitously visible email server controversy that dogged her throughout 2015–2016 certainly had not helped. By contradicting that narrative, the graphic had an opportunity to either persuade detractors or inspire dogged pushback.

Stated formally, our hypotheses are as follows:

H_1: *Exposure to the PolitiFact image is positively associated with perceptions of the fact checkers' reliability among Clinton supporters, but the opposite is the case among Sanders supporters and Republicans, lowering their assessments of reliability.*

H_2: *Exposure to the PolitiFact image is positively associated with higher assessments of Clinton's honesty (relative to that of Sanders or Trump) only among Clinton supporters but not among Sanders supporters or Republicans.*

We also anticipate that populism and education condition the willingness of respondents to update their assessments of Clinton's relative honesty in response to PolitiFact's assertions. Specifically:

---

[18] Again, Republicans could not vote in the Democratic primary, so we only assessed candidate preferences among Democrats and Independents.

[19] See, for example, Chozick and Thee-Brenan 2016, De Pinto 2016.

[20] See, for example, the *Economist*/YouGov poll in Frankovic 2015.

H_3: Among citizens who do not support Clinton, populism heightens negative assessments of the reliability of fact checkers and negative assessments of Clinton's honesty.

H_4: Among non-Clinton supporters, greater education heightens negative assessments of the reliability of fact checkers as well as negative assessments of Clinton's honesty.

Analysis

To test H_1 (and the ability of populism or education to condition it), we dichotomized respondents' perceptions of fact checkers' reliability[21] and estimated a binary probit regression model (identifying the differences in the predicted probabilities of expressions of reliability associated with full range increases in the independent variables).[22]

To test H_2 (and again any conditioning effects of populism or education), we estimated a series of linear regression models. The dependent variables were "difference scores" measuring perceptions of relative candidate honesty (Clinton's honesty minus Trump's honesty and Clinton's honesty minus Sanders' honesty). Given that the honesty measures ranged from 0 to 4, each relative honesty variable ranged from −4 to +4, with negative values favoring Trump or Sanders and positive values favoring Clinton.[23] To ease interpretation in our models, we recoded each variable to range from −1 to +1.[24]

In all of the models, the primary independent variable of interest is the experimental treatment of having been exposed to the PolitiFact graphic. After estimating the effects within the full sample, we split the file to observe differences across the subgroups identified. Specifically, we estimated separate equations for (1) Democrats and Independents who planned to vote for Clinton in the June primary, (2) Democrats and Independents

---

[21] 0 = somewhat or very unreliable, 1 = somewhat or very reliable; mean = .27, standard deviation = .44.

[22] We initially estimated this model using ordinal probit regression, finding very similar results to what we report in this chapter; but that model violated the proportional odds assumption of ordinal regression. As such, we report the binary probit results (which also eases interpretation).

[23] It is notable that—even in a California sample—the average respondent's assessment of Clinton's honesty is barely higher than that of Trump's. And it is considerably lower than that of Sanders, even though she would win the California primary a couple of weeks later (perceptions of her experience and electability, unlike perceptions of her honesty, were considerably higher than those of Sanders).

[24] Clinton–Trump honesty, mean = .08, standard deviation = .58; Clinton–Sanders honesty, mean = −.26, standard deviation = .38.

who planned to vote for Sanders in the primary, (3) Democrats and Independents who were still undecided at that point, and (4) Republicans (who had not been asked whom they would have hypothetically supported in the Democratic primary).

Additionally, in the successive models designed to test our hypotheses regarding the conditioning roles of populism and education, we added each conditioning variable to the model in question, along with an interaction term with exposure to the PolitiFact graphic.[25]

To account for potential confounds, we included a series of control variables in all the models.[26] We also controlled for education and for party identification (in all of the models except for the one restricted to Republicans).[27]

Results

Focusing first on how the PolitiFact graphic affected perceptions of reliability, we see in Table 14.1 that exposure *diminished* the probability of citizens calling fact checkers "reliable" by about 19 percentage points in the full sample. Exposure to the fact checker's assessment of the candidates did not boost perceptions of reliability among *any* group. Even Clinton supporters only showed a small and statistically insignificant movement in the positive direction, while all other groups moved distinctly toward

---

[25] PolitiFact * populism, mean = .29, standard deviation = .35; PolitiFact * education, mean = .32; standard deviation = .37. We measured populism by asking two Likert-style questions (0 = strongly disagree; 4 = strongly agree): (1) "I'd rather put my trust in the wisdom of ordinary people than the opinions of experts and intellectuals" (mean = 2.09, standard deviation = 1.14) and (2) "Ordinary people are perfectly capable of deciding for themselves what's true and what's not" (mean = 2.75, standard deviation = 1.09). We summed them to create a single measure analysis (0–8; mean = 3.21, standard deviation = 1.92). We had measured the education variable by asking "What is the highest level of education that you have completed?" (0 = <high school graduate, 1 = high school graduate, 2 = some college, 3 = baccalaureate degree, 4 = postgraduate degree; mean = 2.42, standard deviation = 1.91). Before entering any of these conditioning variables into the models or creating the interaction terms, we converted each to a 0–1 scale to ease interpretation.

[26] Gender (1 = female; mean=.51, standard deviation=.49), race/ethnicity (1 = non-white; mean = .37, standard deviation=.48), age (0 = 18–25, 1 = 26–34, 2 = 35–49, 3 = 5–64, 4 = 65 and older; mean = 2.3, standard deviation = 1.23), and family income (0 = <$15k, 1 = $15.01–$30k, 2 = $30.01–$50k, 3 = $50.01k–$75k, 4 = $75.01k–$100k, 5 = $100.01k–$150k, 6 = $150.01k–$200k, 7 = >$200k; mean = 3.16, standard deviation = 1.9).

[27] 0 = Democrats and Independents who lean Democratic, 1 = Independents who do not lean toward either party, 2 = Republicans and Independents who lean Republican; mean = .80, standard deviation = .90. We clustered the (Huber-White) standard errors according to the specific sampling method that had been used to recruit a particular respondent into the panel, and we weighted the final (post-ranking) sampling weight. After including control variables and deleting missing cases using the listwise procedure, our working sample size for analysis was 599.

TABLE 14.1 Predicting Perceptions of Fact-Checker Reliability

	ALL	SANDERS SUPPORTERS	CLINTON SUPPORTERS	UNDECIDEDS	REPUBLICANS
PolitiFact treatment	-.19 ***	-.14 **	.07	-.22 *	-.35 ***
Female	.00	-.05	-.01	-.11 *	.10 ***
Non-white	-.01	-.01	-.04 *	-.05	-.09 ***
Age	.03	-.20 ***	.19 ***	-.12	-.23
Income	.16 ***	.00	-.24	.63 ***	.20
Education	-.11	.29 **	-.09	-.61 **	-.18
N	599	153	164	91	191

Binary probit regression models. Coefficients are differences in the predicted probabilities of viewing "fact-checking organizations such as PolitiFact as reliable," associated with each independent variable (exposure to the PolitiFact graphic and minimum-to-maximum differences in the other variables). Shaded cells represent statistically significant relationships.

*p < .05, **p < .01, ***p < .001.

negative reactions. Sanders supporters who saw the PolitiFact graphic were approximately 14 percentage points less likely to rate fact checkers as reliable, whereas Republicans who saw the graphic were 35 percentage points less likely to do so. This difference in effect sizes between Sanders supporters and Republicans is consistent with what we know about each group's relative levels of suspicion toward the elite mainstream media in general (of which PolitiFact is an example).

In something of a surprise, undecided Democrats/Independents who saw the graphic were also less likely to rate fact checkers as reliable, which perhaps speaks to how thoroughly the Clinton-as-dishonest narrative had metastasized through the electorate, including those who do not routinely pay close attention to politics.

How did populism condition the pushback against fact checkers? Figure 14.2 displays the conditional effects of populism, focusing on just non-Clinton supporters (Republicans, Sanders supporters, and undecideds, who have a clear motivation to reject the information offered by PolitiFact). After viewing the graphic, citizens with the highest levels of populism (the column at the far right of the figure) were substantially *less* likely to view fact checkers as reliable, while citizens low in populism maintained their relatively high levels of trust in fact checkers. The reduction in perceived reliability was 47 percentage points on average but broken down into 40 points among Republicans (.69 to .29), 65 points among Sanders supporters (.96 to .31), and 77 points among undecideds (.97 to .20).

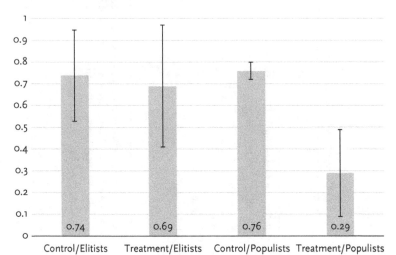

FIGURE 14.2 Perceptions of Fact Checker Reliability, Conditioned by Populism
NOTE: Bars represent 95% confidence intervals.

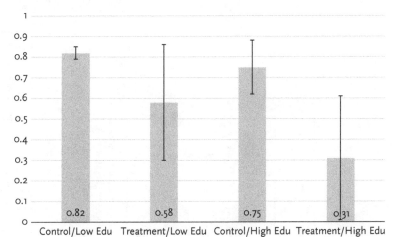

FIGURE 14.3 Perceptions of Fact Checker Reliability, Conditioned by Education

Turning to the conditioning influence of education, we see in Figure 14.3 that among the same group of Republicans, Sanders supporters, and undecideds, greater education leads to greater rejection of fact checkers. Those with a lower degree of formal education rated fact checkers to be somewhat less reliable after seeing the laudatory evaluation of Clinton (24 percentage points, moving from an average of .82 to .58), but this relationship showed a great deal of variation and is not statistically significant. Among the more educated citizens, on the other hand, perceptions of reliability fell significantly by 44 percentage points (.75 to .31).

Perceptions of Candidate Honesty

How did exposure to the PolitiFact graphic affect perceptions of Clinton's relative honesty? The next two tables illustrate the influence of the PolitiFact graphic on assessment of Clinton's honesty compared to Trump (Table 14.2) and compared to Sanders (Table 14.3). Grouping all respondents together, the PolitiFact graphic appears to have no meaningful effect. But among Clinton supporters alone, seeing the image improved their assessments of her honesty relative to Trump (from .63 to .82 on the −1 to +1 scale, a coefficient of .19, or almost 10 percentage points of the full range of the measure, $p < .05$). However, the PolitiFact information did *not* appear to produce a statistically significant boost in assessments of her honesty relative to Sanders (and thus would presumably not have

TABLE 14.2 Predicting Perceptions of Clinton's Honesty, Relative to Trump

	ALL	SANDERS SUPPORTERS	CLINTON SUPPORTERS	UNDECIDEDS	REPUBLICANS
PolitiFact treatment	.10	.04	.19 *	.29 **	.02
Female	.04 *	.03	.11	.08	-.17 ***
Non-white	.04 *	-.16	-.12	.23 *	.21 ***
Age	.25 *	-.03	.34 *	-.18 *	.08
Income	-.24 *	.34 *	-.42 ***	-.27	-.33
Education	.21	.70 *	-.32	.03	-.04
N	599	153	164	91	191

Linear (ordinary least squares) regression model. The unstandardized regression coefficients represent differences in the predicted value of the perceptions of Clinton relative to Trump (coded such that positive figures up to 1 indicate an advantage for Clinton and negative to –1 indicate an advantage for Trump) that are associated with the independent variables on the left side (exposure to the PolitiFact graphic and minimum-to-maximum differences in the other variables). Shaded cells represent statistically significant relationships.

$*p < .05$, $**p < .01$, $***p < .001$.

TABLE 14.3 Predicting Perceptions of Clinton's Honesty, Relative to Sanders

	ALL	SANDERS SUPPORTERS	CLINTON SUPPORTERS	UNDECIDEDS	REPUBLICANS
PolitiFact treatment	.04	.06	.12	.13 *	.02
Female	.05 **	.03	.15 *	-.14 **	-.06
Non-white	.09 *	-.09	.04	.07 **	.17 ***
Age	.08	-.12	-.03	-.11 **	-.09
Income	-.19 *	-.11	-.33 *	-.04	-.35
Education	.13	.34 *	-.02	.10 **	-.26
N	599	153	164	91	191

Linear (ordinary least squares) regression model. The unstandardized regression coefficients represent differences in the predicted value of the perceptions of Clinton relative to Trump (coded such that positive figures up to 1 indicate an advantage for Clinton and negative to –1 indicate an advantage for Trump) that are associated with the independent variables on the left side (exposure to the PolitiFact graphic and minimum-to-maximum differences in the other variables). Shaded cells represent statistically significant relationships.

$*p < .05, **p < .01, ***p < .001$.

boosted enthusiasm or turnout for Clinton in the primary contest that occurred shortly thereafter).

Among potential primary voters who were at that time still undecided, exposure to the PolitiFact graphic seemed to increase the appraisal of Clinton's honesty relative to Trump by about 15 percentage points of the scale (a coefficient of .29). The graphic seems to have provided a smaller but still significant boost to her reputation relative to Sanders, by about 7 percentage points. It seems that fact-checking might have the potential to affect appraisals of candidate honesty among undecided voters. This is somewhat surprising given that this same group of respondents tended to view fact-checking more negatively after seeing the image (see Table 14.1). Unfortunately for the potential beneficiary, though (in this case, Clinton), undecided voters are the least likely participants in elections to pay attention to politics through the media and thus to become aware of such fact-checking information.[28]

As for Clinton's detractors—our real focus—Republicans and Sanders supporters alike were unmoved by the PolitiFact graphic. Exposure to PolitiFact's assessments of the candidates was not associated with evaluations of Clinton's honesty in any way, with respect to either Sanders or Trump. Comparing Sanders supporters' evaluations of Clinton in relation to a candidate of the same party (Sanders) versus an opposing-party candidate (Trump) shows that there is generally no difference. Even partisan or ideological dynamics do not appear strong enough to overcome the reluctance on the part of Sanders supporters to give her some credit, in light of reliable information that could have made it easy to do so.

The remaining questions for us to consider are the extent to which populism and education tend to condition the resistance to fact-checking. In light of our focus on Clinton's detractors and to streamline the analyses, we excluded Clinton's supporters from the sample in these models. Again, while the full results of each of these conditional models can be found in the appendix, we aim to enhance clarity by presenting a series of bar charts (Figures 14.4 and 14.5).

As for our intuition that populism has something to do with detractors' general reluctance to update perceptions based on new (and ostensibly objective) information, we see in Figure 14.4 that among those who revealed the most positive attitudes toward intellectuals and experts, exposure to the graphic was associated with a jump in perceptions of Clinton's

---

[28] See Vavreck 2016.

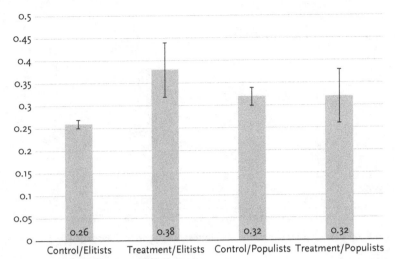

FIGURE 14.4 Perceptions of Clinton's Honesty (Relative to Sanders), Conditioned by Populism

NOTE: The y axis graphs the perceptions of Clinton's honesty relative to that of Sanders. Scores below .5 (all of the scores in the graph) represent mean perceptions that Sanders is more honest than Clinton, whereas scores above .5 would have represented mean perceptions that Clinton is more honest than Sanders. "Treatment" refers to those who were randomly exposed to the PolitiFact graphic; "Control" refers to those who were not. "Elitists" refer to those who scored lowest on the populism scale; "Populists" refer to those who scored highest on the populism scale.

relative honesty of 12 percentage points. By contrast, among those with the most pronounced populist attitudes, exposure to the graphic had no effect whatsoever.

Thus, these results are consistent with H_3: it would seem that populism does indeed drive fact-checking resistance to a substantial degree. By extension, if citizens were to become more trusting in what they are hearing from media, academia, and other sources of traditional authority, it is conceivable that fact-checking might become more successful at influencing perceptions of facts. From where we are sitting, it is hard to imagine that happening anytime soon.

If populism encourages fact-checking resistance, could the efficacy of fact-checking be enhanced by greater educational attainment? Looking at the conditioning role of education, Figure 14.5 illustrates that among those with the lowest levels of educational attainment, exposure to the PolitiFact graphic was associated with a marginally significant 12 percentage-point increase in perceptions of Clinton's honesty relative to that of Sanders ($p < .07$). However, among the most educated respondents, the effect is

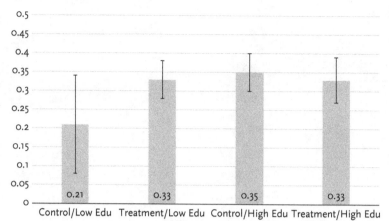

FIGURE 14.5 Perceptions of Clinton's Honesty (Relative to Sanders), Conditioned by Education

NOTE: The y axis graphs the perceptions of Clinton's honesty relative to that of Sanders. Scores below .5 (all of the scores in the graph) represent mean perceptions that Sanders is more honest than Clinton, whereas scores above .5 would have represented mean perceptions that Clinton is more honest than Sanders. "Treatment" refers to those who were randomly exposed to the PolitiFact graphic; "Control" refers to those who were not. "Low Edu" refers to those with the lowest levels of educational attainment; "High Edu" refers to those with the highest levels of educational attainment.

null. So not only does greater educational attainment not appear to enhance the efficacy of fact-checking; it actually seems to weaken it.

Conclusion

Our findings suggest that citizens dismiss fact-checks easily when they have a motivation to do so. For those predisposed against Hillary Clinton—either Republicans or Bernie Sanders supporters—PolitiFact's facts are merely opinions. When presented with PolitiFact's conclusions that Clinton has been more honest than Sanders (and especially more so than Trump), citizens who do not want to accept this message do not allow it to affect their conclusions. However, they *do* allow it to lower their regard for the fact checkers themselves. Citizens may judge fact checkers by the palatability of the facts they offer, more than they judge the facts grounded in the assertions of the professional fact checkers.

The ineffectiveness of fact-checking (and the boomerang effect on trust in the messenger) is conditioned by two important factors: populism and education. Contemporary populism—which focuses on the epistemological lionizing of ordinary folk and the distrust of expertise, the experts who offer it, and the institutions that support them—is related to the rejection of fact-checking. Likewise, increased education is no remedy, merely allowing citizens to reject the conclusions and reliability of fact checkers with more confidence.

We have devoted two full chapters to fact-checking because of its importance to the public discussion and possible correction of dueling fact perceptions. Many commentators and scholars are hopeful that the rise of the fact-check industry and the new emphasis on accountability journalism will bring citizen perceptions of facts toward a consensus. Unfortunately for this hope, the evidence presented in both chapters suggests greater pessimism. The assertions of fact checkers are no match for the predispositions of citizens.

15 | Symmetry, Asymmetry, and Durability

W E HAVE MADE THE CLAIM that DFPs are likely to be durable and difficult to remedy. One reason is the multifaceted psychological foundation of value projection. Another factor is the inability of education and fact-checking to serve as effective reforms. A third factor may be *symmetry across political ideologies*. Some writers have argued that the dueling facts phenomenon is driven disproportionately by the ideological Right: conservatives and Republicans, so the argument goes, are more likely to engage in motivated reasoning and wind up misinformed. As Stephen Colbert famously phrased it, "reality has a well-known liberal bias." Perhaps the best-known proponent of this interpretation is Chris Mooney, but many others have made similar arguments (including one of us).[1] If it were indeed the case that dueling fact perceptions (DFPs) are driven by only one-half of the ideological spectrum, the problem would be more tractable—if for no other reason than that it would be less widespread. Reformers could focus their efforts on correcting conservative misinformation and tailor strategies accordingly.

On first consideration, there are several reasons to anticipate that conservatives might well be more prone to project their values onto their perceptions of reality and to discount contrary evidence. To be sure, an expanse of scholarship documents the *rigidity of the Right*, which suggests that conservatives tend to be disproportionately (1) ideological,[2] (2) suspicious of moderation,[3] (3) uninterested in compromise,[4] (4) prone toward

---

[1] Mooney 2005, 2012; see also Kruglanski et al. 1993, McCrae 1996, Jost et al. 2003, Feygina et al. 2010, Hofstetter and Barker 1999.
[2] See, for example, Grossman and Hopkins 2016, Lelkes and Sniderman 2016, Schufeldt 2018; also see a similar argument by Barker and Carman 2012.
[3] See, for example, McCarty et al. 2006, Barker and Carman 2012, Mann and Ornstein 2012.
[4] See, for example, Dimock et al. 2014, Grossmann and Hopkins 2016.

authoritarianism,[5] (5) cognitively inflexible,[6] (6) lacking in empathy,[7] (7) socially and informationally insular,[8] and (8) hostile toward outgroups.[9]

However, the case for such partisan or ideological asymmetry might not be open and shut. For one thing, much of that research is plagued by methodological shortcomings.[10] Second, in recent years, Democrats appear to have moved rapidly to the Left and now resemble Republicans when it comes to ideological extremism and constraint.[11] Third, when it comes to championing free speech rights for groups they abhor (rather than toward traditionally disadvantaged groups), liberals might not cheer any louder for the First Amendment than conservatives do.[12]

In light of this growing body of evidence, as well as the obvious energy behind movements such as Occupy, Black Lives Matter, #MeToo, Time's Up, and The Resistance (not to mention Bernie Sanders supporters' infamously impassioned defiance of Hillary Clinton's nomination at the 2016 Democratic National Convention), it is worth wondering whether America's new democratic socialists and *multiculturalista* are coalescing into a "Tea Party of the Left," harboring rates of principled intransigence traditionally reserved for the ideological Right.[13]

But even if the rigidity of the Right is outdated or was misplaced to begin with, there is an additional reason to anticipate that conservatives might exhibit disproportionate resistance to what most academics and scientists think of as objective facts, which we detailed in Chapter 12: the long-standing—and intensifying—resentment of and distrust toward traditional sources of informational authority, including non-partisan government agencies, academia, and especially the mainstream media.[14] Republicans tend to hold strong convictions that such mainstream sources of informational authority are liberally biased, which leads them to easily dismiss much of what they see or hear from such sources.[15]

Such disproportionate anti-elitism on the Right might be related to the fact that, holding everything else constant, self-identified conservatives

---

[5] See, for example, Altemeyer 1996, Hetherington and Weiler 2009.
[6] See, for example, Jost et al. 2003.
[7] See, for example, Lakoff 1996, Barker and Tinnick 2006.
[8] See, for example, Mitchell et al. 2014.
[9] See, for example, Roccas and Brewer 2002, Haidt 2012, Kugler et al. 2014, Mitchell et al. 2014. For a good meta-analysis of ideological asymmetries, see Jost 2017.
[10] See Malka et al. 2018.
[11] See Dimock et al. 2014.
[12] See Crawford and Pilanski 2014.
[13] See Foran 2016, Arnsdorf et al. 2016, Hanna and Gee 2017.
[14] See Jones 2004, Ladd 2011, Allcott and Gentzkow 2017.
[15] See Watts et al. 1999, Iyengar and Hahn 2009.

now tend to enjoy lower levels of educational attainment than do liberals, on average (which was not true until very recently).[16] Contemporary liberals are also more likely to work in the "information economy," as educators, journalists, researchers, librarians, publishers, and the like, which may make them more inclined to trust mainstream sources of informational authority.[17] So the people who comprise those mainstream sources are in many cases their colleagues, their family members, their friends, or themselves. White-collar conservatives, on the other hand, are more likely to be employed in business, law enforcement, or the military, whose leaders must demonstrate tremendous cerebral acumen but are not traditional sources of *informational* authority in the way that educators, scientists, and journalists are.

But it is worth considering whether such apparently high-minded embrace of scientific conclusions (and authority) on the Left might be just a coincidence. After all, when it comes to many of the most prominent factual disputes with direct political ramifications—including the existence of climate change, racism's influence, and the origins of sexual orientation—liberals currently benefit from knowing that their perceptions tend to reflect something close to a consensus within scientific or scholarly communities.[18] So what looks like disproportionate erudition on the part of liberals might just relate to the fact that liberals are more likely to agree with the conclusions that scholars and scientists tend to reach on some of the issues that get the most media attention. Perhaps when science leads to less friendly conclusions, liberals tend to express just as much skepticism and resistance to "correction" as conservatives do. To be sure, liberals are not typically in the habit of reflexively deferring to established authorities (indeed, they are typically less so).[19] Why should respect for *informational* authorities be any different?

There are a few studies that lend support to the hypothesis of ideological symmetry as it relates to DFPs. For example, in one line of research, Dan Kahan and his colleagues have shown that traits thought to drive conservative acceptance of congenial facts—dogmatism, aversion to complexity, and need for closure—do not have any relationship with holding specific

---

[16] See Pew Research Center 2018.
[17] See Weeden and Kurzman 2016.
[18] When it comes to sexual preference, as we discussed in Chapter 4, the state of scientific understanding is a bit more complicated. There is no consensus that such preferences are exclusively biological but rather that there is a biological component. But that is good enough for liberals to conclude that the science supports their perspective.
[19] See Hetherington and Weiler 2009, Haidt 2012.

facts (either liberal or conservative).[20] And in a particularly clever study (in our view), Anthony Washburn and Linda Skitka created data presentations (with respect to a range of issues) that could easily be interpreted one way but that actually indicate the opposite when closely examined. When shown these data analyses and asked what they suggest, both conservatives and liberals interpreted the evidence in ways that bolstered their initial attitudes. And when errors of interpretation were pointed out, both sides rejected such inconvenient evidence at the same rate. Thus, contrary to the view that liberals are disproportionately habituated to scientific reasoning, Washburn and Skitka conclude that "liberals and conservatives appear to be similarly motivated to deny scientific claims that are inconsistent with their attitudes."[21]

There is even some theoretical rationale to suspect that liberals are actually *more* likely than conservatives to engage in motivated reasoning—at least in some ways. As we showed in Chapter 12 and as several other studies have shown as well, intellectual sophistication tends to enhance motivated reasoning, so if liberals tend to be more educated and bookish, then they would also be more inclined to engage in motivated reasoning. This might be reflected most clearly in differential perceptions of certainty. After all, it stands to reason that education and broader intellectualism would prompt greater intellectual assuredness—or even hauteur—which would be reflected in a tendency to express greater certainty with regard to specific facts (especially, but not exclusively, with regard to perceptions that reflect scientific consensus).[22]

Such assuredness could, by extension, potentially inspire lopsided hostility toward factual heretics. Indeed, some suggestive evidence supports the notion that those who perceive reality through liberal lenses might be disproportionately inclined to spurn others because of political differences. Separate surveys administered by the Pew Research Center in 2014 and the Public Religion Research Institute in 2016 observed that political liberals are more likely to end a social relationship with someone (whether online or off) for political reasons.[23] In short, liberal open-mindedness and tolerance may be for *morality* but not for *reality*.

---

[20] "Liberals and conservatives were uniformly prone to ideologically motivated reasoning" (Kahan 2013a, page 417). There is only "weak evidence for the asymmetry thesis" (Kahan 2016, page 14).
[21] Washburn and Skitka 2017. See also Peterson et al. 2013.
[22] It is important to reiterate that we are not using *intellectualism* as a synonym for *intelligence*. It refers, primarily, to the fact that liberals disproportionately graduate from college having majored in social sciences, humanities, or education and become employed in those professions.
[23] See Mitchell et al. 2014, Jones and Cox 2016.

So, in sum, there is enough theoretical scaffolding to warrant three competing hypotheses regarding ideological asymmetry and DFPs:

H_0: *Symmetry (null) hypothesis: Those who prioritize liberal values are no more or less likely than those who prioritize conservative values to project those values onto their fact perceptions, to express certainty about those perceptions, and to harshly judge those who disagree with them.*

H_1: *Rigidity of the Right hypothesis: Those who prioritize conservative values are disproportionately likely to project those values onto their fact perceptions, to express certainty about those perceptions, and to harshly judge those who disagree with them.*

H_2: *Sophistication realignment hypothesis: Those who prioritize liberal values are disproportionately likely to project those values onto their fact perceptions, to express certainty about those perceptions, and to harshly judge those who disagree with them.*

In the remainder of this chapter, we consider these competing hypotheses by revisiting several of the analyses we have presented in earlier chapters. We begin by looking again at the basic relationships between value priorities and fact perceptions, to see if the connections we described in Chapter 7 are stronger on one side or the other of the ideological divide. Next, we revisit how people respond to fact-checking, the subject of Chapter 14. From there, we examine how values and partisanship may relate to factual certainty, the subject of Chapter 9. Finally, we ask whether the tendency for factual disagreement to prompt social and professional disdain that we observed in Chapter 11 is stronger on the Right or the Left.

Empirical Tests

Looking first at the basic relationships between value priorities and fact perceptions (the subject of Chapter 7), we start with our 2013 data. Regression results normally describe the effects of a variable as it moves from lower to higher points along its range. For example, looking back at Table 7.1 in Chapter 7, the numbers show that the effect of collectivism–individualism (from strong collectivists to strong individualists) on climate is –.24, which means that strong individualists are 24 percentage points less likely to perceive climate change to be real and caused by humans—*independent* of several other potential confounds like party identification (PID), ideology, and demographic variables. This tells us a great deal about perceptions of climate change but does not tell us anything about symmetry or asymmetry; the effect could be thought of as individualists being much *less* likely to have a specific perception or collectivists being much *more* likely.

To see if the effects are symmetric or asymmetric, we have to break the variable down further. Table 15.1 presents the same analysis as Table 7.1, except that the value variables are recoded to represent very collectivist citizens (22% of the national sample) against all of the other categories. The results represent the changes in perceptions associated with this dichotomous variable (1 = strong collectivist; 0 = all others). The same is the case with the second line in the table representing strong individualists (26% of the sample) versus all others. If the results show relatively similar effects of extremity in either direction, this indicates symmetry, while stronger results in one direction or the other would indicate asymmetry of the influence of that particular value on that DFP.

Regarding climate change, we see that the effect is driven in roughly equal measure by both strong individualists *and* strong collectivists (the difference between the 15 and 11 percentage-point effects is not statistically significant). The same pattern emerges for perceptions of racism. However, in relation to whether sexuality is innate, the lack of any association in the aggregate breaks down into no effect of strong collectivism but

TABLE 15.1 Symmetry and Asymmetry of Value Projection (2013)

	HUMAN-DRIVEN CLIMATE CHANGE IS REAL	RACISM IS INFLUENTIAL	SEXUAL ORIENTATION IS INNATE
Strong collectivism	.11 ***	.14 ***	.00
Strong individualism	−.15 ***	−.13 ***	−.07 †
Strong humanism	.24 ***	.09 **	.24 ***
Strong theism	−.04	−.04	−.21 ***

Analyses are binary probit regressions. Coefficients are percentage-point differences in the probability of perceiving the disputed fact to be true, associated with being a strong holder of a value compared to all others. For example, strong collectivists are 11 percentage points more likely than weak collectivists, weak individualists, and strong individualists combined to perceive climate change to be real and anthropogenic. Shaded cells represent statistically significant relationships. The models also include controls for ideology, PID, gender, race, age, family income, and education; but space constraints preclude their inclusion here.

$†p < .10$, $**p < .01$, $***p < .001$.

a small negative effect of strong individualism ($p = .09$), illustrating some degree of conservative asymmetry regarding perceptions of sexuality,

Humanism–theism tells a very different story.[24] Regarding sexuality, the strong effects are roughly symmetric; both theism and humanism at the extremes predict meaningful changes in perceptions (21 and 24 percentage points, respectively). Turning to climate change, the influence of humanism–theism on perceptions is driven entirely by the humanist side. The 8 percentage-point effect of the entire variable (see Table 7.1) is masking a 24 percentage-point effect of extreme humanism alone but no effect for extreme theism. It is not so much that theists trust more that God will not allow climate change as it is that humanists trust more that scientists must be right.

Finally, with respect to humanism–theism and perceptions of racism, the effect is driven entirely by strong humanism (a 9 percentage-point effect, $p < .01$). That is, humanist thinkers seem to be the ones who are more convinced that racism is to blame for the disparities in contemporary society, rather than theists being more motivated to deny it.

To summarize the initial evidence of symmetry versus asymmetry, the influence of specific values on specific DFPs tends to be symmetric (about half of the time) with some important examples of asymmetry from the conservative direction and some from the liberal direction.[25]

Additionally, when we look at symmetry or asymmetry of the influence of PID on DFPs, the results are similarly mixed. As illustrated in Table 15.2, strong Republicans may demonstrate a slightly stronger relationship to climate, while strong Democrats reveal a slightly stronger relationship to perceptions of racism (while neither are related to sexuality, as in the original analyses).[26]

Of course, as we also pointed out in Chapter 7, an alternate interpretation of these results so far is that Stephen Colbert was right: the truth does indeed have a well-known liberal bias. That is, given that climate, racism, and sexuality are all factual disputes on which the preponderance

---

[24] Strong humanists represent 29% of the sample, strong theists 26%.

[25] In other models that we do not display here, to avoid redundancy, we replicated these results with the 2014 and 2016 data as well.

[26] Importantly, while these results are from the same fully specified models that we described in Chapter 7, which simultaneously model the effects of values, ideology, and PID, they are robust to modeling decisions. That is, when we remove PID and ideology from the model and look just at the independent effects of conservative versus liberal values, the conclusions are the same. The same is true if we remove values and focus on comparing the impact of Democratic PID and Republican PID. Likewise, the results are also not dependent on measurement decisions.

TABLE 15.2 Symmetry and Asymmetry of Partisan Fact Projection (2013)

	HUMAN-DRIVEN CLIMATE CHANGE IS REAL	RACISM IS INFLUENTIAL	SEXUAL ORIENTATION IS INNATE
Strong Democrat	.08 †	.10 ***	.05
Strong Republican	−.10 **	−.05 †	−.04

Analyses are binary probit regressions. Coefficients are percentage-point differences in the probability of perceiving the disputed fact to be true, associated with being a strong partisan compared to all others. For example, strong Democrats are 10 percentage points more likely than weak Democrats, weak Republicans, and strong Republicans combined to perceive racism to be influential. The models also include controls for ideology, gender, race, age, family income, and education; but space constraints preclude their inclusion here. Shaded cells represent statistically significant relationships.

$^\dagger p < .10$, $^{**}p < .01$, $^{***}p < .001$.

of evidence supports the liberal point of view, one might be inclined to interpret these results as supporting the hypothesis that people on the Right (whether measured in terms of values or partisanship) are just disproportionately misinformed and that the relationships we observe between liberal values and fact perceptions simply reflect a liberal tendency to follow the science on these things and a conservative reluctance to do so. For this reason, it is important that we continue our investigation by looking at a broader array of factual disputes, including ones around which there is much less scholarly consensus or for which the evidence may even be more consistent with conservative perceptions.

Fortunately, in our 2017 data collections we did precisely that—analyzing perceptions relating to the national debt, vaccines, false convictions, minimum wage increases, immigration, gun control, and violent crime. Also, the 2017 data collections are uniquely useful for examining asymmetry because, as readers may recall, each value measure (inspired by Haidt's "moral foundations") represents only one side of the ideological spectrum (unlike our 2013 and 2014 measures). Specifically, care and equality are liberal values, whereas proportionality, sanctity, loyalty, and authority are conservative values.

Thus, to examine asymmetry with respect to these additional fact disputes, we can simply look again at the results we presented in Chapter 7. Looking at that presentation in Table 15.3 (with control variables removed from the table), we see that there is no clear pattern of liberal or conservative value dominance. Across the ten fact disputes, at least one liberal value and at least one conservative value is significantly predictive of

TABLE 15.3 Symmetry and Asymmetry of Value Projection (2017)

PREDICTORS	CLIMATE	RACE	SEX	DEBT BAD	VACCINES HARMFUL	FALSE CONVICTIONS COMMON	MINIMUM WAGE HURTS	IMMIGRANTS TAKES JOBS	GUN CONTROL WORKS	CRIME UP
Care	**.10**	**.37**	**.16**	-.04	-.02	**.11**	-.04	**-.22**	**.09**	-.05
Equality	.17	.01	.04	**.09**	**-.16**	**.22**	**-.25**	-.11	.13	-.07
Proportionality	.06	**-.12**	.06	.03	**.13**	**-.13**	**.16**	**.26**	.05	**.22**
Sanctity	.05	-.01	**-.12**	**.13**	**.12**	.02	.05	**.10**	.05	**.13**
Authority	**-.13**	-.02	**-.19**	**.09**	**.10**	**-.11**	**.11**	**.24**	**-.22**	**.26**
Loyalty	.01	.05	.03	**-.10**	.03	**-.08**	.01	.06	.04	.07

Shaded cells represent statistically significant relationships ($p < .05$). Analyses are binary probit regressions. Coefficients are percentage-point differences in the probability of believing the dispute is true that are associated with minimum-to-maximum differences in the independent variable in question. For example, those who prioritize care values are 37 percentage points more likely than those who oppose them to believe that racism is influential. The models also include controls for PID, ideology, news attentiveness, gender consciousness, racial consciousness, age, family income, and education; but space constraints preclude their inclusion here.

TABLE 15.4 Predicting Perceptions of Fact Checker Reliability

	SANDERS SUPPORTERS	REPUBLICANS
PolitiFact treatment	**–.14**	**–.35**

Binary probit regression models. The numbers are differences in the predicted probabilities of viewing "fact-checking organizations such as PolitiFact as reliable," associated with exposure to the PolitiFact graphic. Shaded cells represent statistically significant relationships.

perceptions in nine out of ten cases (crime being the exception). In some cases, liberal values appear to be stronger predictors (racism, convictions, and wages), and in other cases conservative values appear stronger (guns and crime).[27]

Resistance to Fact-Checking

The next question to consider is the extent to which *resistance to fact-checking* is stronger on one or the other side of the red/blue divide. Recalling our experiment from the previous chapter, this provides perhaps an even cleaner test of the asymmetry hypothesis, given that the perception in question—candidate Clinton's relative degree of honesty—transcends ideology; the 2016 nomination season provided an extremely fortuitous context in which to examine this question because Secretary Clinton had the uncommon distinction of being loathed by many on the Left as well as the Right.

Again, to evaluate asymmetry with respect to fact-checking resistance, no additional analyses are necessary. Tables 15.4 through 15.6 are simplified presentations of tables that appear in Chapter 14, which show how Sanders supporters and Republicans, respectively, tended to react to the PolitiFact graphic showing that Clinton's public statements had been deemed more truthful, on average, than any of the other candidates running for president in 2016.

Table 15.4 displays the change in each group's perceptions of fact checkers' reliability, and here we do see some asymmetry: Republicans

---

[27] Again, this conclusion is robust to alternate model specifications that do or do not include ideology or PID. Furthermore, if we examine the question by focusing on ideology or PID as the predictive variable of interest (distinguishing Democrats/liberals from Republicans/conservatives) and omitting values from the model, we observe similar patterns. Additionally, if we combine the liberal values into a single variable and the conservative ones into a single variable (to reduce multicollinearity), we see the same things. Finally, the patterns also hold if we substitute the "intuitive epistemologies" measures from Chapter 8 for the direct moral foundations measures.

	SANDERS SUPPORTERS	REPUBLICANS
PolitiFact treatment	.04	.02

Linear (ordinary least squares) regression model. The numbers are differences
in the predicted value of the perceptions of Clinton relative to Trump (coded
such that positive integers up to 1 indicate an advantage for Clinton and negative
integers to −1 indicate an advantage for Trump) that are associated with exposure
to the PolitiFact graphic.

were more than twice as likely as Sanders supporters to see fact checkers
as unreliable. This difference may reflect differences in populism between
liberals and conservatives—the Sanders supporters were not as ready to
throw PolitiFact under the bus.

However, as Tables 15.5 and 15.6 make clear, *neither Sanders
supporters nor Republicans were moved to update their impressions of
Clintons' honesty*—relative to either Trump or Sanders—after seeing the
graphic contradicting Clinton's long-standing characterization as a dishonest politician. If liberals really are less obstinate than conservatives
are—especially with respect to information coming from a source they are
inclined to trust—we would have expected more movement on the part of
Sanders supporters.

Factual Certainty

Another way to address the question of whether one set of DFP
combatants might have an itchier trigger finger is through the lens
of certainty. As we observed in Chapter 9, those with the strongest
value commitments are also considerably more likely to feel that their
perceptions of the world are "certainly" rather than "probably" true.

TABLE 15.6 Predicting Perceptions of Clinton's Honesty Relative
to Sanders

	SANDERS SUPPORTERS	REPUBLICANS
PolitiFact treatment	.06	.02

Linear (ordinary least squares) regression model. The numbers are differences in the
predicted value of the perceptions of Clinton relative to Sanders (coded such that
positive integers up to 1 indicate an advantage for Clinton and negative integers to −1
indicate an advantage for Sanders) that are associated with exposure to the PolitiFact
graphic.

That pattern also holds, to a lesser extent, with respect to partisan and ideological intensity. But does one or the other side of the red/blue divide tend to feel more "factually self-righteous" than the other? If so, it would suggest that misperceptions would be less correctable on that side of the divide.

To briefly reiterate our earlier hypotheses, conservatives' demonstrable tendency toward moral dogmatism (partly as a function of their frequent identities as evangelical Christians) might make us assume that they tend to express greater factual dogmatism as well. But the steady movement over the last generation of more educated whites out of the Republican Party and into the Democratic Party—and their increasing willingness to identify as "liberals"—suggests that such blue Americans might now be the ones to feel more self-assured and absolutist when it comes to what they believe is empirically true (in contrast to what they believe is normatively true). Or maybe these dynamics on the Right and Left just balance each other out, leaving us with ideologically symmetrical levels of certainty.

If we are going to assess these competing hypotheses fairly, we must not focus disproportionately on factual disputes that have clearly disproportionate evidence in support of liberal perceptions—like climate change, racism's influence, or sexuality's innateness. Accordingly, we used our 2017 data to create a "certainty index," by summing individual propensities toward certainty across ten different fact disputes: climate, racism, sexuality, debt, vaccines, false convictions, minimum wage, immigration, gun control, and crime. With respect to each dispute, the variables are dichotomous (1 = certain), resulting in an index that ranges from 0 to 10 (mean = 4.12, standard deviation = 2.46).

Table 15.7 displays results from four separate regression models that highlight the relationship between the certainty index and (1) PID, (2) ideological identification (liberalism–conservatism), (3) moral values (care, equality, proportionality, sanctity, loyalty, and authority), and (4) all of these measures simultaneously (to maintain consistency and comparability to what we have done through most of this book). We also include our standard complement of demographic and attentiveness controls (but, as we have frequently done, we leave them out of the table to simplify the presentation).

As the table makes clear, when it comes to certainty, we have our first evidence of liberal asymmetry. Whether measured as PID, ideological identification, or value priorities, those on the Left tend to express considerably more certainty than do those on the Right. Specifically, strong

TABLE 15.7 Factual Certainty: Left–Right Symmetry/Asymmetry (2017)

	PID MODEL	IDEOLOGY MODEL	VALUES MODEL	ALL MEASURES
PID (GOP high)	–1.27			–.62
Ideology (con high)		–1.43		–.39
Care			1.71	1.52
Equality			.64	.39
Proportionality			–.05	.07
Sanctity			–.23	–.15
Loyalty			–.80	–.75
Authority			–.31	–.07
N	1,000	1,000	1,000	1,000

Shaded cells represent statistically significant relationships. Analyses are ordinary least squares regressions. Results are differences in the number of fact disputes (out of 10) about which respondents feel "certain" in their perception, associated with minimum-to-maximum differences in PID (GOP high), ideological identification (conservative high), and values (moral foundations). For example, those who strongly prioritize the liberal value Care tend to feel certain on about 1.52 more DFPs than those who do not prioritize care.

Democrats tend to feel certain about 1.27 more disputes (out of ten) than do strong Republicans, a difference of 13 percentage points. Similarly, strong liberals tend to feel certain on about 1.43 more issues than do strong conservatives, a difference of 14 percentage points. The value models provide perhaps the most clarity: those who strongly adhere to the liberal value care tend to feel certain about 1.71 more disputes than those who do not, a difference of 17 percentage points. And those who strongly value equality tend to feel certain about .64 more than those who do not, a difference of 6 percentage points. Meanwhile, those who strongly champion the conservative value of loyalty tend to feel certain about *fewer* disputes, on average, than do those who oppose such values. Finally, as the last column shows, these basic patterns hold even when the roles of values, PID, and ideology are all modeled simultaneously.[28]

These results lend support to the theoretical perspective that liberalism and Democratic PID have become increasingly associated with higher

---

[28] These patterns hold with respect to not only the number of disputes about which respondents feel certain but also the probability of feeling certain with respect to individual disputes. Indeed, when we looked at each fact dispute separately, the only two disputes for which this pattern did not clearly hold were debt and minimum wage, with the former being the only one in which Republicans/conservatives tended to express greater certainty.

levels of educational attainment and disproportionate employment in the information economy, leading to greater feelings of factual certainty. Because such heightened intellectualism has been consistently associated (both in this book and in many other studies) with more automatic motivated reasoning, it follows that those on the Left might increasingly hold more certain perceptions. While we found only limited support for liberal asymmetry when it comes to the tendency to connect values with fact perceptions, we see it clearly as it relates to the certainty one has in those perceptions. With respect to some fact disputes, such liberal certainty may be completely justifiable and appropriate (climate and vaccines may be the two clearest examples, with racism and sexuality also being good candidates). But when it comes to many other disputes about which the objective truth is much less clear, such certainty is really not warranted and is likely contributing to political polarization more broadly.

Social Disdain

Does the asymmetry we observe regarding factual certainty translate into greater disdain toward those who hold different fact perceptions? There are reasons to suspect it might. Although a venerable literature has demonstrated that liberals tend to be more tolerant of *moral* or *cultural* heterodoxy (apparently driven by the tendency to embrace moral, religious, and lifestyle differences on the Left and outsized levels of conformity, hierarchism, and traditionalistic religiosity on the Right), tolerance of *factual* disagreement may well function quite differently.

To elaborate, liberals may be less indulgent of perceptual differences than they are of cultural differences because they may view the former as an illegitimate dismissal of evidence and science. Liberals may perceive specific facts to be beyond debate because they are demonstrated by legitimate authority. They may view tolerance of different lifestyles as a virtue but tolerance of ignorance as a vice. As we showed in Chapter 12, liberals hold much more confidence in universities as a source of informational authority, whereas conservatives tend to distrust the factual utterances from the academy (and the government and the media) as clouded by a liberal bias.

We can test this final hypothesis by simply referring back to our findings from Chapter 11, in which we looked at how people respond to a hypothetical coworker ("Bob Stratford") who posts factual claims on Twitter with which they disagree. Figure 15.1 compares the average percentage-point drop in the probability of being willing to work with Bob associated

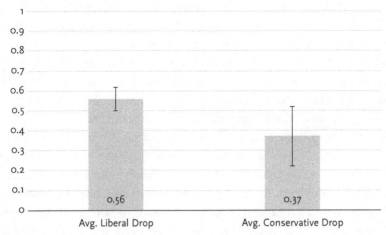

FIGURE 15.1 Drop in Probability of Willingness to Work with Bob, Across All DFP Disputes

with disagreeing with him when he is making liberal claims of fact versus when he is making conservative claims. We see that among those who view the world through liberal-tinted glasses, Bob's contrarian (conservative) tweets produce an average drop in one's willingness to work with him of 56 percentage points. By comparison, among those who see the world through conservative lenses, the average drop in response to one of Bob's liberal tweets is 19 percentage points smaller (though still substantial). The average confidence interval around the effects among conservatives is also much larger—indicating more variability—than is the case with reactions from liberals.

The stronger and more reliable reactions by liberals to factual disagreement support our theory that greater education (which has become associated with the Left in a way that was not true until recently), broader intellectualism, and awareness of the academic support for their perceptions produce disproportionate factual certainty and hence disproportionate disdain toward heretics.

Conclusion

If DFPs were driven primarily by ideological conservatives, as the *rigidity of the Right* hypothesis predicts, then the DFP phenomenon would perhaps be more contained and open to targeted reform. After all, the cultural conservatism that underlies the rigidity of the Right seems to be waning with each successive generation. Millennials and post-Millennials (Democrats and Republicans alike) are far more embracing of sexual and ethnic diversity than their forebears were, which might suggest that an ideological shift of this nature could potentially influence factual depolarization—but only if DFPs were associated with conservatism. And with the exception of a tendency to judge fact checkers more harshly when they produce information that contradicts their perceptions, we have not found any evidence of conservative asymmetry. Instead, we find broad ideological symmetry with respect to the tendency to project one's PID or value priorities onto perceptions of reality. And when it comes to the confidence with which people hold their perceptions of reality, liberals appear considerably more likely to enjoy such confidence, which seems to translate into asymmetrical disdain. These dynamics might relate to the fact that liberalism has become increasingly associated with greater educational attainment and intellectualism more broadly. But whatever may be driving these reactions, one thing is clear: the DFP phenomenon is not merely a conservative phenomenon. It is, rather, a broad condition within American society, which lends further support for our claim that DFPs are probably not going away any time soon.

V | Conclusion

16 | Conclusion

FACTS AND VALUES, KNOWLEDGE AND DEMOCRACY

DUELING FACT PERCEPTIONS (DFPS) ARE a defining characteristic of contemporary American politics. Few citizens see a distinction between *their facts* and *the facts*, while many see the distance between their facts and *your facts*. We suspect this will be the case for a long time. Our first conclusion about DFPs is that their origins are internal as well as external, psychological as well as environmental. Citizens tend to project their core values onto their perceived facts. External factors like partisan leadership and ideological media also contribute to their origins, but the internal factors—the multiple reinforcing psychologies of value projection—will remain regardless of potential changes in the external influences.

This first conclusion bolsters our second, that DFPs are entrenched and deeply resistant to reform. Education is no aid, fact-checking is no comfort, and Democrats are just as susceptible as Republicans (in some ways maybe even more so). DFPs are here to stay, to fight, and likely to polarize behind deeper trenches, with more commitment to the contest. This will cause our policymaking abilities to further calcify, our deliberative capacity to further weaken, and our willingness to even put up with each other to further retreat. Perhaps most importantly, the assumed relationship between knowledge and democracy will bleed and pale as the duel continues.

Concepts, Causes, Consequences, and Correctives

This book employed extensive evidence to illuminate the causes, consequences, and possible correctives of a phenomenon gaining deserved attention in the study of American politics. We began, however, with the concept itself, which has yet to garner an established vocabulary. We offer the term *dueling fact perceptions* as a neutral descriptor. Regardless of underlying truth or facts, the phenomenon is characterized by two competing *perceptions*, and those different perceptions are what influence the political behavior and decision-making of the citizens who hold them. Even when a best approximation of the truth—a fact—is available, there are often two distinct perceptions held by different groups of citizens who believe those perceptions to be facts, which is what causes the trouble.

This approach is different from the focus on *misinformation* and *misperceptions*, which has characterized most research in this area. Those terms suggest that the truth is readily knowable by the public or at least by experts. However, for many of the influential DFPs of contemporary politics, this is not the case, as least not with any kind of certainty. Brute facts like the number of combat casualties in a given conflict or the rate of inflation in a given year may be something on which scholars can claim consensus, but these sorts of facts are relatively unusual within the broader realm of politically influential DFPs.

Even those circumscribed realities require careful framing to gain scholarly consensus on a description of facts. For example, the number of combat casualties in many cases becomes disputed quickly as soon as we include civilian deaths, for which estimates tend to vary greatly. And in the economic realm, the level of inflation demands relative consensus, but the measurement of unemployment does not, given the various ways it can include or exclude certain categories of citizens. Even the level of the national debt does not yield a single number or ratio because some economists only consider the extra-governmental debt owed to American citizens and foreign entities, while others insist that we must also include the intra-governmental debt that some parts of the government owe to each other. The differences in those two numbers describing the national debt are not at all small or inconsequential.

When we move from the size of the national debt to the question of whether it will have negative consequences for the economy or questions like whether raising the minimum wage hurts low-wage workers or whether false convictions are common or rare, even experts who express certainty must recognize that other equally qualified scholars hold opposing views, also often with certainty. Those misguided experts can be written off as idiots or ideologues, but that is very hard for ordinary citizens to sort out; they only hear expert disagreement.

In our view, with some exceptions like the existence of anthropogenic climate change (which may have outsized influence in the conceptualization of DFPs), the broad range of politically influential DFPs are not easily categorized as accurate perceptions and misperceptions but instead reflect uncertainties and public disagreements among experts, to the degree that ordinary citizens cannot arrive easily at a ready conclusion about the facts. This condition that many—not all, but many—of the realities at the heart of contemporary politics are debated among experts and lie outside the realm of ordinary citizens to know for sure creates an environment ripe for dueling perceptions.

Causes

Understanding the causes underlying the broad range of DFPs is perhaps the core inquiry of the book. Unlike the term *partisan facts*, which assumes a specific cause within the term itself, *dueling fact perceptions* as a term allows for a broad range of possible origins. We test and compare possible causal patterns in several empirical studies (Chapters 7, 8, and 9) grounded in several psychological mechanisms (Chapters 5 and 6). One clear origin is the polarization (in its various forms) that has separated Americans from each other. Knowing things is difficult under the best of conditions; hence, epistemology has always been central to social science, if not citizenship. Citizens are free to assume that things are easy to know; scholars know that knowing is hard. Reaching certainty is even harder, almost hubristic. But if knowing things is difficult under positive conditions of consensus values and trusted institutions, it is surely worse under conditions of multifaceted polarization of partisanship, religion, geography, media sources, and especially core values. *The polarization problem has made the epistemological problem more difficult.*

While many psychological theories tell us that under such conditions citizens will be prone to project their priors onto their perceptions, the more controversial question is, *Which priors?* Some scholars have argued that the dominant cause is partisanship, others that it is social identity, others that it is conservative media personalities who guide citizens to their perceptions of facts. These distinctions are important for understanding not just the origins but also the likely future of DFPs and the success of efforts to bring them into consensus. Some possible origins are more internal and others more external. If the causes are fully external—signaling by partisan leaders and conservative media—then DFPs may be changeable or open to reform efforts. On the other hand, if internal origins—core values held by citizens themselves—play a strong independent role, then DFPs will be more durable and difficult to bring into consensus.

Both theory and evidence suggest that DFPs are driven by internal as well as external factors. It is not simply the case that partisan leadership or conservative media are alone to blame (or that the problem will go away if they reform). Value projection results from several interwoven psychological mechanisms representing aspects of both cognitive and social psychology. Selective cognitions—of attention, acceptance, and memory—lead to a highly selective perception of facts. Social conformity reinforces these mechanisms when our close identity groups hold a known consensus perception. Motivated reasoning toward prior beliefs and social norms further reinforces these trends. Other scholars have argued that we are motivated more strongly to be accepted, impressive, or even amusing than to be correct. Accuracy often has far less payoff than social status. Taken together, these interwoven strands of psychology suggest a strong tendency toward value projection.

The empirical evidence from several years of national surveys demonstrates that ordinary citizens project their core values onto their perceived facts, without the intervention of external leadership being necessary. Whether we focus on political values, personal values, or moral values, the results are the same. The connections between specific values and specific perceptions of facts are predictable and strong. Greater individualism predicts the perception that climate change is not real, just as greater collectivism predicts the perception that racism is influential on social outcomes and greater theism predicts the perception that sexuality is not innate. Across several years and several measurement techniques, values are as powerful as partisan identity (PID) in predicting DFPs. These influences remain strong even when controlling for the influence of social identities or attention to ideological media.

We want to be as clear as possible about our positions on the prominent alternative rival hypotheses, which do have important influences on DFPs. Social identities—especially race and gender—do have noteworthy effects on perceived facts, but they frame perceptions less powerfully than values, across a smaller range of DFPs. Identity (and especially pride in that identity) is important for the subset of perceptions that are clearly related to specific identities, but for many others it is not as influential. Ideological media similarly have important effects but not dominant ones.

The most prevalent opposing argument is partisan leadership. However, PID only predicts some DFPs, but some it does not, while values predict *all* of the DFPs we studied. Values also differentiate among them, with specific values being connected to individual DFPs in a predictable fashion. Perhaps most importantly, PID tends to influence DFPs primarily when combined with media attention. Unlike values, PID does not usually frame DFPs among citizens who are less politically attentive. Partisan leadership is a fully external mechanism, unlike the internal and deep-seated effects of value projection.

In addition to these empirical tests and recognized psychological theory, we offer a set of arguments grounded in Tetlockian psychology, about how *intuitive epistemologies* and *sacred values* account for the process of how values are projected onto facts. The core of this theory is that *values carry epistemologies*: citizens do not bring the same approaches to knowledge but hold competing intuitions about the important questions that frame their observations. These intuitive epistemologies vary systematically with value priorities, priming us for divergent perceptions. We do not end up with the same answers because we often do not begin with the same questions. A second argument is that *sacred values lead to sacred facts*. The more absolutist our values are, the more absolutist our facts tend to be, accounting for some of the uncorrectable nature of fact perceptions as well as the overabundance of certainty. And when it comes to certainty of fact perceptions, extremity of PID has little influence compared to the dominant role of value extremity. These facets of intuitive epistemology reinforce the process of value projection. Grounded in this approach as well as the well-established arguments of cognitive and social psychology, we provide a broad accounting of the deep psychological basis of dueling facts.

Consequences

What does it mean if we have a long-term state of DFPs? Other scholars have made several of these consequences clear: greater *public ignorance*, more entrenched *policy gridlock*, and the failure of *deliberation*. In a political environment characterized by DFPs and struggles by elites and masses alike to grasp their implications, we are likely to suffer from a lack of accurate knowledge among citizens, a lack of agreement on public problems and their solutions, and a lack of true deliberation.

Our contribution to the question of consequences focuses on the social (and therefore indirectly political) ramifications. When we examine how the recognition of opposing fact perceptions influences reactions toward those misguided or misinformed fellow citizens, it becomes clear that DFPs have broader consequences for social and professional interactions. Citizens are less inclined to think well of or even work with those who hold opposing perceptions of facts. The reluctance to work next to fellow citizens who perceive facts differently is a noteworthy facet of contemporary polarized America. As citizens retreat more into enclaves of like-minded families and friends, the workplace remains one of the possible spheres of interaction across ideologies, but not if shunning grounded in contrary perceptions becomes normal. Rather than attempting to understand those with opposing perceptions, citizens often react with distrust of their character. Rather than engage in discussion or a search for common ground, they more often retreat further into their own zone of comfort, reinforcing the prevalent worldview bubbles and increasing the existing polarization.

In his study of modern means of understanding reality (*A Social History of Truth*), the historian of science Steven Shapin noted the close connection between facts and civility: "The ultimate incivility is the public withdrawal of trust in another's access to the world and in another's moral commitment to speaking the truth about it."[1] Many Americans have withdrawn this trust, and hence this civility, from their fellow citizens along fault lines of fact perception, with all of the potential for spiraling polarization this suggests. DFPs beget social disdain and disengagement, which beget further polarization, and the cycle continues.

Correctives

Many scholars not only want to understand contemporary conditions but also hope to provide ideas that will influence the future. We wouldn't mind offering that, but the evidence does not support it. While many are hopeful that DFPs are a temporary phenomenon or that they can be corrected by expanded political knowledge or greater education or more fact-checking, the theory and evidence suggest that these potential correctives will not be effective.

Other scholars have observed that as political knowledge rises, DFPs do as well. As citizens gain political sophistication, they employ it to project their priors—both values and partisanship—more adroitly onto their perceptions. Our data reveal the exact same patterns. Political knowledge contributes to value projection rather than leading toward consensus

---

[1] Shapin 1994, page 36.

perceptions. Education is in theory the stronger candidate for a mechanism of reform. Greater education encourages not only specific knowledge but a greater desire for knowledge gathering and the ability to seek out legitimate information, as well as respect for the institutions that promote it. Education *should* be a corrective, but it is not. The empirical analyses demonstrate that as citizens grow in education, they also grow in their ability to filter evidence and to project their values onto their perceived facts. *Citizens employ greater education to cement the connections between values and perceptions more firmly.*

We suspect that this deep problem for democracy is the result of the *explosion of available knowledge* at the same time as the *implosion of trust* in the institutions that create and disseminate it. The amount of available information expanded at the same time that trust in any specific source declined. Under these conditions, deciding which information to accept is difficult, so many citizens default to value-driven perceptions. Even under these problematic conditions of rising data and falling trust, if citizens shared values, they would still likely gravitate to the same perceptions of facts. The current information environment allows them to travel freely, but their values take them down different roads. Favorable conditions may encourage consensus fact perceptions—trust in gatekeeping institutions and shared values that shape our perceptions—but in contemporary America, those conditions do not exist. *Contrary to the hope often voiced, we cannot educate ourselves out of our dilemma of divided perceptions.*

Another potential corrective is the fact-check industry. Like greater education, many reformers hope that fact-checking may lead toward consensus perceptions of facts. But the available empirical studies suggest the opposite—that citizens disregard fact-checks that dispute their prior beliefs, making exposure to fact-checking ineffective when it comes to DFPs. Our own studies confirm these conclusions. The epistemology of the fact-checking enterprise is not as authoritative or unquestionable as its advocates often suggest. The major fact checkers do not always agree on the selection or assessment of political facts. On the contrary, their conclusions sometimes contradict each other, leading to grounds for mistrust. When we look at how ordinary citizens respond to fact-checking, they tend to distrust the source and reject the correction when fact checkers dispute their priors. Even while fact-checking may have some salutary effects, such as influencing the behavior of politicians who seek to avoid ending up on its public scales of truth and falsity, fact-checking is unlikely to alter the trajectory of DFPs.

A final reason we are pessimistic about the potential for correction is the essential ideological symmetry in the origins of fact perceptions. If value projection were only occurring on the Right, then reformers could focus on convincing only one group of citizens, counteracting just the tendencies of conservatives to perceive convenient facts. But the tendency toward the projection of priors is bipartisan, with relatively equal influence among conservatives and liberals. This is not just the case for DFPs on which the dominant evidence favors liberal perceptions but extends to those on which scholars have legitimate divisions. We are not the first to note ideological symmetry in regard to DFPs, but our data bear out the essential similarities in the psychology of perception.

To summarize our arguments about DFPs, the concept is broad, the causes deep, the consequences severe, and the potential correctives ineffective.

Limitations

Of course, as with any investigation, ours is limited in various ways. Two limitations deserve particular attention.

The Historical Problem

We have suggested that polarized fact perceptions are not merely an important problem but a greater problem than they have been in the past. Historical judgments of this nature are hard to avoid but difficult to prove. This is not at heart a historical book grounded in historical data but instead focuses on contemporary empirical evidence. If we have demonstrated that DFPs are quite bad now, are driven by value polarization, are causing broad negative consequences, and seem to be poised to lead to further negative consequences in the future, then we believe our job is done.

DFPs are clearly not *entirely* new. Surely there were some DFPs in the past (just as there were some divided values). Perhaps the most prominent example is perceptions of the Soviet Union during the Cold War: some Americans saw the Soviet Union as fundamentally aggressive and expansionist, while others saw it as fundamentally defensive and not posing a military threat. But we hold that if we compare our current politics to the post–World War Two era of the 1950s or the Vietnam Era of the 1960s and 1970s or the Reagan era of the 1980s or even the Clinton era of the 1990s, there are more DFPs now, across a broader range, more deeply divided, with stronger consequences, than in these previous times. But if the reader is convinced that we have always had DFPs to the same degree as now and we have always suffered from their consequences, that does not dismiss the importance of our arguments. If DFPs are nothing new, they are still important; but the significance of the book rises if DFPs have also risen in their range and potency.

Unfortunately, we have no way to explore this question empirically. We have detailed empirical data for the five-year period from 2013 to 2017, but there are no comparable data for those previous times. One reason no such data exist, even though a great deal of other sorts of polling was conducted, may be that this concept was not on the radar then—which is our point. In the end, however, we cannot show data comparisons, and one's perception of the current era compared to the past is a matter of qualitative historical comparisons. We think the polarized nature of the current era is manifest but also that our core arguments about the concepts, causes, consequences, and corrections of DFPs do not depend on demonstrating historical uniqueness. We are not alone, however, in suspecting historical change. In an interview for the *New Yorker*, an American intimately familiar with contemporary political conflicts expressed the view that

> ideally, in a democracy, everybody would agree that climate change is the consequence of man-made behavior, because that's what ninety-nine percent of scientists tell us. And then we would have a debate about how to fix it. That's how, in the seventies, eighties, and nineties, you had Republicans supporting the Clean Air Act and you had a market-based fix for acid rain rather than a command-and-control approach. So you'd argue about means, but there was a baseline of facts that we could all work off of. And now we just don't have that."[2]

President Obama's sentiments are backed up by a recent study from the Rand Corporation, which conducted a comparison of public disagreements about facts across different historical periods of American history, including the 1880s era of yellow journalism and the 1960s era of civil rights and war protest.[3] It concludes that

> We see no evidence in any of these earlier periods of an increase in disagreement about facts and analytical interpretations of facts and data. This trend

---

[2] Remnick 2016.
[3] Kavanagh and Rich 2018, chapter 3.

appears today in the form of disagreement over scientific findings, data and statistics, and objective facts. . . . Although each of the periods explored in this chapter exhibit a significant rise in disagreement over social, economic, and political policies and norms, there is little evidence that agreement about the veracity and legitimacy of basic facts declined in previous eras.[4]

The Rand study is the only serious historical evaluation of this question of which we are aware. It recognizes that survey data or other quantitative measures of perceptions of facts are simply not available for previous eras and that the best that can be done is to examine newspaper reports, political commentaries, and other media presentations. The historical changes the authors describe comport with our own sense of the evolution of American politics over the past decades. We believe the historical shift is real, but if DFPs were always there and political scholars simply did not notice, that does not lessen their importance in the current day.

The Lack of Solution

This book reaches pessimistic conclusions. Everything we have learned about the causes of DFPs led us to suspect that the commonly suggested corrections—especially greater education and fact-checking—are not effective. All of the empirical studies we have conducted indicate that this is the case. We suspect that the situation will only get worse in the coming years, with no known solution available. We know that many scholars desire or expect a more optimistic conclusion from a book of this nature, but we don't want to pretend to an optimism that seems unwarranted.

We have frequently heard the reaction that surely there is an answer to this problem. We have just not heard a specific or plausible one. We have heard repeatedly that the pendulum will swing back, surely. The pendulum theory of social science—essentially that things tend in one direction but will also swing back the other way over time (so we need not worry)—is not a valid or supported historical theory. Sometimes things do swing back and sometimes they do not, but the idea that most things swing from one pole to the other and maintain a balance in the middle is simply not the case. Often there are long-term trends in one direction, and cultures or institutions move in a discernable path over time.[5]

---

[4] Ibid., pages xiii, 72.

[5] As some have pointed out, we were indeed polarized deeply in previous periods of American history about the facts regarding the nature of non-whites and slavery. This led to a major war that

Moreover, pendulum thinking offers no sense of *when* the return swing will occur or, perhaps more importantly, *how* that would happen. Change requires a mechanism of causation. The current trends and known mechanisms of change point toward greater polarization; it is unknown to us what would reverse the current trend or in what direction greater consensus would be. If we move back to consensus, on what side of each factual divide? Those who assert confidence in a future consensus often assume the consensus will be around *their* perceptions of facts. But any future consensus might also be on the other side. We are not sure what many readers would think worse: greater polarization of fact perceptions or consensus around facts they oppose. An assumption of a pendulum swing toward a favorable consensus is more comforting than real.

Conclusion I: Facts and Values

"The greatest American superstition is belief in facts."

—*Count Hermann von Keyserling*[6]

Facts are fragile. They require trust in the institutions that create them, trust in the media that communicate them, and, perhaps less obviously— but more importantly for contemporary democracy—trust in the values that we share, because without consensus values, consensus perceptions of facts are difficult to maintain. We have demonstrated empirically that facts and values are deeply intertwined, regardless of efforts to maintain a distinction between consensus facts and polarized values. For individual citizens to achieve correspondence with external reality is difficult, but to achieve coherence with internal values is much easier. That is especially true when information is overly plentiful and trusted authorities to sort it out are relatively scarce. Many contemporary philosophers have no confidence in the fact/value distinction, and psychologists have less. We think the wall has surely been breached to the point that little practical distinction remains. Values and facts are hopelessly intertwined.

The painter Paul Gauguin famously represented the world in colors that diverged from the perceptions of others. Many have wondered if he really saw things in vivid alternatives. Others have asked, *Who is right, Gauguin*

---

caused more American casualties than any other war before or since. If the response to DFPs is that we have been here before during the Civil War era, that is not comforting.

[6] Quoted by Gunther 1947, page 907.

or us? When it comes to political facts, do we see what is there or what we project? Or do we see what others tell us is there? The alternative hypotheses about the origins of DFPs are largely external, driven by political and social leadership. In this view, the offer of misinformation by trusted sources creates misperceptions by ordinary citizens. But the availability of conflicting information does not account for the believing of it. Citizens can choose sources and perceptions, and they tend to choose what comports with their own values. Gauguin projected his personal vision onto painted reality; citizens' contemporary projections are more prosaic and less artistic. But they are projections nonetheless. And to the degree that citizens' dueling perceptions of facts are driven by the internal mechanisms of interwoven psychologies, core values, and intuitive epistemologies, they will be deeply entrenched and resistant to reform.

Conclusion II: Knowledge and Democracy

"Democracy does require basic bonds of trust between its citizens.
It doesn't work if we think the people who disagree with us
are all motivated by malice . . .
Democracy grinds to a halt without a willingness to compromise,
or when even basic facts are contested."

—*Barack Obama*[7]

The normal fixes are not working: political knowledge, education, and fact-checking are not creating consensus facts. The bitter pill for democracy is that knowledge and education are working *against* consensus, increasing the problem of DFPs as they empower citizens to follow their internal inclinations more forcefully.

The most controversial consequence of DFPs may be in regard to the nature of democracy itself. In a sense what this book is really about is the paradoxical relationship between facts and democracy. Democracy relies on accurate factual knowledge among the citizens who are entrusted to weigh alternatives and choose leadership. The free exchange of information that democratic rights to freedom of speech and press encourage are expected to lead to the emergence of accurate information in the marketplace of ideas. But the democratization of information has not led to consensus facts that promote the health of democracy.

---

[7] Final State of the Union Address, January 12, 2016.

Education and democracy are most often thought to be reinforcing: education empowers democracy, while democracy empowers education. The Founder and physician Benjamin Rush famously argued that "freedom can exist only in the society of knowledge," and many Americans since the time of the Revolution have agreed that the relationship must always be salutary. But the connections from education to better democratic outcomes, as well as from the democracy of information to consensus perceptions of facts, are faltering. Greater political knowledge and higher levels of education no longer have entirely positive relationships with functioning democracy.

While we would like greater education to lead to positive outcomes, the reality can be quite different. Greater education and political sophistication of the public do not help and may hurt. Those with greater intellectual assets do not wind their way closer to any consensus reality but merely reinforce their predispositions. Under current conditions of multifaceted polarization and fractured authority, DFPs become dominant and the normal relationship between knowledge and democracy no longer applies.

The university traditionally plays a strong role in establishing consensus facts. But that relationship is severed when the university is not a trusted arbiter of reality. The primary institution entrusted to discern and disseminate knowledge is no longer trusted by a large sector of the population who perceive the university to be a partisan institution, leading them to reject university claims to knowledge. Max Weber argued that "the primary task of a useful teacher is to teach his students to recognize 'inconvenient' facts—I mean facts that are inconvenient for their party opinions."[8] Universities have more and more difficulty fulfilling this function. University-sponsored knowledge may be entirely legitimate but has lost verisimilitude—the appearance of truth—to many citizens. This declining trust in the creators of knowledge has led to a fracturing of authority.

We are not served well by simply another call for greater education. In a polarized environment, increasing political knowledge and engagement are now part of the problem. Greater education and knowledge of politics—factors that used to be seen as aids to democracy—are now sources of factual division. We have undergone a realignment of authority, away from traditional sources of consensus facts and toward personal values, personal knowledge, and hence a politics of dueling facts. Its consequences are not

---

[8] Weber 1946.

only miscommunication, distrust, poor policy decisions, and failing deliberation but also the corruption of the relationship between knowledge and democracy.

We opened the book with the observation that facts rely on trust. Humans with no reliable access to truth can nonetheless reach consensus perceptions of facts when they share values and maintain trust in legitimate authority. But facts—our all-too-human approximations of the truth—are as fragile as human failings. We end this book with the conclusion that the psychology of ordinary citizens, who project their priors onto their perceptions, has created a realignment of trust and a fracturing of facts, which no known reform is likely to repair.

Appendix | Measurement Notes

T
HESE NOTES ADDRESS TWO METHODOLOGICAL questions in the survey measurement of perceived facts: the use of a midpoint and the possibility of disingenuous survey responses.

1) No midpoint on fact perceptions

We chose to measure fact perceptions along a four-point scale, including response options of "certainly true" "probably true," "probably false," and "certainly false." This allows us to gauge both the direction of perceptions and the important distinction between certain and probabilistic perceptions. We intentionally avoided including a midpoint for several reasons.

   a. Though some people may lack a clear position on specific facts, they nonetheless may have a working assumption that it is important to gauge, which would be reflected in a "probably true" or "probably false" response.

   b. When a factual question arises in political conversation or decision-making, citizens are often forced to employ such a working assumption, and our goal was to measure that inclination.

   c. A midpoint would likely be overused in the same sense as the midpoint is on questions of party identification; "Independents" are often closet leaners, which requires a branching scale to identify. Space constraints on our surveys did not allow for a branching question for each dueling fact perception (DFP), so we believe that a forced choice is a better measurement technique.

   d. To the degree that some respondents actually have no idea about the fact and are truly in the middle, the forced choice will merely cause random measurement error to either side and downgrade the relationships in our analyses. In other words, this approach militates *against* our hypothesized findings and hence is the appropriate method.

   e. Including a midpoint would also limit dichotomous analyses of the type we employ, which provide clear interpretations of effects. An alternative approach would have been to incorporate a midpoint and exclude those respondents from the analysis, but this would likely have falsely increased the appearance of effects by excluding the more uncertain citizens. By keeping the possibly uncertain respondents in the "probable" categories, we maintain the largest representation of respondents and provide a more valid test of our hypotheses.

2) Disingenuous Survey Reponses

One critique of the research on DFPs is that expressions of polarized perceptions may not be real: participants in surveys or experiments may be expressing perceptions of climate change or the prevalence of racism that they know are not really accurate but are making themselves feel good or perhaps even goading their interlocutors. In this sense, the reasoning is motivated not by empirical accuracy or social acceptance or belief congruence but by expressiveness.

One response to this is that "mere" expressions of belief and preference are all we have in democratic politics. If citizens are arguing in public grounded in certain fact perceptions, it may not matter much if they do not *really* believe them. Timur Kuran refers to this as *preference falsification* and demonstrates its power within democratic politics even when not entirely honest.[1] If public expressions are partly false, they are still equally influential. (See especially Chapter 11 on the ramifications of the public expression of DFPs, which have the same political and social consequences whether fully sincere or partially expressive.)

A second, more empirical response is that there is very little evidence that expressions of polarized fact perceptions are not real. Some research suggests that if citizens are given the right incentive (paid money), they will in fact offer the accurate facts.[2] However, in another study, Adam Berinsky found that there was no difference between unpaid factual responses and those paid for accuracy. Moreover, he suggests that the alteration in paid responses in some studies is due to an acquiescence or demand effect: participants know which answers academics consider to be "correct" and are sometimes willing to offer them for money.[3]

Dan Kahan is likewise not persuaded, grounded in several factors including the samples of participants in the monetary reward studies: "M Turk workers are distinguished from members of the general population by their willingness to perform various forms of internet labor for pennies per hour. They are also known to engage in deliberate misrepresentation of their identities and other characteristics to increase their on-line earnings. . . . Thus, how readily *they* will alter their reported beliefs in anticipation of earning monetary rewards for guessing what *researchers* regard as 'correct' answers furnishes an unreliable basis for inferring how members of the general public form beliefs outside the lab."[4]

Finally, Flynn et al. similarly conclude that there is scant evidence for factual falsification: "the studies find only partial and inconsistent evidence of greater belief accuracy as a result of incentives . . . we do not know of convincing evidence that misperceptions about highly salient facts are insincere."[5]

---

[1] Kuran 1997.
[2] See Bullock et al. 2015, Khanna and Sood 2016, Prior et al. 2015.
[3] Berinsky 2018.
[4] Kahan 2016, page 15, italics in original.
[5] Flynn et al. 2017, pages 133, 139.

TABLE A7.1 Value Projection, Partisan Leadership, and DFPs (2014)

	HUMAN-DRIVEN CLIMATE CHANGE IS REAL	RACISM IS INFLUENTIAL	SEXUAL ORIENTATION IS INNATE
Simple model			
Collectivism–Individualism	−.17 ***	−.22 ***	.05
Humanism–Theism	−.13 ***	−.04	−.27 ***
PID (GOP high)	−.36 ***	−.36 ***	−.08
Interactive models			
Collectivism–Individualism (inattentive)	−.11 ***	−.15 *	.03
Collectivism–Individualism (attentive)	−.23 ***	−.51 ***	.05
Humanism–Theism (inattentive)	−.11 **	.06	−.30 ***
Humanism–Theism (attentive)	−.18 ***	−.15 ***	−.24 ***
PID (inattentive)	−.26 ***	−.24 ***	−.10
PID (attentive)	−.46 ***	−.52 ***	−.08
Controls (from simple model)			
Ideology (con high)	−.20 ***	−.23 ***	−.32 ***
Non-white	.05 †	.11 ***	−.11†
Female	.07 **	.04 †	.09 ***
Education	.01	.00	.02
Age	−.12 *	−.04	.06
Income	.00	.00	.02 *
N	859	862	857

Analyses are binary probit regressions. Coefficients are percentage-point differences in the probability of perceiving the disputed fact to be true, associated with minimum-to-maximum differences in the independent variable in question. For example, individualists are 17 percentage points less likely than collectivists to perceive climate change to be real and anthropogenic.

Shaded cells represent statistically significant relationships.

$^\dagger p < .10$, $^* p < .05$, $^{**} p < .01$, $^{***} p < .001$.

TABLE A8.1 Moral Values and Intuitive Epistemology

	CAREGIVER	CRUSADER	UMPIRE	PURIST	LOYALIST	CONSTABLE	SCIENTIST
Moral values							
Care	-.08 (.08)	.21 (.08) **	-.12 (.07) †	-.10 (.06)	.01 (.06)	-.02 (.07)	.05 (.08)
Fairness (equality)	-.06 (.08)	.27 (.08) **	.13 (.08) †	-.08 (.06)	-.08 (.06)	-.15 (.06) *	-.10 (.08)
Fairness (proportionality)	.16 (.07) *	.00 (.07)	.09 (.07)	.02 (.06)	-.07 (.05)	.00 (.06)	-.11 (.08)
Sanctity	-.18 (.06) **	-.18 (.06) **	.10 (.06) †	.20 (.05) **	.11 (.04) *	.15 (.05) **	-.04 (.06)
Loyalty	-.13 (.06) *	-.07 (.06)	.06 (.05)	.07 (.05)	.19 (.05) **	.11 (.05) *	-.19 (.06) **
Authority	-.10 (.07)	.01 (.06)	.07 (.06)	.02 (.06)	.07 (.05)	.03 (.06)	.05 (.07)
Control variables							
PID (D → R)	-.11 (.04) **	-.23 (.03) **	-.03 (.04)	.07 (.03) **	.05 (.03) †	.08 (.03) **	.11 (.04) **
White	.02 (.03)	-.09 (.03) **	.00 (.03)	.00 (.03)	-.01 (.02)	.01 (.03)	.04 (.04)
Female	.02 (.03)	.05 (.03) †	.00 (.03)	.05 (.03) †	-.04 (.02) †	.00 (.03)	.00 (.03)
Income	.14 (.06) *	-.06 (.06)	.04 (.06)	.01 (.05)	-.02 (.04)	.06 (.05)	-.05 (.07)
Education	.15 (.07) *	.08 (.08)	-.12 (.07)	-.09 (.06)	-.02 (.05)	-.15 (.06) *	.18 (.08) *
Age	-.02 (.05)	.04 (.05)	.05 (.05)	.09 (.04) *	.12 (.04) **	-.06 (.05)	-.24 (.06) **

Results are average changes in the probability of the dependent variable in each column being positive (in this case, indicating each intuitive method) associated with a full range change in the independent variable. Standard errors are in parentheses. For example, the increased probability of identifying the Crusader epistemology associated with moving from low to high on the Fairness moral value scale is 27%.

Analyses were conducted through binary probit regressions of epistemological inclinations against moral values and control variables. N = 862.

Shaded cells represent statistically significant relationships.

†p < .10, *p < .05, **p < .01.

TABLE A8.2 Intuitive Epistemology and DFPs

	CLIMATE	RACISM	SEXUALITY
Intuitive method			
Caregiver	**.08 (.03) ***	.03 (.04)	.00 (.03)
Crusader	**.11 (.03) ****	**.14 (.03) ****	**.08 (.04) ***
Umpire	.04 (.03)	−.02 (.04)	−.04 (04)
Purist	.03 (.04)	−.05 (.04)	−.07 (.04)
Loyalist	.01 (.04)	**−.09 (.05) ***	−.03 (05)
Constable	−.05 (.04)	−.02 (.04)	−.05 (.04)
Scientist	.06 (.03)	.06 (.04)	.05 (.04)
Control variables			
PID (D → R)	**−.27 (.03) ****	**−.24 (.03) ****	**−.20 (.03) ****
White	−.02 (.03)	−.05 (.03)	**.07 (.03) ***
Female	**.05 (.03) †**	.02 (.03)	.03 (.03)
Income	.05 (.05)	.01 (.06)	.07 (.06)
Education	.06 (.07)	.02 (.06)	.07 (.07)
Age	.00 (.05)	.00 (.05)	**−.15 (.05) ****

Results are average changes in the probability of the dependent variable in each column being positive (in this case, the probability of perceiving the DFP to be real) associated with a full range change in the independent variable. Standard errors are in parentheses. For example, the increased probability of perceiving racism to be influential associated with Crusader epistemology is 14%.

Analyses were conducted through binary probit regressions of DFPs against epistemological inclinations and control variables. $N = 862$.

Shaded cells represent statistically significant relationships.

$^{†}p < .10$, $^{*}p < .05$, $^{**}p < .01$.

TABLE A8.3 Intuitive Epistemology and Additional DFPs

	DEBT (HURTS ECONOMY)	TERROR (IS A THREAT)	FALSE CONVICTIONS (ARE COMMON)	VACCINES CAUSE AUTISM
Intuitive method				
Caregiver	-.04 (.03)	-.01 (.03)	.00 (.04)	.04 (.03)
Crusader	-.05 (.04)	-.03 (.04)	.08 (.04) *	.00 (.03)
Umpire	.09 (.04) *	.04 (.04)	-.02 (.04)	.02 (.04)
Purist	-.04 (.04)	.07 (.05)	.03 (.04)	.16 (.04) **
Loyalist	-.06 (.05)	.13 (.05) *	-.08 (.05) †	.07 (.04) †
Constable	-.04 (.04)	.08 (.05) †	-.05 (.04)	-.05 (.04)
Scientist	.02 (.04)	-.01 (.04)	.04 (.04)	-.05 (.04)
Control variables				
PID (D → R)	.18 (.04) **	.15 (.04) **	-.14 (.03) **	.00 (.03)
White	-.03 (.03)	.05 (.03)	-.04 (.03)	-.07 (.03) *
Female	-.01 (.03)	.10 (.03) **	.03 (.03)	-.01 (.03)
Income	.04 (.06)	.02 (.06)	-.09 (.06)	-.05 (.06)
Education	-.17 (.07) *	-.21 (.07) **	-.14 (.07) *	-.16 (.07) *
Age	.04 (.05)	-.22 (.05) **	.08 (.05)	-.01 (.05)

Results are average changes in the probability of the dependent variable in each column being positive (in this case, the probability of perceiving the DFP to be real) associated with a full range change in the independent variable. Standard errors are in parentheses. For example, the increased probability of perceiving vaccines to cause autism associated with Purist epistemology is 16%.

Analyses were conducted through binary probit regressions of DFPs against epistemological inclinations and control variables. N = 862.

Shaded cells represent statistically significant relationships.

†p < .10, *p < .05, **p < .01.

TABLE A11.1 Factual Disagreement and Socio-Professional Disdain (Climate Change)

	BOB "STUPID"	BOB "SHADY"	WORK W/ BOB
	PROB. Δ (z)	PROB. Δ (z)	PROB. Δ (z)
Bob denies–affirms climate change	.36 (1.54)	.31 (2.22)	.03 (.25)
R denies–affirms climate change	.12 (.71)	.10 (.76)	-.05 (.28)
Bob denies–affirms * R denies–affirms	-.80 (2.81)	-.62 (3.52)	.35 (1.95)
PID (GOP high)	-.12 (4.32)	-.21 (3.13)	.09 (5.60)
Female	.12 (2.00)	.15 (3.29)	-.12 (2.40)
White	.05 (1.26)	.07 (1.62)	-.11 (2.70)
Age	-.32 (3.09)	-.41 (6.68)	.18 (1.28)
Income	-.15 (1.22)	.08 (.99)	.04 (.48)
Education	.08 (1.60)	-.18 (10.51)	-.08 (1.96)
Predicted prob. of "1" at means	.44	.46	.69
N	452	424	429

Each cell coefficient represents the increase/decrease in the predicted probability (converted from the binary probit coefficient) of a respondent (a) viewing Bob as "stupid," (b) viewing him as "shady," or (c) being willing to work with him, for a *minimum-to-maximum* difference in the independent variable. The z coefficient, in parentheses, is the ratio of the unconverted probit coefficient to its (Huber-White) standard error.

TABLE A11.2 Factual Disagreement and Socio-Professional Disdain (Racism)

	BOB "STUPID" PROB. Δ (z)	BOB "SHADY" PROB. Δ (z)	WORK W/ BOB PROB. Δ (z)
Bob denies–affirms racism's import	.13 (1.13)	.26 (2.92)	-.42 (3.99)
R denies–affirms racism's import	.02 (.14)	.16 (1.16)	-.38 (1.96)
Bob denies–affirms * R denies–affirms	-.43 (2.71)	-.57 (19.49)	1.03 (4.28)
PID (GOP high)	-.10 (.76)	-.09 (1.64)	.12 (2.84)
Female	.13 (3.28)	.26 (2.34)	-.11 (1.40)
White	.12 (1.50)	.04 (.32)	-.08 (1.14)
Age	-.29 (6.50)	-.18 (3.13)	.06 (.55)
Income	.05 (.66)	-.09 (.91)	-.04 (1.21)
Education	-.15 (3.41)	-.06 (.30)	.17 (.93)
Predicted prob. of "1" at means	.43	.45	.68
N	420	420	422

Each cell coefficient represents the increase/decrease in the predicted probability (converted from the binary probit coefficient) of a respondent (a) viewing Bob as "stupid," (b) viewing him as "shady," or (c) being willing to work with him, for a *minimum-to-maximum* difference in the independent variable.

TABLE A11.3 Factual Disagreement and Socio-Professional Disdain (Minimum Wage)

	BOB "STUPID" PROB. Δ (z)	BOB "SHADY" PROB. Δ (z)	WORK W/ BOB PROB. Δ (z)
Bob: minimum wage hurts–helps	-.03 (.87)	-.17 (6.32)	-.52 (8.68)
R: minimum wage hurts–helps	.02 (1.01)	-.02 (-.97)	-.57 (7.19)
Bob denies–affirms * R denies–affirms	-.06 (1.13)	.16 (3.86)	1.45 (8.99)
PID (GOP high)	-.08 (4.24)	-.09 (5.84)	-.17 (5.87)
Female	.00 (.61)	-.01 (1.46)	-.05 (.77)
White	-.01 (.67)	-.03 (1.87)	-.04 (2.45)
Age	-.00 (.23)	.01 (.45)	.14 (3.01)
Income	-.12 (10.55)	-.07 (5.56)	.09 (1.60)
Education	-.02 (1.21)	-.04 (1.51)	-.16 (.79)
Predicted prob. of "1" at means	.04	.05	.81
N	299	299	299

Each cell coefficient represents the increase/decrease in the predicted probability (converted from the binary probit coefficient) of a respondent (a) viewing Bob as "stupid," (b) viewing him as "shady," or (c) being willing to work with him, for a *minimum-to-maximum* difference in the independent variable.

TABLE A11.4 Factual Disagreement and Socio-Professional Disdain (Free Trade)

	BOB "STUPID"	BOB "SHADY"	WORK W/ BOB
	PROB. Δ (z)	PROB. Δ (z)	PROB. Δ (z)
Bob: free trade hurts–helps	-.12 (4.18)	.02 (.24)	-1.05 (4.63)
R: free trade hurts–helps	.09 (1.98)	.02 (.28)	-1.02 (8.96)
Bob denies–affirms * R denies–affirms	-.14 (2.09)	-.17 (1.03)	2.18 (6.59)
PID (GOP high)	-.06 (2.05)	.01 (.43)	.02 (.20)
Female	-.13 (4.52)	-.06 (2.92)	-.15 (2.45)
White	-.06 (6.94)	.01 (.69)	.18 (2.21)
Age	.07 (.99)	-.00 (.09)	.22 (1.24)
Income	.02 (.36)	.03 (.59)	.08 (.95)
Education	-.30 (4.03)	-.35 (3.45)	-.25 (1.65)
Predicted prob. of "1" at means	.10	.10	.70
N	197	197	197

Each cell coefficient represents the increase/decrease in the predicted probability (converted from the binary probit coefficient) of a respondent (a) viewing Bob as "stupid," (b) viewing him as "shady," or (c) being willing to work with him, for a *minimum-to-maximum* difference in the independent variable.

TABLE A14.1 Exposure to PolitiFact and Changes in Perceptions of Clinton's Honesty: The Conditioning Roles of Populism and Education

	POPULISM	EDUCATION
PolitiFact treatment	.24 *	.24
Populism	.13 **	
Treatment * populism	−.25	
Education	.12	.28
Treatment * education		−.27
Female	−.04 *	−.04 *
Non-white	.04	.03
Age	.05	.00
Income	−.13	−.11
Intercept	−.32	−.30
R^2	.39	.40
N	343	343

Linear (ordinary least squares) regression model. The unstandardized regression coefficients represent differences in the predicted value of the perceptions of Clinton, relative to Trump (coded such that positive figures up to 1 indicate an advantage for Clinton and negative to −1 indicate an advantage for Trump) that are associated with the independent variables on the left side (exposure to the PolitiFact graphic and minimum-to-maximum differences in the other variables).

Shaded cells represent statistically significant relationships.

$*p < .05, **p < .01$.

REFERENCES

Abcarian, Robin, and Kathleen Hennessey. "President Obama Gets Enthusiastic Welcome at L.A. Gay Event." *Los Angeles Times*, June 6, 2012.

Abelson, Robert. "Beliefs Are Like Possessions." *Journal for the Theory of Social Behaviour* 16, no. 3 (1986): 223–250.

Abramowitz, Alan. *The Disappearing Center: Engaged Citizens, Polarization, and American Democracy*. New Haven, CT: Yale University Press, 2011.

Abramowitz, Alan. *The Polarized Public: Why American Government Is So Dysfunctional*. Boston: Pearson, 2013.

Abramowitz, Alan, and Kyle Saunders. "Is Polarization a Myth?" *Journal of Politics* 70, no. 2 (2008): 542–555.

Achen, Christopher, and Larry Bartels. *Democracy for Realists: Why Elections Do Not Produce Responsive Government*. Princeton, NJ: Princeton University Press, 2016.

Ai, Chunrong, and Edward C. Norton. "Interaction Terms in Logit and Probit Models." *Economics Letters* 80 (2003): 123–129.

Allcott, Hunt, and Matthew Gentzkow. "Social Media and Fake News in the 2016 Election." *Journal of Economic Perspectives* 31, no. 2 (2017): 1–28.

Allport, Gordon W. "Values and Our Youth." *Teachers College Record* 63 (1961): 211–219.

Almond, Gabriel, and Sydney Verba. *The Civic Culture: Political Attitudes and Democracy in Five Nations*. London: Sage Publications, 1963.

Altemeyer, Robert. *The Authoritarian Specter*. Cambridge, MA: Harvard University Press, 1996.

Althaus, Scott. "Information Effects in Collective Preferences." *American Political Science Review* 92, no. 3 (1998): 545–558.

Amazeen, Michelle. "Making a Difference? A Critical Assessment of Fact-Checking in 2012." New America Foundation Research Paper, Washington, DC, October 2013.

Amazeen, Michelle. "Revisiting the Epistemology of Fact-Checking." *Critical Review* 27, no. 1 (2015): 1–22.

Amazeen, Michelle. "Checking the Fact-Checkers in 2008: Predicting Political Ad Scrutiny and Assessing Consistency." *Journal of Political Marketing* 15, no. 4 (2016): 433–464.

American Psychological Association. "Understanding Sexual Orientation and Gender Identity." n.d. https://www.apa.org/helpcenter/sexual-orientation.aspx.

Amis, Martin. "The Voice of the Lonely Crowd." *Harper's* (August 2002): 15–18.

Andersen, Kurt. *Fantasyland: How America Went Haywire, A 500-Year History.* New York: Random House, 2017.

Ansolabehere, Stephen, and Douglas Rivers. "Cooperative Survey Research." *Annual Review of Political Science* 16 (2013): 307–329.

Ansolabehere, Stephen, and Brian F. Schaffner. "Does Survey Mode Still Matter? Findings from a 2010 Multi-Mode Comparison." *Political Analysis* 22, no. 3 (2014): 285–303.

Anson, Ian. "Just the Facts? Partisan Media and the Political Conditioning of Economic Perceptions." *Political Research Quarterly* 69, no. 3 (2016): 444–456.

Arceneaux, Kevin, and Martin Johnson. *Changing Minds or Changing Channels? Partisan News in an Age of Choice.* Chicago: University of Chicago Press, 2013.

Arceneaux, Kevin, Martin Johnson, and John Cryderman. "Communication, Persuasion, and the Conditioning Value of Selective Exposure: Like Minds May Unite and Divide But They Mostly Tune Out." *Political Communication* 30, no. 2 (2013): 213–231.

Arnsdorf, Saac, Katie Glueck, and Edward-Isaac Dovere. "Hundreds of Sanders Supporters Walk Out after Clinton Nominated." *Politico*, July 26, 2016.

Aronow, Peter M., and Benjamin T. Miller. "Policy Misperceptions and Support for Gun Control Legislation." *Lancet* 387 (2016): 223.

Asch, Solomon. "Group Forces in the Modification and Distortion of Judgments." In *Social Psychology*, edited by Solomon Asch, 450–501. Englewood Cliffs, NJ: Prentice-Hall, 1952.

Asch, Solomon. "Studies of Independence and Conformity: A Minority of One Against a Unanimous Majority." *Psychological Monographs* 70, no. 9 (1956): 1–70.

Azzimonti, Marina, and Marcos Fernandes. "Social Media Networks, Fake News, and Polarization." NBER Working Paper 24462. Cambridge, MA, 2018.

Baldwin, Alec, and Kurt Andersen. *You Can't Spell America Without Me: The Really Tremendous Inside Story of My Fantastic First Year as President Donald J. Trump (a So-Called Parody).* New York: Penguin, 2017.

Barabas, Jason, and Jennifer Jerit. "Estimating the Causal Effects of Media Coverage on Policy-Specific Knowledge." *American Journal of Political Science* 53, no. 1 (2009): 73–89.

Barabas, Jason, Jennifer Jerit, William Pollock, and Carlisle Rainey. "The Questions of Political Knowledge." *American Political Science Review* 108, no. 4 (2014): 840–855.

Barber, Benjamin R. *Strong Democracy: Participatory Politics for a New Age.* Berkeley: University of California Press, 1984.

Barker, David C. "The Talk Radio Community: Non-traditional Social Networks and Political Participation." *Social Science Quarterly* 79, no. 2 (1998): 273–286.

Barker, David C. *Rushed to Judgement? Talk Radio, Persuasion, and American Political Behavior.* New York: Columbia University Press, 2002.

Barker, David C. "Cognitive Deliberation, Electoral Decision-making, and Democratic Health." *Social Science Quarterly* 99, no. 3 (2018): 962–976. https://doi.org/10.1111/ssqu.12475.

Barker, David C., and David H. Bearce. "End-Times Theology, the Shadow of the Future, and Public Resistance to Addressing Global Climate Change." *Political Research Quarterly* 66, no. 2 (2014): 267–279.

Barker, David C., and Christopher Carman. *Representing Red and Blue: How the Culture Wars Change the Way Citizens Speak and Politicians Listen.* New York: Oxford University Press, 2012.

Barker, David C., and Susan Hansen. "All Things Considered: Systematic Cognitive Processing and Electoral Decision-Making." *Journal of Politics* 67, no. 2 (2005): 319–344.

Barker, David C., and Kathleen Knight. "Political Talk Radio and Public Opinion." *Public Opinion Quarterly* 64, no. 2 (2000): 149–170.

Barker, David C., and Adam B. Lawrence. "Media Favoritism and Presidential Nominations: Reviving the Direct Effects Model." *Political Communication* 23, no. 1 (2006): 41–60.

Barker, David C., and James D. Tinnick. "Competing Visions of Parental Roles and Ideological Constraint." *American Political Science Review* 100, no. 2 (2006): 249–263.

Baron, Jonathan, and Sharon Lesher. "How Serious Are Expressions of Protected Values?" *Journal of Experimental Psychology: Applied* 6 (2000): 183–194.

Baron, Jonathan, and M. Spranca. "Protected Values." *Organizational Behavior and Human Decision Processes* 70 (1997): 1–16.

Baron, Robert, Joseph Vandello, and Bethany Brunsman. "The Forgotten Variable in Conformity Research: Impact of Task Importance on Social Influence." *Journal of Personality and Social Psychology* 71, no. 5 (1996): 915–927.

Barry, Dan, David Barstow, Jonathan Glater, Adam Liptak, and Jacques Steinberg. "Correcting the Record: Times Reporter Who Resigned Leaves Long Trail of Deception." *New York Times*, May 11, 2003.

Bartels, Larry. "Uninformed Votes: Information Effects in Presidential Elections." *American Journal of Political Science* 40, no. 1 (1996): 194–230.

Bartels, Larry. "Beyond the Running Rally: Partisan Bias in Political Perceptions." *Political Behavior* 24, no. 2 (2002): 117–150.

Baum, Matthew A. "Sex, Lies, and War: How Soft News Brings Foreign Policy to the Inattentive Public." *American Political Science Review* 96 (2002): 91–110.

Baum, Matthew A. "Talking the Vote: Why Presidential Candidates Hit the Talk Show Circuit." *American Journal of Political Science* 49, no. 2 (2005): 213–234.

Baum, Matthew A., and Tim Groeling. "New Media and the Polarization of American Political Discourse." *Political Communication* 25 (2008): 345–365.

Benhabib, Seyla. *The Claims of CultureEquality and Diversity in the Global Era.* Princeton, NJ: Princeton University Press, 2002.

Bentley, Arthur. *The Process of Government: A Study of Social Pressures.* Chicago: University of Chicago Press, 1908.

Berger, Peter. *The Sacred Canopy: Elements of a Sociological Theory of Religion.* New York: Anchor Books, 1967.

Berger, Peter, and Thomas Luckmann. *The Social Construction of Reality.* New York: Anchor Books, 1966.

Berelson, Bernard R., Paul F. Lazarsfeld, and William N. McPhee. *Voting: A Study of Opinion Formation in a Presidential Campaign*. Chicago: University of Chicago Press, 1954.

Berinsky, Adam. "Rumors and Health Care Reform: Experiments in Political Misinformation." *British Journal of Political Science* 47, no. 2 (2017): 241–262.

Berinsky, Adam. "Telling the Truth About Believing the Lies? The Prevalence of Expressive Responding in Surveys." *Journal of Politics* 80, no. 1 (2018): 211–224.

Berlin, Isaiah. *Four Essays on Liberty*. New York: Oxford University Press, 1969.

Berlin, Isaiah. *The Crooked Timber of Humanity: Chapters in the History of Ideas*. New York: Knopf, 1991.

Berlin, Isaiah. *Three Critics of the Enlightenment*. New York: Random House, 2000.

Berry, William, Matt Golder, and Daniel Milton. "Improving Tests of Theories Positing Interaction." *Journal of Politics* 74 (2012): 653–671.

Binning, Kevin R., Cameron Brick, Geoffrey L. Cohen, and David K. Sherman. "Going Along versus Getting It Right: The Role of Self-Integrity in Political Conformity." *Journal of Experimental Social Psychology* 56 (2015): 73–88.

Bishop, Bill. *The Big Sort*. New Hork: Houghton Mifflin, 2008.

Blau, Francine D., and Christopher Mackie, eds. *The Economic and Fiscal Consequences of Immigration*. Washington, DC: National Academies Press, 2017. https://doi.org/10.17226/23550.

Bolsen, Toby, James Druckman, and Fay Cook. "The Influence of Partisan Motivated Reasoning on Public Opinion." *Political Behavior* 36, no. (2014): 235–262.

Bonilla-Silva, Eduardo. *Racism Without Racists: Color-Blind Racism and the Persistence of Racial Inequality in America*. 4th ed. Lanham, MD: Rowman and Littlefield, 2014.

Born, Kelly. "The Future of Truth: Can Philanthropy Help Mitigate Misinformation?" Hewlett Foundation, June 8, 2017. https://www.hewlett.org/future-truth-can-philanthropy-help-mitigate-misinformation.

Boudreau, Cheryl. "Gresham's Law of Political Communication: How Citizens Respond to Conflicting Information." *Political Communication* 30, no. 2 (2013): 193–212.

Boxell, Levi, Matthew Gentzkow, and Jesse M. Shapiro. "Is the Internet Causing Political Polarization? Evidence from Demographics." NBER Working Paper 23258. Cambridge, MA, March 2017.

Brambor, Thomas, William Roberts Clark, and Matt Golder. "Understanding Interaction Models: Improving Empirical Analyses." *Political Analysis* 14 (2006): 311–331.

Brewer, Mark, and Jeffrey Stonecash. *Split: Class and Cultural Conflict in American Politics*. Washington, DC: CQ Press, 2007.

Brewer, Paul R., and Xiaoxia Cao. "Candidate Appearances on Soft News Shows and Public Knowledge About Primary Campaigns." *Journal of Broadcasting & Electronic Media* 50, no. 1 (2006): 18–35.

Broman, Clifford L., Harold W. Neighbors, and James S. Jackson. "Racial Group Identification Among Black Adults." *Social Forces* 67 (1988): 146–158.

Brownstein, Ronald. *The Second Civil War: How Extreme Partisanship Has Paralyzed Washington and Polarized America*. New York: Penguin Press, 2007.

Buchanan, Neil. "The Cruel 'Crooked' Caricature that Doomed Clinton." *Newsweek*, November 11, 2016.

Bullock, John G., Alan S. Gerber, Seth J. Hill, and Gregory A. Huber. "Partisan Bias in Factual Beliefs About Politics." *Quarterly Journal of Political Science* 10 (2015): 519–578.

Bybee, Carl. "Can Democracy Survive in the Post-Factual Age?" *Journalism & Communication Monographs* 1 (1999): 29–66.

Campbell, Angus, Philip E. Converse, Warren E. Miller, and Donald E. Stokes. *The American Voter*. Chicago: University of Chicago Press, 1960.

Campbell, David E. *Why We Vote: How Schools and Communities Shape Our Civic Life*. Princeton, NJ: Princeton University Press, 2006.

Campbell, James. *Polarized: Making Sense of a Divided America*. Princeton, NJ: Princeton University Press, 2016.

Campbell, Jeremy. *Liar's Tale: A History of Falsehood*. New York: W. W. Norton, 2002.

Card, David, and Alan B. Krueger. "Minimum Wages and Employment: A Case Study of the Fast-Food Industry in New Jersey and Pennsylvania." *American Economic Review* 84, no. 4 (1994): 487–496.

Carpentier, Megan. "Why Do People Dislike Hillary Clinton? The Story Goes Far Back." *Guardian*, October 18, 2016.

Cassidy, David. "The Reinhart and Rogoff Controversy: A Summing Up." *New Yorker*, April 26, 2013.

Cengiz, Doruk, Arindrajit Dube, Attila Lindner, and Ben Zipperer. "The Effect of Minimum Wages on the Total Number of Jobs: Evidence from the United States Using a Bunching Estimator." CEP Discussion Paper 1531. Center for Economic Performance, London, UK, February 2018.

Chaiken, Shelly, and Durairaj Maheswaran. "Heuristic Processing Can Bias Systematic Processing—Effects of Source Credibility, Argument Ambiguity, and Task Importance on Attitude Judgment." *Journal of Personality and Social Psychology* 66 (1994): 460–473.

Chan, Man-pui Sally, Christopher R. Jones, Kathleen Hall Jamieson, and Dolores Albarracin. "Debunking: A Meta-Analysis of the Psychological Efficacy of Messages Countering Misinformation" *Psychological Science* 28, no. 11 (2017): 1531–1546.

Chen, M. Keith, and Ryne Rohla. "The Effect of Political Advertising and Advertising on Family Ties." *Science* 360 (2018): 1020–1024.

Chong, Dennis, and James N. Druckman. "Public–Elite Interactions." In *The Oxford Handbook of American Public Opinion and the Media*, edited by Robert Y. Shapiro and Lawrence R. Jacobs, 170–188. Oxford: Oxford University Press, 2011.

Chozick, Amy, and Megan Thee-Brenan. "Poll Finds Voters in Both Parties Unhappy with Their Candidates." *New York Times*, July 14, 2016.

Cialdini, Robert B. "Harnessing the Science of Persuasion." *Harvard Business Review* 79, no. 9 (2001): 72–79.

Cohen, Geoffrey. "Party Over Policy: The Dominating Impact of Group Influence on Political Beliefs." *Journal of Personality and Social Psychology* 85 (2003): 808–822.

Colbert, Stephen. "The Word—Truthiness." [Television Series Clip] *Colbert Report*. New York: Comedy Central, October 17, 2005.

Comte, Auguste. *Cours de Philosophie Positive (Course on Positive Philosophy)*, 6 vols. Paris: Rouen, 1830–1842.

Converse, Philip. "The Nature of Belief Systems in Mass Publics." In *Ideology and Discontent*, edited by David E. Apter. New York: Free Press, 1964.

Crawford, Jarret, and Jane Pilanski. "Political Intolerance, Right and Left." *Political Psychology* 35, no. 6 (2014): 841–851.

Curry, Oliver. "Who's Afraid of the Naturalistic Fallacy." *Evolutionary Psychology* 4 (2006): 234–247.

Darwin, Charles. *The Autobiography of Charles Darwin 1809–1882. With the original omissions restored. Edited and with appendix and notes by his granddaughter Nora Barlow*. London: HarperCollins, 1958.

Dawsey, Josh, Damian Paletta, and Erica Werner. "In Fundraising Speech, Trump Says He Made Up Trade Claim in Meeting with Justin Trudeau." *Washington Post*, March 15, 2018.

Delli Carpini, Michael X., and Scott Keeter. *What Americans Know About Politics and Why It Matters*. New Haven, CT: Yale University Press, 1996.

Demo, David H., and Michael Hughes. "Socialization and Racial Identity Among Black Americans." *Social Psychology Quarterly* 53 (1990): 364–374.

De Pinto, Jennifer. "From Trump to Terrorism, the Year in Polls." *CBS News*, December 30, 2016.

Derakshan, Hossein, and Claire Wardle. "Ban the Term 'Fake News.'" *CNN*, November 27, 2017. https://www.cnn.com/2017/11/26/opinions/fake-news-and-disinformation-opinion-wardle-derakhshan/index.html.

Derrida, Jacques. *Positions*. Chicago: University of Chicago Press, 1981.

Dewey, John. "Philosophy and Democracy." In *The Political Writings*, edited by Debra Morris and Ian Shapiro. Indianapolis: Hackett Publishing, 1919.

Dewey, John. *The Public and Its Problems*. New York: Henry Holt and Company, 1927.

Dewey, John. *Liberalism and Social Action*. New York: Putnam, 1935.

Dewey, John. "Democracy and Educational Administration." *School and Society* 45 (1937): 457–467.

Dezhbakhsh, Hashem, and Paul H. Rubin. "Lives Saved or Lives Lost? The Effects of Concealed-Handgun Laws on Crime." *American Economic Review*, 88, no. 2 (1998): 468–474.

DiFonzo, Nicholas, and Prashant Bordia. *Rumor Psychology: Social and Organizational Approaches*. New York: American Psychological Association, 2006.

Dimock, Michael, Carroll Doherty, Jocelyn Kiley, and Russ Oates. "Political Polarization in the American Public: How Increasing Ideological Uniformity and Partisan Antipathy Affect Politics, Compromise and Everyday Life." Pew Research Center, June 12, 2014.

Ditto, Peter, James Scepansky, Geoffrey Munro, Anne Apanovitch, and Lisa Lockhart. "Motivated Sensitivity to Preference-Inconsistent Information." *Journal of Personality and Social Psychology* 75, no. 1 (1998): 53–69.

Dobbs, Michael. "The Rise of Political Fact-Checking." New America Foundation Research Paper. Washington, DC, February 2012.

Dryzek, John. *Discursive Democracy: Politics, Policy, and Political Science*. Cambridge: Cambridge University Press, 1990.

Duggan, Mark. "More Guns, More Crime." *Journal of Political Economy*, 109, no. 5 (2001): 1086–1114.

Dunwoody, Philip. "Theories of Truth as Assessment Criteria in Judgment and Decision Making." *Judgment and Decision Making* 4, no. 2 (2009): 116–125.

Durkheim, Emile. *The Elementary Forms of Religious Life.* 1912.

Dyck, Joshua, Shanna Pearson-Merkowitz, and Michael Coates. "Primary Distrust: Political Support for the Insurgent Candidacies of Donald Trump and Bernie Sanders in the 2016 Primary." *PS* 51, no. 2 (2018): 351–357.

Edelman Trust Barometer. "2017 Edelman Trust Barometer Reveals Global Implosion of Trust." January 15, 2017. https://www.edelman.com/news/2017-edelman-trust-barometer-reveals-global-implosion.

Edwards, Kari, and Edward Smith. "A Disconfirmation Bias in the Evaluation of Arguments." *Journal of Personality and Social Psychology* 71, no. 1 (1996): 5–24.

Egan, Patrick, and Megan Mullin. "Climate Change: US Public Opinion." *Annual Review of Political Science* 20 (2017): 209–227.

Eliade, Mircea. *The Sacred and the Profane.* New York: Harcourt, 1957.

Elster, Jon. *Sour Grapes.* Cambridge: Cambridge University Press, 1983.

Entine, Jon. "AAAS Scientists: Consensus on GMO Safety Firmer Than for Human-Induced Climate Change." *Huffington Post*, January 29, 2015.

Epstein, Robert, and Ronald Robertson. "A Method for Detecting Bias in Search Rankings, with Evidence of Systematic Bias Related to the 2016 Presidential Election." White Paper WP-17-02. American Institute for Behavioral Research and Technology, Vista, CA, June 1, 2017.

Farhi, Paul, and T. Rees Shapiro. "Rolling Stone Retracts Discredited UVA Rape Story." *Washington Post*, April 5, 2015.

Farnsworth, Stephen, and Robert Lichter. "A Comparative Analysis of the Partisan Targets of Media Fact-Checking: Examining President Obama and the 113th Congress." Presented at the American Political Science Association Meeting, Philadelphia, PA, September 2016.

Feldman, Stanley. "Economic Individualism and American Public Opinion." *American Politics Quarterly* 11, no. 1 (1983): 3–29.

Feldman, Stanley. "Structure and Consistency in Public Opinion: The Role of Core Beliefs and Values." *American Journal of Political Science* 32, no. 2 (1988): 416–440.

Feldman, Stanley. "Political Ideology." In *The Oxford Handbook of Political Psychology*, edited by Leonie Huddy, David O. Sears, and Jack S. Levy, 2nd ed., 591–626. Oxford: Oxford University Press, 2013.

Feldman, Stanley, and Marco Steenbergen. "The Humanitarian Foundation of Public Support for Social Welfare." *American Journal of Political Science* 45 (2001): 658–677.

Feldman, Stanley, and John Zaller. "The Political Culture of Ambivalence: Ideological Responses to the Welfare State." *American Journal of Political Science* 36, no. 1 (1992): 268–307.

Festinger, Leon. *A Theory of Cognitive Dissonance.* Stanford, CA: Stanford University Press, 1957.

Feygina, Irina, John Jost, and Rachel Goldsmith. "System Justification, the Denial of Global Warming, and the Possibility of 'System-Sanctioned Change.'" *Personality and Social Psychology Bulletin* 36 (2010): 326–338.

Fingerhut, Hannah. "Republicans Skeptical of Colleges' Impact on U.S., but Most See Benefits for Workforce Preparation." Pew Research Center, July 20, 2017.

Fiorina, Morris, Samuel J. Abrams, and Jeremy C. Pope. *Culture War? The Myth of a Polarized America*. New York: Pearson-Longman, 2005.

Fischhoff, Baruch, Paul Slovic, and Sarah Lichtenstein. "Knowing with Certainty: The Appropriateness of Extreme Confidence." *Journal of Experimental Psychology* 3, no. 4 (1977): 552–564.

Fishkin, James. *Democracy and Deliberation: New Directions for Democratic Reform*. New Haven, CT: Yale University Press, 1991.

Fiske, Alan, and Philip Tetlock. "Taboo Trade-offs: Reactions to Transactions That Transgress Spheres of Justice." *Political Psychology* 18, no. 2 (1997): 255–297.

Flaxman, Seth, Sharad Goel, and Justin M. Rao. "Filter Bubbles, Echo Chambers, and Online News Consumption." Special issue, *Public Opinion Quarterly* 80 (2016): 298–320.

Flynn, D. J., Brendan Nyhan, and Jason Reifler. "The Nature and Origins of Misperceptions: Understanding False and Unsupported Beliefs About Politics." *Advances in Political Psychology* 38, no. 1 (2017): 127–150.

Foran, Clare. "The Never Clinton Campaign." *Atlantic*, May 5, 2016.

Foucault, Michel. *Discipline and Punish*. New York: Pantheon Books, 1977.

Frankfurt, Harry G. *On Bullshit*. Princeton, NJ: Princeton University Press, 2005.

Frankovic, Kathy. "NH Win Boosts Sanders' Image, but Clinton Still Holds Large Lead." Yougov, February 17, 2016. https://today.yougov.com/topics/politics/articles-reports/2016/02/17/nh-win-boosts-sanders-image-clinton-still-holds-la.

Freed, Gary, Sarah Clark, Amy T. Butchart, Dianne C. Singer, and Matthew M. Davis. "Parental Vaccine Safety Concerns in 2009." *Pediatrics* 125, no. 4 (2010): 654–659.

Fridkin, Kim, Patrick Kenney, and Amanda Wintersieck. "Liar, Liar, Pants on Fire: How Fact-Checking Influences Reactions to Negative Advertising." *Political Communication* 32, no. 1 (2015): 127–151.

Friedman, Jeffrey. "Motivated Skepticism or Inevitable Conviction? Dogmatism and the Study of Politics." *Critical Review* 24, no. 2 (2012): 131–156.

Friedman, Jeffrey. *Power Without Knowledge*. New York: Oxford University Press, 2019.

Friedman, Shterna. "Popper, Ignorance and the Emptiness of Fallibilism." In *Routledge International Handbook of Ignorance Studies*, edited by Matthias Gross, 44–52. New York: Routledge, 2015.

Frimer, Jeremy A., Linda J. Skitka, and Matt Motyl. "Liberals and Conservatives Are Similarly Motivated to Avoid Exposure to One Another's Opinions." *Journal of Experimental Social Psychology* 72 (2017): 1–12.

Fukuyama, Francis. "The Emergence of a Post-Fact World." Project Syndicate, January 12, 2017. https://www.project-syndicate.org/onpoint/the-emergence-of-a-post-fact-world-by-francis-fukuyama-2017-01.

Gaiman, Neil. *Norse Mythology*. New York: W. W. Norton, 2017.

Gaines, Brian, James Kuklinski, Paul Quirk, Buddy Peyton, and Jay Verkuilen. "Same Facts, Different Interpretations: Partisan Motivation and Opinion on Iraq." *Journal of Politics* 69 (2007): 957–974.

Galston, William A. "Political Knowledge, Political Engagement, and Civic Education." *Annual Review of Political Science* 4, no. 1 (2001): 217–241.

Garrett, Kristin N., and Alexa Bankert. "The Moral Roots of Partisan Division: How Moral Conviction Heightens Affective Polarization." *British Journal of Political Science* (2018): 1–20. doi:10.1017/S000712341700059X.

Garrett, R. Kelly, Erik C. Nisbet, and Emily K. Lynch. "Undermining the Corrective Effects of Media-Based Political Fact Checking? The Role of Contextual Clues and Naïve Theory." *Journal of Communication* 63 (2013): 617–637.

Gauchat, Gordon. "Politicization of Science in the Public Sphere: A Study of Public Trust in the United States, 1974 to 2010." *American Sociological Review* 77, no. 2 (2012): 167–187.

Gauchat, Gordon. "The Political Context of Science in the United States: Public Acceptance of Evidence-Based Policy and Science Funding." *Social Forces* 94, no. 2 (2015): 723–746.

Gerber, Alan, and Gregory Huber. "Partisanship, Political Control, and Economic Assessments." *American Journal of Political Science* 54, no. 1 (2010): 153–173.

Gerber, Alan, Donald Green, and C. Larimer. "Social Pressure and Voter Turnout: Evidence from a Large-Scale Field Experiment." *American Political Science Review* 102, no. 1 (2008): 33–48.

Gidda, Mirren. "Fear and Rumors Fueling the Spread of Ebola." *Time*, August 12, 2014.

Gift, Karen, and Thomas Gift. "Does Politics Influence Hiring? Evidence from a Randomized Experiment." *Political Behavior* 37, no. 3 (2015): 653–675.

Gilbert, Daniel, Romin Tafarodi, and Patrick Malone. "You Can't Not Believe Everything You Read." *Journal of Personality and Social Psychology* 65, no. 2 (1993): 221.

Gilens, Martin. "Political Ignorance and Collective Policy Preferences." *American Political Science Review* 95, no. 2 (2001): 379–396.

Gilovich, Thomas. *How We Know What Isn't So: The Fallibility of Human Reason in Everyday Life*. New York: Free Press, 1991.

Gimpel, James G., J. Celeste Lay, and Jason E. Schuknecht. *Cultivating Democracy: Civic Environments and Political Socialization in America*. Washington, DC: Brookings Institution Press, 2003.

Godsey, Mark. *Blind Injustice: A Former Prosecutor Exposes the Psychology and Politics of Wrongful Convictions*. Oakland: University of California Press, 2017.

Goldberg, Julie, Jennifer Lerner, and Philip Tetlock. "Rage and Reason: The Psychology of the Intuitive Prosecutor." *European Journal of Social Psychology* 29 (1999): 781–795.

Goren, Paul. "Party Identification and Core Political Values." *American Journal of Political Science* 49 (2005): 881–896.

Goren, Paul, Christopher M. Federico, and Miki Kaul Kittilson. "Source Cues, Partisan Identities, and Political Value Expression." *American Journal of Political Science* 53, no. 4 (2009): 805–820.

Goren, Paul, Harald Schoen, Jason Reifler, Thomas Scotto, and William Chittick. 2016. "A Unified Theory of Value-Based Reasoning and U.S. Public Opinion." *Political Behavior* 38, no. 4 (2016): 977–997.

Gould, Stephen J. *Eight Little Piggies*. New York: W. W. Norton, 1993.

Graham, Jesse, Jonathan Haidt, and Brian A. Nosek. "Liberals and Conservatives Rely on Different Sets of Moral Foundations." *Journal of Personality and Social Psychology* 96, no. 5 (2009): 1029–1046.

Graves, Lucas. "What We Can Learn from the Factcheckers' Ratings." *Columbia Journalism Review*, June 4, 2013a.

Graves, Lucas. "In Defense of Factchecking." *Columbia Journalism Review*, August 9, 2013b.

Graves, Lucas. *Deciding What's True: The Rise of Political Fact-Checking in American Journalism*. New York: Columbia University Press, 2016.

Graves, Lucas. "Anatomy of a Fact Check: Objective Practice and the Contested Epistemology of Fact Checking." *Communication, Culture & Critique* 10, no. 3 (2017): 518–537.

Green, Donald, Peter Aronow, Daniel Bergan, Pamela Greene, Celia Paris, and Beth Weinberger. "Does Knowledge of Constitutional Principles Increase Support for Civil Liberties? Results from a Randomized Field Experiment." *Journal of Politics* 73, no. 2 (2011): 463–476.

Green, Donald, Bradley Palmquist, and Eric Schickler. *Partisan Hearts and Minds*. New Haven, CT: Yale University Press, 2002.

Griffin, Dale, and Amos Tversky. "The Weighing of Evidence and the Determinants of Confidence." *Cognitive Psychology* 24, no. 3 (1992): 411–435.

Gross, Neil, and Solon Simmons, eds. *Professors and Their Politics*. Baltimore: Johns Hopkins University Press, 2014.

Gross, Samuel, Barbara O'Brien, Chun Hu, and Edward Kennedy. "Rate of False Conviction of Criminal Defendants Who Are Sentenced to Death." *Proceedings of the National Academy of Sciences* 111, no. 20 (2014): 7230–7235.

Grossman, Matt, and David Hopkins. *Asymmetric Politics*. New York: Oxford University Press, 2016.

Guess, Andrew, and Alexander Coppock. "Does Counter-Attitudinal Information Cause Backlash? Results from Three Large Survey Experiments." Working Paper, 2017.

Guess, Andrew, Brendan Nyhan, and Jason Reifler. "Selective Exposure to Misinformation: Evidence from the Consumption of Fake News During the 2016 Presidential Campaign." Working Paper, 2018a.

Guess, Andrew, Joshua Tucker, Pablo Barbera, Brendan Nyhan, Cristian Vaccari, Alexandra Siegel, Sergey Sanovich, and Denis Stukal. *Social Media, Political Polarization, and Political Disinformation: A Review of the Scientific Literature*. Menlo Park, CA: Hewlett Foundation, March 19, 2018b.

Gunther, John. *Inside U.S.A.* New York: Harper & Brothers, 1947.

Gunther, Richard, Erik C. Nisbet, and Paul Beck. "Trump May Owe His 2016 Victory to 'Fake News,' New Study Suggests." *The Conversation*, February 15, 2018.

Gurin, Patricia. "Women's Gender Consciousness." *Public Opinion Quarterly* 49, no. 2 (1985): 143–163.

Guthrie, W. K. C. *History of Greek Philosophy*. Cambridge: Cambridge University Press, 1962.

Gutmann, Amy, and Dennis Thompson. *Democracy and Disagreement*. Cambridge, MA: Harvard University Press, 1996.

Habermas, Jurgen. *The Theory of Communicative Action*. Vol. 1, *Reason and the Rationalization of Society*. Boston: Beacon, 1984.

Habermas, Jurgen. *Between Facts and Norms: Contributions to a Discourse Theory of Law and Democracy*. Cambridge, MA: MIT Press, 1996.

Haglin, Kathryn. "The Limitations of the Backfire Effect." *Research and Politics* 5, no. 3 (2017): 1–5.

Haider-Markel, Donald, and Mark Joslyn. "Beliefs About the Origins of Homosexuality and Support for Gay Rights: An Empirical Test of Attribution Theory." *Public Opinion Quarterly* 72, no. 2 (2008): 291–310.

Haider-Markel, Donald, and Mark Joslyn. "Stereotypes in Post-Truth Politics: Enhancing Political and Group Divisions." Presented at the Politics of Truth Conference, American University, Washington, DC, March 18, 2018.

Haidt, Jonathan. *The Righteous Mind: Why Good People Are Divided by Politics and Religion*. New York: Pantheon Books, 2012.

Hamilton, Lawrence. "Education, Politics, and Opinions About Climate Change: Evidence for Interaction Effects." *Climatic Change* 104 (2011): 231–242.

Hammond, Kenneth. "Coherence and Correspondence Theories in Judgment and Decision Making." In *Judgment and Decision Making: An Interdisciplinary Reader*, edited by Terry Connolly, Hal Arkes, and Kenneth Hammond, 53–65. Cambridge: Cambridge University Press, 2000.

Hammond, Kenneth. *Beyond Rationality: The Search for Wisdom in a Troubled Time*. Oxford: Oxford University Press, 2007.

Hanna, Andrew, and Taylor Gee. "Could America's Socialists Become the Tea Party of the Left?" *Politico*, October 1, 2017.

Hardin, Russell. *How Do You Know? The Economics of Ordinary Knowledge*. Princeton, NJ: Princeton University Press, 2009.

Hastorf, Albert, and Hadley Cantril. "They Saw a Game: A Case Study." *Journal of Abnormal and Social Psychology* 49, no. 1 (1954): 129–134.

Helfand, David. *A Survival Guide to the Misinformation Age: Scientific Habits of Mind*. New York: Columbia University Press, 2016.

Hemenway, David. *Private Guns, Public Health*. Ann Arbor: University of Michigan Press, 2006.

Hemingway, Mark. "Lies, Damned Lies, and 'Fact-Checking.'" *Weekly Standard*, December 19, 2011.

Herbst, Susan. *Rude Democracy: Civility and Incivility in American Politics*. Philadelphia: Temple University Press, 2010.

Herndon, Thomas, Michael Ash, and Robert Pollin. "Does High Public Debt Consistently Stifle Economic Growth? A Critique of Reinhart and Rogoff." *Cambridge Journal of Economics* 38, no. 2 (2013): 257–279.

Hersh, Eitan D., and Matthew N. Goldenberg. "Democratic and Republican Physicians Provide Different Care on Politicized Health Issues." *Proceedings of the National Academy of Sciences* 113, no. 42 (2016): 11811–11816.

Herzfeld, Michael. "Factual Fissures: Claims and Contexts." *Annals of the American Academy of Political and Social Science* 560 (1998): 69–82.

Hetherington, Marc. "Turned Off or Turned On? How Polarization Affects Political Engagement." In *Red and Blue Nation? Consequences and Correction of America's Polarized Politics*, edited by Pietro S. Nivola and David W. Brady, 1–54. Washington, DC: Brookings Institution, 2008.

Hetherington, Marc J., and Thomas J. Rudolph. *Why Washington Won't Work*. Chicago: Chicago University Press, 2015.

Hetherington, Marc J., and Jonathan D. Weiler. *Authoritarianism and Polarization in American Politics*. New York: Cambridge University Press, 2009.

Hilliard, David, and Donald Weise, eds. "Black Capitalism Re-analyzed I: June 5, 1971." In *The Huey P. Newton Reader*, 227–233. New York: Seven Stories Press, 2002.

Hindman, Douglas. "Mass Media Flow and Differential Distribution of Politically Disputed Beliefs: The Belief Gap Hypothesis" *Journalism & Mass Communication Quarterly* 86 (2009): 790–808.

Hochschild, Jennifer. *What's Fair? American Beliefs About Distributive Justice*. Cambridge, MA: Harvard University Press, 1981.

Hochschild, Jennifer, and Katherine Einstein. *Do Facts Matter? Information and Misinformation in American Politics*. Norman: University of Oklahoma Press, 2015.

Hofstadter, Richard. *Anti-Intellectualism in American Life*. New York: Vintage Books, 1962.

Hofstadter, Richard. "The Paranoid Style in American Politics." *Harper's Magazine*, November 1964.

Hofstetter, C. Richard, and David C. Barker. "Talk Radio, Information, and Misinformation." *Political Research Quarterly* 52, no. 2 (1999): 353–370.

Holmes, Oliver Wendell, Jr. "The Path of the Law." 10 *Harvard Law Review* 457 (1897).

Hopf, Ted. "The Promise of Constructivism in International Relations Theory." *International Security* 23, no. 1 (1998): 171–200.

Hopkins, Daniel J., and Jonathan M. Ladd. "The Consequences of Broader Media Choice: Evidence from the Expansion of Fox News." *Quarterly Journal of Political Science* 9, no. 1 (2014): 115–135.

Hopkins, Daniel J., John Sides, and Jack Citrin. "The Muted Consequences of Correct Information About Immigration." *Journal of Politics* (forthcoming).

Horkheimer, Max, and Theodor Adorno. *Dialectic of Enlightenment*. Amsterdam: Querido Verlag, 1947.

Huber, Gregory A., and Neil Malhotra. "Political Homophily in Social Relationships: Evidence from Online Dating Behavior." *Journal of Politics* 79, no. 1 (2017): 269–283.

Hulme, Mike. *Why We Disagree About Climate Change: Understanding Controversy, Inaction and Opportunity*. Cambridge: Cambridge University Press, 2009.

Hume, David. *A Treatise of Human Nature*. 1739.

Hunter, James Davison. *Culture Wars: The Struggle to Define America*. New York: Basic Books, 1991.

Hunter, James Davison. *Before the Shooting Begins: Searching for Democracy in America's Culture War*. New York: Free Press, 1994.

Hurtado, Sylvia, Kevin Egan, John Pryor, Hannah Whang, and Serge Tran. "Undergraduate Teaching Faculty: The 2011–2012 HERI Faculty Survey." Los Angeles: Higher Education Research Institute at UCLA, 2011.

Hurwitz, Jon, and Mark Peffley. "How Are Foreign Policy Attitudes Structured: A Hierarchical Model." *American Political Science Review* 81 (1987): 1099–1120.

Intergovernmental Panel on Climate Change. *Climate Change 2014: Synthesis Report*. Fifth Assessment Report of the Intergovernmental Panel on Climate Change. Geneva: Intergovernmental Panel on Climate Change, 2014.

Iyengar, Shanto, and Kyu Hahn. "Red Media, Blue Media: Evidence of Ideological Selectivity in Media Use." *Journal of Communication* 59, no. 1 (2009): 19–39.

Iyengar, Shanto, and Sean J. Westwood. "Fear and Loathing Across Party Lines: New Evidence on Group Polarization." *American Journal of Political Science* 59, no. 3 (2014): 690–707.

Iyengar, Shanto, Tobias Konitzer, and Kent Tedin. "The Home as a Political Fortress: Family Agreement in an Era of Polarization." *Journal of Politics* 80, no. 4 (2018): 1326–1338.

Iyengar, Shanto, Gaurad Sood, and Yphtach Lelkes. "Affect, Not Ideology: A Social Identity Perspective on Polarization." *Public Opinion Quarterly* 76, no. 3 (2012): 405–431.

Jackson, Brooks, and Kathleen Hall Jamieson. *unSpun: Finding Facts in a World of Disinformation*. New York: Random House, 2007.

Jacobson, Gary. *A Divider, Not a Uniter: George W. Bush and the American People*. New York: Pearson Longman, 2007.

Jacoby, William. "Value Choices and American Public Opinion." *American Journal of Political Science* 50, no. 3 (2006): 707–723.

Jacoby, William. "Is There a Culture War? Conflicting Values in American Public Opinion." *American Journal of Political Science* 108, no. 4 (2014): 754–771.

James, William. 1896. "The Will to Believe." *New World*, 1896.

Jamieson, Kathleen Hall. *Dirty Politics: Deception, Distraction, and Democracy*. New York: Oxford University Press, 1992.

Jamieson, Kathleen Hall. "Implications of the Demise of 'Fact' in Political Discourse." *Proceedings of the American Philosophical Society* 159, no. 1 (2015): 66–84.

Jamieson, Kathleen Hall, and Joseph N. Capella. *Echo Chamber: Rush Limbaugh and the Conservative Media Establishment*. New York: Oxford University Press, 2010.

Jardim, Ekaterina, Mark Long, Robert Plotnick, Emma van Inwegen, Jacob Vigdor, and Hilary Wething. "Minimum Wage Increases, Wages, and Low-Wage Employment: Evidence from Seattle." NBER Working Paper 23532. Cambridge, MA, June 2017.

Jarman, Jeffrey. "Influence of Political Affiliation and Criticism on the Effectiveness of Political Fact-Checking." *Communication Research Reports* 33, no. 1 (2016a): 9–15.

Jarman, Jeffrey. "Motivated to Ignore the Facts: The Inability of Fact-Checking to Promote Truth in the Public Sphere." In *Truth in the Public Sphere*, edited by Jason Hannan, 115–135. Lanham, MD: Rowman & Littlefield, 2016b.

Jarrett, Prudence. "You Cannot Bring Facts to a Culture War." Columbia University Mailman School of Public Health, Student Voices. November 11, 2016.

Jerit, Jennifer, and Jason Barabas. "Partisan Perceptual Bias and the Information Environment." *Journal of Politics* 74, no. 3 (2012): 672–684.

Jerit, Jennifer, and Jason Barabas. "Revisiting the Gender Gap in Political Knowledge." *Political Behavior* 39, no. 4 (2017): 817–838.

Jones, David A. "Why Americans Don't Trust the Media: A Preliminary Analysis" *International Journal of Press/Politics* 9, no. 2 (2004): 60–75.

Jones, Jeffrey M. "Six in 10 Americans Say Racism Against Blacks Is Widespread." Gallup, August 17, 2016. http://news.gallup.com/poll/194657/six-americans-say-racism-against-blacks-widespread.aspx. Accessed November 25, 2017.

Jones, Robert P., and Dan Cox. "'Merry Christmas' vs. 'Happy Holidays': Republicans and Democrats Are Polar Opposites." Public Religion Research Institute, December 19, 2016.

Joslyn, Mark, and Donald Haider-Markel. "Who Knows Best? Education, Partisanship, and Contested Facts." *Politics & Policy* 42, no. 6 (2014): 919–947.

Jost, John. "Ideological Asymmetries and the Essence of Political Psychology." *Political Psychology* 38, no. 2 (2017): 167–208.

Jost, John T., Christopher M. Federico, and Jaime L. Napier. "Political Ideology: Its Structure, Functions, and Elective Affinities." *Annual Review of Psychology* 60 (2009): 307–337.

Jost, John T., Jack Glaser, Arie W. Kruganski, and Frank J. Sulloway. "Political Conservatism as Motivated Social Cognition." *Psychological Bulletin* 129 (2003): 339–375.

Kahan, Dan. "Ideology, Motivated Reasoning, and Cognitive Reflection." *Judgment and Decision-Making* 4 (2013a): 407–424.

Kahan, Dan. "A Risky Science Communication Environment for Vaccines." *Science* 342 (2013b): 53–54.

Kahan, Dan. "Climate-Science Communication and the Measurement Problem." *Advances in Political Psychology* 36 (2015): 1–43.

Kahan, Dan. "The Politically Motivated Reasoning Paradigm." In *Emerging Trends in Social and Behavioral Sciences*, edited by Robert Scott and Stephen Kosslyn. Hoboken, NJ: John Wiley & Sons, 2016.

Kahan, Dan, and Donald Braman. "Cultural Cognition and Public Policy." *Yale Law & Policy Review* 24 (2006): 147–170.

Kahan, Dan, Ellen Peters, Erica C. Dawson, and Paul Slovic. "Motivated Numeracy and Enlightened Self-Government." *Behavioural Public Policy* 1, no. 1 (2017): 54–86.

Kahan, Dan, Ellen Peters, Maggie Wittlin, Paul Slovic, Lisa Ouellette, Donald Braman, and Gregory Mandel. "The Polarizing Impact of Science Literacy and Numeracy on Perceived Climate Change Risks." *Nature Climate Change* 2 (2012): 732–735.

Kahneman, Daniel. *Thinking, Fast and Slow*. New York: Farrar, Straus and Giroux, 2011.

Kahneman, Daniel, and Amos Tversky. "Availability: A Heuristic for Judging Frequency and Probability." *Cognitive Psychology* 5, no. 2 (1973): 207–232.

Kahneman, Daniel, and Amos Tversky. "Intuitive Prediction: Biases and Corrective Procedures." *Management Science* 12 (1979): 313–327.

Kahneman, Daniel, Paul Slovic, and Amos Tversky. *Judgment Under Uncertainty: Heuristics and Biases*. New York: Cambridge University Press, 1982.

Kakutani, Michiko. *The Death of Truth: Notes on Falsehood in the Age of Trump*. New York: Random House, 2018.

Kaplan, Jonas T., Sarah I. Gimbel, and Sam Harris. "Neural Correlates of Maintaining One's Political Beliefs in the Face of Counterevidence." *Scientific Reports* 6 (2016): 39589.

Kavanagh, Jennifer, and Michael D. Rich. *Truth Decay: An Initial Exploration of the Diminishing Role of Facts and Analysis in American Public Life*. Santa Monica, CA: Rand Corporation, 2018.

Kerlinger, Fred N. *Liberalism and Conservatism: The Nature and Structure of Social Attitudes*. Hillsdale, NJ: Erlbaum, 1984.

Kessler, Glenn. "Two Conventions, in Parallel Universes of Narratives and Philosophies." *Washington Post*, September 8, 2012.

Kessler, Glenn. "Just the Facts: Politics and the New Journalism." *Foreign Affairs*, January 6, 2014.

Keyes, Ralph. *The Post-Truth Era: Dishonesty and Deception in Contemporary Life.* New York: St. Martins, 2004.

Khanna, Kabir, and Markus Prior. "Different Realities for Different Parties? Measuring Partisan Bias in Perceptions of the National Economy." Presented at the Midwest Political Science Association Meeting, Chicago, IL, April 2014.

Kinder, Donald R. "Opinion and Action in the Realm of Politics." In *The Handbook of Social Psychology*, edited by Gilbert, 2nd ed. New York: Oxford University Press, 1998.

Kinder, Donald, and Nathan Kalmoe. *Neither Liberal Nor Conservative: Ideological Innocence in the American Public.* Chicago: University of Chicago Press, 2017.

Kirkham, R. *Theories of Truth: A Critical Introduction.* Cambridge, MA: MIT Press, 1992.

Kirkland, Anna. *Vaccine Court: The Law and Politics of Injury.* New York: New York University Press, 2016.

Kluckhohn, Clyde. "Values and Value-Orientations in the Theory of Action: An Exploration in Definition and Classification." In *Toward a General Theory of Action*, edited by Talcott Parsons and Edward A. Shils, 388–433. Cambridge, MA: Harvard University Press, 1951.

Kruglanski, Arie W., Donna M. Webster, and Aden M. Klem. "Motivated Resistance and Openness to Persuasion in the Presence or Absence of Prior Information." *Journal of Personality and Social Psychology* 65 (1993): 861–876.

Krugman, Paul. "PolitiFact, R.I.P." *New York Times*, December 20, 2011.

Krugman, Paul. "Nobody Understands Debt." *New York Times*, January 1, 2012.

Krugman, Paul. "Debt Is Good." *New York Times*, August 21, 2015.

Kugler, Matthew, John T. Jost, and Sharareh Noorbaloochi. "Another Look at Moral Foundations Theory: Do Authoritarianism and Social Dominance Orientation Explain Liberal–Conservative Differences in Moral Intuitions?" *Social Justice Research* 27, no. 4 (2014): 413–431.

Kuhn, Thomas. *The Structure of Scientific Revolutions.* Chicago: Chicago University Press, 1962.

Kuklinski, James. "The Limits of Facts in Citizen Decision-Making." *Extensions: A Journal of the Carl Albert Congressional Research and Studies Center* (2007).

Kuklinski, James, Paul Quirk, Jennifer Jerit, David Schweider, and Robert Rich. "Misinformation and the Currency of Democratic Citizenship." *Journal of Politics* 62 (2000): 790–815.

Kull, Steven, Clay Ramsay, and Evan Lewis. "Misperceptions, the Media, and the Iraq War." *Political Science Quarterly* 118, no. 4 (2003): 569–598.

Kunda, Ziva. "The Case for Motivated Reasoning." *Psychological Bulletin* 108, no. 3 (1990): 480–498.

Kuran, Timur. *Private Truths, Public Lies: The Social Consequences of Preference Falsification.* Cambridge, MA: Harvard University Press, 1997.

Ladd, Jonathan M. *Why Americans Hate the Media and How It Matters*. Princeton, NJ: Princeton University Press, 2011.

Lakoff, George. *Moral Politics: How Liberals and Conservatives Think*. Chicago: University of Chicago Press, 1996.

Lane, Robert. *Political Ideology*. New York: Free Press, 1962.

Lasswell, Harold D. *Propaganda Techniques and the World War*. New York: Knopf, 1927.

Layman, Geoffrey. *The Great Divide: Religious and Cultural Conflict in American Party Politics*. New York: Columbia University Press, 2001.

Layman, Geoffrey, and Thomas Carsey. "Party Polarization and 'Conflict Extension' in the American Electorate." *American Journal of Political Science* 46, no. 4 (2002): 786–802.

Lazarsfeld, Paul, Bernard Berelson, and Hazel Gaudet. *The People's Choice: How the Voter Makes Up His Mind in a Presidential Campaign*. New York: Duell Sloan and Pearce, 1944.

Lazer, David M. J., Matthew A. Baum, Yochai Benkler, Adam J. Berinsky, Kelly M. Greenhill, Filippo Menczer, Miriam J. Metzger, Brendan Nyhan, Gordon Pennycook, David Rothschild, Michael Schudson, Steven A. Sloman, Cass R. Sunstein, Emily A. Thorson, Duncan J. Watts, and Jonathan L. Zittrain. "The Science of Fake News." *Science* 359, no. 6380 (2018): 1094–1096.

Lecklider, Aaron. "Inventing the Egghead: The Paradoxes of Brainpower in Cold War American Culture." *Journal of American Studies* 45, no. 2 (2013): 245–265.

Lee, Brandy. *The Dangerous Case of Donald Trump: 27 Psychiatrists and Mental Health Experts Assess a President*. New York: St. Martin's, 2017.

Lelkes, Yphtach, and Paul M. Sniderman. "The Ideological Asymmetry of the American Party System." *British Journal of Political Science* 46, no. 4 (2016): 825–844.

Lenker, Margaret. "Dan Rather on 'Truth': See It and Make Up Your Own Mind." *Variety*, December 21, 2015.

Lerner, Jennifer, and Philip Tetlock. "Accounting for the Effects of Accountability." *Psychological Bulletin* 125 (1999): 255–275.

Leetaru, Kalev. "Introducing RealClearPolitics' Fact Check Review." RealClearPolitics, April 9, 2018. https://www.realclearpolitics.com/articles/2018/04/09/introducing_realclearpolitics_fact_check_review.html.

Levendusky, Matthew. "Clearer Cues, More Consistent Voters: A Benefit of Elite Polarization." *Political Behavior* 32, no. 1 (2010): 111–131.

Levendusky, Matthew. *How Partisan Media Polarize America*. Chicago: University of Chicago Press, 2013.

Lewandowsky, Stephan, Ullrich Ecker, and John Cook. "Beyond Misinformation: Understanding and Coping with the Post-Truth Era." *Journal of Applied Research in Memory and Cognition* 6, no. 4 (2017): 353–369.

Lewandowsky, Stephan, Ullrich Ecker, C. Seifert, N. Schwarz, and John Cook. "Misinformation and Its Correction: Continued Influence and Successful Debiasing." *Psychological Science in the Public Interest* 13, no. 3 (2012): 106–131.

Lewandowsky, Stephan, Gilles E. Gignac, and Samuel Vaughan. "The Pivotal Role of Perceived Scientific Consensus in Acceptance of Science." *Nature Climate Change* 3, no. 4 (2013): 399–404.

Lewis, Charles. *935 Lies. The Future of Truth and the Decline of America's Moral Integrity*. New York: PublicAffairs Books, 2014.

Lewis, Michael. *The Undoing Project: A Friendship That Changed Our Minds*. New York: Norton, 2016.

Lewis-Beck, Michael S., William G. Jacoby, Helmut Norpoth, and Herbert F. Weisberg. *The American Voter, Revisited*. Ann Arbor: University of Michigan Press, 2008.

Lindeman, Marjaana, and Markku Verkasalo. "Measuring Values with the Short Schwartz's Value Survey." *Journal of Personality Assessment* 85, no. 2 (2005): 170–178.

Linkins, Jason. "PolitiFact Has Decided That a Totally True Thing Is the 'Lie of the Year,' For Some Reason." Huffington Post, December 20, 2011.

Lippmann, Walter. *Public Opinion*. New York: Free Press, 1922.

Lippmann, Walter. *The Phantom Public*. New York: Macmillan, 1925.

Lipset, Seymour Martin. "Some Social Requisites for Democracy: Economic Development and Political Legitimacy." *American Political Science Review* 53 (1959): 69–105.

Liu, Brittany, and Peter Ditto. "What Dilemma? Moral Evaluation Shapes Factual Belief." *Social Psychological and Personality Science* 4 (2012): 316–323.

Locke, John. *Essay Concerning Human Understanding*. 1690.

Long, Scott, and Jeremy Freese. *Regression Models for Categorical Variables Using Stata*. College Station, TX: Stata Press, 2014.

Lord, Charles, Lee Ross, and Mark Lepper. "Biased Assimilation and Attitude Polarization: The Effects of Prior Theories on Subsequently Considered Evidence." *Journal of Personality and Social Psychology* 37, no. 11 (1979): 2098–2109.

Lott, John. *More Guns, Less Crime*. Chicago: University of Chicago Press, 1998.

Lupia, Arthur. *Uninformed: Why People Know so Little About Politics and What We Can Do About It*. Oxford: Oxford University Press, 2016.

Lupia, Arthur, and Mathew McCubbins. *The Democratic Dilemma*. Cambridge: Cambridge University Press, 1998.

Malka, Ariel, Yphtach Lelkes, and Nissan Holzer. "Rethinking the Rigidity of the Right Model: Three Suboptimal Methodological Practices and Their Implications." *The Politics of Social Psychology*. New York: Routledge, 2018.

Manjoo, Farhad. *True Enough: Learning to Live in a Post-Fact Society*. New York: John Wiley & Sons, 2008.

Mann, Thomas E., and Norman J. Ornstein. *It's Even Worse Than It Looks*. New York: Basic Books, 2012.

Marietta, Morgan. "From My Cold, Dead Hands: Democratic Consequences of Sacred Rhetoric." *Journal of Politics* 70, no. 3 (2008): 767–779.

Marietta, Morgan. "The Absolutist Advantage: Sacred Rhetoric in Contemporary Presidential Debate." *Political Communication* 26, no. 4 (2009): 388–411.

Marietta, Morgan. "Value Representation: The Dominance of Ends over Means in Democratic Politics." *Critical Review* 22, no. 2 (2010): 311–329.

Marietta, Morgan. *A Citizen's Guide to American Ideology: Conservatism and Liberalism in Contemporary Politics*. New York: Routledge, 2011.

Marietta, Morgan. *The Politics of Sacred Rhetoric: Absolutist Appeals and Political Persuasion*. Waco, TX: Baylor University Press, 2012.

Marietta, Morgan, and David C. Barker. "Values as Heuristics: Core Beliefs and Voter Sophistication in the 2000 Republican Nomination Contest." *Journal of Elections, Public Opinion and Parties* 17, no.1 (2007): 49–78.

Marietta, Morgan, and David C. Barker. "Conspiratorial Thinking and Polarized Fact Perceptions." In *Conspiracy Theories and the People Who Believe Them*, edited by Joseph E. Uscinski. New York: Oxford University Press, 2018.

Marietta, Morgan, David C. Barker, and Todd Bowser. "Fact-Checking Polarized Politics: Does the Fact-Check Industry Provide Consistent Guidance on Disputed Realities?" *The Forum: A Journal of Applied Research in Contemporary Politics* 13, no. 4 (2015): 577–596.

Martin, Gregory J., and J. McCrain. "Yes, Sinclair Broadcast Group Does Cut Local News, Increase National News and Tilt Its Stations Rightward." *Washington Post*, April 10, 2018.

Martin, Gregory J., and A. Yurukoglu. "Bias in Cable News: Persuasion and Polarization." *American Economic Review* 107, no. 9 (2017): 2565–2599.

Maslow, Abraham. "Fusions of Facts and Values." *American Journal of Psychoanalysis* 23 (1963): 117–31.

Mason, Liliana. *Uncivil Agreement: How Politics Became Our Identity*. Chicago: University of Chicago Press, 2018.

McCarty, Nolan, Keith T. Poole, and Howard Rosenthal. *Polarized America: The Dance of Ideology and Unequal Riches*. Cambridge, MA: MIT Press, 2006.

McClosky, Herbert, and John Zaller. *The American Ethos: Public Attitudes Toward Capitalism and Democracy*. Cambridge, MA: Harvard University Press, 1984.

McConnell, Christopher, Neil Malhotra, Yotam Margalit, and Matthew Levendusky. "The Economic Consequences of Partisanship in a Polarized Era." *American Journal of Political Science* 62, no. 1 (2018): 5–18.

McCrae, R. R. "Social Consequences of Experiential Openness." *Psychological Bulletin* 120 (1996): 323–337.

McCright, Aaron, and Riley Dunlap. "The Politicization of Climate Change and Polarization in the American Public's Views of Global Warming, 2001–2010." *Sociological Quarterly* 52, no. 2 (2011): 155–194.

McIntyre, Lee. *Respecting Truth: Willful Ignorance in the Internet Age*. New York: Routledge, 2015.

McIntyre, Lee. *Post-Truth*. Boston: MIT Press, 2018.

Mercier, Hugo. "The Functioning of Reasoning: Argumentative and Pragmatic Alternatives." *Thinking & Reasoning* 19 (2013): 488–494.

Mercier, Hugo, and Dan Sperber. "Why Do Humans Reason? Arguments for an Argumentative Theory." *Behavioral and Brain Sciences* 34 (2011): 57–111.

Mercier, Hugo, and Dan Sperber. *The Enigma of Reason*. Cambridge, MA: Harvard University Press, 2017.

Miller, Joanne M., Kyle L. Saunders, and Christina E. Farhart. "Conspiracy Endorsement as Motivated Reasoning: The Moderating Roles of Political Knowledge and Trust." *American Journal of Political Science* 60, no. 4 (2016): 824–844.

Miller, Warren E., and Donald E. Stokes. "Constituency Influence in Congress." *American Political Science Review* 57, no. 1 (1963): 45–56.

Milton, John. *Areopagitica*, 1644.

Mitchell, Amy, Jeffrey Gottfried, Jocelyn Kiley, and Katerina Eva Matsa. "Political Polarization and Media Habits: From Fox News to Facebook, How Liberals and Conservatives Keep Up with Politics." Pew Research Center, October 2014.

Molden, Daniel, and Tory Higgins. "Motivated Thinking." In *The Cambridge Handbook of Thinking and Reasoning*, edited by Keith J. Holyoak and Robert G. Morrison, 295–320. New York: Cambridge University Press, 2005.

Mooney, Chris. *The Republican War on Science*. New York: Basic Books, 2005.

Mooney, Chris. *The Republican Brain: The Science of Why They Deny Science—And Reality*. New York: Wiley, 2012.

Moore, G. E. *Principia Ethica*. Cambridge: Cambridge University Press, 1903.

Morris, Debra. "'How Shall We Read What We Call Reality': John Dewey's New Science of Democracy." *American Journal of Political Science* 43, no. 2 (1999): 608–628.

Morris, J. S. "The Fox News Factor." *Harvard International Journal of Press/Politics* 10 (2005): 56–79.

Motta, Matt. "Republicans Are Increasingly Antagonistic Toward Experts. Here's Why That Matters." *Washington Post*, August 11, 2017.

Moynihan, Daniel Patrick. *Secrecy: The American Experience*. New Haven, CT: Yale University Press, 1998.

Mutz, Diana. *Hearing the Other Side: Deliberative Versus Participatory Democracy*. Cambridge: Cambridge University Press, 2006.

Mutz, Diana. "Effects of In-Your-Face Television Discourse on Perceptions of Legitimate Opposition." *American Political Science Review* 101 (2007): 621–635.

Mutz, Diana. *In-Your-Face Politics: The Consequences of Uncivil Media*. Princeton, NJ: Princeton University Press, 2015.

Mutz, Diana, and Jeffrey Mondak. "The Workplace as a Context for Cross-Cutting Political Discourse." *Journal of Politics* 68, no. 1 (2006): 140–155.

Mutz, Diana, and Brian Reeves. "The New Videomalaise: Effects of Televised Incivility on Political Trust." *American Political Science Review* 99 (2005): 1–15.

Nalder, Kimberly. "The Paradox of Prop. 13: The Informed Public's Misunderstanding of California's Third Rail." *California Journal of Politics and Policy* 2, no. 3 (2010): 1–21.

Neumark, David, and William L. Wascher. "Minimum Wages and Employment." *Foundations and Trends in Microeconomics* 3, nos. 1–2 (2007): 1–182.

Nichols, Tom. *The Death of Expertise*. Oxford; Oxford University Press, 2017.

Nicholson, Stephen P. "Dominating Cues and the Limits of Elite Influence." *Journal of Politics* 73, no. 4 (2011): 1165–1177.

Nicholson, Stephen P. "Polarizing Cues." *American Journal of Political Science* 56, no. 1 (2012): 52–66.

Nicholson, Stephen P., Chelsea M. Coe, Jason Emory, and Anna V. Song. "The Politics of Beauty: The Effects of Partisan Bias on Physical Attractiveness." *Political Behavior* 38, no. 4 (2016): 883–898.

Nielsen, Rasmus Kleis. "Social Media and Bullshit." *Social Media + Society* 1, no. 1 (2015): 1–3.

Nieminen, Sakari, and Lauri Rapeli. "Fighting Misperceptions and Doubting Journalists' Objectivity: A Review of the Fact-Check Literature." *Political Studies Review, forthcoming* (2019).

Nietzsche, Friedrich. *Writings from the Late Notebooks*, edited by Rudiger Bittner. 1886. Cambridge: Cambridge University Press, 2003.

Nisbet, Matt, and Ezra M. Markowitz. "Understanding Public Opinion in Debates over Biomedical Research: Looking Beyond Political Partisanship to Focus on Beliefs About Science and Society." *PLoS One* 9, no. 2 (2014): e88473.

Noel, Hans. *Political Ideologies and Political Parties in America.* Cambridge: Cambridge University Press, 2014.

Norton, Michael, and Samuel Sommers. "Whites See Racism as a Zero-Sum Game That They Are Now Losing." *Perspectives on Psychological Science* 6, no. 3 (2011): 215–218.

NPR/PBS News Hour/Marist Poll, 1 October 2018.

Nyhan, Brendan. "Why the "Death Panel" Myth Won't Die: Misinformation in the Health Care Reform Debate." *The Forum* 8, no. 1 (2010): 1–24.

Nyhan, Brendan, and Jason Reifler. "When Corrections Fail: The Persistence of Political Misperceptions." *Political Behavior* 32, no. 2 (2010): 303–330.

Nyhan, Brendan, and Jason Reifler. "The Effects of Fact-Checking on Elites: A Field Experiment on U.S. State Legislatures." *American Journal of Political Science* 59, no. 3 (2015a): 628–640.

Nyhan, Brendan, and Jason Reifler. "Displacing Information About Events: An Experimental Test of Causal Corrections." *Journal of Experimental Political Science* 2, no. 1 (2015b): 81–93.

Nyhan, Brendan, and Jason Reifler. "Does Correcting Myths About the Flu Vaccine Work? An Experimental Evaluation of the Effects of Corrective Information." *Vaccine* 33, no. 3 (2015c): 459–464.

Nyhan, Brendan, and Jason Reifler. "Do People Actually Learn from Fact-Checking: Evidence from a Longitudinal Study During the 2014 Campaign." American Press Institute, Arlington, VA, September 2016.

Nyhan, Brendan, Ethan Porter, Jason Reifler, and Thomas Wood. "Taking Corrections Literally but Not Seriously? The Effects of Information on Factual Beliefs About Candidate Favorability." *SSRN Electronic Journal* (2017). doi: 10.2139/ssrn.2995128.

Nyhan, Brendan, Jason Reifler, and Peter A. Ubel. "The Hazards of Correcting Myths About Health Care Reform." *Medical Care* 51, no 2 (2013): 127–132.

Oliver, Eric, and Wendy Rahn. "Rise of the *Trumpenvolk*: Populism in the 2016 Election." *Annals of the American Academy of Political and Social Science* 667 (2016): 189–206.

Osmundson, Joseph. "'I Was Born This Way': Is Sexuality Innate and Should It Matter?" *LGBTQ Policy Journal at the Harvard Kennedy School* (2011).

Ostermeier, Eric. "Selection Bias? PolitiFact Rates Republican Statements as False at Three Times the Rate of Democrats." Smart Politics, February 10, 2011.

Page, Benjamin, and Robert Y. Shapiro. *The Rational Public: Fifty Years of Trends in Americans' Policy Preferences.* Chicago: University of Chicago Press, 1992.

Pateman, Carole. *Participation and Democratic Theory.* Cambridge: Cambridge University Press, 1970.

Pasek, Josh, Gaurav Sood, and Jon Krosnick. "Misinformed About the Affordable Care Act? Leveraging Certainty to Assess the Prevalence of Misperceptions." *Journal of Communication* 65, no. 4 (2015): 660–673.

Peffley, Mark, and Jon Hurwitz. "A Hierarchical Model of Attitude Constraint." *American Journal of Political Science* 29 (1985): 871–890.

Peffley, Mark, and Jon Hurwitz. *Justice in America: The Separate Realities of Blacks and Whites*. Cambridge: Cambridge University Press, 2010.

Peterson, M. B., M. Skov, S. Serritzlew, and T. Ramsoy. "Motivated Reasoning and Political Parties: Evidence for Increased Processing in the Face of Party Cues." *Political Behavior* 35 (2013): 831–854.

Pew Research Center. "Political Polarization in the American Public." June 12, 2014.

Pew Research Center. "Sharp Partisan Divisions in Views of National Institutions." July 10, 2017.

Pew Research Center. "Wide Gender Gap, Growing Educational Divide in Voters' Party Identification: College Graduates Increasingly Align with Democratic Party." March 20, 2018. http://assets.pewresearch.org/wp-content/uploads/sites/5/2018/03/20113922/03-20-18-Party-Identification.pdf.

Pinker, Steven. *The Better Angels of Our Nature: Why Violence Has Declined*. New York: Viking, 2011.

Pjurko, Yuval, Shalom H. Schwartz, and Eldad Davidov. "Basic Personal Values and the Meaning of Political Orientations in 20 Countries." *Political Psychology* 32, no. 4 (2011): 537–561.

Plato. *The Republic*. 381 BC.

Pluviano, Sara, Caroline Watt, and Sergio Della Sala. "Misinformation Lingers in Memory: Failure of Three Pro-Vaccination Strategies." *PLoS One* 12, no. 7 (2017): e0181640.

Polanyi, Michael. *Personal Knowledge: Towards a Post-Critical Philosophy*. Chicago: University of Chicago Press, 1958.

Popper, Karl. *The Logic of Scientific Discovery*. Vienna: Springer Verlag, 1935.

Popper, Karl. *Conjectures and Refutations*. New York: Harper, 1963.

Price, Vincent, and Mei-ling Hsu. "Public Opinion About AIDS Policies: The Role of Misinformation and Attitudes to Homosexuals." *Public Opinion Quarterly* 56, no. 1 (1992): 29–52.

Prior, Markus. *Post-Broadcast Democracy: How Media Choice Increases Inequality in Political Involvement and Polarizes Elections*. New York: Cambridge University Press, 2007.

Prior, Markus, Gauruv Sood, and Kabir Khanna. "You Cannot Be Serious: The Impact of Accuracy Incentives on Partisan Bias in Reports of Economic Perceptions." *Quarterly Journal of Political Science* 10, no. 4 (2015): 489–518.

Pulido, Laura. "Rethinking Environmental Racism: White Privilege and Urban Development in Southern California." *Annals of the Association of American Geographers* 90 (2000): 12–40.

Putnam, Hillary. *The Collapse of the Fact/Value Dichotomy and Other Essays*. Cambridge, MA: Harvard University Press, 2002.

Ramsay, Clay, Steven Kull, Evan Lewis, and Stefan Subias. "Misinformation and the 2010 Election: A Study of the US Electorate." World Public Opinion, Washington, DC, December 10, 2010.

Rasmussen Reports, "Who Do You Believe–Kavanaugh or Ford? It's a Tie," 1 October 2018.

Redlawsk, David. "Hot Cognition or Cool Consideration? Testing the Effects of Motivated Reasoning on Political Decision Making." *Journal of Politics* 64 (2002): 1022–1044.

Redlawsk, David P., Andrew J. W. Civettini, and Karen M. Emerson. "The Affective Tipping Point: Do Motivated Reasoners Ever 'Get It'?" *Political Psychology* 31, no. 4 (2010): 563–593.

Reedy, Justin, Chris Wells, and John Gastil. "How Voters Become Misinformed: An Investigation of the Emergence and Consequences of False Factual Beliefs." *Social Science Quarterly* 95, no. 5 (2014): 1399–1418.

Reinhart, Carmen, and Kenneth Rogoff. "Growth in a Time of Debt." *American Economic Review* 100 (2010): 573–578.

Reinhart, Carmen, Vincent Reinhart, and Kenneth Rogoff. "Public Debt Overhangs: Advanced Economy Episodes Since 1800." *Journal of Economic Perspectives* 26, no. 3 (2012): 69–86.

Remnick, David. "Obama Reckons with a Trump Presidency." *New Yorker*, November 28, 2016.

Rescher, Nicholas. *The Coherence Theory of Truth.* Oxford: Oxford University Press, 1973.

Rigney, Daniel. "Three Kinds of Anti-Intellectualism: Rethinking Hofstadter." *Sociological Inquiry* 61, no. 4 (1991): 434–451.

Ritov, Ilana, and Jonathan Baron. "Protected Values and Omission Bias." *Organizational Behavior and Human Decision Processes* 79, no. 2 (1999): 79–94.

Rivers, Doug. "Second Thoughts About Internet Surveys." Pollster.com, September 6, 2009.

Roccas, S., and M. Brewer. "Social Identity Complexity." *Personality and Social Psychology Review* 6, no. 2 (2002): 88–106.

Rogowski, Jon. "Electoral Choice, Ideological Conflict, and Political Participation." *American Journal of Political Science* 58, no. 2 (2014): 479–494.

Rohan, Meg. "A Rose by Any Name? The Values Construct." *Personality and Social Psychology Review* 4, no. 3 (2000): 255–277.

Rokeach, Milton. *The Nature of Human Values.* New York: Free Press, 1973.

Rorty, Richard. *Philosophy and the Mirror of Nature.* Princeton, NJ: Princeton University Press, 1979.

Rothman, Stanley, Robert Lichter, and Neil Nevitte. "Politics and Professional Advancement Among College Faculty." *The Forum* 3, no. 1 (2005): Article 2.

Schaffner, Brian, and Cameron Roche. "Misinformation and Motivated Reasoning: Responses to Economic News in a Politicized Environment." *Public Opinion Quarterly* 81, no. 1 (2017): 86–110.

Scherer, Michael. "Blue Truth, Red Truth." *Time Magazine*, October 15, 2012, pages 24–30.

Schier, Steven. *Polarized: The Rise of Ideology in American Politics.* Lanham, MD: Rowman & Littlefield, 2016.

Schuck, Peter H. *One Nation, Undecided: Clear Thinking About Five Issues that Divide Us.* Princeton, NJ: Princeton University Press, 2017.

Schufeldt, G. "Party-Group Ambivalence and Voter Loyalty: Results from Three Experiments." *American Politics Research* 46, no. 1 (2018): 132–168.

Schulz, Kathryn. "Pond Scum: Henry David Thoreau's Moral Myopia." *New Yorker*, October 19, 2015.

Schumpeter, Joseph. *Capitalism, Socialism, and Democracy*. New York: Harper, 1942.

Schwartz, Shalom H. "Universals in the Content and Structure of Values: Theoretical Advances and Empirical Tests in 20 Countries." *Advances in Experimental Social Psychology* 25 (1992): 1–65.

Schwartz, Shalom, and W. Bilsky. "Toward a Theory of the Universal Content and Structure of Values: Extensions and Cross-Cultural Replications." *Journal of Personality and Social Psychology* 58 (1990): 878–891.

Schwartz, Shalom, and K. Boehnke. "Evaluating the Structure of Human Values with Confirmatory Factor Analysis." *Journal of Research in Personality* 38 (2004): 230–255.

Schwartz, Shalom, Gilla Melech, Arielle Lehmann, Steven Burgess, Mari Harris, and Vicki Owens. "Extending the Cross-Cultural Validity of the Theory of Basic Human Values with a Different Method of Measurement." *Journal of Cross-Cultural Psychology* 32 (2001): 519–542.

Searle, John R. *The Construction of Social Reality*. New York: Free Press, 1995.

Sears, David O. "An Ignorant and Easily Duped Electorate?" *Perspectives on Politics* 15, no. 1 (2017): 137–141.

Shani, Danielle. "Can Knowledge Correct for Partisan Bias in Political Perceptions?" Paper presented at the annual meeting of the The Midwest Political Science Association, Chicago, IL, April 2006.

Shapin, Steven. *A Social History of Truth: Civility and Science in Seventeenth Century England*. Chicago: University of Chicago Press, 1994.

Shapiro, Robert, and Yaeli Bloch-Elkon. "Do the Facts Speak for Themselves? Partisan Disagreement as a Challenge to Democratic Competence." *Critical Review* 20, no. 1 (2008): 115–139.

Sherif, Muzafer. "A Study of Some Social Factors in Perception." *Archives of Psychology* 27, no. 187 (1935): 1–60.

Sherman, D., and G. Cohen. "The Psychology of Self-Defense: Self-Affirmation Theory." *Advances in Experimental Social Psychology* 38 (2006): 183–242.

Shermer, Michael. "Is Truth and Outdated Concept? Are We Living in a Post-Truth World?" *Scientific American*, March 1, 2018.

Sides, John. "Stories or Science? Facts, Frame, and Policy Attitudes." *American Politics Research* 44, no. 3 (2015): 387–414.

Silverman, C. "This Analysis Shows How Viral Fake Election News Stories Outperformed Real News on Facebook." BuzzFeed, November 16, 2016.

Sinclair, B. *The Social Citizen: Peer Networks and Political Behavior*. Chicago: University of Chicago Press, 2012.

Singer, Peter. *The Expanding Circle: Ethics and Sociobiology*. New York: Farrar Straus and Giroux, 1981.

Skurnik, Ian, Carolyn Yoon, Denise C. Park, and Norbert Schwarz. "How Warnings About False Claims Become Recommendations." *Journal of Consumer Research* 31, no. 4 (2005): 713–724.

Smaiya, Ravi. "Rolling Stone Article on Rape at University of Virginia Failed All Basics, Report Says." *New York Times*, April 5, 2015.

Smith, Ben. "Facts Checked," *Politico*, May 19, 2010.

Sobieraj, Sarah, and Jeffrey M. Berry. *The Outrage Industry: Political Opinion Media and the New Incivility*. New York: Oxford University Press, 2013.

Southwell, Brian, and Emily Thorson. "The Prevalence, Consequence, and Remedy of Misinformation in Mass Media Systems." *Journal of Communication* 65 (2015): 589–595.

Southwell, Brian, Emily Thorson, and Laura Sheble. *Misinformation and Mass Audiences*. Austin: University of Texas Press, 2018.

Sperber, Dan, Fabrice Clement, Christophe Heintz, Olivier Mascaro, Hugo Mercier, Gloria Origgi, and Deirdre Wilson. "Epistemic Vigilance." *Mind & Language* 25, no. 4 (2010): 359–393.

Spohr, D. "Fake News and Ideological polarization: Filter Bubbles and Selective Exposure on Social Media." *Business Information Review* 34, no. 3 (2017): 150–160.

Sproule, M. J. *Propaganda and Democracy*. Cambridge: Cambridge University Press, 1997.

Stahl, Lori. "Dan Rather Still Defends His Report on George W. Bush." *Washington Post*, April 17, 2012.

Steinmetz, Katy. "Oxford's Word of the Year for 2016 Is 'Post-Truth.'" *Time*, November 16, 2016.

Stelter, Brian. "No One Fired at Rolling Stone. *Really?*" CNN Online, April 6, 2015.

Strange, Jeffrey, and Elihu Katz, eds. *The Future of Fact*. Thousand Oaks, CA: Sage Press, 1998.

Suhay, Elizabeth, and Cengiz Erisen. "The Role of Anger in the Biased Assimilation of Political Information." *Political Psychology* 39, no. 4 (2018): 793–810.

Suhay, Elizabeth, and Jeremiah J. Garretson. "Science, Sexuality, and Civil Rights: Does Information on the Causes of Sexual Orientation Change Attitudes?" *Journal of Politics* 80, no. 2 (2018): 692–696.

Sunstein, Cass R. *On Rumors: How Falsehoods Spread, Why We Believe Them, What Can Be Done*. Farrar, Straus and Giroux, 2009.

Sunstein, Cass R., and A. Vermeule. "Conspiracy Theories: Causes and Cures." *Journal of Political Philosophy* 17, no. 2 (2009): 202–227.

Swire, Briony, Adam Berinsky, Stephan Lewandowsky, and Ullrich K. H. J. Ecker. "Processing Political Misinformation: Comprehending the Trump Phenomenon." *Royal Society of Open Science* 4 (2017): 1–21.

Taber, Charles, and Milton Lodge. "Motivated Skepticism in the Evaluation of Political Beliefs." *American Journal of Political Science* 50, no. 3 (2006): 755–769.

Taber, Charles, and Milton Lodge. *The Rationalizing Voter*. New York: Cambridge University Press, 2013.

Taber, Charles S., Damon Cann, and Simona Kucsova. "The Motivated Processing of Political Arguments." *Political Behavior* 31, no. 2 (2009): 137–155.

Taleb, Nassim Nicholas. *The Black Swan: The Impact of the Highly Improbable*. New York: Random House, 2007.

Tetlock, Philip. "Accountability: A Social Check on the Fundamental Attribution Error." *Social Psychology Quarterly* 48 (1985): 227–236.

Tetlock, Philip. "A Value Pluralism Model of Ideological Reasoning." *Journal of Personality and Social Psychology* 50 (1986): 819–827.

Tetlock, Philip. "An Alternative Metaphor in the Study of Judgment and Choice: People as Politicians." *Theory and Psychology* 1, no. 4 (1991): 451–475.

Tetlock, Philip. "Social Functionalist Frameworks for Judgment and Choice: Intuitive Politicians, Theologians, and Prosecutors." *Psychological Review* 109, no. 3 (2002): 451–471.

Tetlock, Philip. "Thinking the Unthinkable: Sacred Values and Taboo Cognitions." *Trends in Cognitive Sciences* 7, no. 7 (2003): 320–324.

Tetlock, Philip. *Expert Political Judgment: How Good Is It? How Can We Know?* Princeton, NJ: Princeton University Press, 2005.

Tetlock, Philip, and Dan Gardner. *Superforecasting: The Art and Science of Prediction.* New York: Crown Publishing, 2015.

Tetlock, Philip, Orie Kristel, Beth Elson, Melanie Green, and Jennifer Lerner. "The Psychology of the Unthinkable: Taboo Trade-offs, Forbidden Base Rates, and Heretical Counterfactuals." *Journal of Personality and Social Psychology* 78, no. 5 (2000): 853–870.

Tetlock, Philip, Randall Peterson, and Jennifer Lerner. "Revising the Value Pluralism Model: Incorporating Social Content and Context Postulates." In *The Psychology of Values: The Ontario Symposium,* edited by Clive Seligman, James Olson, and Mark Zanna. Mahwah, NJ: Lawrence Erlbaum Associates, 1996.

Theriault, Sean. *Party Polarization in Congress.* New York: Cambridge University Press, 2008.

Thoreau, Henry David. *Walden, or Life in the Woods.* 1854. New York: Library of America.

Thorson, Emily. "Belief Echoes: The Persistent Effects of Corrected Information." *Political Communication* 33 (2016): 460–480.

Tversky, Amos, and Daniel Kahneman. "Belief in the Law of Small Numbers." *Psychological Bulletin* 76, no. 2 (1971): 105–110.

Ulbig, S. G., and Cary L. Funk. "Conflict Avoidance and Political Participation." *Political Behavior* 21, no. 3 (1999): 265–282.

Uscinski, Joseph. "The Epistemology of Fact Checking (Is Still Naïve): Rejoinder to Amazeen." *Critical Review* 27, no. 2 (2015): 243–252.

Uscinski, Joseph, and Ryden Butler. "The Epistemology of Fact Checking." *Critical Review* 25, no. 2 (2013): 162–180.

Uscinski, Joseph, and Joseph Parent. *American Conspiracy Theories.* New York: Oxford University Press, 2014.

Uscinski, Joseph, Casey Klofstad, and Matthew D. Atkinson. "What Drives Conspiratorial Beliefs? The Role of Informational Cues and Predispositions." *Political Research Quarterly* 69, no. 1 (2016): 57–71.

Vaccari, Cristian, Augusto Valeriani, Pablo Barbera, John T. Jost, Jonathan Nagler, and Joshua A. Tucker. "Of Echo Chambers and Contrarian Clubs: Exposure to Political Disagreement Among German and Italian Users of Twitter." *Social Media + Society* 2, no. 3 (2016).

Vales, Leinz. "Fareed Zakaria: Trump 'Indifferent to Things that Are True or False." CNN, March 19, 2017. http://edition.cnn.com/2017/03/18/politics/zakaria-wiretap-trump-don-lemon-cnntv.

Vavreck, Lyn. "So Just Who Are These Undecided Voters?" *New York Times,* September 30, 2016.

Vico, Giambattista. *Principij di scienza nuova*. 1725. Naples: Stamperia Muziana.

Walzer, Micheal. "On the Role of Symbolism in Political Thought." *Political Science Quarterly* 82, no. 2 (1967): 191–204.

Washburn, Anthony, and Linda Skitka. "Science Denial Across the Political Divide: Liberals and Conservatives Are Similarly Motivated to Deny Attitude-Inconsistent Science." *Social Psychological and Personality Science* (2017): doi:10.1177/1948550617731500.

Watts, Mark D., David Domke, Dhavan Shah, and David P. Fan. "Elite Cues and Media Bias in Presidential Campaigns: Explaining Public Perceptions of a Liberal Press." *Communication Research* 26, no. 2 (1999): 144–175.

Weaver, David, Lars Willnat, and G. Cleveland Wilhoit. "The American Journalist in the Digital Age: Another Look at U.S. News People." *Journalism and Mass Communication Quarterly* (2018): doi: 10.1080/1461670X.2017.1387071.

Weber, Max. "Science as a Vocation." In From Max Weber: Essays in Sociology, edited by H. H. Gerth and C. Wright Mills. New York: Oxford University Press, 1946.

Webster, Steven, and Alan Abromowitz. "The Ideological Foundations of Affective Polarization in the U.S. Electorate." *American Politics Research* 45, no. 4 (2017): 621–647.

Weeden, J., and R. Kurzman. "Do People Naturally Cluster into Liberals and Conservatives?" *Evolutionary Psychological Science* 2, no. 1 (2016): 47–57.

Weeks, Brian. "Emotions, Partisanship, and Misperceptions: How Anger and Anxiety Moderate the Effect of Partisan Bias on Susceptibility to Political Misinformation" *Journal of Communication* 65, no. 4 (2015): 699–719.

Wells, Chris, Justin Reedy, John Gastil, and Carolyn Lee. "Information Distortion and Voting Choices: The Origins and Effects of Factual Beliefs in Initiative Elections." *Political Psychology* 30, no. 6 (2009): 953–969.

Wendt, Alexander. "Anarchy Is What States Make of It: The Social Construction of Power Politics." *International Organization* 46, no. 2 (1992): 396–399.

White, John Kenneth. *The Values Divide: American Politics and Culture in Transition*. Washington, DC: CQ Press, 2002.

Wilson, Edward O. *Sociobiology*. Cambridge, MA: Harvard University Press, 1975.

Wintersieck, Amanda. "Debating the Truth: The Impact of Fact-Checking During Electoral Debates" *American Politics Research* 45, no. 2 (2017): 304–331.

Wintersieck, Amanda, and Kim Fridkin. "The Rise of Fact Checking in American Political Campaigns." In *The Praeger Handbook of Political Campaigning in the United States*. New York: Praeger, 2015.

Wintoki, M. Babajide, and Yaoyi Xi. "Political Partisan Bias in Mutual Fund Portfolios." (2017).

Wood, Thomas, and Ethan Porter. "The Elusive Backfire Effect: Mass Attitudes' Steadfast Factual Adherence." *Political Behavior* (2019).

Yeager, David S., Jon A. Krosnick, LinChiat Chang, Harold S. Javitz, Matthew S. Levendusky, Alberto Simpser, and Rui Wang. "Comparing the Accuracy of RDD Telephone Surveys and Internet Surveys Conducted with Probability and Non-Probability Samples." *Public Opinion Quarterly* 75, no. 4 (2011): 709–747.

Young, Dannagal G., Kathleen Hall Jamieson, Shannon Poulsen, and Abigail Goldring. "Debunking: A Meta-Analysis of the Psychological Efficacy of Messages Countering Misinformation." *Psychological Science* 28, no. 11 (2017): 1531–1546.

Young, J. "A Defense of the Coherence Theory of Truth." *Journal of Philosophical Research* 26 (2001): 89–101.

Zaller, John. *The Nature and Origins of Mass Opinion*. Cambridge: Cambridge University Press, 1992.

INDEX

Abelson, Robert, 79, 88
Adair, Bill, 232, 235, 236, 237–38
Adams, John, 2–3, 29, 58
Adorno, Theodor, 210
affective polarization, 181–82, 198
Andersen, Kurt, 54–55
Asch, Solomon, 84
authority, 5, 10, 13, 52–53, 202–3, 216, 217, 225, 226, 266, 295
authority moral value, 126, 127, 128, 135, 148, 164–66

Barry, Marion, 175–76
Berger, Peter, 23–24
Berinsky, Adam, 298
Berlin, Isaiah, 23, 93–94, 95
Bernstein, Carl, 36
Brown, Michael, xi–xii, 177
bullshit, 41, 43, 91
Bush, George W., 11, 64–65
Bybee, Carl, 33, 39, 57–58

CALSPEAKS Panel, xiii, 145, 183, 250
care moral value, 126, 128–29, 134, 135, 144, 148, 164–66, 272
certainty, 157, 275
Chambers, Whitaker, 176–77
climate change, 59, 102–3, 119, 124–25, 128–29, 183, 189–91, 241, 244
Clinton, Hillary, 61, 249, 252, 253, 266, 274

CNN, 3, 212
cognitive psychology, 80, 81, 91, 109–10, 167
coherence, 35, 44, 83, 156, 293
Colbert, Steven, 58, 85, 91, 265, 271–72
Cold War, xii, 290–91
collectivism, See values
confirmation bias, 81, 82, 85, 90–91
conformity, 13, 80, 83, 88, 93, 100–1, 109–10, 141–42, 167, 278, 286
Converse, Philip, 31, 45
correspondence, 35, 44, 156, 293
crime, 51–52, 114, 134, 135, 272–74

Darwin, Charles, 73, 144, 158–59
Declaration of Independence, 2, 227
deliberation, 167, 172, 173, 180, 181, 198, 287, 295–96
Delli Carpini, Michael X., 46
Dewey, John, 31, 36, 39, 44, 204
disconfirmation bias, 82
disdain, 181, 278
dress controversy, 74

echo chamber, 112–13, 181–82
education, ix, 12–13, 14, 17–18, 34, 50–52, 58–59, 92, 149–51, 201, 248, 257, 261–62, 265, 266–67, 268, 277–78, 279, 283, 288–89, 292, 294–96
epistemology, 74, 139

Mercier, Hugo, 89, 141
mere contemplation effect, 161
Milton, John, 2
minimum wage, 133–34
misinformation, ix–x, xiii, 9, 15, 47, 50–52,
265, 284, 293–94
misperceptions, ix–x, xiii, 9, 15, 47, 50–52,
265, 284, 293–94
Mooney, Chris, 217, 224, 265
moral fallacy, 100, 161
moral foundations, 98–99, 115–16, 126,
145, 146, 164, 272. See authority,
care, equality, fairness, loyalty,
proportionality, sanctity
motivated reasoning, 13, 17, 80, 85, 89,
100, 104, 109–10, 141, 167, 218,
265, 268, 276, 286, 298
Mutz, Diana, 173–74
myside bias, 85

Nalder, Kimberly, 247
national debt, 132
natural fallacy, 100
news media, See media
Nichols, Tom, 216
Norse mythology, 22, 25, 44, 77
Nyhan, Brendan, 47, 86–87

Obama, Barrack, 113, 171, 232, 243–44,
291, 294
Odin, 22, 77

partisan facts, 9, 16, 46, 48, 50, 108, 285
personal knowledge, 74
Pinker, Steven, 228
Plato, 7, 22, 25, 31–32, 140–41
Polanyi, Michael, 78
polarization, ix, 12, 13–49, 14–, 15–16,
18, 50–51, 58–59, 175, 180, 194–95,
198, 223–24, 285, 288, 293
PolitiFact, 227, 247
epistemology, 233
origins, 232
Popper, Karl, 8–159, 180
populism, 209, 214, 248, 249, 252–53,
256, 260–63, 274–75

postmodernism, 36–37, 39–40, 54
post-truth, x–xi, 57–58
pragmatism, 36–37, 39, 40, 210
preference falsification, 298
proportionality moral value, 126, 127,
129, 135, 144, 164–66, 272, 276
Putnam, Hillary, 26–27, 28–29, 161–62

racism, xi–xii, 57, 61, 68–69, 103, 114, 116,
119–20, 121–22, 124–26, 127–29,
130–31, 151, 152–53, 162–63, 177,
178–79, 183, 184, 185, 191, 206,
240–59, 86
Rand Corporation, 53–54, 171,
211, 291–92
Rather, Dan, 11, 212
realignment of authority, 202, 225,
226, 295–96
reasoning is for arguing (Mercier
thesis), 89
Reifler, Jason, 86–87
Rigidity of the Right, 79, 265–66, 269
Roberts, Chief Justice John, 61,
205, 240–41

sacred values, 16, 157
sanctity moral value, 126, 127, 128, 129,
135, 143, 144–45, 147–48, 149,
164–66, 276
Sanders, Bernie, 249, 266
scandal, 11, 175
Scarface, 43–44
Schwartz, Shalom, 98–99, 115–16,
123–24, 143
Searle, John R., 23–24
selective cognitions, 13, 15–16, 81–83,
85, 88, 91–92, 93, 105, 109–10, 167,
210, 286
sexual orientation, xii, 59, 63, 69, 104–5,
109, 119–20, 124, 128, 151,
207–8, 270
Shakespeare, 41–42, 86, 100, 159–60, 209
Shapiro, Robert, 47
Shermer, Michael, 230
Simpson, OJ, 62
Skitka, Linda, 267–68